THE
UNEXPLAINED

THE
UNEXPLAINED

**ABBEYDALE
PRESS**

This paperback edition published in 2006
by Abbeydale Press
An imprint of Bookmart Limited
Blaby Road, Wigston
Leicestershire, LE18 4SE

© 1993 Bookmart Limited

ISBN: 1-86147-190-4

1 3 5 7 9 10 8 6 4 2

Originally incorporated in *The Encyclopedia of the Unexplained*
and
Mysteries of the Mind published by Bookmart Limited.

Production by Omnipress Ltd, Eastbourne

Printed in India

Contents

UFO Investigation

Life After Death

Poltergeists and the Paranormal

Nostradamus and Visions of the Future

Monsters and Mysterious Places

UFO
INVESTIGATION

HOW LONG HAVE THEY BEEN HERE?

On a bright summer's day an ordinary man witnessed an extraordinary sight. Kenneth Arnold's cautious reports unwittingly launched the age of the flying saucer. His was only one in a long series of inexplicable sightings.

At about 7 p.m. on the evening of 2 April 1991, Dick Feichtinger was driving to work in Faribault, Minnesota, when he saw a curious, white, long and narrow rectangular object apparently hanging in the sky above the town. 'It seemed to be hanging up and down. Rather than horizontal it was vertical,' he told reporter Paul Adams of the *Faribault Daily News*. 'The fact that it wasn't horizontal is strange… the configuration and the way it was hanging, that was what drew my attention to it.'

Still more remarkable was the fact that the object was there again when Feichtinger returned home from work late in the evening. Now, instead of being simply white, it was red and green. Once home, Feichtinger, naturally somewhat excited and more than intrigued, urged his wife and children to come and look at what he had seen. His family rushed to join him. As the Feichtingers watched, the object hanging mysteriously in the sky changed colour from red and green to solid white. By this time, neighbours had come out to see what the fuss was about, and were equally astonished to see the weird rectangle in the sky – which, they later agreed, 'seemed to be intelligently guided'.

At this point something very strange happened: two aircraft came cruising incredibly low over the houses. Said neighbour Steve Kelly: 'I thought they were going to land on my house.' And they were flying extremely slowly – so slowly that Dick Feichtinger commented: 'I couldn't figure out what was keeping them up there.' Undaunted, he waved at them as he stood under a street light, and one of the planes seemed to acknowledge the wave by briefly turning on a set of floodlights - possibly its landing lights.

Before long, more aircraft were on the scene. Some witnesses said they counted up to 11 planes, including helicopters and two large aircraft. When the local military were contacted, however, they had no knowledge of any aircraft in the area besides a pair of National Air Guard C-I30 Hercules cargo planes – one of which, spokesman Lt. Kevin Gutknecht admitted, had indeed turned on its landing lights, although why was not explained. However, the C-I30 pilots did not report seeing any strange lights in the vicinity of the town. A puzzled Lt. Gutknecht was reported as saying: 'I have no idea what it is. It doesn't sound like anything we have in the Minnesota military inventory.'

This case has all the ingredients of a certain kind of classic UFO sighting. There is the bizarre light in the sky, changing colour but seemingly under intelligent control, witnessed by a number of independent observers, none of whom apparently has any reason to lie, let alone organize a neighbourhood conspiracy. There are unexplained terrestrial aircraft associated with the sighting. The military deny all knowledge, as usual, although they give away a tantalizing and inexplicable detail: why did the Hercules pilot turn on his landing lights?

The role of the military in UFO lore is a subject on its own, but this case, like the hundreds of others reported each year, serves to illustrate that the UFO phenomenon is as strong as it ever was. But how long have UFOs been seen in our skies?

SUPER INTELLIGENCE

The modern history of UFOs is traditionally considered to begin in 1947, when Idaho businessman Kenneth Arnold saw nine weird disks of light flashing through the air while he was flying over the Cascade Mountains in Washington State, USA. This extraordinary encounter is worth recounting in detail, for it is a key episode in any attempt to understand what UFOs are – and what they have been. For Arnold's experience was by no means the first recorded instance of unexplained aerial objects and ordinary humanity coming into contact with each other. The great difference between his and previous sightings was the interpretation that was very soon put on it – that the lights Arnold saw were extra terrestrial craft.

Hardly anyone in the Western world was immune to this belief. Even US President Harry S. Truman could say, at a press conference on 4 April 1950, 'I can assure you that flying saucers... are not constructed by any power on Earth.' Just a few years later, in June 1954, at another conference in Innsbruck, Austria, Dr Herman Orberth - often called the 'father' of the German V-2 rocket, precursor of all the spacecraft launched from Earth – stated his conviction unmistakably: 'These objects are conceived and directed by intelligent beings of a very high order. They probably do not originate in our Solar System, perhaps not even in our galaxy.'

Whether or not UFOs are indeed material craft from outer space, messengers from alien civilizations, or the vehicles of galactic 'guardians' of humanity – or possibly even evidence of something far less benign that has a presence here on Earth – is a question that still vexes experts. The important point for the moment is that in the late 1940s, there was no other interpretation that made sense to most observers. Yet this was not Kenneth Arnold's own belief, and was certainly not the way that earlier witnesses saw the strange and bewildering lights and seemingly solid objects that from time to time have filled the skies throughout history and at the same time have filled the witnesses, too, with awe and wonder.

Harry S. Truman, US President during the first sightings of 'flying saucers' after World War Two. Truman publicly stated his belief that UFOs were from outer space, and some ufologists believe that he instigated research into the phenomenon – research that remains super-secret even today.

FLYING SAUCERS

Kenneth Arnold unwittingly launched the age of the flying saucer on the clear sunny afternoon of 24 June 1947. He was an experienced pilot, and that day was flying east across the Cascade Mountains from Chehalis to Yakima, Washington. Arnold had been enticed by the offer of a $5,000 reward to spend an hour or so during his journey searching for a C-46 transport aircraft belonging to the US Marine Corps that had recently come down near Mount Rainier with 32 men on board. The Callair aircraft Arnold was flying was specially designed for working in the mountains. He took off from Chehalis airport at about 2 p.m. and made straight for the plateau of Mount Rainier.

Arnold was in the midst of his search at an altitude of about 9,200 ft above the town of Mineral (about 25 miles south-west of the peak of Mount Rainier), and was making a 180° turn when 'a tremendously bright flash lit up the surfaces of my aircraft'. Understandably startled, Arnold thought at first that he was about to collide with another aircraft. He spent an anxious half-minute or so searching the sky for the source of the flash of light, but the only other plane in the vicinity was a Douglas DC4 airliner, which he judged to be on the airlane from Seattle to San Francisco. Arnold then figured that he had seen the flash of the sun on the wings of a close flying fighter; he thought he had been buzzed by a gung-ho young USAF lieutenant in a P-51, better known as the North American Aviation Mustang, the most powerful piston-engined fighter then in common service with the USAF.

Before he had time to start searching for a fast-moving Mustang, however, Arnold saw another flash – and this time saw where it came from. 'I observed,' he reported drily, 'far to my left and to the north, a formation of very bright objects coming from the vicinity of Mount Baker, flying very close to the mountain tops and travelling at tremendous speed.' Watching the craft near Mount Rainier, Arnold at first thought that he was watching a formation of nine jets at, he calculated, a distance of over l00 miles. 'What startled me most at this point was… that I could not find any tails on them.'

The formation was flying almost directly across Arnold's own flightpath, which made it easy to make a rough calculation of the objects' speed, using the clock in his instrument panel, Mounts Rainier and Adams as markers, and reckoning the formation would pass about 23 miles in front of him. Arnold was amazed to discover that the nine craft were travelling at over 1,700 mph – an astonishing speed for the time (it was only later that year that the sound barrier, about 750 mph, was first broken by a jet aircraft). What made this phenomenal speed all the more extraordinary was the way the craft were flying, Arnold said:

'They didn't fly like any aircraft I had seen before... they flew in a definite formation, but erratically... their flight was like speed boats on rough water or similar to the tail of a Chinese kite that I once saw blowing in the wind... they fluttered and sailed, tipping their wings alternately and emitting those very bright blue-white flashes from their surfaces – At the time I did not get the impression that these flashes were emitted by them, but rather that it was the sun's reflection from the extremely highly polished surfaces of their wings.'

By the time the nine craft had flown beyond the southernmost crest of Mount Adams, Arnold had decided to abandon his search for the missing C-46 and make for Yakima to report what he had seen. Landing there at about 4 p.m., Arnold told his story to an airline manager and discussed it with other professional fliers, before taking off once more for Pendleton, Oregon. The news had travelled ahead of him: among the crowd of people to greet him there was Bill Becquette, from the local newspaper, the *East Oregonian*. It was during this time that Arnold described the craft he had seen as flying 'like a saucer would if you skipped it across the water'. This description was slightly garbled by Becquette, who thus originated the phrase 'flying saucers'. Then, with other pilots, Arnold cautiously recalculated his estimate of the UFOs' extraordinary speed. But even the most conservative reckoning still put their velocity at over 1,350 mph. From talking to other airmen, Arnold was now convinced that he had seen a flight of guided missiles, 'robotly controlled'. He concluded that the government had chosen this way to announce the discovery of 'a new principle of flight'.

Then the story broke, put out on the Associated Press wire by Bill Becquette. For three days at Pendleton Arnold was besieged with enquiries. Finally, exhausted and unable to work, Arnold flew the 200 miles across the state line to his home in Boise, Indiana. It was shortly after arriving there that Arnold had a telephone call from Dave Johnson, aviation editor of the *Idaho Statesman*. That conversation changed everything for Arnold. As he put it:

'The doubt he displayed of the authenticity of my story told me, and I am sure he was in a position to know, that it was not a new military guided missile and that if what I had seen was true it did not belong to the good old USA. It was then that I really began to wonder.'

ALIEN CRAFT

Arnold might well have wondered, for in the three days that he was being harassed by newshounds he discovered that his was by no means the only, or even the first, sighting of such mysterious flying objects. ('I thought it wouldn't be long before there was one of these things in every garage,' he commented wryly, at the stage when he still believed that he had seen a flight of government-sponsored machines.)

In April 1947, a meteorologist tracking a weather balloon saw a saucer-shaped object fly by – a neat irony, as so many later UFO sightings have been explained away as, and sometimes have really been, misidentifications of weather balloons. On 5 May, a 'silvery object' was reported to have dropped out of the sky over Washington State and disintegrated before reaching the ground. On 12 June, shortly before Arnold's own experience, another chain of UFOs was seen over Weiser, Idaho, and on 14 June a pilot named Rankin also observed a flight of ten saucer-like objects flying in triangular formation. At about the same time as Arnold saw 'his' flying disks, a prospector in the Cascades also witnessed a similar group of UFOs, whose presence made his compass needle go wild. Arnold's sighting in fact took place in the midst of a major UFO 'flap' – a flurry of sightings – in the late spring and summer of 1947. Between the beginning of June and 16 July that year, the US authorities received over 850 reports of UFOs from all over the USA. By September, the USAF had set up Project Sign to evaluate the reports and, among other things, consider the possibility that these were extraterrestrial craft.

What made Arnold's report different was that it sparked an equally monumental flap in the media – whose underlying assumption throughout was that 'flying saucers' were indeed alien craft, and were probably not very friendly.

Curiously enough, Arnold himself did not share this view of the origins of UFOs. In 1962, in the magazine *Flying Saucers*, he published his own conclusion: 'the so-called unidentified flying objects that have been seen in our atmosphere are not space ships from another planet at all, but are groups and masses of living organisms that are as much a part of our atmosphere and space as the life we find in the depths of our oceans. The only major difference [is] that they have a natural ability to change their densities at will.'

Arnold, perhaps, was not a man of his age; but this was not the first time that UFOs had been identified with living things in the sky. On the other hand, the belief that they were nuts-and-bolts machines was not entirely new, either.

MACHINES OF DEATH

Probably the earliest report of a UFO on record is to be found in (of all places) a treatment of architecture and civic planning called the *Samarangana-Sartradhara*, an ancient Indian text that dates back at least to 500 BC. In this, one passage describes curious machines called vimanas, which can fly, and are controlled by pilots. There follows a number of lengthy descriptions of how the vimanas' various power systems work, but they are tantalizingly obscure. The same devices are also mentioned in the great Hindu epics in Sanskrit, the *Mahabharata* and *Ramayana*, where they are described as military machines with the range to 'carry death' anywhere in the world – an assertion that, like so many aspects of unexplained and paranormal phenomena, raises as many questions as it answers. One researcher has even gone so far as to say that 'we cannot but be struck [when reading these works] by the modernity of certain passages, where we seem to be reading an account of a nuclear war'.

Roman writers noted visitations by UFOs: Livy (59 BC–AD 17) described a sighting in 214 BC at Hadria in Italy that looked like an altar in the sky, while Pliny the Elder (AD 23–79) refers to 'gleaming beams in the sky' in his *De Rerum Naturae*, and describes how in 66 BC a 'spark' fell from a star to the Earth, became as large as the Moon, and then – shrinking in size – returned to the sky. And in his *Historia Naturalis*, Pliny makes an intriguing assertion:

'A light from the sky by night, the phenomenon usually called "night suns" was seen in the consulship of Gaius Caecilius and Gnaeus Papirius and often on other occasions causing apparent daylight in the night. In the consulship of Lucius Valerius and Gaius Marius a burning shield scattering sparks ran across the sky at sunset from east to west.'

The fascinating part of this passage is the words 'usually called'. Pliny seems to assume that 'night suns' were, if not commonplace, at least well-enough known to have a common name. And, although he was one of the first naturalists, Pliny was enough a man of his time to accept such wonders without comment.

The literature of medieval Europe abounds in UFO reports of various kinds. Among the earliest are to be found in the works of St Gregory, Bishop of Tours in France in the 6th century. In his *Historia Francorum* ('History of the Franks'), the saint related how in AD 584 'there appeared in the sky brilliant rays of light which seemed to cross and collide with one another', while the following year 'in the month of September, certain people saw signs, that is to say rays or domes such as are customarily seen... to race across the sky'. Elsewhere he describes 'golden globes' that, on several occasions, flashed at speed across the skies of France. St Gregory also wrote seven volumes concerning miracles and - in keeping with his devout Christianity – seems to have been in little doubt that these were heavenly signs. The interpretation, in short, fitted the preconceptions of the chronicler.

In the same way, in AD 793, the *Anglo-Saxon Chronicle* reported: 'In this year terrible portents appeared in Northumbria, and miserably afflicted the inhabitants; these were exceptional flashes of lightning, and fiery dragons were seen flying through the air.' The Chronicle was written by secular scribes, and their report reflects the still thickly pagan atmosphere of 8th-century England – for both people and places were far less orthodox in their Christianity than the monasteries of France had been two centuries previously. What today would have been called a UFO or even a 'flying saucer' was to them a dragon. It flew in the air, it lit up the sky, and it was fearsome and inherently inexplicable; it was a dragon because that was the nearest thing in human knowledge to match what people actually saw. This unconscious mental process also helps to explain why diehard sceptics, confronted with a UFO, will always believe they have seen the planet Venus, or a weather balloon – indeed, anything other than an inexplicable and possibly alien craft.

Just as people see UFOs today, people saw dragons then. Kenneth Arnold was not the first to suggest that UFOs, in the most literal sense of being unidentified flying objects, were members of the animal kingdom. In England in 1113, a group of churchmen from Laon in France were going from town to town in Wessex (south-west England), bearing with them relics of the Virgin Mary, which they used to perform miracles of healing. At the coastal town of Christchurch, Hampshire, they were astonished to see a dragon come up out of the sea, 'breathing fire out of its nostrils'. There are plenty of reports of modern UFOs rising out of the sea, as well.

The 12th-century chronicler Ralph Niger recounts that on 9 March 1170, at St Osyth in Essex, south-east England, 'a wonderfully large dragon was seen, borne up from the Earth through the air. The air was kindled into fire by its motion and burnt a house, reducing it and its outbuildings to ashes.'

Dragons and UFOs show some interesting parallels. Whatever form UFOs take, they are always perceived as being on the very edge of human knowledge as it exists in any particular era, including some alluring extras that we can imagine but cannot (yet) achieve – such as faster-than-light travel today, or heavier-than-air flight in the Middle Ages.

Like UFOs today, dragons were familiar as ideas, but were also regarded as 'impossible' in practical terms. To the medieval mind, dragons occupied a strange no-man's land between reality and imagination. Most people had not seen one – though they might know someone who had, or who knew someone else who had. But everyone was familiar with dragons and what they did (which was guard treasure, breathe fire and fly), and everyone knew what a dragon looked like. Medieval people would have had no difficulty in identifying one if it landed in a bustling market place and snorted smoke and flame. But actual dragons remained elusive and magical, neither quite real nor quite imaginary, possible but improbable. Today, most of the same things could be said about UFOs, except that they are only magical in the sense that they are 'otherworldly' or paranormal.

An astonishing aerial battle breaks out over the city of Nuremberg on 4 April 1561. A contemporary account speaks of a 'very frightful spectacle', in which luminous globes, crosses and tubes appeared to fight one another for about an hour in broad daylight.

AERIAL CONFLICT

As time went on, and the old Anglo-Saxon myths disappeared from memory in an England conquered by the Normans, the identification of UFOs with dragons faded too. The persistent appearance of inexplicable lights and objects in the sky did not fade with them, however. In his *Historia Anglorum* ('The History of the English'), another English chronicler, Matthew of Paris, tells how at sunset on 24 July 1239, 'a great star like a torch appeared. It rose in the south and climbed the sky giving out a great light ... it left behind it smoke and sparks. It was shaped like a great head, the front part was sparkling and the back part gave out smoke and flashes.' And in his memoirs the French Duke of Bourgogne recalled that on 1 November 1461, an object appeared in the sky 'as long and wide as a half-moon; it hung stationary for about a quarter hour, clearly visible, then suddenly… spiralled, twisted and turned like a spring and rose into the heavens'.

Such accounts were not limited to Europe: records of strange lights over Japan go back at least to the 10th century, while in May 1606 the former capital of Japan, Kyoto, saw a succession of fireballs in the sky. One of them hovered near the Nijo castle in front of a host of witnesses, spinning like a red wheel.

And so the records continue: blue, black and blood-red balls, along with disks and blood-red crosses and two huge cylinders, battled together in the skies over Nuremberg, Germany, on 4 April 1561, and there was a similar aerial conflict a little more than five years later over Basel, Switzerland, between black spheres: 'many became red and fiery, ending by being consumed and vanishing', wrote the 'student in sacred writings and the liberal arts', one Samuel Coccius, who reported the weird events of 7 August 1566 in the city's gazette.

A SKY OF FLAMES

In the centuries that followed, observers, including the astronomer Edmund Halley (1656–1742), continued to note a host of bizarre aerial phenomena. But now the tone of the reports starts to change yet again: as the so-called 'Age of Reason' dawned in the late 17th century and rigorously 'logical' scientific observation became the order of the day, so different explanations for sightings of what we would now call UFOs began to creep in to the accounts. At Sheffield, England, on 9 December 1731, for instance, at about 5 p.m., Thomas Short saw what he later described as 'a dark red cloud, below which was a luminous body which emitted intense beams of light… the light beams moved slowly for a while, then stopped. Suddenly it became so hot that I could take off my shirt even though I was out of doors [this in the dead of winter!]. This meteor was observed over Kilkenny, Ireland, where it seemed like a great ball of fire. It was reported that it shook the entire island and that the whole sky seemed to burst into flames.'

In the afternoon of the next day, local manuscript records show, this 'meteor' appeared over Romania: ' there appeared in the west a great sign in the sky, blood red and very large. It stayed in place for two hours, then separated into two parts which then rejoined, and the object disappeared towards the west.' To the Romanian mind of the time, this was 'a sign'; to the cultured gentleman of Augustan England, it was a 'meteor', if a very strange one by our modern standards of judging meteors. The tendency to interpret such events according to the most easily available existing explanation – and one that at the time was the most acceptable socially – is even clearer in another account from 18th-century England.

On 18 August 1783, a small crowd of the gentry that included Dr James Lind (whose pioneering dietary work resulted in the eradication of scurvy from the Royal Navy), the renowned water-colour painter Thomas Sandby and the scientist Tiberius Cavallo, were on the terrace at the royal residence of Windsor Castle enjoying the summer evening when, according to Cavallo's

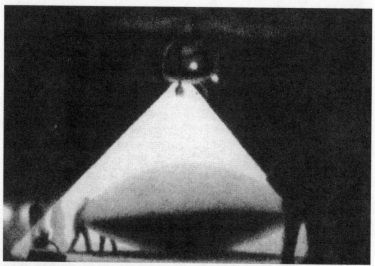

Many ufologists have concluded not only that UFOs are alien, but that the US goverment has retrieved crashed saucers like this one (artist's impression), which allegedly was taken to Fort Riley, Kansas, in November 1964.

account published the next year by the Royal Society, at about 9.45 p.m. they 'suddenly saw appear an oblong cloud moving more or less parallel to the horizon. Under this cloud could be seen a luminous object which soon became spherical, brilliantly lit, which came to a halt... This strange sphere seemed at first to be pale blue in colour, but its luminosity increased and soon it set off again towards the east. Then the object changed direction and moved parallel to the horizon before disappearing to the south-east... the light it gave out was prodigious; it lit up everything on the ground. Before it vanished it changed its shape, became oblong, and at the same time as a sort of trail appeared, it seemed to separate into two small bodies. Scarcely two minutes later the sound of an explosion was heard.'

To the scientist Cavallo the group had clearly witnessed a meteor: the proof was in the explosion, presumably made as the thing crashed to earth. The astonishing thing to modern eyes is the similarity between the cloud and the object beneath it seen in 1783, and the almost identical nature of the other so-called 'meteor' that visited England, Ireland and Romania some half a century before. But a person trained to look out for meteors will see them when something like one appears in the sky, however remotely like an actual meteor it may seem from our later perspective.

THE ALIENS HAVE LANDED

True to form, the next century saw another, no less consistent, interpretation of unexplained aerial phenomena. The Victorian era saw an astonishing leap forward in works of engineering, especially in transport – from the spread of railways around the globe to the introduction of iron steamships capable of crossing the Atlantic, and the production of the first cars. Land and sea had been conquered: but not the air. Airships seemed the most promising means of achieving sustained, controlled flight, but the major problem was power. It was not until light, compact internal combustion engines appeared in the late 1890s that airships became truly practicable. By then, they were being discussed everywhere – both as the next great advance in engineering, and as something more strange.

On 6 November 1896, the citizens of Sacramento, California, were amazed to see a light moving sedately through the night sky, apparently carried by a cigar shaped craft. During the month further reports of this machine poured in from all over California. From March 1897, the American Great Lakes states and Texas were plagued by reports of lights in the sky, some like 'electric arc lights', others shaped like balls or wheels, that were attached to a huge craft - which was at once dubbed an airship – shaped like a cigar, an egg, or a barrel, and apparently powered by propellers. On a number of occasions these machines landed, and the occupants, who appeared to be ordinary human beings, spoke to bemused witnesses on the ground. Then, at the beginning of May 1897, the reports dried up.

An airship as large as the objects that witnesses described would have had to be rigid, or it would have been uncontrollable. But it was not until 1900 that the development of rigid airships – 'dirigibles' – began, and that was in Germany. No airship then flying, either in the USA or elsewhere, was capable of the feats performed by these machines - if that is what they were. The first dirigible to fly in the USA was Thomas Baldwin's California Arrow, which took off from Oakland, near San Francisco, California, in 1904.

In August 1946, the Swedish authorities received nearly 1,000 reports of mysterious rockets in their skies, some of which crashed spectacularly into the country's inland lakes. One theory was that the Soviets were testing captured German V-2 rockets – which, in the public eye at least, were the most advanced technology of the day. But Swedish aviation engineers, who by then had considerable knowledge of the V-2, failed to find any plausible explanation. Similar displays of rocket-like behaviour by mysterious aerial objects were reported early the following month by British Army units in Greece, especially around Thessaloniki. Midway through September they were seen in Portugal, and then in Belgium.

THE WATCHERS IN OUTER SPACE

UFOs have been seen in the form of dragons, meteors, airships, rockets… and as 'flying saucers'. To the sceptic, all these bizarre sightings are either natural phenomena, errors of perception or plain hallucination. Some, perhaps most, UFO sightings certainly are no more than that. There is certainly good evidence that many truly strange lights in the sky are the product of little-known and rarely seen natural forces, which seem to be released in areas of geological disturbance – along fault lines in the Earth's crust, for example. Such a theory may well explain a proportion, at least, of the long history of mysterious airborne lights over Japan, which is notoriously prone to earthquakes. But these explanations don't account for the UFO phenomenon as a whole.

The common belief since Kenneth Arnold's sighting in 1947 has been that UFOs are extraterrestrial craft built by a civilization that is technologically far in advance of our own. There are very strong grounds for questioning this assumption but it remains a possibility. Some of the people who claim to have spoken to aliens and extra-terrestrials also maintain that this civilization has been watching the Earth for a very long time. Presumably, there have been occasions when – for reasons we can only guess at – they have been unable to conceal their presence entirely. Or perhaps they have deliberately shown themselves, as part of a centuries-long programme of gently introducing themselves to us. In either case, when they have been obliged or have chosen to reveal themselves, they have come in clever disguises: just far enough within the bounds of human understanding, carefully matching the mood of the times, to be acceptable, if strange – and just far enough beyond normality to deter unwanted investigation or interference.

And we may just be living in the age when they decide to reveal their true purposes to us.

MESSENGERS FROM OUTER SPACE

George Adamski had spent years observing the skies on the lookout for UFOs. An impulse drew him into the desert where a figure beckoned him from the opening of a ravine... but with a sudden chill of fear he wondered whether his long vigil had been wise.

Is someone – or something – inhabiting the Solar System besides ourselves? Are they out there watching us, for some mysterious purpose of their own, or are they simply our elusive neighbours? Are they friendly or are they hostile?

The answers to these questions – the most perplexing and, many would say, the most crucial in the whole debate about UFOs - should have become apparent in the decades since UFOs first revealed themselves as inexplicable flying disks. For in that time numerous people have claimed to have had direct contact with the occupants of UFOs. One might expect a clear picture to emerge from these undoubtedly traumatic experiences of who the aliens are, where they are from, and what – if anything – they want. Yet cases of contactees, and more especially those of people who have been abducted by UFOs, present some of the most conflicting and perplexing evidence of all the vast array of data in the field of ufology.

There are, essentially, three kinds of witness who might help answer some of the fundamental questions.

First, there are those people who have come so close to UFOs that they have seen and described the occupants.

Second, there are those who have been approached by aliens in a friendly spirit and have come away with what amounts to 'a message for mankind' – not necessarily of enormous cosmic import, but at least containing some explanation of what the aliens are doing and why they are here.

Third, there is a small group of people who seem to have been forcibly abducted by aliens. These cases are the most difficult to assess and contain the most astounding claims: that the contactees were subjected to some kind of medical examination, for example, and in some cases were sexually used or abused.

EVADING CAPTURE

One of the most frustrating aspects of the UFO enigma is the inconsistency of the evidence. This is particularly apparent in the descriptions of alien beings given by those who claim to have seen them.

The first such contactee to come to public attention was George Adamski, a part-time caterer who described himself as a 'philosopher and teacher' and who lived in Palomar Gardens, on the southern slopes of Mount Palomar, California. Adamski's passion was astronomy; he had a 15in and a 6in reflector telescope set up at home to watch the stars. He was also convinced that the other planets of our Solar System were inhabited. On 9 October 1946, while watching a meteor shower from his home, he saw what he later believed to be confirmation of his conviction. Along with others he saw 'a gigantic space craft' that was 'hovering high above the mountain ridge to the south of Mount Palomar, toward San Diego'. It was 'a large black object, resembling a gigantic dirigible'.

In his book *Flying Saucers Have Landed*, Adamski reports that he was first alerted to the possibility that this was 'a ship from another world' by a military officer, shortly after this sighting. From then on, Adamski spent hours every day on the lookout for another UFO. Between the winter of 1949–50 and the summer of 1952, he photographed a number of UFOs both with and without his 6in telescope, some 18 of the photos being of high quality. Adamski began giving lectures on UFOs and extraterrestrials to various interested groups, and as a result of these contacts began to hear rumours that flying saucers had been landing in 'various desert areas not a great drive from Mount Palomar'.

Adamski, with John Nebel and the 'mother ship' and attendant saucers that he claimed to have photographed in March 1951.

On 20 November 1952, Adamski, his secretary Mrs Lucy McKinnis, and the proprietor of Palomar Gardens, Mrs Alice K. Wells, met up with four such contacts – Mr and Mrs Al C. Bailey of Winslow, Arizona, and Dr and Mrs George H. Williamson of Prescott, Arizona – on the highway near Blythe, California, to go into the desert in the hope of seeing a UFO land. Adamski gives no reason for having chosen this day rather than another, but admits to following a hunch as to where they should start their vigil – about 11 miles down the highway from Desert Center toward Parker, Arizona. The group was richly rewarded.

After a stroll and a light lunch, the party sat scanning the sky. The only thing of note was the passage of a two-engine plane apparently on a routine flight. Then: 'Suddenly and simultaneously we all turned as one [sic] looking again toward the closest mountain ridge where just a few minutes before the first plane had crossed. Riding high, and without sound, there was a gigantic cigar-shaped silvery ship, without wings or appendages of any kind.'

The craft moved as if drifting in the direction of the group, then stopped, hovering. Adamski felt that the ship had come specifically for him, and on another hunch demanded to be taken down the road – the spot they were in, next to a well-travelled highway, was too conspicuous, he thought, and would discourage a landing.

With Lucy McKinnis at the wheel and Al Bailey accompanying, Adamski was driven off the highway onto a dirt road, while all the time the giant ship followed them silently. After half a mile or so they stopped. Here, Adamski set up his smaller telescope and a camera and then, fearing the presence of his companions would deter the aliens, sent them back to their original parking spot, to watch from there. As they left, a number of aircraft – presumably fighters – roared into sight and tried to circle the huge craft above. In response, the ship 'turned its nose upward and shot out into space'. Wondering if the planes had chased it away for good, Adamski settled down to wait.

Before five minutes was up, he saw a flash in the sky and 'almost instantly a beautiful craft appeared to be drifting through a saddle between two of the mountain peaks'. It settled on a ridge, and Adamski took photographs. Then it lifted and flew back across the saddle, as two more aircraft came into sight, circled, and flew on.

Apparently the saucer had evaded them. After some minutes Adamski realized that a man was beckoning him from the opening of a ravine about 450 yds away. Wondering who this was, Adamski made his way toward the figure. Only when he was within arm's length of the man did Adamski realize that he was looking at a visitor from another world.

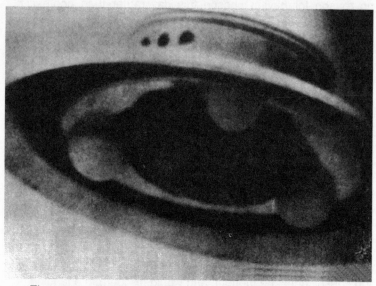

The extraordinary craft, Adamski maintained, flew over his house in Palomar Gardens on 13 December 1952. Surprisingly, no other witnesses reported the event.

A WARNING

'The beauty of his form surpassed anything I had ever seen,' he wrote later. That form was unmistakably human. The man was about 5 ft 6 in tall, weighed about 135 lb, and appeared – in earthly terms – to be about 28 years old. He had shoulder-length, sandy-coloured wavy hair 'glistening more beautifully than any woman's I have ever seen'. His skin was the colour of a suntanned Caucasian's. His face was round, and he had an extremely high forehead, 'calm, grey-green eyes' that slanted slightly at the corners, high cheekbones, and a 'finely chiselled' nose. He seemed to be beardless. The alien was wearing a single-piece, finely woven chocolate-brown suit with no visible fasteners or pockets, but with a broad waistband and a close-fitting high collar. His shoes were ox-blood red and had blunt toes. Adamski thought the outfit was a uniform of some kind.

His attempts to speak to the creature failed, but by concentrating his efforts Adamski succeeded in communicating with a mixture of hand signals and telepathy. The first thing the alien told Adamski in this manner was that he was from the planet Venus. The Venusians were here, he said, because they were concerned about radiation from atomic explosions: too many of these explosions would destroy all of Earth.

And so it went on. The saucer which brought the Venusian – who did not divulge his name – to Earth had been launched from within the atmosphere by the giant 'mother ship' that Adamski had seen earlier. The craft was powered by 'magnetism'. Asked if he believed in God, the spaceman replied yes, but observed that Venusians lived according to the laws of the Creator and not the laws of materialism as Earthmen did. People from the other planets in the Solar System – all of which were inhabited – and from other systems too, were visiting Earth. Some of their craft had crashed on Earth, shot down by 'men of this world'. Saucers landed only in remote places to avoid panicking people, but the time would come when they would land near centres of population. There were many aliens living in our midst already, and for this reason the Venusian refused to be photographed, lest his features become recognizable. All aliens were essentially human in form.

Adamski was then allowed to approach the saucer hovering nearby, but was not permitted inside it. After this, the Venusian climbed aboard his craft, and it glided silently away.

DESOLATE OF LIFE

It is interesting, to say the least, that as Earth's own space programme developed during the 1960s, and probes reported with monotonous regularity that our neighbouring planets were incapable of supporting life as we know it, so the occupants of UFOs have stopped claiming to come from our Solar System. They would certainly feel uncomfortable on Venus, which has an atmospheric pressure 94.5 times higher than our own – which alone would cause any Venusian lacking massive pressurized body armour to explode the moment he set foot on Earth – while temperatures are commonly around 900°F (five times hotter than the boiling point of water). Venusian rain consists largely of hydrochloric and sulphuric acid, and the 'air' is almost entirely carbon dioxide.

However, bearing in mind that one of the few consistent aspects of the UFO phenomenon is its habit of staying just within the borders of the human imagination, it makes some sense for an alien to suggest that he comes from a place that the apparently rather backward terrestrials can immediately recognize as habitable. And in 1952 many people did believe that Venus could support life. Even then, they were wrong – for as early as the 1920s scientists had deduced that Venus could either support 'only low forms of life… mostly belonging to the vegetable kingdom' or was a desert planet plagued by dust storms. By 1932 the Venusian atmosphere was known to be mainly carbon dioxide. This meant that even vegetation was absent.

By 1975, hardly anyone in the Western world was ill-informed about space: six years earlier, the first attempt to put men on the Moon had succeeded brilliantly, while a host of unmanned craft had been sent out to explore remote space, sending back extraordinary pictures of the Solar System along with a mass of information about its planetary environments. All were clearly desolate of any known forms of life.

AN INSANE SOCIETY

Just after 2 p.m. on 28 January 1975, a one-armed farmer named Eduard 'Billy' Meier was walking near his home at Hinwel, in the canton of Zurich in Switzerland, when he saw a silvery, disk-shaped craft swoop down out of the sky with a strange throbbing sound and land about 100 yds away from him. Intrigued, he began to run toward it, but some invisible force halted him after about 50 yds. A figure then emerged from the disk, which was about 25 ft in diameter, and approached him. When it and its vehicle departed an hour and 45 minutes later, Billy Meier knew he had met a cosmonaut from the Pleiades star cluster (of which seven are visible to the naked eye), 430 light years away from the Sun in the constellation of Taurus.

In all, between January 1975 and April 1978, Meier met five Pleiadians – Semjase, Ptaah, Quetzal, Plaja and Asket – in 105 encounters, photographed their five different types of flying disk on numerous occasions, and took 3,000 pages of notes on their conversations and general wisdom. According to Meier, the Pleiadians look like terrestrial Scandinavians, although their lifespan stretches to the equivalent of 1,000 of our years. They came from a planet named Erra 'in the system of Taygeta' in the Pleiades, and before that from a planet in the constellation of Lyra, from which they had emigrated millions of years previously. They had reached Earth thousands of years ago, as part of a continuous programme of space exploration, in ships capable of travelling faster than light through 'hyperspace'. Their general message for mankind was that we should concentrate on the arts

'A giant leap for mankind' – one of the Apollo 11 crew on the Moon. As human knowledge of the Solar System became more accurate and detailed, visiting UFO occupants stopped claiming to have come from neighbouring planets and made more and more extravagant claims.

An artist's impression of an encounter with ufonauts that occurred near Cennina, Arezzo, Italy, on 1 November 1954. Note the craft – few real UFO encounters conform to the 'flying saucer with little green men' stereotype.

of peace and cultivating the life of the spirit – otherwise, Earth was 'an insane society rushing headlong to our own destruction'. The Pleiadians communicated with Meier both through telepathy and by speaking his own dialect.

By astronomical standards, the Pleiades is young: a mere 150 million years old. Its 500-odd stars are virtually all 'B' type – ferociously hot, very large blue stars that burn themselves out very rapidly – most, in fact, have already consumed most of the hydrogen in their cores. In contrast, our Sun, a relatively cool, slow-burning 'G2' yellow dwarf, is some 4.49 billion years old, and it took a further 2.5 billion years or so before conditions on Earth were able to support even the most primitive forms of life. The chances that any planet in the Pleiades is habitable are about zero.

Assuming that extraterrestrial entities of some kind did make contact with Meier, one can only conclude that they were lying about their present galactic address. The obvious question is: why? And if they lie about that, why should we take anything else they say seriously?

The claims made by the aliens in the Meier case are as incredible as those in another, almost equidistant in time between Adamski's encounter in California and the events in Switzerland, that occurred in New York State. On 24 April 1964, farmer Gary Wilcox of Newark Valley, Tioga County, noticed something shiny about 800 yds away, among some trees on a hill where he was working. He drove his tractor up the hill, dismounted, and approached a cigar-shaped object that was hovering just off the ground.

Wilcox kicked it. It felt, he said, like metallic canvas. Then, out from under it, came two 4 ft tall but otherwise featureless creatures who, in the conversation that followed, claimed to be Martians. After an innocent conversation in which the two entities made two predictions that turned out not to be true (one foretold the death of astronaut John Glenn within the year), they departed in their noiseless, 20 ft long craft. This occurred at a time when no space scientist believed that any life form more complex than bacteria might be able to survive in Martian conditions.

VOLUPTUOUS FORMS

These contacts were elaborate and detailed for those who experienced them. They also contain elements of absurdity, illogic and falsehood on the part of the interstellar visitors, but one of the more surprising facets of ufology is the frequency with which these occur. The veteran ufologist and former editor of the internationally respected journal *Flying Saucer Review*, the late Charles Bowen, once offered his readers a few of the choice messages that ufonauts offer to witnesses.

For instance, in 1968 two beings with transparent legs handed an Argentinian farmer's son a written message that translated as 'You shall know the world' and was signed 'F. Saucer'. In 1964, a Venezuelan contactee, confronted by a pair of creatures who were hardly inconspicuous, in that they stood between 7 and 8 ft tall and sported long yellow hair and bulging eyes, asked – with commendable wit, in the circumstances – if any other 'human beings' like them were living on Earth. The reply was 'Yes. Two million, four hundred and seventeen thousand, eight hundred and five.'

Perhaps the most surreal of these utterances came in 1954, when a Frenchman came across a glowing, saucer-shaped UFO, in front of which was standing a diminutive entity who kept repeating, in a mechanical tone: *'La verité est refusée aux constipés'* ('Truth is denied to the constipated'), and *'Ce que vous appelez le cancer vient des dents'* ('What you call cancer comes from the teeth').

If these beings, who seem habitually to lie about their origins and occasionally make obscurely hilarious observations to the humans they meet, are indeed aliens visiting Earth from other planets, one would expect some consistency at least in their appearance. In fact, they take many more forms than the voluptuous young man who greeted Adamski, or the shapely Nordic blondes of Meier's acquaintance. And they are by no means as friendly or concerned for our welfare as the beings that Adamski and Meier met.

A HEADLESS FIGURE

Walter Andrus, director of the Mutual UFO Network, studied thousands of contactee cases and concluded that there were four major categories of UFO occupants. These were: small humanoids; 'experimental animals'; human-like entities; and robots. ('Little green men', the staple mocking term of the media, however, are hardly ever seen in real UFO contacts.) But these broad categories blur a multitude of differences found from one witness's report to the next.

The term 'human-like entities' encompasses extremes as far apart as the two gigantic beings seen filling a sphere as tall as a two-storey house over the Canary Islands on 22 June 1976; the blue, scaly-skinned, 6 ft tall creature that confronted 19-year-old Maria Eliada Pretzel in Córdoba, Argentina, on 13 June 1968; the creature inside a UFO seen by William Bosak near Frederic, Wisconsin, in December 1974 that had a tan-coloured, furry body, a flat nose and mouth, protruding eyes and 'calf-like' ears; and the truly nightmarish creature that in November 1976 emerged from a UFO near Winchester, England, and stared into a car in which Joyce Bowles and Terry Pratt sat in terror: the thing was human in all visible details but for its eyes, which were entirely pink, with neither irises nor pupils, and luminescent.

The animal forms can be unexpectedly horrible. In 1960, during

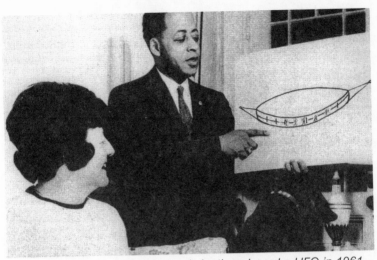

Betty and Barney Hill, whose abduction aboard a UFO in 1961 has been the subject of innumerable analyses. None has entirely explained what the couple experienced, or why they were apparently chosen for alien experiment.

a UFO sighting at Yssandon, France, giant white maggots were seen crawling across a road. On 16 November 1963, two couples walking near Sandling Park in Saltwood, Kent, saw a bright golden oval UFO come down from the sky and then hover among some trees nearby. A figure emerged and approached them, but the foursome fled when it was close enough for them to make out its features: it was entirely black, had wings like a bat, and no head.

Perhaps the most common form taken by UFO occupants is the classic 'small humanoid' – figures on which Steven Spielberg based both 'ET' and the creatures seen emerging from the giant spaceship in *Close Encounters of the Third Kind* (for which Spielberg used the late Dr J. Allen Hynek, a global authority on UFOs who invented the title phrase, as a consultant). Even these pale, huge-headed, hairless, soft-eyed and innocent-looking entities, which so much resemble human foetuses, vary enormously in detail, according to the witnesses' reports.

They may stand from 1 to 5 ft in height. Their eyes may be like ours, or slitted like a cat's. Sometimes they appear apparently naked; at other times in shiny black, yellow or blue garb, possibly with a cloak. Some have pointy ears, others none. Betty and Barney Hill, of New Hampshire, believed that in 1961 they had been taken aboard a craft belonging to such creatures (who were clothed in black) and given medical examinations; while in August 1990, five such beings, of various heights, apparently without clothes and with grey skin, and with only three toes on each foot, were seen walking along a main highway in Puerto Rico by numerous witnesses, but made no attempt to molest anyone. These did have the virtue of slightly resembling the creatures seen at Rio Piedras, Puerto Rico, on 3 March 1980, when teenagers Vivian and José Rodriguez surprised two pointy-eared creatures who were clothed and had webbed feet.

On other occasions, such creatures have paralysed witnesses with lightbeams from their craft – or their eyes – or physically attacked people in daylight. In the hair-raising episode experienced by Lorenzo Flores and Jesús Gómez near Carora, Venezuela, on 10 December 1954, a band of humanoids tried to drag Gómez away until his companion retaliated with his shotgun (the pair were on a hunting trip).

Most bizarre of all the perceived occupants of UFOs have been the so-called robot figures, and possibly the weirdest of all were reported by Jerry Townsend, a radio station employee from Minnesota. On the evening of 23 October 1965 he was driving toward Long Prairie when his car's electrical systems went totally dead and the engine stopped. In front of him on the road was a V-2-style 'spaceship', between 30 and 35 ft tall and resting on the tips

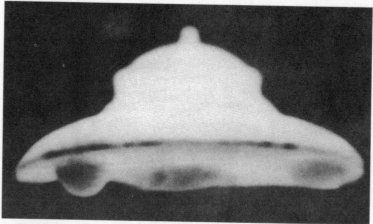

'Typical' flying saucers, like these, in fact make up a minority of real UFO encounter reports.

of three fins, that might have featured in any 1950s sci-fi movie. Undaunted, Townsend got out of the car to investigate and saw, coming from beneath the rocket, three ludicrous objects walking towards him. They were no more than 6 in tall, reeling like drunken sailors on two fins, and shaped like beer cans. When they halted, a third, rear fin descended to keep them upright. In due course they tottered back to their antiquated 'rocket' and it took off – which part of the incident was also witnessed by two hunters who were some distance away.

MIND CONTROL

None of this catalogue of strangeness – which only scrapes the surface of the cases on file – suggests that the being that was encountered by George Adamski in the California desert in 1952 was representative of its type. The brutal fact is that there is no 'type' at all when one is dealing with UFO entities, and no general conclusion to be drawn from the available evidence about their intentions and still less where they come from. So what are they?

Ufologist and specialist in radiation medicine Maxwell C. Cade once suggested that UFO occupants deliberately monitored, and reflected, what was in the mind of the witness: in some cases, homing in on their fears. Thus, the sceptics' dismissal of the contactee phenomenon that 'It's all hallucination' may be true, but with a significant and unexpected twist. According to Cade's hypothesis, the hallucinations are generated from within the UFO, not directly by the witness.

This would explain the huge variations in the degree of sympathy or hostility that contactees encounter among aliens, as well as the bewildering variety of shapes, sizes, colours and textures the entities display. And it would also explain the quality of alien behaviour so shrewdly noted by ufologist Peter Hough – that they 'act less like "aliens" than as if they are fledgling temporary beings hastily assembled and scripted to act out a brief scenario'.

If Cade's hypothesis is correct, it has a clear corollary: whatever they are and wherever they are from, the occupants of UFOs are doing everything in their power to prevent us seeing their true forms or learning their real intentions.

ENCOUNTERS WITH THE UNKNOWN

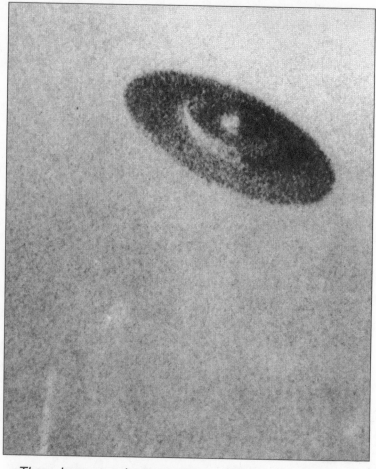

There have now been so many close encounters with UFO phenomena that it is very hard to deny their existence. Terrible injuries have been inflicted on some of the witnesses – but were these encounters with rogue military hardware, or with alien craft on a mission?

Dr J. Allen Hynek (1910–86) was one of the most dedicated, and one of the best-informed, of ufologists the world has seen. A professional astronomer, long a professor, and in due course head of the astronomy department at North Western University in Evanston, Illinois (a suburb of Chicago), Hynek was also one of those fortunate beings who always happen to be in the right place at the right time. In the late 1940s, when still in his early thirties, Hynek was recognized as a rising star (so to speak) and appointed astronomical consultant to the USAF's Project Sign, the official – if not the only – government body established to gather and assess UFO reports. Sign collapsed in 1949, its belief in the extraterrestrial origins of UFOs disbelieved and savagely discredited by the USAF establishment, to be succeeded by Project Grudge and in due course by the long-standing Project Blue Book, which was eventually wound up in 1969.

Hynek survived these political shifts and upheavals, and remained a USAF consultant right through until the end of Project Blue Book, when the USAF officially proclaimed the end of its interest in UFOs. Always, from his earliest professional acquaintance with UFOs until his dying day, Hynek rejected the extraterrestrial hypothesis – the belief that UFOs and their occupants come from some reach of space beyond this Earth – but in the course of 20 years spent investigating UFO reports on behalf of the USAF came to be convinced that something indubitably real lay behind the UFO phenomenon.

In 1984, in a brief survey of the subject, Hynek summed up his own belief concerning UFOs as follows:

'It is far from certain that UFOs represent a single phenomenon, despite the similarity in patterns of reports from all over the world... Perhaps I may presume to intrude my own opinion on these matters, based on more than 30 years of study. I believe that the UFO phenomenon is in some way directing us to consider an aspect of reality of which we have been hitherto largely unaware – an aspect, indeed, that may eventually be incorporated into our science and may prove to be of great value to the progress of mankind.'

During the International Symposium of the Center for UFO

Studies (of which he was founder and director) in Chicago in 1981, Hynek confided to the author of this book that he believed that UFOs were directed by some kind of intelligence. 'That intelligence may be our own,' he added, but did not expand on his conclusion. Perhaps he felt he did not have to.

CLOSE ENCOUNTERS

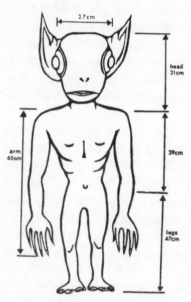

A diagrammatic representation of one of the goblin-like entities that besieged the Sutton farm at Kelly, near Hopkinsville, Kentucky, in August 1955.

So far in this survey of the UFO phenomenon, we have seen that while there is little doubt that the phenomenon itself is real, the hard evidence that it is a physical reality is singularly elusive. The proof, in the form of a solid and indisputable example of a grounded UFO or a captured alien, does not exist. Nevertheless, UFOs of considerable size, apparent complexity and the ability to affect the environment around them continue to be seen and reported. How should one start to sort this kind of evidence?

One of Hynek's most useful contributions to the often confused debate about UFOs was a scheme for analysing the evidence: a standard and non-controversial classification of UFO sightings that any interested party could use as a starting point from which to approach the subject. Hynek divided UFO reports into two basic categories, 'distant' sightings and 'close' encounters. 'Distant' meant that the perceived object was further than 500 ft from the observer; a 'close' encounter is one that takes place less than 500 ft away from the witness.

42

Under distant sightings he listed three sub-categories:

(1) Nocturnal lights – which qualify as UFOs when they make unusual manoeuvres, change speed or direction, show unorthodox configurations, colours or intensity of lights, in such a way as to rule out the presence of conventional aircraft or natural phenomena.

(2) Daylight disks – unusual flying objects seen in daylight. Their shapes may be like cigars, spheres, triangles, boomerangs, eggs, and even pinpoints.

(3) Radar visuals – a comparatively rare event, when there is instrumental evidence of an unidentified object that correlates with the witness's 'subjective' report. Hynek rejected UFOs detected solely by radar because of the high proportion of 'clutter' that can appear on radar screens, especially those scanning near ground level. This distinction has perhaps become less important since many aircraft, civil and military, are now equipped with transponders that identify them individually on air traffic control and military radar screens. A consistent 'unknown' appearing in commercial or military airspace with no such electronic tag may well be a UFO.

Hynek also listed three 'kinds' of close encounter:

(1) Close encounters of the first kind: UFOs are witnessed at close quarters but do not affect the environment.

(2) Close encounters of the second kind: the UFO has physical effects on animate and or inanimate objects around it - animals are frightened, the ground is burned, electromagnetic systems such as radios or car lights and engines cease to function, and so on.

(3) Close encounters of the third kind entities are seen in or near the UFO. Initially Hynek rejected reports that people had had intelligent communication with the occupants of UFOs, and reports of abductions, as never being made by 'sensible, rational and reputable persons', but did come to accept some experiences of this kind. Such cases are now often referred to as 'Close encounters of the fourth kind' in deference to the fact that his classification has now become standard among UFO analysts.

Hynek also referred to some UFO reports as having 'high strangeness', although he never made this term part of his system of ordering as such.

THE BLACK SQUADRON

The nocturnal light is the most commonly reported UFO and is the sighting most prone to misidentification, wishful thinking or even, in extreme cases, fantasy. The number of advertising planes, their sides ablaze with some promotional message, is legion in the USA, and so is the number that have been proved to be the source of the most authentic-sounding UFO reports.

Even the most orthodox aircraft, seen at night at an unexpected angle, especially if it is large and replete with tail illuminations, landing lamps and anti-collision beacons, can become a veritable festival of light – and look very strange indeed.

Proof of alien contact and government cover-up this picture, taken in Germany in the 1950s, shows a tiny alien corpse from a saucer that crashed near Mexico City and had been sent to Europe for analysis.

Daylight disks – unless the sighting is supported by high quality photographs – can be equally ambiguous. The editor of the British partwork magazine *The Unexplained* once recounted how, in the late 1970s, he had been driving the sparsely travelled US Route 95 between Beatty and Las Vegas, Nevada, when around mid-afternoon he saw streaking across the sky an object that looked like no aircraft known to him (the son of an aviation engineer and inventor, he is familiar with a wide range of aircraft).

The craft performed no bizarre manoeuvres or aerobatics, but it was oval-shaped, with a slight bulge at the rear end, apparently wingless and tail-less, and 'the colour of dried blood'. Its speed was 'no greater than might be expected from a large, fast strike aircraft – say an F-15 Eagle – at that apparent distance. That would by most standards be very fast – the F-15 can top 1,800 mph in level flight. But there was in any case no way of knowing whether the mystery object was very small and very near, or very large and very distant; the featureless desert terrain was no help in deciding how far away the craft was, or in giving some clue as to its real size. But he was intrigued to find himself, some miles further on, passing the entrance to the USAF's Indian Springs base. Such installations seem to attract UFOs.

This picture of a UFO over Paris was taken by an engineer, Paul Pauline, at around 3.45 a.m. on 29 December 1953.

As it happened, the witness soon had a clue to what he may have seen: returning to Phoenix, Arizona, where he was the guest of a former USAF pilot, he learned that Indian Springs is indeed out of the usual run of USAF bases: it is the home of the USAF's 'black squadron' of covertly acquired Soviet aircraft, and over the years has been host to a number of experimental aircraft. The apparent size and, most particularly, the wingless shape and unusual colour of the object he had seen matched that of an aerofoil designed and built by NASA as part of its development programme for the space shuttle. The first shuttle was launched about a year after this sighting, so why a one-off experimental craft should still be flying, in such a location, so late in the life of NASA's programme is anyone's guess. But the point of this account was to illustrate the ambiguous nature of daylight disk sightings – even partly explained ones!

HIDDEN PURPOSES

Radar/visual cases, when they occur, offer much richer pickings to the ufologist, but they still offer no clear-cut clues as to the nature of what has caused the sighting, or what the purpose of the UFO may have been at the time.

At around 9 p.m. on 10 October 1990, residents around Skibo, Minnesota, began reporting unusual lights in the sky that were appearing to the south-east of nearby Hoyt Lakes. Two police officers who were sent to investigate saw, as did other witnesses, numerous objects 'of indeterminate shape, alternately hovering and darting about'. A little over an hour after the first reports were received, the Federal Aviation Authority's air traffic controllers at Duluth, the area's major airport, confirmed radar echoes from the Hoyt Lakes area, and for more than an hour after that one of the ATCs at Duluth monitored the echoes. There were between three and five objects registering intermittently, in roughly circular formation. The local National Air Guard radar also picked up the same returns.

Further confirmation came from the pilot of a commercial aircraft flying at 11,000 ft about 45 miles west of Hoyt Lakes, who reported seeing two steady, distinct and unidentified lights at an estimated 1,000 ft below him. They were a few miles apart and a deep, glowing red. Investigators noted that no other conventional aircraft were in the area, and 'no known weather factors accounted for the anomalous radar returns'.

HARD EVIDENCE

The most spectacular UFO cases are without doubt the 'close encounters', and it is in these, especially in encounters of the second kind, that we might best be able to judge whether Hynek was on to something in speculating that the UFO phenomenon is 'in some way directing us to an aspect of reality of which we have hitherto been largely unaware'. For here, the normal and the paranormal seem to meet at an interface – as they do to a lesser extent in radar/ visual cases, but as they do not in the almost wholly paranormal and possibly entirely psychological experiences that constitute close encounters of the third kind.

This is not to say that something real does not happen in such encounters, but they are one crucial stage further removed from the everyday material world than those of the second kind. And this

Close encounters of the third kind, as shown in artist's impression – a meeting between a French farmer, two entities and their egg-shaped craft in a lavender field in the 1950s.

makes encounters of the third kind exceptionally difficult to analyse, for we are again, immediately, confronted with the old riddle about the kind of reality we are dealing with. In close encounters of the second kind we have at least a modicum of 'hard' evidence to add to the witnesses' accounts of their subjective experience. Hynek himself said close encounters of the second kind 'bear a special importance, for when it is reported that a UFO left tangible evidence of its presence… we find the real challenge to scientific enquiry'.

RED INSIGNIA

One of the classic such cases occurred at Socorro, New Mexico, in 1964 - the same town near which, in 1947, Grady L. Barnett reputedly found a crashed UFO. At about 5.45 p.m. on 24 April 1964 - a clear, sunny day with a strong wind blowing – patrolman Lonnie Zamora, on duty in the Socorro Two police cruiser, gave chase to a speeding Chevrolet. While in pursuit, he heard a brief roar and saw a flame in the sky to his right. Zamora knew there was a shack containing dynamite in the vicinity, and his first thought was that it had blown up. He abandoned his chase and headed for the shack.

During this time the flame – blue and orange in colour, smokeless, long and narrow, and broadening toward the bottom – was descending toward the ground. The base of the flame was invisible behind a low hill to Zamora's left. Concentrating on his driving, he did not notice any object atop the flame and, besides, the sun was in his eyes.

While looking out for the shack, he noticed 'a shiny-type object to [the] south' between 100 and 200 yds off the road and below him in a gully. 'It looked', Zamora told FBI agent J. Arthur Bymes Jr later the same day, 'like a car turned upside down… standing on [its] radiator or trunk.'

Next to the object were 'two people in white coveralls… One of these persons seemed to turn and look straight at my car and seemed startled – seemed to quickly jump somewhat.' They 'appeared normal in shape – but possibly they were small adults or large kids'. Zamora radioed Sgt Sam Chavez at the sheriff's office in Socorro that he was about to investigate a possible accident, then, as he got out of the car, his radio mike fell. While he turned back to replace it, he heard 'two or three loud thumps... a second or less apart'.

Zamora approached to within 75 or 100 ft of the object, which he now saw was oval and smooth, with no windows or doors, on girder-like legs. He also noted red insignia on its side, about $2^1/_2$ ft wide. Then the roar began again, low frequency at first, rising rapidly and getting 'very loud'. The object was emitting a flame and kicking up dust. There was no sign of the 'persons' he had seen before.

Zamora thought the object might explode, and ran. The roar stopped, and he looked back to see the UFO 'going away from me in a south-west direction... possibly 10 to 15 ft above the ground, and it cleared the dynamite shack by about 3 ft'. The UFO, now travelling very fast but no longer emitting either noise or flame, rose up and sped away. It 'just cleared' a mountain in the distance and disappeared.

When Sgt Chavez arrived on the scene, he and Zamora went to investigate the spot where the UFO had landed, and where the brush was still burning. They were soon joined by FBI Agent Byrne, in Socorro on another case – and Deputy Sheriff James Lucky. They found four burn marks, and four V-shaped depressions, between 1 and 2 in deep and roughly 18 in long, in the ground in an asymmetrical diamond pattern around the burns. These corresponded to the 'legs' Zamora had seen on the mystery craft, and an independent engineer's analysis later declared that each would have been bearing a load of at least 1 ton to press so deeply into the dense earth of the district. Five other, smaller marks nearby were labelled 'footprints'. All these marks were photographed the following day.

Hynek arrived in Socorro on 28 April to investigate the sighting on behalf of the USAF's Project Blue Book. His first task was to establish the truth of Zamora's testimony, and that he could not fault. At his instigation, the USAF checked – to no avail – whether any aerospace company had been privately developing such a craft. The USAF did not, however, follow up Hynek's request that they attempt to trace the car driver who told the manager of a gas station on US Highway 85 (since superseded by Interstate 25) that he had seen some kind of aircraft just south of town, obviously in trouble and landing – and a police car was approaching it.

Sceptics have had some difficulty in trying to dispose of the Socorro case, imputing motives for a hoax to the town's mayor and suggesting that otherwise Zamora saw a 'ball of plasma' and imagined the rest. The USAF initially thought that a lunar exploration module, then being developed, was somehow responsible, but no such vehicle resembles what Zamora saw; Blue Book finally classified the sighting as 'unidentified'. Hynek himself concluded that 'a real physical event' occurred in Socorro that day.

HYSTERICAL WITH FEAR

A less celebrated but no less intriguing case occurred in England three and a half years after the events at Socorro. Sometime between 1 and 2 a.m. on 6 November 1967, Carl Farlow was driving his truck on the A338 trunk road between the villages of Sopley and Avon in Hampshire. He was approaching a junction when his lights died. The truck's diesel engine (which does not depend on an electrical ignition system) kept running and, assuming a simple short circuit of some kind, Farlow pulled up to investigate.

Before he could climb down from the cab, he was astonished to see a bizarre egg-shaped object move from right to left across the road in front of him at about 25 ft from the ground. It was magenta-coloured, with a white base, and was perhaps 80 ft long – big enough to overhang both sides of the road as it passed, exuded a smell 'like a drill boring through wood' and made a sound 'like a refrigerator'. As it crossed the road it accelerated gradually, then disappeared.

Farlow then realized that a Jaguar sedan, which had been coming in the opposite direction, was stranded on the other side of the UFO's path. Its driver, who was a veterinarian, approached Farlow, explained that his vehicle was out of action and his lady passenger hysterical, and suggested they call the police. The police arrived at the scene shortly afterwards. Their preliminary inspection of the site showed that the surface of the road seemed to have melted. The vet's passenger was taken to hospital to be treated for shock, while the two men were questioned first by police and later by a member of the Ministry of Defence.

Next day, Farlow returned to his truck. A bulldozer was at work levelling the road, the phone booth was being repainted, and other people seemed to be investigating the area with instruments. A week or so later, taking the same route in his truck, Farlow saw that some 70 yds of that particular stretch of road had been resurfaced.

BURNT BY RADIATION

Betty Cash, Vickie Landrum and her seven-year-old grandson Colby Landrum were driving home to Dayton, near Houston, Texas, on the evening of 29 December 1980, after a meal in nearby New Caney. Around 9 p.m. the trio, with Betty at the wheel, were on Highway FM1485, which runs through a forest of oak and pine. Then, Colby pointed to a bright light moving over the trees ahead of them. The light grew larger and larger – until it became 'like a diamond of fire', in Vickie Landrum's words – while every so often flames burst from beneath it. Suddenly, it was right in their way.

Betty braked hard. The three watched as the UFO hovered above the road about 60 yds away. From treetop level it sank to within 25 ft of the highway, gave out a blast of fire, and rose again. It did this several times, mesmerizing the car's occupants. They actually climbed out to see the object, which was lighting up the trees and the highway all around it, more clearly. It seemed to be made of dull aluminium, and the four points of its diamond shape were rounded. A row of blue dots ran across its centre. Now and then it emitted a beeping sound. A terrific heat was coming from the UFO, and Colby begged his grandmother to get back in the car. She and he both did, but Betty stayed outside until the object moved up and away. The car was now so hot that she could not touch the door with bare hands. Then a crowd of helicopters appeared. 'They seemed to rush in from all directions,' said Betty. 'It seemed like they were trying to encircle the thing.'

They drove on another five miles to where they could see the UFO in the distance, and the swarm of helicopters around it. One, a giant, twin-rotor CH-47 Chinook, roared right over them. They counted a total of 23 machines of various types apparently in pursuit of the clearly visible UFO.

But worse was to follow. Over the next few hours, the trio developed painful swellings and blisters on their skin and had severe headaches and stomach upsets. Vickie's hair began to fall out. Colby suffered a sunburn-like rash. Over the following week or so, Betty's eyes also became swollen to the point that she could not see, and she had to be hospitalized. In a few weeks all three had lost some hair and were developing eye problems. Their hair eventually grew again, although it was different from their original hair. Since their experience, none has entirely recovered their former good health. Doctors said that the symptoms shown by the three victims were consistent with exposure to intense electro-magnetic radiation in the ultra-violet, microwave and X-ray bands.

The NASA space shuttle may easily be taken for UFOs by witnesses unfamiliar with the shapes of such machines.

Investigators later established that other witnesses could confirm the UFO's flight path and appearance, and the presence of unusual numbers of CH-47 helicopters – which are quite distinctive – in the sky that night. Yet local civil airfields and military airbases deny that such a fleet used their facilities or showed on their radar. Vickie Landrum was convinced that a secret military device run haywire was responsible for her injuries, and she and Betty Cash sued the US government for $20 million in that belief. In 1986, the case was dismissed on the grounds that 'no such object was owned, operated or in the inventory' of the US Army, Navy, Air Force or NASA.

However, what the US government has not said may be significant, for it has not been obliged to admit whether or not it knows what the object was, irrespective of who owns it. So the origin and nature of the Texas UFO – like that of all other UFOs – remains an enigma. That is precious little comfort to those it affected, or to those trying to solve the mystery of UFOs as a whole. The Texas UFO case is perhaps the most baffling and frustrating of modern times, for what starts with solid evidence for a notoriously elusive phenomenon peters out in a maze of dead ends, official denials, and perhaps even deviousness.

Nonetheless, the three classic close encounters of the second kind discussed here show significant similarities. In the Avon and Texas cases there is a strong indication of military involvement, and it is possible, if by no means proven, that the military may have had some connection with the Socorro case – for by 1964, the White Sands Missile Range had acquired a further 883,910 acres of land that extended the range northwards, east of the town. There are certain physical similarities between the Texas UFO and the Socorro craft. And it is apparent that the authorities had no wish to admit to the existence of either the Avon or the Texas UFO – both of which involved multiple witnesses. And in all cases there were real physical effects, either on people or on the environment.

Are we dealing here with secret military hardware gone wrong, bursting disastrously into public gaze? Or were the UFOs alien craft that were busy trying to escape military scrutiny? Or – the wildest scenario of all, but one that some ufologists take seriously – was the military already well aware that the craft were alien, and simply trying to hide their knowledge, or even their collusion with the UFOs?

UFOS: THE PHYSICAL EVIDENCE

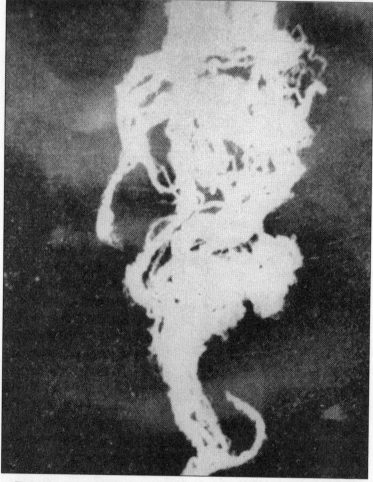

Evidence of UFOs is dramatic and varied but too often the trail goes cold. Are the scientists being silenced? And, if so, is the controlling force a human mind or something far more powerful?

The three cases considered in the last chapter demonstrate that one part at least of the UFO phenomenon involves actual hardware – since we have to assume that only physical, mechanical objects have the capacity to melt road surfaces, crush compacted, dried-out desert earth, and maim witnesses.

It is also clear from that evidence that these cases do not really illuminate ufologist J. Allen Hynek's remark late in his life that 'the UFO phenomenon is in some way directing us to consider an aspect of reality of which we have been hitherto largely unaware – an aspect, indeed, that may eventually be incorporated into our science and may prove to be of great value to the progress of mankind'. Nor do they bear out his belief that close encounters of the second kind 'bear a special importance, for when it is reported that a UFO left tangible evidence of its presence... we find the real challenge to scientific enquiry'.

For here were three classic close encounters that seem to be all too real in worldly terms to indicate that some other order or aspect of reality is involved (although it may well be in other kinds of encounter, of course). Scientific enquiry bore very little fruit in the two American cases. If it was permitted in the English case, the scientists involved were clearly silenced by the Official Secrets Act. What they already knew, or what they discovered – if anything – is still under wraps.

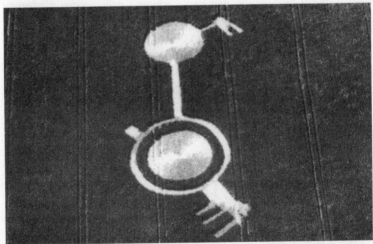

Crop circles were once taken to be UFO 'nests' or landing sites.

The manner in which the scientific trail peters out in these cases is typical of the UFO phenomenon as a whole: the most promising clues to at least part of the phenomenon are leads only to dead ends. Even when investigators are presented with quite dramatic evidence, or material that can be put into a laboratory and analysed, the conclusions raise as many questions as they answer. Not the least baffling aspect of the physical traces that UFOs leave behind is that they are as varied as reports of the appearance of UFOs and their extraordinary occupants – as the following, necessarily brief, survey shows.

ANGEL HAIR

French ufologist Aimé Michel recounted this instance (of many on record) of the gossamer-like material called 'angel hair' that has occasionally fallen from the sky during a UFO sighting.

At about 12.50 p.m. on 17 October 1952, a M. Prigent, the headmaster of a school at Oloron, France, was having lunch with his family when they saw a small fleet of UFOs and a 'mother ship' flying a zigzag course. The latter was a white cylinder, apparently tilted into the sky, at an estimated altitude of 8,000 ft. Travelling in pairs ahead of it were some 30 spherical objects that, M. Prigent saw through binoculars, were red spheres with yellow planetary rings around them, like smaller editions of Saturn. From time to time all these objects seemed to give out puffs of smoke, but they also left long trails of some other substance, which drifted to the ground. A large number of witnesses testified that for hours afterwards the material kept falling; it was gelatinous at first, but eventually vaporized and disappeared.

Scientists could offer no clue as to its nature – and, of course, could not examine it.

STEALTH TECHNOLOGY

One of the most dramatic reports of a radar/visual UFO sighting, with radical physical effects as well, hit the Russian press (including the district military newspaper *Za Rodinu*) in 1990, after a series of bizarre events at the long-range radar tracking station near the city of Samara (then called Kuybyshev) in Russia.

At 12.07 a.m. on 13 September 1990, the radar watch saw a blip 'comparable to that of a strategic bomber' at a range of 60 miles appear on their screens. The station's automatic electronic IFF (Identify Friend or Foe) system then failed, preventing the watch from identifying whether the aircraft was hostile or not. Two and a half minutes after its first appearance, the large blip then scattered into a host of smaller returns. By the time these were within 25 miles or so of the station, the largest of them was showing as a triangular-shaped object, and heading straight for the radar post. As it approached, a team of soldiers was scrambled to investigate: the thing shot over their heads, less than 35 ft up, as they came into the open. Then it stopped, hovering about 100 yds beyond a barbed wire barrier that lay less than 50 yds from a mobile, short-range radar array known as Post No. 12. There was a flash, and No. 12's paired aerials caught fire; the upper one collapsed to the ground. Later inspection revealed that all the steel parts had been melted.

Witnesses - both officers and enlisted men – described the mystery triangle as black and 'smooth… not mirror-like – it was like a thick layer of soot'. Its sides were each about 45 ft long, and it was about 10 ft thick. There were no openings or portholes. The machine remained hovering for about 90 minutes after destroying the radar, while the post soldiers covered it – somewhat optimistically – with small arms. Then it took off.

After the press reports came official denials, and the announcement on 23 September 1990 that the story was a hoax perpetrated by a reporter on *Za Rodinu*. But it seems that a Soviet Defence Ministry commission investigated the site on 18 September, and removed the wrecked upper aerial of Post No. 12 for study. Unnamed military sources claimed to have examined the site of the event and seen tapes of the initial series of radar returns.

The description of both these on-screen radar effects and the craft itself suggests all the characteristics of 'stealth' technology – another instance of a UFO suddenly adopting an ultra-modern but little understood technological disguise. While the 'flash' and the destruction of the radar post could have been caused by a plane missile, it seems unlikely that an American stealth aircraft would have perpetrated such a provocation. And the USAF is the only military force known to have that kind of advanced aircraft in service.

Cameras can lie. This apparent formation of four UFOs was photographed by a US coastguard at the Salem, Massachusetts, Air Station in August 1952. Analysis has shown that the 'lights in the sky' are actually reflections of terrestrial lights on to the camera lens.

SCORCHED EARTH

The notorious crop circles that plagued British farmers during the 1980s and early 1990s were very soon identified by some enthusiastic devotees of the paranormal as traces of UFO activity. However, the increasing elaborateness of the circles, the emergence of possible scientific explanations and finally the confessions of hoaxers have somewhat reduced the strength of the 'UFO hypothesis'. While hoaxers were certainly not responsible for all the circles, and even the scientists admit their explanation is far from complete, the evidence for UFOs in the usually accepted sense of the term being involved seems remote.

Among the commonest ground effects left by UFOs, however, is evidence of burning.

Over a period of two hours or so during the day of 8 October 1978, various members of the Sturgess family noticed 'something' in a field close to their house (the property is near Jenkins, Missouri) but thought little of it until it rose in the air. Six family members saw the object move away and meet another object; both then vanished, in broad daylight. Inspection of the site where the thing had been resting revealed a 4 ft circle of scorched grass, within which were three smaller circles burnt into the ground. Scientific analysis showed nothing unusual about the samples taken, however.

Samples of earth taken from a site at Medford, Minnesota, after a UFO was seen landing there on 2 November 1975 did, however, reveal some curious qualities. In radiation tests conducted by the Space Technology Laboratory at the University of Kansas, Lawrence, the samples showed ten times the thermo-luminescence of control samples from near the site, but appeared identical under the microscope. Dr Edward Zellner, the university's professor of geology, physics and astronomy, called these variations 'unusual' and 'an anomaly', but added: 'Like so much of the other data [that] has been obtained on the UFO phenomenon, the results… are inconclusive.'

On 30 September 1980, an extraordinary series of effects accompanied the UFO witnessed by 'Mr B', a farmhand and caretaker on a 600-acre property five miles from Rosedale, Victoria, in Australia. At about 1 a.m., Mr B woke to the sound of the farm's cattle going wild – accompanied by 'a strange screeching whistling'. He got up to investigate. There was no wind, and the moon was out; Mr B saw a domed object about 15 ft high and 25 ft broad with a white top, showing blue and orange lights. For a while it hovered over a concrete water tank about 450 yds from the house, then came to rest on the ground 15 or 20 yds further on.

Mr B clambered on a motorcycle and drove to within 50 ft of the object. There was no effect on his machine, but the whistling from the UFO suddenly rose to deafening heights, there was a huge bang, and the thing lifted off. At the same time, a blast of hot air nearly knocked Mr B over. The UFO dropped some debris and then flew away to the east, holding a height of no more than 100 ft.

Mr B examined the site early next day. He found a ring of blackened grass, flattened in an anti-clockwise direction. Inside the ring was green grass, but flowers that had been growing there had disappeared. In a line to the east outside the ring was a trail of debris - stones, weeds and cow dung. For some days after the sighting Mr B suffered from headaches and nausea, and his watch refused to work normally. Strangest of all, the water tank over which the UFO had paused had been emptied of 10,000 gallons of water.

BIZARRE PHENOMENA

One of the most common physical reactions to a UFO is the collapse of electrical systems, radios and similar equipment in cars driven by witnesses. This is sometimes, but not always, accompanied by witnesses suffering rashes and nausea after the sighting, a medically recognized reaction to certain kinds of electro-magnetic (EM) radiation. Two cases, more than six years apart and widely separated geographically, show a weird variation on this theme.

Ronald Sullivan was driving on a long, straight stretch of road nine miles east of Bealiba, Victoria, Australia, during the night of 4 April 1966 when his headlight beams suddenly and inexplicably

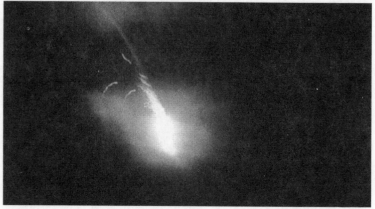

Ball lightning, photographed in Austria in summer 1978. Some researchers believe that all alleged UFOs are little-known or poorly understood natural phenomena such as this.

bent part way along their length to the right - as if they had been pieces of pipe. Sullivan screeched to a stop, and was then treated to a brilliant display of coloured lights coming from a field by the road. After that, an object rose up from the field and vanished. Sutherland had his lights checked before reporting the incident to the police; they were in perfect order. When the police investigated the site they found a circular depression about 5 ft across and 5 in at its deepest in the field. Sullivan reported that he 'did not believe in UFOs'.

Six and a half years later, something similar occurred at Taizé, in eastern France. At about 1 a.m. on 11 August 1972, a group of about 30 people gathered at the Protestant monastery there, witnessed a 90 ft long UFO hovering against a hillside opposite the building. This then gave a bizarre light display that involved apparently solid beams of light extending slowly to the ground. Four of those present decided to take a closer look, and went across the fields toward it armed with torches. After about 600 yds they came across a dark mass about 20 ft high and shaped like a haystack. When they shone their torches at it, the beams turned upwards at right angles just a foot or so from the object.

Neither case has been satisfactorily explained, although it is perhaps worth noting that the EM effects here occurred on an unusual frequency – that of visible light – rather than on the longer radio wavelengths that more commonly are affected by UFOs. Even this is not much help, since so many of the data on UFOs are concerned precisely with bizarre phenomena involving light.

MARKS OF THE MIND

The disparate forms of the different entities seen around UFOs, the variety of shapes and sizes of the craft themselves (if craft they are), the rarity and ambiguity of the physical evidence: all these suggest that the UFO is not one thing, but several – and possibly many.

How does the UFO phenomenon divide up, given the evidence we have? What kinds of UFO are there?

The first essential distinction to make is that in many cases something undoubtedly physical has presented itself to witnesses.

But what kind of physical thing is it? There are six possibilities worth serious consideration:

UFOs are alien craft from planets in outer space.

UFOs are alien craft from a shy and elusive culture that shares our Earth and perhaps our Solar System.

UFOs are secret terrestrial craft, probably military in origin, which hide behind a screen of 'flying saucer myths'.

UFOs are not 'nuts and bolts' craft of any kind, but some kind of biological phenomenon – although some (those without apparent occupants) may possibly be wild creatures, while those with occupants may have been domesticated.

UFOs are natural phenomena that are related to ball lightning, plasma, and other little-understood manifestations of physics.

UFOs are intrusions, accidental or deliberately engineered, from other physical dimensions or parallel universes.

As the reported behaviour of UFOs is so varied, it is quite possible that each of these hypotheses is true for a particular set of circumstances – although some of them are more probable than others. But there is no law to say that if UFOs are physical objects, they have to be all the same kind of object.

On the other hand they may not be objects at all. Not all UFOs leave physical traces, and many are seen by only a single witness, even over highly populated areas. So it is not inconceivable that the UFO phenomenon is an entirely psychological – even psychic – one. There are three major hypotheses that attempt to account for UFOs as immaterial phenomena:

UFOs are hallucinations, triggered by some actual event but confined in reality to the mind of the witness.

UFOs are indeed hallucinations, but the mental event has been induced by an alien intelligence, either from deep space or from nearer at hand. Both this and the previous suggestion would explain why UFOs present themselves in forms that are appropriate to the particular era in which the witness lives.

UFOs are material objects – but they are brought into being only by the unconscious psychic working of the witness – or even by the working of the mass unconscious.

Once again it is not outside the bounds of possibility that all three explanations are true, one or another applying to differing circumstances and different sets of evidence.

Researchers in the 1950s used a chart of basic UFO types to help classify sightings. Note the variety of shapes and configurations – an aspect of UFOs that remains unchanged to this day.

However, there is another possibility. All nine of the hypotheses offered here may be correct – in other words, it may be the case that some UFOs are indeed hallucinations, while some are natural physical and biological phenomena, some are alien craft, others are military in origin, and so on. Just as there is no rule that dictates that all UFOs must be physical objects, so there is no law to say that UFO sightings must be either physical or psychic events. They may be one or the other; they may on occasion even be a mixture of both, the product of an interaction between physical and psychological states, planes of being, or even dimensions.

Judging from a number of remarks that he made in private, it is likely that it was some such insight that J. Allen Hynek had in mind when he suggested that UFOs should make us 'consider an aspect of reality of which we have been hitherto largely unaware'. The UFO phenomenon is almost unique in exhibiting almost every aspect of the paranormal there is; the physical traces that we have been considering in this chapter may, in fact, be the marks left by the mind – although whether it is the human mind at work here, or the mind of someone or something else, we cannot be certain.

ABDUCTED BY ALIENS

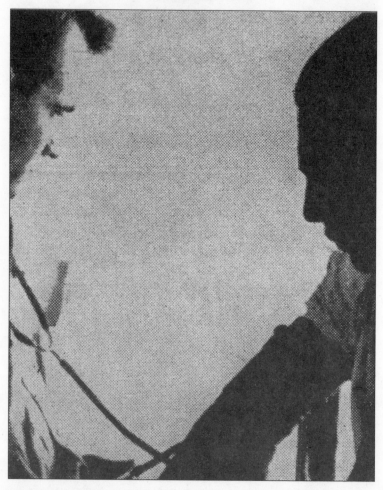

Sensational stories of abduction and grotesque sexual experiments carried out by aliens may be easy to discount, but how do the 'experts' discredit the consistent testimony of a respected sober-suited lawyer?

At the age of 23, Antonio Villas Boas lived a hard but simple life with his parents, his brothers and sisters-in-law on a small farm near the town of São Francisco de Salles, in the Brazilian state of Minas Gerais. With his brothers, Villas Boas worked the farm: while the family had hired help in during the day, Antonio worked at night. On the night of 15–16 October 1957, he was out alone, ploughing the fields by the light of his tractor's headlamps.

He may not have been entirely surprised when, at about 1 a.m., he saw what he described as a 'large red star' descending out of the sky toward the end of the field he was working. At about 9.30 p.m. the previous evening, he had been out ploughing with his brother, and the pair had seen a dim red ball of light hovering about 300 ft above the northern end of the field they were working. He had then tried to get close to the light to see what was behind it, but it eluded him, darting from one end of the field to the other.

But this time Villas Boas was alone, and petrified, for as the red light came down to about 150 ft above him, he could see that it was an apparently egg-shaped object. Its brilliant glow drowned out the lights of his tractor as it landed – lowering three shafts as an undercarriage - no more than 50 ft from where he was sitting. The machine had a definite rim, in which were set purple lights. Three spurs were set at the front, lit up with red light. The upper, domed part of the machine was spinning anti-clockwise, and as it slowed to land, it changed colour from red to green.

Antonio tried to escape on his tractor, but the engine died after a few yards. He jumped from the seat and started to struggle across the ploughed field. Then someone grabbed him from behind. He knocked the creature flying, but was grabbed by three others – none higher than his shoulder, and he is only 5 ft 5 in tall – and dragged to the waiting craft. He was taken struggling up a flexible ladder into the machine, and found himself in a small, square, brightly lit room with metallic walls.

He realized that there were five small entities present: two kept a firm hold on him. They were wearing tight-fitting suits of thick, soft, unevenly striped grey material, and large, broad helmets reinforced with bands of metal. Pipes led down from the helmets to their clothes, two going under each armpit and one down their backs. Thick-soled 'shoes' seemed to be integral to their suits, as did thick, unwieldy gloves. All Villas Boas could see of the creatures' features through the helmets were their small, pale blue eyes.

He was then taken into another bright room, this time oval-shaped. Here, the aliens first attempted a conversation with their captive. Villas Boas later recalled that the sounds they made 'were so totally different from anything I had heard.. .They were slow barks and yelps, neither very clear nor very hoarse, some longer, some shorter, at times containing several different sounds all at once… But they were simply sounds, animal barks… I still shudder when I think of those sounds. I can't reproduce them – my voice just isn't made for that.'

Failing to communicate in words, the five diminutive aliens then proceeded to strip the protesting farmer of his clothes. One of the beings rubbed a wet sponge-like thing over his skin, and then he was led through still another door. This had an inscription over it in red 'letters', which he was able to reproduce later for investigators. (At first glance, this looks very like hastily scribbled Arabic, but it seems to relate to no known terrestrial alphabet.) In this chamber, sparsely furnished with a few chairs and a couch, the aliens produced 'a sort of chalice', which they used to take a blood sample. Then Villas Boas was left alone – only to find a weird odour filling the room, which soon had him rushing to a corner of the room to be sick. After that he began to calm down. But then came the most bizarre part of his experience aboard the alien ship.

A sign over one of the doors which Antonio Villas Boas saw, when he came in contact with an alien craft.

SEXUAL ENCOUNTERS

He had been standing there naked for perhaps half an hour when the door to the room opened - to reveal a woman 'whose body was more beautiful than any I have ever seen before'. This was something Antonio could hardly help noticing, for she was entirely nude.

The woman stood shoulder-high to him. Her hair was parted in the middle, and reached halfway down her neck before it curled inward. It was smooth, fair, almost white, except for her armpits and pubic hair, which was bright red. She had a pointed chin, straight nose, high cheekbones, and large blue eyes. Her arms were freckled. Her body, said Villas Boas, was 'slim, and her breasts stood up high and well separated. Her waistline was thin, her belly flat, her hips well developed, and her thighs were large.' What happened next was perhaps inevitable, and best told in Antonio Villas Boas's own words:

'The woman came toward me in silence, looking at me all the while as if she wanted something from me, and suddenly she hugged me and began to rub her head against my face from side to side. At the same time I also felt her body glued to mine and it also was moving.'

Villas Boas wondered if the liquid the aliens had spread on him had been some kind of stimulant, but he, at least, needed none:

'We ended up on the couch, where we lay together for the first time. It was a normal act and she reacted as any other woman would. Then we had some petting, followed by another act, but by now she had begun to deny herself to me, to end the matter.'

At that, Antonio too lost interest – and became angry, as it dawned on him that 'all they wanted [was] a good stallion to improve their stock... but [I] decided not to attach any importance to the fact, for anyhow I had spent a few agreeable moments with the woman'. His impression that he was being used in a quite calculating fashion may have been reinforced by the fact that the woman never kissed him, although she did bite him gently on the chin.

Shortly after this (it seems not to have occurred to Villas Boas that his activities were possibly being monitored), the woman was

67

called away. Before she left, she pointed to her stomach, and then at the sky, which he interpreted as meaning that sooner or later she, and the other aliens, would return to take him away. Brazilian investigators persuaded him, however, that she had simply meant that she would bear their child on her home planet. After this, Antonio Villas Boas was given back his clothes and taken on a guided tour of the alien craft, during which he tried, and failed, to purloin an instrument as a keepsake. Then he was carried back down the ladder to the ground, from where he saw the UFO take off, listing slightly to one side and then disappearing into the sky like a bullet. He had been aboard the craft for 4 hours, 15 minutes.

The Villas Boas case boggled the UK investigators who heard about it so much that it was not until 12 years after these events that the witness's name was published. While the case became a classic in ufology, little was heard about Villas Boas himself. But in 1978 he surfaced again on a TV programme in Brazil – no longer a simple peasant farmer, but Dr Antonio Villas Boas, a sober lawyer with a practice in a small town near the nation's capital, Brasilia, happily married and with four children. The only item of his testimony that he changed was minor: the woman had taken a sperm sample from him during their second act of intercourse.

To the determined sceptic, the Villas Boas case has always been the fantasy of a simple Brazilian rustic. Yet the person who experienced what he did in October 1957, and the man who had gained academic distinction and a respected place in his community 21 years later, were essentially one and the same. Intelligent, articulate, educated and determined, Dr Villas Boas was revealed as a person who cannot be dismissed any more as a mere 'peasant' – which is to say, ignorant, superstitious, and clod-hopping. And he did not change his mind, or contradict himself, when questioned 21 years later about his abduction.

Perhaps most important, his first account of that bizarre, frightening, yet exciting night was given straight from his conscious memory, and less than four months afterward. Unlike many who have claimed to recall – sometimes more than 20 years after the alleged events – being abducted by aliens and having sometimes grotesque sexual experiences while in their custody, Antonio Villas Boas did not need to be hypnotized to be able to give the most detailed account of what happened to him.

THE 'MISSING TIME'

The 'AVB' case, as it was known among ufologists, was long regarded as almost unique in the annals of abductions in that it involved a sexual encounter – although still more astounding claims were published in Germany in 1977, by South African Elizabeth Klarer. She maintained that between 1954 and 1963 she had numerous meetings with the two-man crew of a craft from the planet Meton, in the solar system of Proxima Centauri, the nearest star to the Sun, 4.3 light-years away. One of the aliens, the astrophysicist Akon, became the father of her child, and Klarer says she spent four months on Meton before her son was born, after which she was obliged to return to Earth while he remained on Meton with his father. Few ufologists took Klarer's claims seriously – as so often with contactees who allege they have visited

A UFO approaches a witness and disgorges three aliens during a close encounter near Pirassununga, São Paulo, Brazil, in September 1976.

known star systems, the laws of celestial mechanics spoil her story. Proxima Centauri is part of the triple-star system of Alpha Centauri, and as such is highly unlikely to have any planets. And even if it did, the star is a red dwarf – too small and too feeble to support life of any kind.

The typical pattern of abductee accounts did not, until the 1980s, involve any specifically sexual component at all. The classic scenario is reflected in the well-known accounts given by Betty and Barney Hill (abducted in New Hampshire in 1961), Betty Andreasson (in Massachusetts, 1967), Calvin Parker and Charlie Hickson (in Mississippi, 1973), David Stephens (in Maine, 1975), Whitley Strieber (in New York State, 1985) and others.

The events reported by these witnesses followed this basic pattern: first came a UFO sighting, sometimes involving electro-magnetic effects or other physical effects on the witnesses' vehicles. A key factor in the vast majority of such cases emerges after the UFO has departed: the events of what seem like a few minutes' duration turn out to have taken an hour or more. The witnesses duly report their sighting to the police, local military authorities or the sheriff's office. Of their own accord, or encouraged by their family or members of a UFO investigation organization, witnesses then undergo hypnosis in an attempt to bring out the buried memory of what transpired in the crucial 'missing time' during their UFO encounter.

However, a handful of abductees do have clear memories of this part of their experience and need no such prompting or psychological dredging. But their descriptions of what happened to them in this segment of 'missing time' closely match the reports of hypnotized subjects, even though the physical appearance of the aliens and the exterior of their ships often differ wildly from case to case.

Interiors of alien craft are, according to these witnesses, usually brightly lit, clinically clean, often shiny, with white or metallic appurtenances. The reason for this soon becomes clear, for the next stage in the abduction is a medical examination of some kind – usually a painful one.

Betty Hill and Betty Andreasson independently reported that they were examined with a machine from which needle-like wires protruded. Charles Hickson said his body was 'scanned' by a floating instrument resembling a large eye. Betty Hill and Betty Andreasson also said that needles were inserted into their navels for a 'pregnancy test'. Betty Hill had skin scrapings, samples of ear wax, hair and clippings from her fingernails taken from her. David Stephens had two blood samples taken, and was undressed and examined from head to toe with 'a box-like device'. Whitley Strieber maintained that 'an enormous and extremely ugly object', triangular in structure and with a tangle of wires at one end, was inserted into his rectum.

After this, the witnesses report, they are either allowed to dress and leave the ship – some are 'transferred' directly from the craft or 'floated' back to where the aliens first took them captive – or, occasionally, given a guided tour around the ship first. Once the victims have been returned to their starting point, the UFO leaves at high speed.

GENETIC SAMPLING

The reality, or otherwise, of UFO abductions became a major controversy among ufologists in the 1980s, and excited massive public attention as well. Budd Hopkins, a New York artist who as a result of his own UFO sighting became fascinated by abduction stories, used hypnotic techniques to uncover numerous witnesses' hidden memories of such experiences, and the bestselling book (later made into a film) *Communion* by novelist Whitley Strieber, in which he recounted his own gruesome and humiliating experiences as an abductee, was based on events recalled under hypnosis.

Undoubtedly, Hopkins's book received huge attention in the media because of the new element he had discovered in the cases he had investigated: and that was a constant sexual slant to the stories. Men reported having devices applied to them that relieved them of their sperm. Still greater numbers of women, notably one named Kathie Davis, told stories under hypnosis that suggested to Hopkins that aliens were conducting a deliberate and sustained programme of genetic sampling and possibly even manipulation among the human race, who were mostly unaware of what was being done to them.

According to Hopkins, hypnosis revealed that aliens first visited Kathie Davis when she was a child, and had implanted a device in her head so that they could keep track of her. (She and other members of her family had similar, mysterious scars on their legs, which Hopkins attributed to cell-sampling by the aliens, noting that other alleged abductees bore similar marks.) As a teenager, Kathie became pregnant, but the pregnancy ended suddenly and mysteriously. Hypnosis revealed that before her pregnancy, aliens had visited Kathie, performed an 'uncomfortable' and intimate procedure, and departed. Some months later they returned and removed her foetus. Years later, after she had married and had two children, the aliens returned again and briefly presented her with a little girl who 'looked like an elf or an... angel'. This was, apparently, her extraterrestrially induced daughter. Kathie Davis was not the only woman who, according to Hopkins's research, had been impregnated by ufonauts.

A FLAWED TOOL

Many serious ufologists – across the whole spectrum of the subject, from ardent 'believers' to those who border on scepticism – have had serious doubts about the validity of abduction accounts ever since George Adamski claimed to have met a Venusian in the California desert.

If, however – as is at least possible – the 'UFO experience' is a peculiar blend of material and psychic realities, there may be a kernel of truth in many abduction reports – though it may be truth of a very strange kind. But there is a vast difference between the account of a man like Dr Antonio Villas Boas and the stories that Budd Hopkins has put into mass circulation – and the key to that difference is the use of hypnosis.

Despite its many virtues in other contexts, hypnosis is notoriously unreliable as a tool for probing the memory, unless the hypnotist is scrupulously careful in the style and content of the questioning. One particular problem is that a false memory unconsciously and even innocently suggested to the subject by the hypnotist through a leading question, will become part of ordinary conscious memory – and its impression, its apparent reality, will grow stronger the more the subject returns to it under hypnosis.

There is a powerful feeling among ufologists that Hopkins's conclusions from his hypnosis of apparent abductees are severely flawed. Critics say that he is too biased in his own beliefs to make a good examiner. Hopkins is not trained as either hypnotist or a psychologist, and critics say he asks blatantly leading questions – letting the subject know the kind of answer that would please him most – and that he breaks all the other rules, too, that expert hypnotists observe.

Most damning of all to his case that for decades aliens have been performing genetic experiments on human subjects, is that a number of Hopkins's star witnesses have publicly repudiated the idea that they have been abducted. In 1987, the central character in his book *Intruders*, Kathie Davis, said bluntly at the US Mutual UFO Network's symposium in Washington DC: 'I can live with it because I don't believe it. I really don't. There's got to be something else' – in other words, another explanation.

Whitley Strieber, who in 1987 received $1 million in advance royalties for his bestselling book *Communion*, admitted in 1991 that there might be some quite different explanation for his experience besides an 'alien abduction'. Attentive readers of the book itself might have guessed as much, for in it Strieber recounts how he used to tell a number of dramatic stories about himself as truth but now candidly admits they were fantasies.

UFO photographed by contactee Elizabeth Klarer in South Africa in the 1950s. Klarer was not abducted by ufonauts – she went willingly and, she claimed, lived with one on his home planet, where she gave birth to their child.

PUZZLING RESULTS

Still more serious is the discovery that under hypnosis, even people who have no knowledge or interest in UFOs will create essentially the same details of an abduction story as are reported by people who believe that they have actually been abducted.

This astonishing and potentially devastating piece of research was conducted in 1977 by Prof. Alvin Lawson, Dr W.C. McCall and ufologist John DeHerrerra at Anaheim Memorial Hospital, near Los Angeles. The experiment was inspired by the puzzling results of an investigation that DeHerrerra had conducted into a UFO sighting. In the hope of gaining further details of the event, the witness, Brian Scott, had agreed to be hypnotized and 'regressed' (that is, was taken back in time) to the time of his encounter. In his hypnotic trance he had described being abducted by aliens. But in his normal waking state, Scott vehemently insisted that no such abduction had taken place.

Lawson and his colleagues recruited 16 volunteers who, in Lawson's words, 'knew little and cared less' about UFOs. They were given the bare bones of a typical abduction story: seeing a UFO land, being taken aboard and seeing the inside of the spacecraft, and being 'examined' by the aliens. The subjects of the experiment were simply asked, at each stage, what they saw or felt happening. And in detail after elaborate detail, the volunteers poured out images and experiences that were uncannily similar to those described by 'real' UFO abductees.

Lawson also noted that the alien figures described by both genuine claimants and his innocent creators of fictional abductions fitted with basic archetypes that the pioneering psychologist C.G. Jung suggested were part of everyone's unconscious imagery. It would be easy enough to conclude from this that people claiming to have been abducted by UFOs were simply calling on imagery that is buried deep in everyone's unconscious mind. But, interestingly, Lawson did no such thing. In answer to his own question, 'Do these similarities prove that close encounter cases are illusory?', Lawson cited four reasons why abduction reports might still be genuine.

First, he pointed out, many abductions and close encounter reports involve multiple witnesses; that they all would have identical hallucinations seems highly unlikely. Second, the physical scars that many abductees can show to be a result of their experiences 'suggest that something happened'. Third, close encounter witnesses recognize how unlikely the events are that unfold during their experience, yet are convinced of their reality. Fourth, psychologists can identify the 'trigger' that sets most hallucinations running in the human mind, but there is no consistent factor in abduction or encounter cases that lets investigators pinpoint an unmistakably imaginary experience.

Lawson's experiment has been cited time and again by sceptics who claim that it disposes of all abduction claims. But Lawson himself was not so convinced. 'I myself feel certain', he wrote, 'that accounts given by witnesses reflect what their senses have reported - that is, they do actually perceive humanoids... and so on. But if [the entities they perceive are] already in the collective unconscious, they are already... in the mind of the witness before his close encounter.' The real mystery, Lawson suggested, was not what the witness saw but what stimulated those archetypal images to arise from the witness's unconscious in the first place. Neither he nor his experiment, he admitted, could answer that question.

A BRUTAL ORDEAL

Even if one rejects Budd Hopkins's belief that a secret alien programme of genetic sampling is under way in our midst, a genuine mystery remains – indeed more than just one mystery. One riddle is posed by that handful of abduction cases that have been reported by sober and upright citizens without recourse to hypnosis.

Antonio Villas Boas is not alone in this category. At about 11 p.m. on 16 October 1973, a 43-year-old woman (who, understandably, insisted on anonymity) was driving along a road near Langford Budville, Somerset, when the electrical system of her car failed. She climbed out to investigate, felt something touch her, and turned to see a 6 ft tall robot-like figure. She fainted on the spot. When she came round, a domed vehicle some 20 ft long and

One of the frightening goblin-like creatures that besieged the Sutton farm at Kelly, Hopkinsville, Kentucky, in 1955, makes a determined attack on one of the family members.

perhaps 40 ft high had appeared next to her. Again she fainted, and came round to find herself tied naked to a metallic table in a room with glowing walls, inside the craft. When three humanoids – also about 6 ft tall – had finished examining her, two left the room. The third then raped her, and she fainted once more. She came to finally to find herself back in her car - which was now in perfect working order. By now it was 2 a.m.

But not all conscious abductions have a lurid sexual element. Brazilian military policeman José Antonio was on a fishing trip at a lake north of Belo Horizonte, Minas Gerais, one Sunday afternoon in May 1969, when he was paralysed by a burst of light and borne off to an upright, cylindrical craft by two 4 ft tall creatures in masks. Once inside, he was tied up and given a helmet to wear. The machine then took off and after an 'interminable' period, landed. José Antonio was next blindfolded and taken to a brilliantly lit room, in which he saw the bodies of four other humans, one of them a Negro, to be interrogated in front of about 15 of the tiny creatures. They removed samples of his fishing gear, and used drawings and sign language to suggest that he be 'their guide among men'. When he refused, he was blindfolded again and returned to Earth. Once on the ground he collapsed, and woke to find himself near Vitoria, in the state of Espirito Santo, 200 miles from where he had been fishing. He subsequently discovered that four and a half days had elapsed between his initial abduction and his return.

If abduction experiences were purely hallucinatory, a pattern would emerge within them, just as patterns are clear enough in states of neurosis and madness. The fact that Budd Hopkins perceives patterns in the abduction cases he has investigated is, in fact, almost as good as a danger sign. The genuine UFO case often signals itself by the way it only partly conforms to a pattern, and has only some aspects in common with previous cases of its kind.

Taken together, what the most genuine sounding accounts of abduction by aliens most resemble, in fact, is not a pattern of deliberate and calculated intrusions by beings from elsewhere, but a series of bizarre accidents as they might appear to some innocent victims, only partly aware of the full circumstances in which they have been caught up. If there is anything to the notion that UFOs are not extraterrestrial craft from within our own Universe, but exist in parallel with it, this image may prove highly fruitful in both comprehending, and coming to terms with, the entire perplexing enigma.

And not the least important of the answers to these mysteries lies hidden in the human mind, its nature, and its abilities.

VISITS FROM GOD

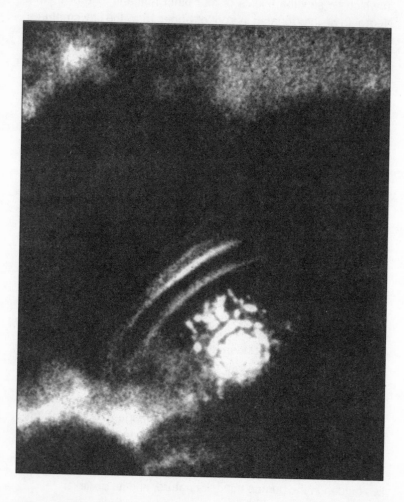

For centuries individuals have accepted the possibility of alternative realities and other worlds. As humanity rushes headlong to its fate, many wonder about the nature of the beings that may control these realities.

Most people in the West have grown up with some knowledge of a reality that is quite different from that of the everyday world. Some believe in it without question; and while others would deny its existence altogether, the majority probably fall into a grey area of more or less nervous uncertainty. But everyone has an opinion about it, however vague. That other reality is, of course, the religious dimension, which encompasses the notion of God as all-seeing and all-powerful, includes the possibility of an evil power opposed to God, and involves images and traditions concerning the survival of the soul after death.

Whether or not each of us continues to exist in some conscious form when the body dies has little bearing on the problems thrown up by UFOs, but it is absolutely relevant that most people have no hardship in accepting the possibility that another order of reality besides our own may exist – and some people are absolutely convinced of it. (Convinced and committed atheists, on the other hand, are surprisingly hard to find.) This other reality is, besides, by definition beyond our comprehension. Moses hid his face in the presence of God, whose 'explanation' of Himself as I AM WHAT I AM can be understood only intuitively, not rationally.

The age-old battle between the forces of good and evil. In this illustration from a 13th-century manuscript, Satan attempts to seize a magician with whom he has made a pact, while a lay brother defends the wizard. Some ufologists believe that UFOs are part of this eternal struggle between the powers of light and the powers of darkness.

Many people feel similarly awed when confronted by the utterances of the secret priests of our own epoch, scientists and mathematicians. Physicists blithely tell us that certain sub-atomic particles may be seen travelling backwards in time, and that time itself may be stretched, shrunk, or bent. Indeed, built into Einstein's theories of relativity is the concept of not a single universe – the one that visibly fills the night sky – but an infinite multiplicity of universes.

Such concepts are extraordinary, but they are grounded in extremely rigorous mathematical proofs. The immemorial claims of religions the world over that there is at least another plane of existence beyond the reach of our immediate senses has thus, in this century, been paralleled by the discoveries of science – although these are no more than parallel ideas: not even the most religious scientist would maintain that he or she has found the source of the Creator.

There are people, however, who would say that the mysteries of religion, of good versus evil, the ultimate fate of humankind, and the mysteries of UFO phenomena, are closely related. To an impartial observer, it may seem that such ideas result from a confusion between the scientific concept of other distinct but equal planes of being, and the religious apprehension of an absolute reality that underpins, justifies and verifies our life on Earth. It would also appear that if genuine UFO entities are really communicating messages of cosmic import, the ufonauts have a singularly cruel sense of humour. These suspicions may seem more reasonable after a survey of what various religious cults have made of the UFO phenomenon.

TELEPATHIC MESSAGES

The longest-lived UFO organization to recognize the religious significance of flying saucers is undoubtedly the Aetherius Society. The society was founded by Western Master of Yoga Sir George King in 1955 following an alleged instruction proclaiming 'Prepare yourself! You are to become the voice of Interplanetary Parliament!'

Sir George King then set up the Aetherius Society in response to growing interest in his messages from a being from Venus called Aetherius. The information that he allegedly received telepathically was, according to the Aetherius Society, relayed over millions of miles of etheric space for the benefit of mankind.

The Aetherius Society believes there is a strong link between man's nuclear activity and the presence of flying saucers. It is claimed that the occupants of these UFOs are concerned that a nuclear disaster on Earth could affect the Solar System too. Therefore, the Aetherius Society considers that part of the role of these aliens is to act as 'guardians' who impart information to mankind which would help avert such a catastrophe.

One of the major missions of the Aetherius Society is to charge 'prayer batteries' designed by Sir George King. In collaboration with various 'space agencies' the prayer energy, often amounting to 2,500 'prayer hours', is frequently discharged to areas of the world which are, according to the Aetherius Society, in desperate need of spiritual energy. Pilgrimages are often made to charge these batteries from the tops of holy mountains in various parts of the world, where the adherents form a circle and recite mantras. The society says that often as a result of these efforts, extraterrestrials then add their own energy.

At 2 p.m. on 4 February 1990, schoolboy Dima Girenko took this photograph of a UFO in the Achtyrka District of the Ukraine. The Moscow Aviation Institute declared that it was no hoax.

PROPHECIES OF DOOM

Few UFO religious cults have lasted as long as the Aetherius Society. More than one has come to an abrupt end through making grandiose prophecies about future events that then fail to come to pass. One such was Human Individual Metamorphosis (HIM), founded in the mid-1970s by a couple known variously as The Two, Him and Her, Bo and Peep and, to previous acquaintances (who included their former fellow inmates within the Texas penitentiary system, and others at the mental hospital where they met, he as patient and she as nurse), as Marshall Herff Applewhite and Bonnie Lu Nettles. Seized by a sense of destiny, the pair turned up unannounced in small communities around the southern and western states to divulge their message, which Applewhite had received through mediumistic contact with a 19th-century monk.

Unholy alliance – a 17th-century representation of witches, imps and Satan. Some ufologists would now add UFOs and aliens to the forms that evil may take.

This was in essence that 'the level above human' was a physical place, and could be reached by UFO. This would happen only when Bo and Peep – who said they were themselves aliens, millions of years old, in human form – had first been assassinated, and left dead in the street for three and a half days: they would then return to life and at this point the UFO would arrive and bear them away. Others could join The Two on the trip to salvation, on condition that they renounced all private possessions and family ties. Astonishingly enough, The Two soon gathered about 1,000 disciples.

Unfortunately, at an inaugural meeting of HIM in Waldport, Oregon, on 14 September 1975, Bo and Peep had promised that their deaths, resurrection and translation by UFO would occur within six months. When no assassin obliged with the necessary act, they hastily revised their timetable and announced they would remain on Earth for at least a further ten years. The number of devotees soon declined drastically and, 15 years later, Bo and Peep were still on Earth, living a nomadic existence with their few remaining followers in Wyoming and Texas.

A similar fate befell the cult that grew up around the British Columbian channeller Robin McPherson (a.k.a. Estelle), whose extraterrestrial contact Ox-Ho predicted that prodigious natural disasters would begin on Earth on 22 November 1969. The 'Chosen' – i.e. members of the cult, Light Affiliates – would be removed beforehand by the Space Brothers and returned when the Earth had recovered. No major disaster of any kind began on Earth that day.

John Ashton's intriguing volume **The Devil In Britain And America**, *published in 1986, contains this curious script, which purports to be 'the only known specimen of the Devil's handwriting'.*

It remains to be seen whether the prediction of Ruth E. Norman, channeller for an entity called URIEL (Universal Radiant Infinite Eternal Light) will come true. According to URIEL, spacecraft from the 33 members of the Interplanetary Confederation landing in the year 2001, would usher in a 1000-year epoch of peace, contentment and cultural achievement.

SUBVERSIVE INVASIONS

The cosmologies of the various UFO cults are wildly different – far more incompatible with each other than any established earthly religion. The California-based One World Family, for instance, declare that they will one day take over the government of the USA and the administration of the United Nations – but not before all professing Christians have been 'eliminated'. In contrast, the Aetherians have no political ambitions, and maintain that the Christian prophet is recognized as an intergalactic 'Master' who lives on, or near, Venus – which happens also to be the alleged abode of Ashtar, the One World Family's extraterrestrial contact. Alien-Michael Noonan, the leader of the sect, claims to be the sole authentic mouthpiece for Ashtar – but Tuella, of the Utah-based cult, Ashtar Space Command, regularly channels messages of a gentler nature from an 'interplanetary space commander' of the same name.

All these cults differ fundamentally, however, from the small band of commentators who see UFOs not as harbingers of peace and plenty, but as unambiguously evil. Chief among these is probably linguist and former diplomat Gordon Creighton, editor of the international UFO journal *Flying Saucer Review*. Creighton's own theory is that djinns, supernatural creatures who work on behalf of the forces of evil and can take on human form, are UFOs in appropriate cultural disguise. Curiously, Creighton has an apocalyptic view of the present era that is not far removed from the beliefs of some 'space brother'-types of UFO cult who are expecting the End Times to begin at any moment:

'Time is running out fast. All the indications are that before the close of this century, cataclysmic and apocalyptic events will rend the planet. As the waves of senseless, irrational violence rise higher and higher on the Earth... who can doubt that certain of the "UFO entities" have a hand in the wrecking, and in the stirring of the nauseating brew?'

How he knows these things, Creighton does not reveal. But there is a long fundamentalist Christian tradition of identifying UFOs with the work of the Devil. As early as 1954 Gordon Cove offered the novel insight that 'Satan is the cleverest military genius ever known'. Exactly which battles in history he has planned and won, Cove did not say, but was certain that the aliens aboard UFOs were possessed by the Devil, even when appearing to be most benign.

Commentator Dan Lloyd likewise sees the UFO cults who look forward to mass contact with our intergalactic guardians as deluded: their 'distorted religious longings' are directed toward entities who merely appear benign in order to win our trust and thereby subvert humanity. He follows ufologist Jacques Vallee's suggestion in his book *Messengers of Deception* that the UFO phenomenon is 'a control system which acts on humans and uses humans'.

Vallee points to recurrent patterns in UFO cases that echo patterns of behaviour by evil spirits, goblins and other creatures from folklore, and suggests that something – perhaps human, and

Scale model of a UFO constructed by the Aetherius Society. Note the resemblance to the UFO that George Adamski claimed to have seen in California in the early 1950s.

perhaps not – is making such patterns. Lloyd first argues that UFOs are not from another physical dimension, but are 'deliberately distorted etheric effects, and it should surprise no one to learn that such effects can influence physical matter and create, in turn, physical effects' and then identifies the maker of the patterns noted by Vallee: 'Behind whatever human group may be active in this area, there hovers the invisible presence of... the cosmic being who has been known since ancient Persian times as Ahriman. In the Bible he is known as Satan.'

EXTRATERRESTRIAL SALVATION

From this brief survey of the various points of contact between UFOs and religious beliefs, a number of things emerge. We previously suggested that such beliefs rest on a confusion between the scientific concept of other planes of being, distinct from but equal to our own, and the religious apprehension of a quite different kind of 'other dimension', the absolute reality that informs all existence.

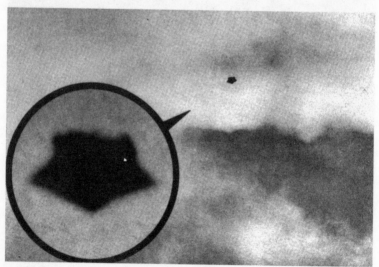

A UFO, caught on film by Guy B. Marquand, skims the hills near Riverside, California.

This confusion is nowhere more evident than in the message of The Two, who seemed to think that Heaven, or something like it, could be reached in a spaceship. Such a literal, physical religious cosmology has not been contemplated by any major religion since the Middle Ages.

In conventional religious terms, there is no conflict between the levels of reality inhabited by God and those of parallel universes or additional dimensions. The Creator of one universe is still the Creator of all the others; and the God that created humanity also created ufonauts. But what, in effect, many of the cultists have done is to create a kind of substitute set of gods - the aliens, 'space brothers' and the rest, who will come down like cosmic cavalry to save humanity from itself.

Leaving aside the question of how many of the major world religions would regard this belief as heresy, the UFO cults actually have little in common besides a common faith in some kind of extraterrestrial salvation. If all these cults have any claim to truth, the immediate regions of space around Earth must be unusually crowded with our intergalactic brethren.

If these cults are in touch with genuine UFO entities, there are only a few logical conclusions to draw. One is that diehard ufonauts themselves are confused, with no greater claim to the truth than anyone on Earth. Or they themselves are at the mercy of rival systems of thought, and for all we know may be deeply hostile to one another's beliefs. Or they may simply be hopeless at prophecy, which also puts them on much the same level as anyone on Earth. Or, worst of all, they are cosmic cats, playing with the dying mouse of humanity.

This leads us to one further possible explanation. We have seen in previous chapters how both UFOs and their occupants, in all kinds of context, indulge in apparently meaningless, often contradictory, and most often simply incomprehensible behaviour: disguise, trickery, deceit, cruelty that, if the reports are to be believed, does not balk at rape or murder. One does not have to believe that UFOs are evil to wonder if the 'messages to mankind' and the cults they inspire are not simply another facet of this taunting game. If, that is, it is a game.

HARVEST FESTIVAL

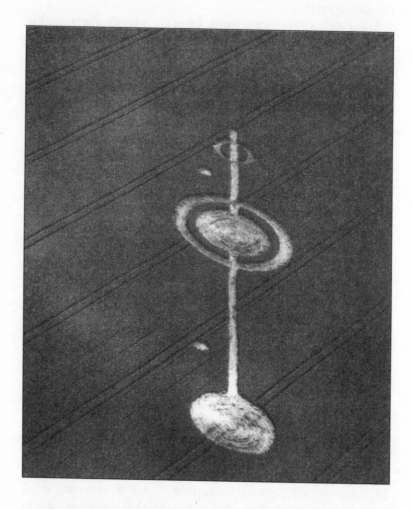

*Crop circles became big news in the 1980s; as the
sightings multiplied, so did the complexity of markings.
But are these weird phenomena the work of hoaxers,
UFOs, or some freak of nature? The cautious British
army major preferred to reserve judgement, despite what
he had witnessed with his own eyes...*

Just after 4.30 a.m. on 10 August 1965, a truck driver, heading south on the Warminster–Westbury road in Wiltshire, came around the bend at a point called Colloway Clump and drove straight into a UFO. The object was a huge crimson ball of light. To the driver's amazement the thing seemed to fasten itself to the windscreen, generating 'enormous vibrations'. The driver swerved, and the truck ended up by the fence on the verge, and on the wrong side of the road. At this point, the object spun away with a whistling sound.

'It was so huge,' the driver said, 'much larger than my truck. I would say it measured a good 30 to 40 ft across at the base.'

Almost a month later, at about 7.30 p.m. on 7 September, a British army officer, Major Hill, was driving past the same spot at about 45 mph when his car engine suddenly cut out. As the car came to a stop it was seized by huge vibrations. The body swayed, and Major Hill jumped out. Around him the air was pulsating, and there was a noise 'on a par with the sounds of high-powered refrigeration units or deep-freeze equipment, but... magnified many times'.

Less than three minutes later, he said, 'everything was back to normal. I pressed the starter button, and the car purred away perfectly, just as if nothing had happened at all.'

These reports bear all the hallmarks of classic kinds of UFO encounter. And, in the field just by that bend in the road, precisely circular depressions have been found and photographed in the crops – what, in 1965, many ufologists would immediately have dubbed 'UFO nests'. The question is: what connection is there between UFO reports like the two cited above, and what are now known as 'crop circles'? Are they made by UFOs, or by some freak of nature – or are the UFOs concerned themselves some kind of natural phenomenon?

COMPLEX PICTOGRAMS

Crop circles became big news in the 1980s. From the early years of the decade, more and more of them seemed to be appearing each year, especially in southern England, while reports came in too from Australia, New Zealand, Argentina, Brazil, South Africa, Mexico, the USA, Canada, France, Spain, Switzerland, Austria, Germany, Sweden, the former Soviet Union and, by no means least as to numbers, Japan.

In 1990, more than 1,000 circle formations were reported in England alone.

As, year by year, the number of sightings multiplied so, it seemed, did the complexity of the markings. At the beginning of the decade people found only plain circles. Their sizes ranged from the diameter of a cartwheel to that of a circus arena. Sometimes the circles were laid out in tantalizingly neat patterns, but as the years passed – and especially from 1990 onward – the marks became noticeably weirder and consequently posed more difficult questions for researchers to answer.

From simple circular depressions, the phenomenon developed into circles with rings around them, or consisting entirely of rings. There were symmetrically placed circles, or single large ones with minor precisely aligned 'satellites'. Towards the end of the decade, astonishing pictograms appeared: some resembled the more elaborate and mysterious ground markings at ancient sites like Nazca, Peru. Perhaps the most astonishing of these later patterns was the 'Mandelbrot set' found in August 1991 at Ickleton, about ten miles south of Cambridge – which consisted of a closely connected pattern of circles that exactly matched one of the visual depictions of the currently fashionable chaos theory in mathematics. The forgivable presumption that it was a fake was confused by the fact that the wheat stalks were reported to be 'laid in multiple swirled layers to create the characteristic plaited effect which no human imitators of crop circles have been able to reproduce'. And as the mysteries grew so did the number and kind of speculations about the circles' origins. Believers in paranormal explanations became increasingly bold in their assertions, while most scientists became progressively more sceptical. But all wanted to know – whatever suspicions they harboured - how the increasing complexity of the circles could be reconciled with the rising number of reliable eyewitnesses – who, perplexingly, persisted in seeing only simple circles being made?

HORDES OF RUTTING HEDGEHOGS!

Some researchers suspected hoaxers were hard at work, while the more imaginative sceptics produced some of the most surreal 'rational explanations' ever to adorn an anomalous phenomenon. The least of these blamed deer, who had supposedly trampled the crops with geometrical exactitude in order to give birth and raise their young in orderly surroundings. Deer – and vixens, too – have been known to use the circles as 'nurseries', but they are rather more likely to have taken advantage of the shelter they had found, than to have trampled circles of such precision. The most baroque 'solution' to the mystery put the circles down to hordes of stampeding hedgehogs – or to rutting hedgehogs, still more amazing.

Others developed extraordinary mystical 'New Age'-style theories that, in essence, saw the circles as 'signs of the times' – as if something (perhaps the Earth itself) was writing urgent coded messages to us on the ground. From this point of view it was possible to see esoteric cosmic symbols in the circles, from 'the Divine Hermaphrodite' to signs of the zodiac.

Other researchers, notably Colin Andrews and Pat Delgado, concluded in their book *Circular Evidence* that 'the circles are created by an unknown force field manipulated by an unknown intelligence', and that 'Nothing in the current state of conventional science can account for all that has been described in this book.' What that hypothetical intelligence was could perhaps be guessed from Delgado's research summaries in *Flying Saucer Review*. At the end of 1986 he wrote there: 'Maybe these circles are created by alien beings using forcefields unknown to us. They may be manipulating existing Earth energy...'

That there are UFOs, and that UFOs have been seen at around the same time that crop circles have been created, is not in doubt. But the idea that such UFOs are necessarily under 'intelligent' control has yet to be proved.

ANCIENT SITES

Other 'rationalist' attempts to explain the circles have blamed the downdraft from helicopters – but the effect from chopper rotors does not create a precise 'edge' typical of the circles – and spreads of fungus, which do create exact circles as they reproduce (as in fairy rings of toadstools and mushrooms); but field investigators found no evidence of fungoid growth or disease among the crops in the circles. Some archaeologists have suggested that the circles were forming over ancient prehistoric sites, which were often circular in form. There may well be a connection with these sites, but the proponents of this form of the theory failed to explain why an ancient site should make an area of crops fall down.

Other scientists entered the fray with the hypothesis that the biochemistry of the soil had been disturbed (perhaps by overindulgence in pesticides), so that the crop had weakened. But that did not explain the random appearance of the circles, their exact construction, the complex patterns, or the fact that circles would sometimes appear in the same field at widely spaced intervals.

Still other researchers took a strictly scientific but less prejudiced line and made steps toward explaining the phenomenon in terms of unusual, but perfectly natural and explicable, meteorological conditions – Delgado's and Andrews's claims that this was impossible notwithstanding. This last group also suspected that hoaxers were muddying the waters by producing the most complicated of the patterns found in the fields.

'EVERYONE HAS BEEN FOOLED'

Then, in September 1991, Douglas Bower and David Chorley hit the headlines. The pair, both artists in their sixties, claimed that since 1978 they had been faking crop circles in England. 'Everyone has been fooled,' they crowed. The two hoaxers showed a delighted press contingent how they had done it: using nothing but wooden boards and lengths of twine, they repeated a complex insect-like pattern that researcher Pat Delgado (promoter of the 'unknown force/unknown intelligence' hypothesis) had declared indubitably genuine at a private showing three days earlier.

Most circle researchers were underwhelmed by the claim that everyone had been fooled. Delgado and other officers of the Centre for Crop Circle Studies and other organizations whose leaders had embraced paranormal explanations for the phenomenon rejected the idea that hoaxers – including Bower and Chorley – could be responsible for creating crop circles.

But even before Bower and Chorley had dropped their bombshell, members of the scientific organization CERES (Circles Effect Research Group) already knew, in founder Dr Terence Meaden's words, that 'pranksters were rampant', and that some had nearly been caught. CERES had spent the entire 1991 season seeking out and exposing hoaxed circles – and netted some 150 fraudulent patterns in the process.

THE MOWING DEVIL

It was also apparent that Bower and Chorley were not merely pretending to be hoaxers, as the paranormalists preferred to believe. Since 1978, the pair had created hundreds of circles, but they had worked in only a small part of southern England. And they never claimed they had fabricated any of the pre-1978 circles already known to researchers.

In his book *The Circles Effect And Its Mysteries* Dr G. Terence Meaden cites cases that occurred in Britain as early as 1918 – this

93

actually appeared in a Kentish field of beans, rather than corn – but the earliest detailed instance on record from Britain is the so-called 'mowing devil' report of 1678.

In August that year, according to a contemporary four-page pamphlet, a Hertfordshire farmer had three half-acres of oats standing ripe and in need of harvesting. He approached 'a poor mower' to do the job, but the mower's price was too high for the farmer, and they exchanged a few sharp words. Infuriated, the farmer snapped that 'the Devil himself should mow his oats before he should have anything to do with them'. The pamphlet continues:

'that same night this poor mower and farmer parted, his field of oats was publickly beheld by several passengers to be all on a flame, and so continued for some space, to the great consternation of those that beheld it, which strange news being by several carried to the farmer next morning... the inquisitive farmer no sooner arrived at the place where his oats grew, but to his admiration he found the crop was cut down ready to his hands, and as if the Devil had a mind to show his dexterity... he cut them in round circles, and plac't every straw with that exactness that it would have taken up above an age for any man to perform what he did in one night – and the man that ow[n]s them is as yet afraid to remove them.'

Here, once again, we have the peculiar, luminous, UFO-like phenomena that are associated with later circles. What is odd is the report that the oats were cut, as in genuine crop circles the stalks are bent over just above the ground. But one might also surmise that no one was prepared to approach 'the Devil's work' that closely, and certainly the bent stalks can look as if they have been cut. The neat arrangement, too, suggests the characteristic outward swirling of the crops from the centre noted by modern investigators.

If the hoaxers could not have produced these circles from times past, nor could they possibly have created the many hundreds of circles reported elsewhere in the world.

A crop circle found in 1967 in the north-eastern USA was featured in the infamous Condon Report on UFOs. The circle was 30 ft in diameter and had affected a small swamp: 'cattails had been squashed down and found to lie in a clockwise spiral pattern,' said the report. A lady eyewitness had seen a large glowing light at that spot the night before. Another instance is the 45 ft-wide ringed circle that appeared at Orebro in Sweden in April 1972. Witnesses in this case saw a red light descend prior to the discovery of the circle. Within the mark, the crops were swirled clockwise. Its overall shape was oval, but within it was a 10 ft-wide anti-clockwise ring.

In 1975, geologist Dr Alan Wells photographed a series of overlapping swirled circles at the snow-covered foot of a mountain in a remote part of the Munzur range in Turkey. Each circle was about 35 ft in diameter. In 1968, Dr Wells had also found similar swirled, circular markings in snow in the Elburz Mountains near Tehran, Iran.

Crop circles appear in huge numbers in Japan. Recent incidents include the 10 ft rayed and blasted circle that formed in reeds on 9 August 1986, in Yamagata prefecture, and interfered with TV signals. Another formed within the double-fenced grass compound of a Nippon Radio station in the early hours of 1 September 1991. It seems to have been responsible for the massive amount of radio interference that occurred at the same time. There are, too, many Japanese reports from long before the 1980s, some dating back centuries.

It seems a reasonable conclusion that the more complex and elaborate 'circles' and their attendant patterns are hoaxes, while

A fascinating account of a crop circle, the case of the 'moving devil', appeared in a four-page pamphlet published in 1678. The circle appeared in a field of oats on the night after a dispute between a mower and a farmer: angered by the price the mower had quoted, the farmer declared that he would rather the Devil himself should mow his oats than that the poor mower should have anything to do with them.

the simpler ones are not. In these simpler formations, a typical pattern can be seen in the bent crops: an outward swirling of the stalks (noted above), interwoven layers of stalks, twisted straws and, occasionally, a centre with crops still standing.

But that still leaves the fundamental question unanswered: what causes the circles to form in the first place?

A RUSTLING VORTEX

Some people have actually witnessed crop circles coming into existence, and the best clues to the solution of the mystery have come from examining what they have seen. And it is worth noting that not one of these eyewitnesses, nor any other known witnesses of the making of a crop circle, reported supernatural experiences.

In July 1982, at Westbury, Wiltshire, Ray Barnes saw a huge circle take shape close by him, within a mere three or four seconds, to the accompaniment of a weird humming noise. Late one evening in 1983 Melvyn Bell saw a circle appear in wheat as dust spun in a typical whirlwind. Near Dundee, Scotland, in 1989, Sandy Reid was out at dawn one morning when he heard a tremendous noise in the air; then he saw a crop circle take rapid shape.

At about 9 p.m., as the sun was setting on 17 May 1990, Gary and Vivienne Tomlinson were walking along the edge of a wheatfield in Surrey, when a vortex formed next to where they were standing. From a soft rustling, the sound of the wind changed to something like a high-pitched flute. Pressure of the air from above and beside them forced them into the corn, where they found themselves right in the centre of a corn circle as it formed. Gary Tomlinson's hair was standing on end from static electricity; both were almost knocked to the ground by the force of the wind roaring around them. But in seconds, it was all over. As the mass of swirling air drifted away it cut out a second circle and then a third, further off.

In Gloucestershire, at dusk one day in July 1988, Tom Gwinnett saw a large orange-yellow ball of light spinning just above a field of wheat. A crop circle was found next day at the spot where he judged the light to have been.

SPECTACULAR LIGHTS

It seems, then, that comparatively simple circles are formed from a combination of wind and electrical effects, and that at night an associated spinning ball of light may develop – or at any rate, be more obvious: it is this that forms the 'UFO' component in crop circles.

For such a vortex to form, the air has to be virtually calm, which happens more often in the evening, at night, or early in the morning than by day. When a wind butts against a hill, the downward airflow can produce vortices that, within a small area, can be quite violent. And when the air is also humid, they become visible as the whirling columns or hollow spheres that witnesses have also on occasion reported.

According to Professors John Snow and Tokio Kikuchi, when eddies of wind 'break down', they move towards the ground and sweep out the circles in the crops. Professor G. Terence Meaden suggests that, as this happens, friction in the moving air separates and concentrates existing electrical charges in the atmosphere. This accounts for the humming noises reminiscent of high-tension power

This crop circle is one of three that appeared in Cornwall between 11 July and 10 August 1991. In each case, a bluish-white light was reported over or inside the circle.

lines (a sound not unlike a deep-freeze unit at work, incidentally) and for the sometimes spectacular lights that have been seen accompanying the high-powered winds. Alarmed witnesses have taken the lights to be UFOs – which in the strict sense they were, until this explanation for their presence was put forward.

SACRED BURIAL GROUNDS

Whatever the origin of real crop circles, they have always been with us. There is evidence the prehistoric people, too, noticed circle-making vortices, and the seemingly magical nature of the phenomenon may well have made them sacred in those people's eyes. The crop circle effect may even account for the circular shape of so many prehistoric sacred sites. The peoples of Neolithic and Early Bronze Age Britain built some 40,000 round burial mounds, around 1,000 stone circles and many thousands of ring ditches, timber circles and the like. Many were not exactly circular. Like crop circles, some were oval, others elliptical in shape. It may be that the rings of stone, burial mounds and so on were laid on top of sites made sacred by the visitation of whirling winds and inexplicable lights, and that burials took place at the crop circle centre. It is possible that Stonehenge was built on just such a site.

And here, too, may be an explanation of the association so often noted between ancient sites and UFOs, for certain features of the landscape seem to favour the formation of crop circle vortices – similar features to those so frequently chosen by the ancient builders for their sacred places.

In the opinion of one of the world's most eminent scientists, Professor Stephen Hawking, crop circles are entirely explicable by natural atmospheric vortices on the one hand and hoaxing on the other. Circle researcher Paul Fuller remarked, no less pertinently, after Bower and Chorley went public: 'When the media stop promoting the phenomenon as a supernatural mystery, the hoaxers will go away and leave us with the real circles.' Those two comments make a fair conclusion. And they do not make the existence of crop circles any less a matter for wonder.

LIFE
AFTER DEATH

GHOSTS AND APPARITIONS

*A troubled lady, haunting the place she was bound to in life;
a dead father, unable to rest easy until his will is carried
out; a piratical sailor whose love of adventure defeats even
death – the many shades of ghosts present intriguing, if
inconsistent, evidence for survival beyond the grave.*

In 1968, Frances Little and her husband were delighted with the adobe house they had bought in the desert setting of California's Kern County, but after a few weeks, Mr Little became disturbed at seeming to see his wife in two places at once. He'd leave her in one room, or outside, only to see her immediately afterwards, wandering around at the other end of the house. Finally, it dawned on him that the 'other woman' must be a ghost. But whose ghost? And why was she haunting the house?

Then, alone at home one night, Frances Little herself saw a 'tall thin woman in a long dark old-fashioned dress' come out of a back room and go into her bedroom. From there, she went into the family room and Mrs Little was able to see her features quite clearly.

Not long after this, Mrs Little was sorting through some junk that had been left in the garage by the previous owners. To her amazement, she came across a photograph of a woman who looked exactly like the ghost she had seen. Careful enquiries revealed that this was Alice Margaret Kolitisch who, with her husband, had had the adobe house built in the 1920s. She was, Frances Little felt, still concerned about the house she had loved when alive.

This is a ghost story in a classic mould: the troubled shade of the dead haunts a place it had been bound to emotionally in life. But not all ghost stories are like this, and because hauntings are so varied in kind, they make intriguing, if inconsistent, evidence for some kind of life after death.

Legend says that US President Abraham Lincoln had a strong belief in ghosts: he apparently consulted a medium during the worst days of the American Civil War and, according to W.H. Crook, one of his bodyguards, Lincoln had a number of psychic experiences. At the beginning of April 1865, he told Crook that he had had a dream in which he had been in the hall of the White House, and had seen a coffin draped in black there. When he asked who it was for, he was told: 'The president.'

On 11 April, Lincoln told Crook that he had dreamed of his own assassination; and on the morning of 14 April he had a vision of a ship carrying him to some unknown place. That night, against the advice of Crook and other members of his staff, Lincoln went to Ford's Theater in Washington. There, he was shot dead by John Wilkes Booth. Within months of Lincoln's death, rumours began to circulate that his ghost was haunting the White House.

Lincoln's spectre took a long time to take visible form. Theodore Roosevelt, president from 1901 to 1909, maintained that he 'felt the presence' of Lincoln at 1600 Pennsylvania Avenue. The first person actually to see his ghost was Grace Coolidge, wife of Calvin Coolidge, the 30th president, who was in office between 1923 and 1929. Mrs Coolidge saw the ghost standing at the window of the Oval Office, staring out on to Pennsylvania Avenue in the attitude of a man deep in thought. Staff members and presidential aides have reported the same thing – and the apparition always appears at the same window.

The next president, Herbert Hoover (at the White House from 1929 to 1933), heard no more than 'odd sounds' but said that 'many of them were fantastic'.

Between 1933, when Franklin Delano Roosevelt became president, and 1945, when he died, Lincoln's ghost was allegedly seen many times. On one occasion Queen Wilhelmina of The Netherlands, who had long had an interest in spiritualism, had gone to bed in the Lincoln Room – formerly used by Lincoln himself

Robert (left) and John F. Kennedy. Both brothers saw the Lincoln spectre at the White House during John's presidency, although neither wa noted for his interest in psychic or spritual matters.

as a dressing room – when she heard a gentle tap on the door. She opened it, and there stood the dead president, gravely doffing his famous stovepipe hat; then the apparition vanished. When the queen told Roosevelt of her encounter the next morning, he confessed that he knew the room was haunted; Winston Churchill had also seen the ghost of Lincoln while sleeping there, and Mrs Roosevelt had detected Lincoln's presence on several occasions.

Harry S. Truman, who succeeded to the presidency on Roosevelt's death and lived in the White House from 1945 to 1952, often joked to his guests about Lincoln's ghost. He once admitted that though he had never seen it, he was certain that he had heard it, in the form of footsteps which approached his bedroom door, followed by a knocking.

There had certainly been no rational explanation for these sounds, he said, and they always occurred in the early hours of the morning. A White House stenographer who served both Roosevelt and Truman allegedly saw Lincoln frequently. The first time was in the Lincoln Room; the spectre was sitting on the bed pulling on his boots. The girl was badly scared, although with repeated appearances she seems to have got used to seeing the ghost. Both John and Robert Kennedy saw the spirit of Lincoln, according to friends of the Kennedy family.

The White House ghost is intriguing for several reasons. First, it hardly seems likely that several presidents, their wives, a queen, and a statesman like Winston Churchill would lie about seeing the wraith of Lincoln: 'seeing ghosts' might call their fitness for high office into question. The credentials of the witnesses, then, are beyond question.

But is this ghost really the spirit of Abraham Lincoln, bound to the scene where he worked and thought so hard and so deeply? Or is the apparition brought into being by something else? Could it be the result of a collective feeling that the White House really ought to be haunted by Lincoln, the greatest of all the men who lived there, and who died so tragically – so that those who have seen him, presidents included, somehow projected the 'spirit' to suit their own unconscious wishes? Or might the apparition be some kind of recording of Lincoln, impressed upon the place somehow and played over and over again? Or is the Lincoln ghost not one ghost, but several – sometimes one thing, sometimes another, depending on the circumstances and the person who perceives it?

Such questions take us to the heart of the mystery surrounding ghosts of all kinds.

HOARSE WHISPERS

What is a ghost? That the belief that a ghost is present and active can be created by circumstances is beyond doubt. Given some specious evidence, a credulous collection of witnesses, and a background of fear, a ghost will make itself heard, seen or felt. This is very clear from the story told by New Zealander Frank Brookesmith, who until his death in 1991 was one of the last few survivors from the age of square-rigged sailing ships.

In his book *I Remember the Tall Ships*, Brookesmith recalled a haunting that briefly afflicted the tanker *Orowaiti* on a voyage across the Pacific from Wellington, New Zealand, to San Francisco, in the early 1920s. What happened was this. After one of the sailors on board the ship had committed suicide, the rest of the crew, understandably distressed at the incident, swore that the dead man was haunting the bow end of the ship. The ghost was invisible, but its constant, eerie whisper could clearly be heard. Determined to find out what was really going on, Brookesmith went forward at about four o'clock one morning to investigate.

'The ship was rolling quite moderately and I paced the deck from right forward to the after rail on the weather side. I heard nothing. I walked along the lee side and paused by the windlass.

'I froze, and the hairs on the back of my neck stood on end... It felt as if all my hair was standing on end. Someone was talking in a hoarse whisper!... I ran down the ladder to the foredeck and I walked into the space under the focsle head. It was all as dark as the inside of a cow but I knew what was there... I stood quite still and listened. There was no sound save the usual creaks and cracks of a ship in a seaway.. .

'I went back... to the after rail and I could hear a faint whispering. I could not distinguish the words but there was no mistaking the sound... My skin crept. I knew that I could easily imagine words but I simply had to find the source of the sounds. I moved about and found that, the nearer I was to the gypsy [a small winch], the clearer was the sound. It was an indistinct asthmatic whisper.

'I put my hand on the [anchor] chain where it went down the pipe into [its] locker and I felt it! As the ship rolled the rusty links moved against each other to make this harsh sound.

'Rub two pieces of rough iron together and you will hear what we heard,' Brookesmith wrote many years later. 'Add to it unhappiness and superstitious fears and you will have a haunting.' He silenced the 'ghost' by lashing the chain down with rope. 'I've found the ghost and I've bound him hands and feet,' he reported with a certain grim satisfaction.

Frank Brookesmith was, on that occasion at least, driven to get to the root of the shipboard 'haunting' partly by curiosity and partly by a determination not to be prey – or to be in thrall – to what he called 'superstitious fears'. But he also told his family of another and quite different experience of the supernatural that he had as a young man, before he went to sea, in the last years of World War One.

He was then working as a clerk in a bank in Christchurch, New Zealand; one of the few perks of the job was a free flat above the bank premises. The perk in turn had its price – which was that he had to be on the alert for any attempt to raid the bank. To help terminally dissuade any villains intent on relieving the bank of its customers' cash – or perhaps simply as a psychological support – he was issued with a hefty British Army officer's .455 Webley revolver and several boxes of ammunition. He used most of the ammunition practising with the pistol in the deserted hills outside the town, but he slept with the weapon loaded at his bedside every night.

One night he awoke suddenly, inexplicably disturbed. Peering warily at first down the length of his bed through half-closed eyes – half-expecting, half-fearing to find an intruder in his room - he found himself staring round-eyed at the figure of a young woman, dressed in white, kneeling as if in prayer beside his bed – and leaning her weightless arms on the covers over his knees.

This apparition, he swore, bore no relation to any image from any dream he had been having immediately prior to waking up. In fact he had been in a dreamless period of sleep when he was so strangely disturbed. What he saw, he admitted, frightened him. But his reaction to this extraordinary sight was weirdly rational: he wondered if it were not some outlandish decoy – the gangster's moll pretending to be a ghost! – set up by some particularly cunning set of burglars. With unusual presence of mind, he reached for his gun. As he swung it into aim, the image of the girl kneeling by his bedside faded away.

Brookesmith found himself rather foolishly waving a heavy revolver at his own bare feet. Making the best of a bad job, he salved his wounded pride by creeping around his flat and then the ground floor – the working area of the bank – looking for any sign of a break-in. He found nothing out of order, but neither could he explain the apparition that had woken him up.

Here we have a witness to two very different kinds of haunting, and a witness, to boot, with a certain rather startlingly logical reaction to both. Unfortunately, we don't know (because he did not say) whether Brookesmith made any attempt to discover if anyone else had ever seen the female phantom that rested so lightly on his bed, or if he made any effort later to find out whose phantom she may have been.

However, the real importance of these two stories, side by side and from the same source, is that someone can on one occasion believe he is really seeing a ghost and accept it as such, and on another occasion, confronted by another apparent haunting, take a thoroughly sceptical view and investigate and effectively exorcise it. To that person – and this is the point – the existence of false ghosts does not preclude the existence of real ones. And no one can say that Brookesmith's extraordinarily cool reaction was essentially different from one case to the other. On each occasion he responded according to a certain logic (despite his fright). The witness, if not the phenomenon, was consistent throughout.

DEATH-OMEN

Does any of this get us any nearer the answer to the question: what is a ghost?

In a way, no, this last story does not, because there is no evidence to suggest that the phantom lady seen by the conscientious bank guard and bluff, no-nonsense sailor Frank Brookesmith was not, in any case, a figment of his own momentarily disorientated imagination. But it does tell us that the most sceptical and practical of people can believe that they have genuinely seen a ghost. In short, the key to ghost stories may be the witness, not the ghost. And these two stories together also tell us that the most common presumption about ghosts is that they are the spirits – or at least the inexplicably immaterial records – of people once alive and now dead.

Before sorting out the vexed question of the role of the witness in ghost reports, it's as well to establish how varied the phenomenon of hauntings itself can be.

Ghosts of people may or may not be images of the spirit world, but they are not always apparitions of dead people, or even of animals.

Christina Hole comments in *Haunted England*: 'There is scarcely an old road in England along which the Spectral Coach has not trundled at some time or another. It may be either a genuine coach or a hearse; but whatever form it takes, it bears certain distinguishing marks [that] prove it to be something from another world. It is always black, and so are the driver and his horses. Often both are headless. It appears suddenly on the roadway and moves very fast and usually without noise. Only in a few cases do we hear of the rumble of wheels on the road or the clattering of horses' hoofs to give warning of its approach. Like

The spectral coach and coachman, of whom it has been said that 'scarcely an old road in England' lacks an example. But how does a coach acquire a 'spiritual' form, if ghosts are the shades of the dead?

most apparitions of its kind, it... often serves as a death-omen for those unlucky enough to encounter it.'

Why vehicles should take on spectral form, no one knows (let alone how), but phantom conveyances appear time and again in accounts of ghosts and hauntings. Furthermore, this is a tradition that refuses to die (so to speak). Modern accounts of ghost vehicles are rife with phantom trains, buses, ships, cars, and even aircraft.

SPECTRAL SHIP

In the winter of 1942, the destroyer USS *Kennison* was returning from an antisubmarine patrol along the California coast, coming up to the Golden Gate at the mouth of San Francisco Bay, when a heavy fog came out of nowhere. The *Kennison's* engine-room bells rang for dead slow, and the ship began to nose carefully through the water, its foghorn sounding.

Then the fantail lookout, torpedoman Jack Cornelius, yelled into the ship's tannoy for everyone to look aft. Cornelius and another seaman, who was on the aft gundeck, both reported that a huge, derelict, two-masted sailing ship had passed within a few feet of the destroyer's stern. They had had the hulk in full view for about half a minute before the fog closed in around it. The radar operators, however, had not seen a thing before, during, or after the sighting of the seemingly immaterial ship.

There is one ghost ship that has been seen dozens of times over the years by sailors. In a letter to *Occult Review* in 1921, F.G. Montagu Powell recounted an incident that had occurred many years previously, when he was serving with the Royal Navy:

'Somewhere in July 1859, when I was on HMS *Euryalus*, we were off the Cape of Good Hope when a curious thing happened. It was about six bells (11 a.m.) in the forenoon, and I was midshipman of the watch, when a dull and heavy mist fell upon us. We were under steam and sail and very light airs from the south were hardly filling our sails, the sun breaking out through the mist like a fiery copper ball every now and then, when we sighted a sailing ship right ahead of us, lying in fact right across our track and so close that before we could hail her or alter our course we were on top of her and in fact cut clean through her.

'Her sails seemed to me flat, lifeless and discoloured, no "bellying to the breeze" about them. Her crew, clad in sou'westers and tarpaulins and the traditional breeches, moved lifelessly about the decks, coiling up ropes or leaning over the hammock netting, and paying not the slightest attention to us, not nearly so much as we paid to them.

'I remember the curious vague look she had as, apparently undamaged by this tremendous impact (though of course there was no impact, it was just like cutting through a shadow or a cloud) she vanished slowly astern, the mist overwhelming and enfolding her like a shroud. I remember hearing one bluejacket saying to another, "Yon's the Flying Dutchman, I expect."'

The Flying Dutchman, Hendrik Vanderdecken, blasphemed against God and was condemned to sail the seas until the Last Judgement. That is a legend. But here we have dates, names, a specific location – and an account of a genuine personal experience. Was this spectral ship the *Flying Dutchman*? Or did the legend spring up to explain all such ghostly encounters at sea?

Two phantom faces, photographed from on board the oil tanker SS Watertown in December 1924. The ghost faces apparently had the features of two sailors who had died in an accident on the voyage down the Pacific coast of the USA and had been buried at sea. The faces appeared for days afterwards, though only for brief periods each day.

RECORDINGS OF THE PAST

In their way, steam trains are no less romantic than full-rigged ships – although no less problematic when it comes to explaining how ghost trains could be in any sense 'spiritual'. But there is no lack of them in the annals of ghost lore.

John Quirk, of Pittsfield, Massachusetts, reported that he and several customers at the Bridge Lunch café saw a phantom train hauled by a steam engine one afternoon in February 1958. The train consisted of a baggage car and five or six coaches, which the witnesses described in great detail. A month later, a similar train passed the same location at top speed, barrelling towards Boston, at 6.30 one morning.

Railroad officials insisted that no steam engine had run on that line for years. On yet another occasion when the phantom train was reported, the railroad stated categorically that no train of any material kind had been on that section of track at that time.

As trucks have largely replaced trains for hauling freight – and as the trucker and his big rig have become romanticized as modern exemplars of the great American tradition of rugged individualism – so ghost trucks have appeared on the highways.

In *Fate* magazine for February 1986, truck driver Harriette Spanabel of Brooksville, Florida, recalled an experience that unnervingly echoes Steven Spielberg's eerie movie *Duel*:

'I drive a tractor trailer and haul produce from Florida up the East Coast and west as far as Texas. For the past year and a half, always on my return run, a phantom truck follows me at least part of the time. At first I thought it was my imagination. One minute nothing would be behind me but the next minute a tractor trailer would be there.

'This truck has followed me on both Interstate highways and narrow two-lane roads. It is always behind me at night, moving over every once in a while so that its left headlight hits my left mirror directly. It disappears just as quickly as it appears.

'I now know for sure that I am not imagining the truck because I have a witness who also watched my mystery vehicle. I recently took my friend Kelly Rose with me to Miami to make a delivery. I picked up the load in Philadelphia on March 8, 1985. It was a load of dry freight with two drops. It was when we were coming back from Miami that the truck first joined us at approximately 11:30 the evening of the 12th. I drove out of Lakeland, Fla, on US 98 going north. I planned to turn onto [State Route] 471 which runs through the middle of the Green Swamp. The phantom truck first appeared behind us on US 98 about two miles before I made my turn onto [State Route] 471. It followed us from there until we had almost reached [State Route] 50 where I turn to go west into the town where I live.

'On a narrow two-lane road which runs through a state forest, about 50 miles from my house, the truck again appeared behind us. Kelly immediately asked where it had come from. Of course I couldn't tell her but it followed us for 30 miles before it disappeared this time.

'Kelly, who had been watching the truck intently in her mirror, was astounded. I stopped my truck on 471 and we got out and looked for the other truck. It was completely gone. On this road there are no side roads where a truck could pull on or off. There are no shoulders where a truck could pull off without either tipping over or ending up tangled in a mass of big trees. And let me add there was no other traffic on 471 going in either direction.'

The image of a ghost that appeared in a picture taken inside Newby Church, Yorkshire, by the vicar, the Revd K.F. Lord, in the early 1960s. The ghost was not visible to the priest when he took the photograph.

There is no difficulty in believing that these various witnesses are telling the truth – especially as in each case there was more than one witness to the strange events they describe. But these phantoms of the inanimate can hardly be spirits of something dead – since they weren't alive in the first place. So we may be forced to conclude that many ghosts are some kind of recording of the past. But then the problem still remains as to why a particular train, ship or even mighty, snarling 18-wheel semi-trailer should record itself on a particular place: why them, and not any of the hundreds of others that have passed that way?

GHOULISH APPEARANCE

Probably the most frequently told of all kinds of ghost story are those concerning apparitions of people at the moment of their death. Here at least the ghost is inextricably linked with the notion of a life after death – or, at least, with some kind of spiritual existence that is able to project itself across time and space from the dying person to someone near or dear to them. Two instances of this kind of haunting – if that is the word – show how different they can be.

One morning in the spring of 1973, 58-year-old Mrs Martha Beckwhite was doing one of the things she liked best – working in her garden in Blandford, Dorset. Without warning she felt, without knowing how she could identify it, the presence of one of her youngest daughter's friends, Luke Fore. Then, she distinctly heard his voice say 'Goodbye, Martha'. Again without knowing why, she knew that he had died. When the telephone rang in the evening of that day and she heard her daughter's voice on the line, she said: 'Don't worry, darling; I know why you've called. Luke's just died, hasn't he?'

Indeed he had, of cancer of the liver. Two things about this case are intriguing, however. First was that she had met Luke Fore only once or twice (he was the husband of one of her daughter's closest friends at the time). Second was that she had no idea that Luke was ill. For various reasons Luke's cancer had been kept a secret from everyone but his immediate family:

no one outside that small circle knew that he even had a cold, let alone was terminally ill.

There are two ways of stating the mystery here. Whatever the ultimate answer, there may be some clue in the fact that Martha Beckwhite and Luke Fore got along famously together on the few occasions that they met, although they were perhaps 20 years apart in age. Why did he appear to her, though, whom he had met but a few times? Or perhaps the problem should be put another way: why and how did she alone of all the people who knew Luke (and many knew him more intimately) 'tune in' to the fact of his death? Whatever the answer, there is no doubt that Martha Beckwhite received and understood, by some paranormal means, a message from someone who was dying, and whom she had no reason to suppose was even remotely at risk of death.

A much more typical case of a near - death apparition was recounted in the October 1957 edition of *Fate* magazine.

Mary Travers was sitting up late waiting for her husband George, who was an insurance salesman, to come home. Shortly after the clock struck 11, she heard a cab coming down the street. It stopped in front of the house, and Mrs Travers heard a voice, presumably the driver's, call out 'Good night!' Then she recognized the familiar sound of her husband's steps on the porch. She hurried to the front door to welcome him home.

He came in silently, with his hat pulled down over his eyes, and then he stood with his back to his wife while she shut the door. She thought he was behaving oddly, and asked did he feel all right? He turned to face her – and in place of George's face she saw a hideous white death-mask. She screamed, and continued to scream, so that the neighbours rushed in to see what was wrong. By then, the apparition had vanished. Minutes later the phone rang: the caller regretfully announced that George Travers had been killed in a train crash.

It is difficult to account for such an apparition except as a spirit of the dead. It seems unlikely that by sheer coincidence Mrs Travers imagined his ghoulish appearance on the very night he died. It makes more sense to assume that the spectre was indeed her husband's spirit, or at least a projection from his mind, sent to warn Mrs Travers – albeit silently and shockingly – of what had happened to him.

THE DEAD MAN'S WILL

The classic example of a haunting that seems to prove the continued existence of an individual in some form after death is the famous case of the 'lost' will of the North Carolina farmer James L. Chaffin. This is one of the best-documented cases in all psychic research. As several writers have remarked, even the lawyers involved seem to have been honest.

James L. Chaffin, a farmer of Davie County, North Carolina, had four sons: John, James, Marshall and Abner. On 16 November 1905 he made a will, attested by two witnesses, leaving everything he owned to his third son, Marshall. Why he singled out Marshall, no one knows. But, a little over 13 years later, the old man had a change of heart. He made a new will. It read:

'After reading the 27th chapter of Genesis I, James L. Chaffin, do make my last will and testament and here it is. I want, after giving my body a decent burial, my little property to be equally divided between my four children... and if she is living, you must take care of your mummy. Witness my seal and hand. James L. Chaffin. This January 16, 1919.'

This second will lacked the signatures of any witnesses, but would be legally valid under the laws of North Carolina if it could be established that the whole of the document was in the testator's own handwriting. Chaffin, unknown to anyone at the time, put the will between two pages of the family Bible on which were printed the 27th chapter of Genesis. The paper was folded over to make a kind of pocket. Chaffin never mentioned the second will to anyone, but he did scribble on a roll of paper, which he stitched into an inside pocket of his overcoat, a note that said: 'Read the 27th chapter of Genesis in my daddie's old Bible.'

On 7 September 1921, James L. Chaffin died unexpectedly after a fall. Marshall, the third son, obtained probate without fuss; there was no reason for anyone to challenge the will, and there was no enmity or rivalry among Chaffin's children.

But in June 1925 the second son, James P. Chaffin, began having vivid dreams that his father was standing silently beside his bed. A week or so later the apparition, dressed in the old black overcoat his son knew so well, spoke: 'You will find my will in my overcoat pocket.' James was convinced this was significant, and hurried to his mother's house.

His father's coat, however, had been given to her eldest son, John, who lived some 20 miles away. James went to John's home, and explained the situation. The two brothers examined the coat together. They found that the inside pocket had been stitched closed; when they cut it open, they found inside the rolled-up strip of paper in their father's handwriting. 'Read the 27th chapter of Genesis in my daddie's old Bible' was not a will, as James's dream had indicated, but the two brothers felt they must follow the message up.

John felt he could not look at the family Bible without independent witnesses, and took a neighbour, the neighbour's daughter, and his own wife and daughter with him. After a long search in his mother's house the old Bible was discovered in a top drawer in an upstairs room and, as it was being taken out, it fell into three pieces. The neighbour picked up the front section containing Genesis, and it opened automatically at the place indicated in the cryptic message. There lay the second will.

This will was tendered for probate in 1925. Marshall Chaffin had died a year after his father, but his widow contested the application on behalf of her young son.

The court assembled in December 1925 to decide the issue: the public areas were crowded at the prospect of seeing a classic family squabble burst into open view. The scandal-hungry locals were to be disappointed. On the advice of her lawyer, Marshall's widow withdrew her opposition when she saw the will itself, unmistakably in the old man's handwriting.

There are really only two stark alternatives in explaining this case. Either the Chaffin brothers were lying, and set up the whole elaborate hoax in order to lay their hands on their share of their father's estate, or the story is true from start to finish. But the business of the Chaffin will is one of the best-documented and best-attested cases in ghost lore; and as such it stands as reasonable proof that in some cases, at least, ghosts do represent the consciousness of the dead – and that the physically dead do survive in some form of afterlife.

LOVE OF ADVENTURE

Some famous hauntings, however, leave one wondering to what extent some ghosts are purely subjective entities, existing solely in the mind of the witness.

Captain Joshua Slocum, the great American sailor, had a remarkable experience in July 1895, while on his historic solo voyage around the world in his sloop *Spray*. In the Atlantic, between the Azores and Gibraltar, he ran into squally weather. At the same time he began to suffer an attack of severe stomach cramps. These so distracted him that he went below – without taking in sail as he should have done. He threw himself on the floor of the boat's cabin, in great pain. In his account of the voyage he described what happened next:

'How long I lay there I could not tell, for I became delirious. When I came to, as I thought, from my swoon, I realized that the sloop was plunging into a heavy sea, and looking out of the companionway, to my amazement I saw a tall man at the helm. His rigid hand, grasping the spokes of the wheel, held them as in a vice. One may imagine my astonishment. His rig was that of a foreign sailor, and the large red cap he wore was cockbilled over his left ear, and all was set off with shaggy black whiskers. He would have been taken for a pirate in any part of the world. While I gazed upon his threatening aspect I forgot the storm, and wondered if he had come to cut my throat. This he seemed to divine.

'"Senõr," said he, doffing his cap, "I have come to do you no harm." And a smile, the faintest in the world, but still a smile, played on his face, which seemed not unkind when he spoke. "I am one of Columbus's crew, the pilot of the *Pinta*, come to aid you. Lie quiet, senor captain, and I will guide your ship while you have a calentura [a reference to the stomach cramps] but you will be all right tomorrow... You did wrong to mix cheese with plums..."

'I thought what a very devil he was to carry sail. Again, as if he read my mind, he exclaimed, "Yonder is the *Pinta* ahead, we must overtake her. Give her sail, give her sail!"'

Next day Slocum found that the *Spray* was still on the same heading as he had left her when he staggered below in his 'swoon'.

'Columbus himself could not have held her more exactly on her course,' he wrote. 'I felt grateful to the old pilot, but I marvelled some that he had not taken in the jib. I was getting much better now, but was very weak.. .I fell asleep. Then who should visit me but my old friend of the night before, this time, of course, in a dream. "You did well last night to take my advice," said he, "and if you would, I should like to be with you often on the voyage, for the love of adventure alone." He again doffed his cap, and disappeared as mysteriously as he came. I awoke with the feeling that I had been in the presence of a friend and a seaman of vast experience.'

Perhaps so. And perhaps, in his delirious state, Slocum imagined, or hallucinated, the whole thing. But if he did, another small miracle seems to have occurred: the *Spray* kept her course, with no one at the wheel, through a long bout of foul weather and a hostile sea.

Borley Rectory, dubbed 'the most haunted house in England', showing the gates at which a ghostly nun was allegedly seen. The dubious nature of the phenomena at Borley has led many to wonder since if the legend of the house lingers on.

'MERE' COINCIDENCE?

The best evidence that some ghosts present proof of a life after death comes from pacts made between friends or relatives in which each party promises that whichever dies first will 'come back' to the other to show that they still survive.

The best-known of these cases is that of Henry, Lord Brougham (1778–1868), the famous and fiery British reformer. Brougham made just such a pact with his old college friend Geoffrey Garner, one that eventually unravelled in a manner so hilarious that it has to be true. Some years after making this agreement, Brougham went travelling in Sweden with a group of friends.

'Arriving at a decent inn, we decided to stop for the night,' he recalled. 'I was glad to take advantage of a hot bath before I turned in, and here a most remarkable thing happened to me – so remarkable that I must tell the story from the beginning.

'After I left the [Edinburgh] High School, I went with Garner, my most intimate friend, to attend the classes in the University… We frequently discussed and speculated upon many grave subjects – among others, on the immortality of the soul, and on a future state. This question, and the possibility, I will not say of ghosts walking, but of the dead appearing to the living, were subjects of much speculation: and we actually committed the folly of drawing up an agreement, written in our blood, to the effect that whichever of us died the first should appear to the other, and thus solve any doubts we had entertained of the "life after death".

'After we had finished our classes at the college, Garner went to India, having got an appointment there in the Civil Service. He seldom wrote to me, and after a lapse of a few years I had almost forgotten him; moreover, his family having little connection with Edinburgh, I seldom saw or heard anything, and I had nearly forgotten his existence.

'I had taken a warm bath, and while lying in it and enjoying the comfort of the heat, after the late freezing I had undergone, I turned my head round, looking toward the chair on which I had deposited my clothes, as I was about to get out of the bath. On the chair sat Garner, looking calmly at me.

'How I got out of the bath I know not, but on recovering my senses I found myself sprawling on the floor. The apparition, or whatever it was, that had taken the likeness of Garner, had disappeared.'

On his return to Edinburgh after this farcical episode, Brougham learned that Garner had died in India on 19 December, the precise date of the apparition. Many years after the event, Brougham tended to be sceptical about it:

'Singular coincidence! Yet when one reflects on the vast numbers of dreams which night after night pass through our brains, the number of coincidences between the vision and the event are perhaps fewer and less remarkable than a fair calculation of chances would warrant us to expect. I believe every such seeming miracle is, like every ghost story, capable of explanation.'

Others, too, have suggested these cases are the result of 'mere' coincidence. But in their monumental collection *Phantasms of the Living*, published in 1886, the Society for Psychical Research described nine examples of an apparition following a pact of this kind. It is surely stretching scepticism to breaking point to suggest that all these apparitions are purely 'coincidental' with the death of the parties concerned, especially when such a pact is involved. And even if they are, the sceptics still cannot satisfactorily explain what those phantasms are or where they come from.

Nevertheless, it is clear from the apparitions and spectres we have discussed in this chapter that ghost stories, however well documented and however fascinating they may be, do not make the best or most consistent evidence for life after death. That evidence comes in subtler and, often, even stranger forms.

ANOTHER TIME, ANOTHER LIFE

The ancient Celts were terrible in battle as they had no fear of death – they would even lend money on the understanding that if it were not repaid in this life, it would be in the next. What made them so sure that this was not the only life?

The idea that the soul may journey through time, using successive human bodies as vehicles for the journey and the lives of those personalities it adopts as food for its spiritual journey to perfection, is foreign to Western thought. Judaism, Christianity and Islam differ widely in their notions of the kind of afterlife that awaits us, and of heaven and hell, but their broad message is the same.

'It is appointed for men to die once,' says St Paul in his epistle to the Hebrews, 'and after that comes judgement.' If we live in an upright, tolerant and kindly fashion, we shall be rewarded in the life to come – and if we do not, we shall be punished. The fundamental belief is that this is the only life each of us has, and that this life is the only chance we have to prove ourselves morally and spiritually.

So deep is this idea ingrained in Western thought that even in the increasingly irreligious 21th century it has actually proved possible to make money by gently mocking any idea of reincarnation at all. The New York journalist Don Marquis made a small fortune from regaling an eager public with the adventures of his characters Archie, the cockroach who had formerly been a *vers libre* poet but continued to write his versified diary by jumping up and down on the keys of a typewriter, and Mehitabel, the alley cat who 'once accused herself of being Cleopatra.'

However, belief in reincarnation is widespread, ancient and powerful, and the religions of some of the world's greatest civilizations have held that reincarnation may be combined with transmigration - the entry of the soul into the body of an animal. Such beliefs were common in the West before the rise of Christianity. One reason why the ancient Celts were so devastating as warriors was that they had absolutely no fear of death – so convinced were they of the reality of reincarnation and the continuity of their consciousness. They would even lend money on the understanding that if it could not be repaid in this life, it surely would be in a future one.

DEATH AND BIRTH

In ancient Greece, belief in reincarnation was not incompatible with belief in the orthodox pantheon of gods. The Orphic sect, which flourished about 100 years before the golden age of Athens, had a view of earthly life that for gloom and self-punishment matched that of the most zealous medieval Christian flagellator. The Orphics called human existence a 'sorrowful weary wheel', and the only way to escape it was to live with the utmost self-denial and asceticism. Even then, only after many physical deaths and rebirths in both animal and human form would the soul be free.

The belief in reincarnation as such in ancient Greece was not confined to such killjoy cults, however. The mathematical genius Pythagoras, who lived around 500 BC, claimed to know that in former lives he had been variously a fisherman, a peasant, a shopkeeper's wife and a (female) prostitute. Pythagoras, it is true, also held fast to many quite eccentric beliefs, including some concerning the certain fearsome consequences of eating beans.

But Plato, one of the most profoundly original minds of the ancient world, was convinced of the truth of reincarnation. He held that the soul chose its new life at the moment of death, and might enter one of nine levels of being. Plato believed that this was not an endless cycle, and the soul was neither eternal nor did it necessarily progress, or even learn, spiritually from one life to another. Progress could be made if a soul chose its next life wisely, but Plato held that in creating a new physical body for its next life, the soul expended energy. Once its energy was finally consumed, the soul itself died out.

The Roman notion of reincarnation was somewhat different; the 1st-century AD political thinker Sallust, for example, maintained that children born with handicaps were bearing punishments for evils they had committed in former lives.

The other great ancient culture that firmly believed in reincarnation was Egypt. At first, the Egyptian religions held that only 'great souls', destined to lead mankind, were born again, but this belief gradually relaxed and expanded to include everyone from the highest to the lowest social classes. By the time the Book of the Dead came to be compiled, matters had, become distinctly formalized. The book contains incantations that would free the soul from its earthly prison in the tomb and prepare it for reincarnation. And it might come back as a plant – a lotus, say, or a sycamore – or as an animal; after 3,000 years of such transmigrations it would be ready to be reborn as a human being once again.

RETURN OF THE GODS

Christianity gradually expunged such ideas as it spread west from the Middle East, and seven centuries later Islam suppressed them as it began to spread south and east. But in places where these religions have arrived only within the last few centuries, native faiths continue to hold fast in their belief in reincarnation.

Throughout the Pacific, for instance, reincarnation is a bulwark of most native religions. The religions of many American Indian tribes endorse reincarnation, too. It has even been suggested that one reason why the 16th-century Spanish conquistadores found it so easy to conquer huge tracts of South and Central America, despite the existence of highly developed civilizations there, was the prevailing local belief in reincarnation. The Spanish leaders were seen as reborn, returning gods: in Mexico as Quetzalcoatl, and in Peru as Virochas. The Spanish lost no time in taking advantage of this 'heathen' error, and laid the country waste.

In Alaska, where gold and oil rushes have had more effect on local culture than any missionaries, the indigenous Tlingit people have retained to this day a powerful reverence for reincarnation, which they regard as a direct and immediate continuity from one life to another. Tlingit women pay careful heed to their dreams

A wealthy household in ancient Athens. The Greeks, for all their famous rationalism and philosophy, believed both in a pantheon of gods notorious for uproarious behaviour, and in personal reincarnation.

when they are pregnant, for it is then, in dreams, that a previously incarnated but now disembodied soul announces its intention to them to be reborn in the body of the new baby. At birth, diviners take great care to ascertain whose soul has been reborn, and then the baby is given the tribal name of the person it had been before. The child then takes credit for the good deeds done by its predecessors – but also has a powerful moral example that it must live up to.

THE WHEEL OF REBIRTH

In India, attachment to the idea of reincarnation has never wavered since the Hindu religion took hold and, some 3,000 years ago, its sacred writings began to reflect a belief in rebirth and reincarnation. In the Bhagavad-Gita ('The Song of Krishna'), the warrior, hero and god Krishna explains that he is the eighth incarnation of the god Vishnu, saying to Arjuna: 'Both I and thou have passed through many births. Mine are known to me, but thou knowest not of thine.' Hindus call reincarnation samsara, 'the wheel of rebirth'.

For Hindus, the number of reincarnations one may go through is infinite (and may include transmigration to lower forms of life, or even into rocks and stones), for the purpose of them is to give the soul the opportunity to rid itself of the imperfections that inevitably afflict it from its creation. Between each incarnation the soul enjoys a period of rest, in which it ponders on its progress towards moksha, the Absolute, which is also perfection and liberation – from which, paradoxically, the soul first emerged.

To rid oneself of these congenital flaws requires turning one's back on the world and realizing one's best, true nature. At the same time karma, the law of cause and effect, is at work: in essence this means that good is rewarded and evil is punished, and what is good or evil for the soul is judged on deeds and effects, not (as in Western religions) on intentions. Thus the Upanishads say quite clearly, 'Those whose conduct has been evil will have an evil birth as a dog, a pig, or an untouchable outcast.'

Earthly life is regarded as a burden, and at the same time as an illusion, called maya. The opportunities that this ostensibly unworldly outlook, combined with the rigid Hindu caste system, have offered for the exploitation of the poor by the rich have been plentiful, and usually avidly grasped.

The Sphinx, with the Great Pyramid in the background. These monuments were part of the ancient Egyptians' massive and elaborate system of belief and ritual concerning the afterlife.

THE SEARCH FOR THE DALAI LAMA

This observable corruption of a high ideal may have contributed to the inspiration of Siddartha Gautama, born a Brahman, the highest Hindu caste, around 566 BC. He was the heir to the crown of the Sakya clan on the Ganges in India, and is now known universally as Buddha.

The legend says that as soon as he was born Buddha vowed to end birth, old age, suffering, and death – in short, to break the endless grip of earthly life upon the soul. By the age of 29 he had realized that all were inescapable, and eventually propounded his Four Truths: that existence is suffering, and suffering is inevitable;

that suffering is caused by desire; that eliminating desire will rid one of suffering;, and that the right conduct – the Eightfold Path – will rid one of desire.

Central to these principles was the belief that the soul was not (as Hinduism taught) an individual and personal thing, which drove the cycle of reincarnation. Rather, reincarnation was fuelled by the ego, which was constantly changing from life to life, and was an illusion besides. Rid oneself of ego, therefore, and one would attain nirvana – which does not mean heaven or the absolute, but simply extinction. Buddhism thus rejects any connection between social caste and the condition of the soul, although successive rebirths are inevitable if one is to work off the burden of karma from previous existences. But this is a matter of purifying the life force, in redeeming the individual.

One of the most fascinating ways in which the Buddhist belief in rebirth has practical effect is in the search for a successor to the Dalai Lama, leader of Tibet's Buddhists, when he dies.

The Dalai Lama is regarded as the incarnation of Chenrezi, the Buddhist god of grace, and he has taken earthly form 14 times

Constantine, Emperor of Rome early in the 4th century AD. According to testimony given under hypnosis by Welsh housewife Jane Evans, she had once lived as the wife of Constantine's tutor during his residence in Britain.

since 1391. Each time the Dalai Lama (the term means 'greatest teacher') dies, the lamas of Tibet have the task of finding his reincarnated form – a small child born after the death – who will then be brought up to take on the leadership of the Tibetan Buddhist community. When the 13th Dalai Lama died in 1933, it took the monks six years to find his successor.

The search involves sifting a variety of normal and paranormal clues: the lamas scrutinize astrological signs, visions, dreams and other omens to establish when they should start their quest. After the 13th Dalai Lama's death, the corpse itself offered one clue. It turned its head toward the north-east. Then, in the mausoleum where he was laid, a star-shaped fungus grew on the north-east wall. In the mail courtyard of the monastery housing the tomb, a dragon flower unexpectedly grew by the north-east wall.

The lamas decided that it was in this direction that they should begin their search. To help them came a vision in a dream granted to one of the monastery's monks. He saw a place sacred to Buddhists – the lake at Chos Khorgyal, in China, and also a house with carved gables and eaves painted blue. Near here, the lamas concluded, they would find the child they were seeking.

In 1937 a group of lamas and monks set off for China to find the house. Two years later, at the village of Takster, they found it. One of the high lamas in the party disguised himself as a servant and went into the house. He found inside a two-year-old boy, Tenzin Gyatso, who instantly demanded the rosary that, beneath his disguise, the lama was wearing around his neck. This was not the lama's – but it had belonged to the Dalai Lama. Tenzin Gyatso then identified – or recognized – other rosaries, a drum and a walking-stick that had also belonged to the former Dalai Lama.

Encouraged by these initial signs, the lamas went on to look for physical confirmation that the boy was the current embodiment of Chenrezi. The various bodily characteristics, moles and birthmarks found on every Dalai Lama were indeed in place, and the lamas set about making arrangements for the boy and his family to travel to Tibet. Among these was paying a $300,000 ransom to the provincial governor for allowing Tenzin Gyatso to leave China, but eventually the infant Dalai Lama was installed in the Potala Palace above Lhasa to begin his long and arduous training to become the spiritual and temporal leader of the Tibetan nation.

The alleged reincarnation of the Tibetan Dalai Lama is not, in itself, proof of the reality of repeated rebirth. Without casting doubt on the sincerity of those involved, one could if one wanted pick holes in a number of aspects even in this one case. And the key to the matter, here, is profound religious belief; driven by that, a sceptic would assert, the law of averages says that sooner or later the lamas are bound to find a suitable child to proclaim as their reincarnated leader.

On the other hand, there are many cases from the West, where there is no established traditional belief in reincarnation or rebirth, of people who, to their own surprise, have discovered that they have apparently lived more than one life on Earth.

THE SECRET MEMORY

The evidence for these claims has been gathered exclusively from hypnotic regression – that is, from subjects who have been hypnotized and then led back into the past to recall what they can of any former lives. Unfortunately, the most plausible of these – notably the alleged reincarnation of the Irish woman Bridey Murphy (1798–1864, according to the account given under hypnosis) as Wisconsin housewife Virginia Tighe (born in 1923), and the various lives recounted by Welsh housewife Jane Evans – have fallen apart in the light of detailed research.

Of these, the claims of Jane Evans were the most transparent. Once researcher Melvin Harris had burrowed into them, they looked more like a highly aerated Swiss cheese than evidence for reincarnation.

Jane Evans produced an astonishing wealth of detail about (for instance) life as the wife of the tutor to the young Constantine (later to be Emperor of Rome) in 4th-century Britain, or as a young Jewess caught up in the massacre of the Jews in York in 1190. This latter account in fact contained a wealth of thoroughly inaccurate information both about York and about the Jews of the 12th century, and most of it seems to have come from a play broadcast on BBC radio.

Jane Evans's life as 'Livonia' in 4th-century Roman Britain was taken almost word for word from a novel called *The Living Wood* by Louis de Wohl. It seems that Jane Evans had, quite honestly, forgotten that she had ever read any of the books on which her 'former lives' were based, but retrieved her memories of them from her subconscious while in a hypnotic trance. This phenomenon, known as cryptomnesia (from the Greek for 'secret memory') is familiar to hypnotherapists, and has indeed proved useful in digging out facts – often traumatic – about their subjects' early lives that they have often deliberately forgotten.

Another detailed recall of an actual historical event was provided by a subject known only as 'Jan' when she was put into trance by hypnotist Joe Keeton. Jan became 18-year-old Joan Waterhouse who, she said, was tried for witchcraft at Chelmsford Assizes, Essex, in 1556. All the details were proven to be historically correct – including the existence of Joan Waterhouse and her presence in the dock. The only original source for Jan's – or Joan's – account that survived in the 20th century was a contemporary pamphlet, and the only surviving copy was in the library of the Archbishop of Canterbury's London residence, Lambeth Palace. Jan swore that she had never been there and had never seen the document.

But there was one bizarre anomaly. As Joan, Jan insisted that she had been tried in the reign of Queen Elizabeth I. Unfortunately, the English monarch in 1556 was Queen Mary I; Elizabeth did not accede to the throne until 1558. Given the ferment in religious life at the time, the supreme importance of the monarch in deciding and directing what religious practices were acceptable, and the sensitivity to such matters of people at the local level and their readiness to act in their own obsessive interests, this seems an extraordinary confusion.

And, indeed, there was an extraordinary confusion – in the mind of Joe Keeton and his subject 'Jan' – about what constitutes proper research. For the Lambeth Palace pamphlet had been reprinted during the 19th century, its solid black-letter type substituted by a fair attempt to reproduce a more legible typeface and design of Shakespeare's time. But there was one crucial error. The 19th-century printer had set the date of the Chelmsford witchcraft trial as 1556 – the date insisted upon by Jan and Joan. But the original plainly reads 1566 – by which time Queen Elizabeth had been on the throne for eight somewhat tempestuous years.

The only logical conclusion is that Jan had not, as she and Joe Keeton thought, once existed as Joan Waterhouse, accused of witchcraft, but had read, absorbed and – to be charitable – forgotten the reprint of the 16th-century trials at Chelmsford. But Keeton did not do this fundamental piece of research: a sceptic had to do it, and so debunk the case.

Perhaps the final word on hypnosis and progressive reincarnation should go to a travel courier who, in the late 1980s, was accompanying a group of middle-aged American ladies on the Nile steamer from Port Said to Luxor. In the middle of a conversation about the politics of the Middle East, she said to this author: 'You think you got problems? I've got nine Cleopatras on this tour with me. You try keeping them from fighting.'

An engraving from Zucchero's portrait of Queen Elizabeth I of England. The date of her accession to the throne, 1558, was the key to revealing the alleged reincarnation of the Cheltenham witch Joan Waterhouse.

A MATTER OF FAITH

Is there, then, any real evidence for reincarnation?

Actually, and sadly for those of us who would like to have another crack at life in the hope that we might not make the same terrible mistakes again, the answer is most likely a resounding 'No'.

Some of the most apparently convincing evidence for reincarnation has come from the researches of Dr Ian Stevenson, professor of psychology at the University of Virginia. Dr Stevenson has travelled the world, conducted innumerable in-depth interviews, and assiduously researched and reported a huge collection of cases that are, in his cautious words, 'suggestive of reincarnation'.

The British historian Ian Wilson has noted a number of problematic inconsistencies in Stevenson's evidence, and has also pointed out two particular but telling consistencies.

First, Stevenson has had to rely, during his extensive travels, on interpreters who generally already shared a belief in reincarnation with those he was interviewing. In some cultures people will tend to tell foreign visitors what they think the stranger wants to hear rather than the precise truth as they know it.

Second, Wilson has completed a careful analysis of the social backgrounds of the children claiming to have been reincarnated and compared them with the families of the people they allegedly once were. In an astonishing preponderance of cases, the family that the 'reincarnated' child has claimed to belong to has been of higher social status – from anything to an artisan (as opposed to a peasant) to a millionaire (as opposed to – a peasant). In a society in which belief in reincarnation is basic, and that is also circumscribed by a class system that is deeply underwritten by religious orthodoxy, any evidence that offers escape from certain wretched individual circumstances will surely be grasped at the earliest opportunity. Wilson does not say so directly, but it is not difficult to suspect from his evidence that the families involved in the claims Dr Stevenson has investigated have perhaps coached the children in question.

The truth or otherwise of reincarnation, then, has to remain, for the time being at least, a matter of faith. This does not mean that reincarnation does not occur – perhaps only for some people and not for others – but it does mean that there is no conclusive evidence for it at the moment. It is still an attractive idea. And it remains a bulwark of many ancient and respected cultures around the world.

THE MOVING HAND

The lady was ashamed of what had happened in the second-class compartment of the express train, and had intended to tell no one about her unpleasant experience. The famous journalist uncovered her guilty secret in a most unexpected manner…

The great 19th-century British journalist William T. Stead, the founder of the *Review of Reviews*, was also a spiritualist. Appropriately enough for a professional writer, he was also adept at automatic writing – which he used as a vehicle for telepathic communication with a certain lady friend. As proof of its efficacy, he recounted the following incident:

'[My friend] was to lunch with me on the Wednesday if she had returned to town. On the Monday afternoon I wished to know about this, so taking up my pen I asked the lady mentally if she had returned home. My hand wrote as follows:

'"I am sorry to say that I have had the most unpleasant experience, which I am almost ashamed to tell you. I left Haslemere at 2.27 p.m. in a second-class compartment in which there were two women and a man. At Godalming the women got out and I was left alone with the man.

'"He came over and sat by me. I was alarmed and pushed him away. He would not move, however, and tried to kiss me. I was furious and there was a struggle, during which I seized his umbrella and struck him with it repeatedly, but it broke, and I was afraid I would get the worst of it, when the train stopped some distance from Guildford. The man took fright, left me before the train reached the station, jumped out and took to his heels. I was extremely agitated, but I kept the umbrella."'

Author Alex Haley discovered when helping Malcolm X to write his autobiography that the Black Muslim leader habitually committed his unconscious thoughts to paper.

Stead immediately wrote to his friend to commiserate, and explained how he had come by the information. He also asked her to call on him, and bring the broken umbrella with her. She wrote back, slightly disturbed that she had, apparently unconsciously, communicated the details of this event to him: she had intended not to mention it to anyone. She added that there was one incorrect detail in the account his automatic writing had produced – the umbrella had been her own, not her assailant's.

THE HAND THAT BETRAYS

This is an unusual case of communication by automatic writing, if not indeed a unique one, in that the person generating the message was alive at the time. Communication by automatic writing is usually thought of as the preserve of the dead.

In itself, automatic writing is not paranormal. Alex Haley, who assisted with the autobiography of the Black Muslim and political activist, Malcolm X, noted very early in their collaboration that 'while Malcolm X was talking, he often simultaneously scribbled with his red-ink ballpoint pen on any handy paper… I began leaving two white paper napkins by him every time I served him more coffee [which he drank in enormous quantities], and the ruse worked…'

Haley admitted that the projected autobiography 'got off to a very poor start', but by reading Malcolm X's scribblings (which, Haley said, 'documented how he could be talking about one thing and thinking of something else'), he was able to latch on to Malcolm X's real interests at the time, and steer their discussions so that the Black Muslim leader finally abandoned his reserve. Through these scraps of automatic writing, too, Haley was able to tell Malcolm X's true reactions to current events in his life – which were often quite different from what he would be saying publicly and to Haley. When he was officially silenced by the leader of the Black Muslims, for instance, he wrote: 'I was going downhill until he picked me up, but the more I think of it, we picked each other up.' Before he was assassinated, Malcolm X had set up his own rival mosque and militant black political organization.

The example of Malcolm X demonstrates clearly what Dr Brian Inglis has remarked – that automatic writing is 'the outcome of a different level of consciousness' rather than anything intrinsically paranormal. But that level of consciousness has often proven to be one that is sensitive to paranormal information: whether it is received from other people through extrasensory perception or whether it 'tunes in' to entities on a quite different level of being – for instance, those who have died.

DEAD CERTAINTIES

In *The Paranormal*, Dr Inglis cites two fascinating examples of automatic writing that seem to have come from dead people and that produced information that no one living could have known by any normal means.

Sir Edward Marshall Hall (1858–1927), reckoned the premier English barrister of his day, was staying with his sister; among the guests was her friend Miss K. Wingfield, who was adept in automatic writing. When she agreed to give a demonstration of her gift, Hall took a letter that he had had from South Africa the previous day, sealed it in a fresh envelope, handed it to Miss

Sir Edward Marshall Hall, who received news of his brother's death through automatic writing, three weeks before official notification of his loss reached him.

Wingfield and asked her where it came from. The immediate response was: 'The writer of that letter is dead.' After further questions the automatic writing answered the original question: the letter had come from South Africa. What Sir Edward had not told anyone present (not even his sister) was that it had in fact come from his brother, and had been posted three weeks previously. Three weeks after his visit to his sister's house, Sir Edward received another letter from South Africa – telling him that his brother was dead. He had died in his bed the day before the session with Miss Wingfield.

The English healer Matthew Manning found that, when he was a teenager, automatic writing helped divert whatever psychic energy was wreaking havoc in his parents' home through poltergeist attacks. On one occasion the Manning family decided to get in touch with the spirit of Manning's great-grandfather, Hayward Collins, who had been a racehorse owner. They asked if he could give them the winners at a race meeting scheduled for the following day. None of the family had read what horses were running then, and deliberately did not do so until the end of the next day's racing. They found that great-grandfather Collins – or his shade – had correctly 'named six horses, which turned out to be runners: two came in first, one second, and two third, which would have netted a good each-way profit, had money been put on them'.

Collins, later, also gave this message through automatic writing: 'Put your money on Red Rum which will come in first, and on Crisp which will come in second. The third will be a tight spot so leave well alone.' Red Rum won the race. Crisp was second. The third place, a photofinish, was won by a short nose.

THE GLASTONBURY QUEST

One of the most dramatic indications that automatic writing may genuinely come from entities in the world hereafter resulted in the uncovering of Glastonbury Abbey. In the process, the career of the archaeologist concerned was ruined.

From 1191 onward Glastonbury Abbey flourished, as pilgrims flocked to the site of King Arthur's tomb, which was – so the monks said – discovered that year. The Abbey had a long history: it had been founded early in the 5th century by St Patrick before his mission to Ireland, which began in AD 432. In 1539, however, the powers behind the English Reformation cast their eyes on Glastonbury. King Henry VIII's commissioners executed the abbot, Richard Whyting, confiscated the Abbey's lands and wealth, and wrecked the building. Over the next four centuries its stones sank from sight under the encroaching loam and a tangle of weeds.

In 1907 the Abbey ruins were bought by the Church of England. By then the neglected, overgrown site had become an enigma. The Church appointed 43-year-old archaeologist and architect Frederick Bligh Bond to excavate it. Bond was recognized as one of the leading English experts on Gothic architecture and a past master at restoring medieval buildings. Unknown to his new employers, he was also a devotee of psychic studies.

Bond's brief included the task of locating two chapels whose whereabouts were by that time a complete mystery. They were the Loretto and the Edgar chapels, built by Richard Bere, the last abbot

Red Rum, named as a sure-fire winner in a race described through automatic writing by the shade of an English healer's long-dead great-grandfather.

but one at Glastonbury. Bere had also revived and promoted the legend that Joseph of Arimathea, the uncle of Jesus of Nazareth, had visited Glastonbury twice – first with Jesus when he was a child, and later, after the crucifixion, bearing the Holy Grail – the vessel from which the disciples had drunk at the Last Supper.

Bond was faced with a big problem: he had insufficient funds for a full-scale dig, and breathing down his neck was a rival architect, officially appointed to preserve the ruins Bond found, but in reality deeply interested in finding them first, and taking credit for the fact. Bond decided to undertake what he politely called a 'psychological experiment' to aid him in a job whose success otherwise depended on guesswork. The experiment was, in fact, a direct appeal to the spirit world through automatic writing.

DISTINCTIVE HANDWRITING

In the afternoon of 7 November 1907, Bond and his friend John Alleyne Bartlett sat down at a plain wooden table in Bond's Bristol office. They were about to make their first attempt to communicate with the dead.

Bartlett had had considerable experience with automatic writing. He held a pencil lightly over a sheet of blank paper, while Bond rested his fingers lightly on Bartlett's other hand. After a false start, the pencil traced an outline that Bond recognized as the plan of Glastonbury Abbey. Then, curiously, it added a rectangle at the eastern end, beyond the high altar. Asked for more detail, the pencil – or whatever entity was behind it – confirmed that this building was the Edgar Chapel. It had been built, the writing continued, by Abbot Bere; Abbot Whyting had made additions to it. The pencil also traced another chapel to the north of the main Abbey building.

Asked who was writing, the entity replied: 'Johnannes Bryant, monk and lapidator' (i.e. monk and stonemason). Four days later, they learned that he had died in 1533, and had been curator of the chapel during the reign of Henry VII, and that the monks were 'very eager' to communicate. Further sessions of automatic writing with Bartlett over the following months produced a mass of information about the original Abbey buildings. It all came ostensibly from a number of long-dead monks, each of whom had his own distinctive handwriting, faithfully reproduced by Bartlett's pencil.

When Bond finally started work at Glastonbury in May 1909, he was faced with a dilemma: either he could follow the information he had acquired through psychic means, or he could take the view that he and Bartlett had invented it all, and depend on his own luck and guesswork. But in a sense Bond had no choice: the leads provided by the 'dead monks' were as good as any intelligent guess he could make, and they might be just what they appeared to be. He staked his reputation on the monks, and started digging according to their advice.

THE COMPANY OF AVALON

Bond's workmen duly dug trenches at the east end of the visible ruins and discovered a huge wall, more than 30 ft long, whose existence no one had suspected. Further digging revealed the whole of what could only have been the remains of the lost Edgar Chapel, precisely where the monks – who were now calling themselves 'the Company of Avalon' and 'the watchers from the other side' – had said it was.

Bond found time and again that the monks' automatic writing was absolutely reliable. For example, they told him that the chapel roof had been painted in gold and crimson, and Bond's workers dug up arch mouldings with the red and gold paint still intact on them. The monks said the chapel windows were stained azure, and Bond found fragments of blue stained glass among the ruins – to his own surprise, since most glass of the period was stained white or gold. Still more unusual was the monks' claim that at the east end of the chapel was a door leading to the street. Most churches simply don't have doors behind the altar, but the Edgar Chapel, it turned out, did indeed. The monks even told Bond the precise dimensions of the chapel, although he was sceptical when he first read them, for they seemed enormous. But they were correct.

The 'Company of Avalon' produced a mass of other information that explained finds at the Abbey; but Bond could not reveal what he was sure were the facts without revealing his sources. One of the more mysterious finds, as far as conventionally available knowledge went, was the skeleton of a 7 ft tall man found buried – without a coffin – just outside the walls of the Abbey church on the south side of the nave. Stranger still, between the giant's legs was another human skull.

According to the Company of Avalon, the skeleton had belonged to a monk named Radulphus. He had come to England in 1087, after the Norman invasion led by William the Conqueror. William had installed a Norman abbot, named Thurstan, at Glastonbury. Radulphus had been Thurstan's treasurer. Before the giant monk died at the extreme old age of 103, he had asked to be buried as near as possible to the church he loved. But what about the extra skull?

A curious tale attached to this, the shades of the monks informed Bond. Abbot Thurstan and his Norman monks were notoriously cruel to the Saxon monks who had had charge of Glastonbury before their arrival, and at one point incited, or engineered, the slaughter of a number of the Saxons by Norman soldiers. A local earl, Eawulf of Edgarley, had led a reprisal attack against the Normans. In the battle he came up against Radulphus – whom he managed to wound severely with his axe – and then Radulphus slew him. He was buried in the Abbey grounds. When, decades later, the brothers were digging Radulphus's grave, they came upon Eawulf's bones. By chance he had been buried at the same spot that was chosen for Radulphus. The former enemies had been joined in death, their bones mingling in the same plain grave.

Bond spent months poring over old manuscripts to uncover some surviving documentary evidence of what the 'watchers' had told him through automatic writing. There was no known record of Eawulf, no scholar of the period had heard of him. But at the end of this odyssey through the crumbling chronicles of Saxon and Norman England, Bond had established that there had indeed been an earldom of Edgarley in Somerset in the 9th century at least; the obvious inference – at least it was Bond's – was that this was an ancestor of the Eawulf whose story had been told him by the dead monks of Glastonbury.

A DOOMED MAN

For more than ten years Bond kept secret the source of his seemingly – and, in fact – uncanny ability to unearth the most surprising new facts about the Glastonbury site. His discretion was not the result of any lack of faith in what he and Barrett had been told – the times his scepticism had been confounded were too many for that. The problem was the Church of England, which had always been hostile to spiritualism. Bond, already surrounded by jealous colleagues and suffering from a reputation for a dictatorial, even cranky, style of managing the Glastonbury project, would be bound to suffer if he described his experiments with automatic writing – no matter how fruitful they had proved.

In the end, the strain of remaining silent grew too great, and he decided, fatefully, to go public with the truth. In 1918 he published *The Gate of Remembrance*, which detailed the whole saga of his communications with the 'watchers' through automatic writing since 1908. As soon as it went on sale, Bond was a doomed man as far as his professional life was concerned.

The budget for the Glastonbury dig was slashed. Bond was saddled with an unsympathetic co-director, whose job was, plainly enough, to keep him in line. A monstrous Church bureaucracy suddenly took a singularly obstructive interest in his work at Glastonbury. Toward the end of his direct association with the Abbey he was demoted to cataloguing his finds for a miserly stipend of £10 a month. In 1922 he received a letter that, in the scrupulously polite but utterly chilling language of officialdom, summarily fired him from even that lowly position. His career, all too literally, was now in ruins. Even the most scholarly of his books were banned from sale within the Abbey precincts. Bond spent much of the rest of his life in the USA, pursuing psychical research rather than archaeology. He died alone, impoverished and embittered, in 1945.

Do Bond's and Barrett's ventures into automatic writing constitute reasonable proof of survival of death? That is certainly what they seem to offer, but one of the many ironies in the way the Establishment treated Bond lies in the sobering fact that he himself came to believe that they did not. Bond himself maintained that he and Barrett had gained access not to the words of the dead but to a storehouse of buried – perhaps racial – memory. This was something akin to psychologist Carl J. Jung's notion of the 'collective unconscious', but one specific to England and the English and their peculiar myths and traditions. The gateway of remembrance was his own intuition, released to run free through the discipline and concentration of preparing for his experiments in automatic writing. The power of intuition, he wrote, 'from the depths of the subconscious mind… has evoked these images'.

Such an argument is appealing, but its attraction may be somewhat specious. Because 'intuition' is familiar to us all, and because so many of Jung's ideas have acquired a kind of veneer of truth because they have been successful in treating people in psychotherapy, many people feel more comfortable with this form of words as they seem to describe the inexplicable rather than proof of survival of death. In a rigidly secular age, it may even be that most people do not wish to survive after the death of their physical bodies: perhaps their worst fears will come true. Perhaps, even, they fear that they could not cope with their deepest yearnings coming true, either. But to argue that 'intuition' is a better explanation than straightforward communication with the dead, for what Bond and Barrett discovered, is merely to substitute one unknown for another.

Sometimes things really are as simple as they seem. The evidence from the 'Glastonbury scripts' for life after death is probably as good as any we will ever have. That is until we die.

RULING PASSION

Frederick Bligh Bond, curiously enough, was instrumental in a case of apparent communication with the dead that, in contrast, throws up almost every question possible about the nature of psychic communications with the hereafter – ones that do not, however, seem relevant in his own involvement with the former tenants of Glastonbury Abbey.

In 1963, three years after the author's death at the age of 92, an intriguing book titled *A Tudor Story* by an Anglican clergyman, a canon of Peterborough Cathedral named William Packenham-Walsh, was published. It was in essence the record of one man's obsession with a woman who had died 332 years before he was born: in short, Packenham-Walsh's passion for Anne Boleyn, the second wife of King Henry VIII of England, born in 1507 and executed, after Henry had successfully pressed rather dubious charges of high treason, which included claims of adultery with her own brother, who was executed with her, on 15 May 1536.

Packenham-Walsh's interest in Anne Boleyn had first been aroused when, as a missionary in China, he read a biography of the dead queen in 1917. By the time he returned to England, the cause of Anne Boleyn – 'a queen who has been much misunderstood' – had become a ruling passion in his life. In August 1921 he instigated the first of many sittings with mediums that supposedly put him indirectly in touch with the dead queen – and with her husband, who was as temperamental in death, it seems, as he ever was in real life.

A modern Italian medium, Anita, at work. Although normally right-handed, she uses her left hand to receive messages.

This first session, with a medium called Mrs Clegg, did not involve automatic writing, but it did produce a wealth of information, unknown to the canon until his own researches confirmed it, about Anne Boleyn. For the disinterested observer it also raised the most fundamental questions about the nature of Mrs Clegg's mediumship. This is not to imply that she was in any way a fraud or a charlatan, but to question whether she herself understood the real nature of her gift (a problem we shall meet again in discussing other mediums and their alleged communications with the dead). There are two reasons for waving this flag of warning.

In the first place, during the sitting, Packenham-Walsh was unable to restrain himself from telling Mrs Clegg the reason for his visit: she soon learned who her visiting 'spirit' was supposed to be, so breaking a cardinal rule of objective psychical research. In the second place (at a later sitting), the purported Anne Boleyn made a curious prediction. The canon, she said, would be 'offered a parish with the snowdrops' and would 'go to it with the daffodils'. Not long after this Packenham-Walsh was offered the living of Sulgrave, Northamptonshire. When he first visited the parish it was covered with snowdrops. When he took up residence there, daffodils were everywhere. The vicarage gardener, according to Packenham-Walsh, said he had never seen anything like it in 40 years' service in his craft.

Even assuming that Packenham-Walsh's account is accurate and uncoloured by his deep desire to prove his particular point, and presuming a great deal of other things as well, there is no particular reason to infer from all this that Mrs Clegg actually was in contact with the shade of Anne Boleyn. She knew of Packenham-Walsh's interest and it seems much more likely that she was picking up information about the dead queen from Packenham-Walsh's own mind, and was dramatizing it as the word of the dead, than that she was in direct contact with Anne Boleyn herself. This is if anything borne out by the prediction that came true. Mrs Clegg was probably clairvoyant in a wide degree, but her understanding of her gifts had to be translated in terms of her spiritualist beliefs in survival after death. So, she was bound to present - just as Packenham-Walsh, for his own reasons, was bound to accept her precognition of the canon's future through the secondary medium of Anne Boleyn's allegedly discarnate soul.

SIMPLE DECEPTION

Frederick Bligh Bond became involved in Packenham-Walsh's psychical researches into Anne Boleyn because another medium, a Miss Eleanor Kelly, had received messages through automatic writing mentioning both himself and Bond. In due course, Bond introduced Packenham-Walsh, Miss Kelly had received messages through automatic writing concerning Anne Boleyn and Henry VIII, indicating their emotional states in the afterlife. Whether she knew of Packenham-Walsh's interest in Henry's second queen – in other words, whether she was guilty of drawing Packenham-Walsh to her through simple deception - Packenham-Walsh himself does not, of course, say. But the world of psychics is a small one, now as then. News, which cynics would call news of opportunities, travels fast.

On the other hand, if Miss Kelly's interest was genuine and disinterestedly concerned, and if these communications were equally genuine, it remains as likely that clairvoyance was responsible for the initial messages as for the later ones received in sittings with the canon. For nothing in the later messages revealed anything that Packenham-Walsh himself may not have concluded from his, by then, encyclopedic reading on the subject of the Tudor king and his tragically misused and betrayed second wife.

The basic matter of these sittings boiled down to the apparent fact that Henry was still locked in his ego – 'stuck', as modern psychobabble has it – and was busy either justifying his earthly actions or roundly abusing his 20th-century interlocutors. Anne Boleyn, not surprisingly, approved the canon's record of these proceedings as 'one of the ladders… by which many may climb to true knowledge'. By June 1924 - this time with two other and different mediums – King Henry was wanting it known that he had repented of his misdeeds. Few things can have been more musical to the ears of William Packenham-Walsh, but even by his own account few desires can have been less secret than his to rescue Anne Boleyn's reputation or to know that Henry had admitted how dreadfully he had used her.

Automatic writing, as such, then, is as ambiguous as any other means of communication in establishing the reality of life after death. But the experience of Frederick Bligh Bond remains to tantalize us with its implication that sometimes, somehow, we really can get in touch with those who have died – but who live on elsewhere.

GIFTS FROM THE OTHER SIDE

The investigator had checked for any sign of trickery and was convinced that the spiritualist was concealing nothing. Then, as he watched in astonishment, a fresh carnation materialized and began to fall from the medium's lips...

The late Anita Gregory was a distinguished scholar, a stalwart of the Society for Psychical Research in Britain, and by no means gullible when it came to paranormal matters – she spent considerable energy on showing how weak she believed the evidence was that anything truly strange had happened in the famous Enfield poltergeist case, for example. But at a seance held by medium Paul McElhoney in London in the early 1980s, Mrs Gregory was astonished and baffled when a small, metal model of Cologne cathedral landed in the palm of her hand 'from nowhere'.

McElhoney's spirit control, which called itself Ceros, explained through McElhoney that the model was a gift to Mrs Gregory from her dead father. At the time, this made little sense to her. Only later did she discover that her father and mother had spent their honeymoon in a hotel that looked out on to Cologne cathedral.

Paul McElhoney was a relatively rare phenomenon himself for the late 20th century: a spiritualist medium who produced physical phenomena. His peculiar talent was to produce objects, as Mrs Gregory so plainly put it, apparently 'from nowhere' – otherwise known as apports. His speciality was to bring forth flowers, often from his mouth; however he managed this feat, there was no doubt among the witnesses that they were all fresh. Unlike many other mediums, McElhoney would do this as often in good light as in the more traditional – and for sceptics, more suspicious – circumstances of a darkened seance room.

In November 1981, Michael Cleary reported in *Psychic News* how – through a relieving spiritualist — he had carefully searched both Paul McElhoney's person and his seance room for any sign of trickery before 'Ceros' had come through and entranced the medium.

Cleary noted: 'When Ceros brought the first flowers, the lights were on. I looked into Paul's mouth. There was nothing there then a flower began to fall from his mouth. Carnations are very significant in my Family. I had previously asked my mother in the spirit world to bring that kind of flower. When Ceros apported a carnation for me he said it was a present from a woman in the spirit world.'

SPIRIT GUIDES

It is a paradox of spiritualism that apports of material objects are regarded as proof of an immaterial life after death – immaterial, at least, as we understand the term. Mediums who produce such objects, and who create a wide variety of other physical effects during seances, are called, plainly and unsurprisingly enough, 'physical' mediums.

The hey day of the physical medium was the 19th century; spiritualism actually had its beginnings in the late 1840s in the most basic of physical-cum-spiritual phenomena – paranormal rappings that gave every sign of being intelligently controlled by someone, or something, who had survived death. Over the next two decades, mediums developed the ability to create an extraordinary repertoire of physical effects with the aid of spirits. (Mediums themselves would say, of course, that the spirits did this, and that they were indeed no more than the media through which these phenomena were produced.)

An outside observer would say that individual physical mediums tended to specialize in particular effects. A sceptic would say that that is because it is easier and better to perfect one kind of

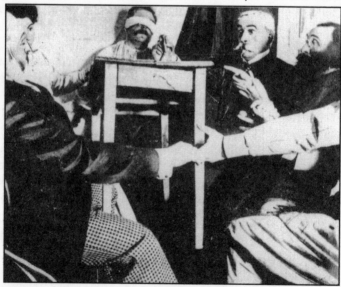

One of the most basic effects witnessed at seances in the 19th century and even today – the levitation of a table.

conjuring trick than to take on a number and suffer indifferent results. Mediums would reject both those ways of describing what happens, preferring to account for the difference between one and another medium's phenomena as the result of the predilections of their spirit guide, and as a matter outside their own personal control.

No medium claims to get directly in contact with a spirit on the 'other side'. It has become a convention, almost, among mediums, to have a 'guide' or 'control' – itself the spirit of a dead person but one seemingly more advanced than others – with whom they initially make contact, and who in turn mediates between the medium and the rest of the world of spirit. No one seems to have addressed the question of why this should be so (perhaps everyone has such a 'guardian angel' from the afterlife, but only mediums have the good fortune to be able to communicate with theirs). But mediums find that that is the way things are, and seem to have no difficulty in accepting it. Nor do they seem to balk at the remarkable number of American Indian medicine men or Zulus who seem to figure among spirit guides. That is the way things are. And if one wants to argue about the truth or falsehood of mediums, these are details; there are better and larger grounds for dealing with the truth of their claims.

'THE STUFF OF THE UNIVERSE'

Some mediums hear the voices of the dead; some communicate through automatic writing; some receive in the mind's eye photographic visions of pertinent material; and some produce physical phenomena which, they or the spirits believe, offer a concrete proof that spiritual life continues after physical death. The very fact that such phenomena are outside the bounds of normal physical possibility is deemed to be proof that only the spirits could have produced them.

Physical mediums have demonstrated an enormous range of such phenomena to prove their point. Among the effects that staid and reliable witnesses have reported are paranormal and apparently intelligently produced raps, as mentioned before; table tilting; disembodied voices speaking through 'trumpets' (essentially no more than paper or cardboard megaphones), or directly through the mediums themselves (a phemonenon closely related to modern 'channelling'); levitations of any number of objects from pieces of paper through pieces of furniture to the persons of those present at seances, witnesses as well as the mediums themselves; elongation of the medium's body; materializing detached and disembodied limbs; playing musical instruments that were well outside the reach of either medium or witnesses; and, most frequently of all in the 19th century, the production of that mysterious substance ectoplasm, which has been claimed to be the formative 'stuff of the Universe', the prototype of matter before it coalesces into recognizable physical form, from its original, allegedly spiritual state.

There have been reports too about individual mediums who have shown still more extraordinary capacities when under the influence of the spirits: they have been immune to the effects of fire, for example, or have produced materializations of their own spirit controls so real that those who saw them could not tell them apart from living flesh.

Here, we review a selection of the more interesting physical mediums from the great days of the seance room. If their manifestations were genuine then, according to them, so is the existence of an afterlife of some kind.

IMPERFECT HARMONY

Among mediums who produced apports, one of the most remarkable during the 19th century was undoubtedly Madame Elizabeth d'Esperance, actually a lady of English origin, whose more astonishing effects were produced through the spirit of a 15-year-old Arab girl named Yolande, who actually materialized as an entire physical form during Madame d'Esperance's seances.

At a seance held on 28 June 1890, this medium and the materialized Yolande produced a flower – not just any flower, or some sparkling cut hothouse bloom, but the seedling of a golden lily that in front of the astonished sitters grew before their eyes to a height of 7 ft, and in the process seven of the eleven flowers on the plant came into bloom and exuded a powerful scent. If this had been some species of vaudeville act, a professional conjuror would have made sure that the plant was either whisked away from prying eyes and sceptical inspection or equally 'magically' made to vanish. In this case, the spirit form of Yolande was disconcerted when she announced sadly that the giant lily could not remain in the material world, and then found that it refused to dematerialize.

Finally she told the sitters to keep the recalcitrant plant in a darkened room until they next met – a week later, on 5 July. The instructions were obeyed, and at the next seance the oversize lily was put squarely in the centre of the seance room at 9.23 p.m. Within seven minutes it had disappeared, but not before two of the flowers had been kept as mementoes of its brief existence and photographs had been taken of the massive plant in company with the medium.

Another reasonable proof, in the eyes of spiritualists, that the dead were able to communicate paranormally with the living was their apparent ability to play musical instruments without the

Ectoplasm pours from a medium's mouth. According to one unimpeachable source, its characteristic smell was of body odour.

assistance of any visible musician. Such phenomena were recorded from the earliest days of spiritualism. In the early 1850s, for instance, the Ohio farmer Jonathan Koons was, by his own account, instructed by the spirits to build a specially dedicated log cabin alongside his farmhouse in which to demonstrate his powers as the 'greatest medium on Earth', in company with his eight children.

The cabin was not the humble abode from which American country boys traditionally set out to crown their achievements with a spell in the White House. It was constructed like a miniature theatre, and had room for an audience of 30 people. Musical instruments were placed around the tiny auditorium. In this setting Koons and his children would take their places on a small stage. The lights would be put out, and Koons himself would take up his fiddle and play hymn tunes. Gradually, the spirits would take up the other instruments dotted about the room and join in – not, according to reports, always in perfect harmony. At the same time, a tambourine would be seen circling above the heads of the audience, trumpets floated into the air, and ghostly voices were heard speaking.

Koons did not make money from his bizarre presentations, and indeed actually encountered outright and aggressive hostility to his demonstrations from his neighbours. His motives seem to have been genuine and, in the light of the persecution he and his family received – the children were set upon, his fields and barns were attacked by arsonists, until in the end the Koonses left the district to become missionaries for spiritualism – it seems unreasonable to assume that the phenomena were not genuine too.

SPEAKING WITH MANY TONGUES

It's almost a commonplace today to see mediums 'channelling' the voices of the dead – reproducing the accents and idioms of the individuals coming through from the 'other side'. The seance rooms of 19th-century and early 20th-century Europe and America witnessed a similar phenomenon – but with a distinct and remarkable difference. For the 'direct voice' mediums who have emerged from time to time in the history of spiritualism have neither used their own voice-boxes to convey the words of the communicating spirits, nor have they been limited to being the channel for a single voice at a time. The voices, sometimes several at once, have come straight out of thin air to deliver their messages to the living.

New York medium George Valiantine demonstrated just such powers in 1924 in England. In seances held virtually every day over a period of five weeks, Valiantine was the medium for over 100 different voices. Numbers of them spoke simultaneously – and not only in English. The Welsh novelist Caradoc Evans held fluent, idiomatic conversations with his dead father in his native language (not an easy tongue to learn, with its difficult inflexions and unique system of mutations, and hardly one a New Yorker could mug up at short notice), while other spirits spoke with equal facility in German, Spanish and Russian.

The clinching demonstration of Valiantine's mediumship came in the late 1920s in New York. At a number of seances some voices that were frankly meaningless to the sitters had come through. On the off chance that he might be able to identify the language, the orientalist scholar Dr Neville Whymant, though sceptical of claims for the paranormal, agreed to attend a seance. He pricked up his ears and became strangely interested, however, when he heard a voice speak the name K'ung-fu-T'Zu – Confucius - in an impeccable Chinese intonation and accent.

Whymant responded by quoting a passage from the works of the ancient sage. This was more than a matter of finding out whether the shade of the long-dead philosopher would recognize his own work. Whymant was reasonably sure that the passage, though it made good sense, had been altered as it had been copied by generations of scribes. He had got no further than the first line when 'the words were taken out of my mouth, and the whole passage was recited in Chinese, exactly as it is recorded in the standard works of reference. After a pause of about 15 seconds the passage was... repeated, this time with certain alterations [that] gave it new meaning. "Thus read," said the voice, "does not its meaning become plain?"'

Whymant could hardly fail to be impressed. He reckoned there were perhaps half a dozen scholars in the West besides himself who knew enough Chinese – and were sufficiently familiar with the writings of Confucius – to have picked up his quotation with such ease, let alone subtly shifted the reading to give it a different sense. None of these learned men was in the USA at the time of the seance – and there was no question that any of them would have lent themselves to cheap trickery in the seance room.

A CURIOUS CHEAT

One of the more consistent exponents of physical mediumship in the 19th and early part of the 20th century was Eusapia Palladino. Born to peasant parents near Bari, Italy, in January 1854, Palladino made a name for herself as the focus of the most extraordinary physical manifestations during seances held in Naples. In 1891 the first of a series of tests and controlled observations, held all over Europe, were made of her powers by Cesare Lombroso, professor of psychiatry at the University of Turin.

Lombroso had had nothing but contempt for mediums, but came away from his encounters with Palladino remarking that he was ashamed to have disbelieved reports of what happened in spiritualist seances, adding, 'I am still opposed to the theory. But the facts exist, and I boast of being a slave to facts.'

The facts were indeed astonishing. Unlike the vast majority of mediums at the time, Palladino did not insist on working under cover of darkness, and did not hide herself away in a 'cabinet' (a small chamber, rather like an enclosed pew, with a curtain across the front) as so many mediums did – often in order to hide the mechanics of their hoaxes. Palladino always allowed those present to tie her hands and feet if they wished, or take other precautions against her cheating. Another Italian scientist, Dr Ercole Chiaia, reported what he saw at her seances: 'Either bound to a seat, or firmly held by the hands... she attracts to her the articles of furniture which surround her, lifts them up, holds them suspended in the air... and makes them come down again, with undulatory movements, as if they were obeying her will. She increases their height or lessens it according to her pleasure. She raps or taps upon the walls, the ceiling, and the floor, with fine rhythm and cadence...

'This woman rises in the air, no matter what bands tie her down. She seems to lie upon the empty air, as on a couch, contrary to all the laws of gravity; she plays on musical instruments – organs, bells, tambourines – as if they had been touched by her hands or moved by the breath of invisible gnomes...'

The French astronomer Camille Flammarion reported that in one of her seances Palladino became irritable for some reason. As a result:

'The sofa came forward when she looked at it, then recoiled before her breath; all the instruments were thrown pell-mell upon the table; the tambourine rose almost to the height of the ceiling; the cushions took part in the sport, overturning everything on the table; [one of those present] was thrown from his chair. This item – a heavy dining-room chair of black walnut, with a stuffed seat – rose into the air, came up on the table with a great clatter, then pushed off.'

One of Palladino's most bizarre talents was to extrude, or somehow materialize, human limbs around her. On occasion she could produce entire human forms. In March 1902, one of the many scientists who investigated Palladino, Professor E. Morselli, had tied her carefully and thoroughly to a camp bed before a seance in which no less than six materialized forms appeared and disappeared. As each one vanished, Morselli checked the medium: he was still tied firmly to the bed.

One reason why Palladino was happy to be constrained in this somewhat undignified way was that she was, she freely admitted, incapable of controlling her actions when in trance. She claimed that in the presence of sceptics she would even react to their unconscious or conscious suggestions – and cheat. She was in fact caught cheating on at least two occasions: once during a visit to Cambridge, England, in 1895, and again in New York in 1910. This last occurrence ended her international career as a medium. But it is a curious kind of hoaxer who admits to her own propensity for fraud, and is caught only when a researcher deliberately lets go his guard to see what will happen – as was the case during the Cambridge series of tests administered by the Australian lawyer Richard Hodgson.

ENORMOUS REPERTOIRE

The greatest of the Victorian physical mediums was without doubt Daniel Dunglas Home, who impressed a huge range of witnesses from all walks of life from emperors to elevator attendants, who never took money for his seances, and who was never caught in any deception or hoax.

Home believed himself to be the illegitimate son of a member of the Douglas-Home family — better known as the Earls of Home — and he pronounced his name as they do, to rhyme with 'spume'. He was born in Scotland in 1833, but was brought up by an aunt in Connecticut, in the USA. In 1855 he was told by doctors that his consumptive lung condition would worsen if he remained in America, and in the spring of that year he left for England.

Home had very little money, but he did have a wealth of psychic talent. He began giving seances when he was 17, after a classic spasm of poltergeist raps and hangings in his aunt's home had left him with powers of clairvoyance and healing. Within a very few years Home was to develop an enormous repertoire of bizarre and astonishing physical effects in the seance room.

In August 1852, Home levitated for the first time, at a sitting in the house of a Connecticut silk manufacturer, Ward Cheney. The editor of the *Hartford Times*, Frank L. Burr, described what happened:

'Suddenly, without any expectation on the part of the company, Home was taken up into the air. I had hold of his hand at the time and I felt his feet – they were lifted a foot from the floor… Again and again he was taken from the floor, and the third time he was carried to the ceiling of the apartment, with which his hands and feet came into gentle contact.'

Then, Home began to materialize disembodied hands. Burr told how one – 'very thin, very pale, and remarkably attenuated' – first took up a pencil and wrote. 'The hand afterwards came and shook hands with each one present. I felt it minutely,' he wrote. 'It was tolerably well and symmetrically made, though not perfect; and it was soft and slightly warm. IT ENDED AT THE WRIST.' Another chronicler of Home's feats described how one of these weird limbs picked up a handbell, rang it, and brought it to him. He tried to grab the hand: 'I had no sooner grasped it momentarily than it melted away, leaving my hand void, with only the bell in it.'

Home gave many demonstrations of such phenomena in London but, lacking an income, had to depend on the hospitality of his friends until 1858, when he married his first wife Alexandrina, one of the Czar of Russia's god-daughters. With this, material insecurity vanished, and his social standing instantly changed. Home was lionized by the most brilliant and fashionable, as well as

Daniel Dunglas Home levitates himself above the heads of his astonished onlookers.

many of the weightiest intellectual members, of London society. The witnesses to his extraordinary powers thus included some of the least impressionable men and women of his day.

BIZARRE ABILITY

Home's seances were often held in good light, and he never hid inside a cabinet. He produced all the usual phenomena of the seance room: tables tilted or levitated (one, an occasional table with a single leg and claw feet, even managed to 'walk' up onto another table, 'exactly like a child trying to climb up a height'); an accordion that played by itself even when others held it in bemusement, watching the keys worked by invisible fingers; pens that wrote without visible assistance; materializations of human faces as well as his famous disembodied hands; raps and bangs; currents of air; and apports – among many others.

The Russian novelist and poet Count Alexey Tolstoy reported on the plethora of phenomena at a typical Home sitting, in a letter to his wife written in 1859. Besides the ringing bells, the levitations of furniture, the mysterious floating (and dissolving) hands, Tolstoy told how: 'The piano played with no one near it; a bracelet unclasped itself from the arm of Mrs Milner-Gibson, and fell on the table, where it lay surrounded by a luminous appearance. Home was raised from the ground… a cold wind passed round the circle very distinctly, and perfumes were wafted to us.'

But perhaps most striking of all his phenomena was not what Home did with other things, but what he did with his own body.

The levitations of Home, rising above the sitters – 'as if', as he put it himself, 'I were grasping the unseen power which slowly raises me from the floor' – were part of the standard Victorian medium's fare. One of Home's truly original effects was his quite bizarre ability both to elongate himself and to shrink. He normally stood about 5 ft 7 in tall. At one seance at the home of the art magazine editors Mr and Mrs S.C. Hall, a journalist – a hardbitten species of witness – reported that:

'Mr Home was seen by all of us to increase in height to the extent of some eight or ten inches, and then sank to some six or eight inches below his normal stature. Having returned to his usual height, he took Lord Adare and the Master of Lindsay, and placing one beside each post of the folding door, lay down on the floor, touching the feet of one with his head and the feet of the other with his feet. He was then again elongated, and pushed both Lord Adare and the Master of Lindsay backward along the floor with his head and feet as he was stretched out...'

Hall, measuring the distance between the two startled noblemen, found that a space of more than 7 ft now separated them.

A GREAT WIND RUSHING

Still more extraordinary was Home's relationship with fire. On one particularly memorable occasion he created a kind of parody of the Pentecost. Tongues of flame darted from his head and he spoke in some unknown foreign language while, according to Lord Adare, 'we all distinctly heard... a bird flying round the room, whistling and chirping. There then came the sound of a great wind rushing through the room...'

This was not all. Numerous witnesses testified how Home was able to handle live coals for minutes at a time without feeling any pain. The supremely eminent physicist William Crookes reported one instance:

'Home removed from the grate a red-hot piece [of coal] nearly as big as an orange, and putting it on his right hand, covered it with his left... and blew... until the lump of charcoal was nearly white hot, and then drew my attention to the lambent flame which was flickering over the coal and licking round his fingers.'

Was any of this proof of life after death? Home certainly believed so. He had been a committed spiritualist since 1850, when he saw a vision of his mother dying in Scotland; the mail brought confirmation later that this happened on the day of her death. She continued to appear to Home throughout his life, giving him useful and moral advice. But he believed that his psychic powers were the work of several spirits – the chief among them was called 'Bryan' – over whom he had no control. His work was spirit work. And no one ever caught him cheating.

CONVERSATIONS
WITH THE DEAD

Lord Archibald turned down an invitation to visit his tenant farmer that fateful evening. The blood-curdling events of the night were to make him regret that decision…

One snowy winter's afternoon some time before 1885, Lord Archibald Zealand had been out with his wife, visiting their acquaintances. As their carriage rolled up the drive to Zealand Manor, Lord Archibald saw one of the tenant farmers on his estate coming away from the front door, having found his landlord not at home. Lord Archibald stopped to talk to the farmer for a while and, before he went, the farmer invited him to drop in at his farmhouse later that evening. Lord Archibald had a busy evening ahead of him, and turned the offer down.

Later that night, at about 10 p.m. Lord Archibald was in his breakfast room, working. He described what happened next to the editors of *Phantasms of the Living*, published by the Society for Psychical Research in London in 1886:

'I distinctly heard the front gate opened and shut again with a clap, and footsteps advancing at a run up the drive. When opposite the window, the steps changed from sharp and distinct on gravel to dull and less clear on the grass slip below the window, and at the same time I was conscious that someone or something stood close to me outside, only the thin shutter and a sheet of glass dividing us.

'I could hear the quick panting and laboured breathing of the messenger, or whatever it was, as if trying to recover breath before speaking. Had he been attracted by the light through the shutter?

'Suddenly, like a gunshot, inside, outside, and all around, there broke out the most appalling shriek – a prolonged wail... Of my [own] fright and horror I can say nothing – [but they] increased tenfold when I walked into the dining room and found my wife sitting quietly at her work close to the window, and in the same line and distant only ten or twelve feet from the corresponding window in the breakfast room. She had heard nothing.'

Too unnerved by this experience to go outside immediately to look for whatever had made this blood-curdling sound, Lord Archibald waited till morning. No fresh snow fell in the night, but there were no signs of any footprints on the ground outside. Later that day, news came to the house that the tenant farmer Lord Archibald had spoken to the afternoon before had killed himself – apparently as the result of an unhappy love affair. He had ended his life by drinking prussic acid – and Lord Archibald's groom, who lived near the farm, had heard the man scream as he took the fatal dose and died.

The groom heard the dying man's cry at about 10 p.m. – 'as near as I can ascertain,' said Lord Archibald, 'at the exact time when I had been so alarmed at my own home'. The farm and the manor, however, were too distant from each other for him to have been able to hear the actual scream of the suicide. Lord Archibald's wife, after all, had heard nothing.

Surrounded by his family and a guard of honour, John F. Kennedy goes to his last long home.

THE BANSHEE

Occurrences like this are known as cases of clairaudience – involving information that is passed on psychically through sound rather than through visual information. There are many cases of spontaneous, one-off clairaudience that, like the one above, occur only at moments of crisis and most often involve someone's death, but some people persistently and repeatedly hear information that they can only be receiving paranormally. And a few people claim to be able to hear the voices of the dead, speaking to them from the other side.

Among a number of old Irish families there is a tradition of clairaudience that is highly specialized, and not always welcome. This is otherwise known as the visitation of the banshee, which lets out a chilling howl as it announces the imminent death of a family member – though some say it comes to collect the departing soul.

The banshee is not only particular as to whose death it foretells; it is usually heard only by members of the family concerned. Irish tradition says that the banshee may also be seen – either in the form of an old hag or in the shape of a beautiful young woman – but reliable accounts of actually seeing the banshee are so rare as to be nonexistent. The term itself comes from the Irish *bean sidhe* - 'woman of the fairies' – but the notion that the banshee is female seems to have arisen from the sound of its voice.

That, by all accounts, is unmistakably feminine, though the sound of its cries ranges from the most wistful, gentle and seductive entreaties to the most spine-chilling and vengeful shrieks. The difference in the nature of these sounds apparently depends on the attitude of the banshee toward the dying individual and his family. That in turn depends on whose spirit the banshee represents, and how the family treated them in earthly life, for it is reckoned always to be the spirit of a long-dead member of the family concerned.

DEMENTED WOMAN

Tales of the banshee's howl are not confined to the misty Irish past. The banshee howled in the late 20th century as loud and clear as it ever did – and its eerie voice is by no means confined to Ireland. One Irish-American businessman from Boston, Massachusetts, who preferred to hide behind the pseudonym 'James O'Barry', told journalist Frank Smyth of three occasions on which he had heard the unearthly voice. The first time, when he was but a small boy, he was unaware even of the existence of anything called the banshee.

'I was lying in bed one morning when I heard a weird noise, like a demented woman crying,' said O'Barry. 'It was spring... I thought for a moment that a wind had sprung up, but a glance at the barely stirring trees told me that this was not so. I went down to breakfast and there was my father sitting at the kitchen table with tears in his eyes. I had never seen him weep before. My mother told me that they had just heard, by telephone, that my grandfather had died in New York. Although he was an old man he was as fit as a fiddle, and his death was unexpected.'

In 1946, O'Barry heard the banshee the second time, when his father died; he himself was in the Far East, serving with the US Army Air Force. He was woken up at 6 a.m. by 'a low howl': 'The noise got louder, rising and falling like an air raid siren.' On the third occasion, O'Barry was alone in Toronto, Canada, on a combined business trip and vacation. His account:

'I was in bed, reading the morning papers, when the dreadful noise was suddenly filling my ears. I thought of my wife, my young son, my two brothers and I thought: "Good God, don't let it be one of them." But for some reason I knew it wasn't.'

Indeed it was not. The time was just before noon, on 22 November 1963: the time that US President John F. Kennedy was assassinated in Houston, Texas. The president was a close friend of O'Barry's – and he was of Irish descent.

UNEARTHLY VOICES

As with other paranormal phenomena, there is nothing new about clairaudience. The ancient Greek philosopher Socrates was familiar with the promptings of what he called his 'daemon'. They were, he told his judges at his trial, 'constantly in the habit of opposing me even about trifles, if I were going to make some slip or error'. He had decided to stand trial for his life (albeit on somewhat frail charges) because his voices had not positively advised him to flee from Athens and, as he remarked to the court, he took this as a sign that 'those of us who think death is an evil are in error'.

Socrates, thus, seemed to think that his voices came from somewhere beyond this earthly life. In the Christian era Socrates would probably have been made a saint, and as such would have been in the company of two fascinating Christian women who, too, heard voices from unearthly realms.

One was Catherine of Siena (the Italian city where she was born in 1347). Catherine not only believed, like other mystics of her time, that among the voices she heard one came directly from God; she seems to have been actually clairvoyant, with the voices giving her information about ordinary human affairs. Some time after she had converted an aristocrat, Francesco Malevolti, to Christianity – and so taken him from a life of singular debauchery – the young man slid back into his former depraved existence. Catherine told him bluntly that she knew from her voices everything he did, and then recited to him a catalogue of his latest doings, sayings and sins. 'When I heard her tell me precisely all that I had done and said,' commented Malevolti, 'confused and shamed, and without an answer, at once and heedfully I fulfilled her command.'

DIVINELY INSPIRED

Possibly the most outstanding clairaudient in history was St Joan of Arc. Born in 1412 into a peasant family and illiterate all her life, Jean la Pucelle, 'the Maid of Orleans', first heard voices when she was only 13 years old. They told her that she could save her country from its enemies – France was then at war with England and the Duchy of Burgundy. Four years later, by sheer force of character, she persuaded the Dauphin (crown prince) of France to let her join the French army that was attempting to relieve the siege of Orleans by the English. She effectively took command of the army, and 10 days later the English were defeated.

Other victories followed, and Joan persuaded the Dauphin to be crowned as Charles VII of France. He, however, did not follow up the moral and military advantage Joan had created, and when she attempted to break another siege more or less alone, she was captured by the Burgundians, who sold her to the English. They tried her for witchcraft, and – conviction being a foregone conclusion – she was burned at the stake in Rouen in 1431, still not yet 20 years old.

Such a career would be astonishing enough, but it is all the more extraordinary that it was based on psychic ability. Joan's voices did not limit themselves to inspiring her to battle or to mystical utterances: they provided specific information. They directed her to the one man likely to introduce her to the Dauphin, for instance, and she impressed him less by her patriotic and religious fervour than by her ability to tell him, in a courtier's words, 'matters so secret and hidden that no mortal except himself could know them save by divine revelation'. These 'matters' had been revealed to her by her voices.

There are many other instances of the efficacy of Joan's voices, from her – or their – accurate prediction (recorded a fortnight before the event actually occurred) to the Dauphin that she would

The ancient Greek philosopher Socrates, whose profound, still-relevant thought was prompted not by deep meditation, but by inner voices entirely outside of his control.

be wounded by an arrow at the siege of Orleans, to the information that there was a sword behind the altar in the church of St Catherine at Fierbois. She wrote to the clergy in Fierbois, telling them to look there; and they found a rusty sword.

Joan of Arc made no secret of her clairaudience, and it was this that condemned her in the eyes of the English court that tried her for witchcraft. As a later commentator put it, she died because of her 'resolute insistence on the truth of the very phenomena which were being used to destroy her'. Joan, naturally enough for anyone of her time, believed her voices were divinely inspired. To 21st-century eyes, she was a psychic, but there seems no doubt of her integrity or truthfulness concerning those voices and what they had to say, and little doubt either that they spoke with uncanny accuracy.

PHANTOM STEPS

Clairaudience, as these historical examples have shown, does not limit itself to precognition, telepathy – or to communication with the dead. Clairaudience is really the auditory awareness of all kinds of extra sensory perception, and only a portion of recorded instances of the phenomenon can be said to offer any evidence at all of life after death.

Socrates seems to have taken his voices as implying that life continued in some form after death, although he did not assume that they came from the realm of the dead itself. St Catherine of Siena and Joan of Arc certainly attributed their voices to spirits, but they were very particular spirits indeed – the Archangel Michael, for instance, was among them. And it was perhaps inevitable that these two women, of such profound and visionary Christian belief, should have identified their clairaudience with the hosts of God. To the medieval Christian there was only one alternative – they were the work of the Devil.

The most commonly reported clairaudient communications with the dead have actually occurred at the point of death.

Karl von Linne (1707–78), the Swedish botanist who established the modern system of classifying living things by Latin names, was not so coldly scientific that he was immune to such events. His house in Uppsala contained a botanical museum, and one night in 1776 he and his wife were woken by loud footsteps pacing about the gallery. No one should have been there at all, since von Linne had locked the doors and, in fact, had the key with him. Then he recognized the footsteps as those of his closest friend, Karl Clerk, but he found neither Clerk nor anyone else in his museum. A few days later, he learned that his friend had died 'at precisely the same hour' as he had heard the phantom steps in his house.

A still surer indication that clairaudience acts as a channel between the living and the dead was recorded by Camille Flammarion in his 1922 book *Death and Its Mystery*.

In response to an appeal for such experiences, Flammarion had been told the story of a French girl named Clementine, who had suffered such a terrible life in the company of her alcoholic father that she decided to escape by entering a nunnery. Clementine's aunt gave her shelter when she first fled her father's house, but the older woman had a presentiment that Clementine did not have long to live. And she told the girl so.

Clementine seems to have had the same intuition, but made light of it. She knew she didn't have long to live, she said, but she would make sure her aunt knew when she died. 'I'll make an outrageous racket for you,' she promised.

Clementine in due course entered a convent, safe at last from the predations of her father. Some time after this, the aunt's entire household was disturbed one night around its usual bedtime by an 'outrageous racket' indeed. There were sounds from the roof as if it were caving in, and the very housebricks seemed to be slamming against one another. At the same time, there was no movement to be seen and no actual damage to the fabric of the house. Clementine's aunt guessed in a flash what had happened.

'Clementine is dead,' she said in a firm voice. At once, the uproar stopped as abruptly as it had begun. The next day, a telegram arrived at the house from the convent, breaking the news of Clementine's death – which had occurred at exactly the time that the clearly paranormal 'racket' had broken out.

UNCANNY VISIONS

By far the most renowned clairaudient of modern times was Doris Fisher Stokes, who for millions of people all over the world came to personify mediumship and contact with the next life. She was a natural star of television chat-shows and stage 'demonstrations' precisely because she was so natural – down to earth, unpretentious, unburdened by any New Age claptrap or desire to surround her talent with occult significance. Talking to the dead through Doris Stokes was an extraordinary experience just because she made it seem so everyday – and at the same time, she seemed hardly able to believe her own success.

In her early life she certainly had no reason to expect it. Doris Fisher Stokes was born the daughter of a blacksmith and a washerwoman, Tom and Jen Sutton, just after the end of World War One, in Grantham, Lincolnshire.

In World War Two Doris Stokes joined the Women's Royal Air Force and worked in operations rooms plotting the progress of Allied bombing raids on Europe. She found she had an uncanny and disconcerting foreknowledge of which aircraft would not return from their missions. It was only in 1944, after her husband John, a sergeant in the elite Parachute Regiment, failed to return (along with so many others) from the disastrous airborne assault on Arnhem in Holland, that Doris Stokes began to take either her own paranormal talent or evidence of survival after death very seriously.

Camille Flammarion, French astronomer and sometime president of the British Society for Psychical Research, among whose voluminous writings on psychic matters was an especially poignant case of clairaudience.

At that time she had a vision of her father, who had died when Doris was only 13 years old. He told her two things: that John was alive, though a prisoner of war, and that their new-born son would shortly die. Both proved true. After that, she began attending her local spiritualist church. Her sensitivity developed, and she was soon practising as a medium herself.

TALKING TO THE DEAD

Doris Stokes said that she had two means of knowing when a soul from 'the other side' wanted to communicate. Either her spirit control – an entity claiming to be a deceased Tibetan Lama called 'Ramonov' (which is not the form of any known Tibetan name) would tell her 'in her ear', or she would see a small blue light appear over the head of a sitter, which indicated that someone close to them was trying to 'come through'.

Doris Stokes captivated huge audiences and many individual sitters too. She did so because time and again she produced information from the 'other side' that could have been known only to the individual she was talking to on 'our side' and to her unseen communicators. Yet some odd doubts remain about whether she was in fact able to converse in the easy way she had with the dead.

Doris Stokes has been accused of fraud since her death. She admitted to cheating once or twice during her lifetime. But to offer some perspective on her mediumship, one has to give personal testimony.

The author of this book saw Doris Stokes in action three times: once at a private sitting in 1981, once at a press conference to launch one of her several books in 1982, and once (while on a flying visit to London) at a stage 'demonstration' in front of a packed house at the London Palladium late in 1985. The first two were highly impressive. The third was not, for reasons that will become clear.

The first occasion was as much a social one (in which I hoped to get some measure of Doris Stokes) as a formal 'sitting' as such. I was not the sitter (an old business colleague was) but over dinner before the sitting began, Doris Stokes made a number of casual observations about my life that were entirely accurate, although she had never met me before and as far as I know heard my name for the first time that evening. Two remarks in particular stand out: 'You've been a soldier, haven't you, love,' she said, 'and you don't know whether to be proud of what you've done or not, do you? But you don't talk about it.' All three of these statements were (and are) true.

Her second memorable remark concerned a ring I was wearing: 'That doesn't belong on that finger! You've moved that, haven't you, love?' The ring was on the little finger of my left hand. It was, in fact, my wedding ring. When my wife and I broke up, I moved it from the ring finger of my left hand to the pinkie, for a mass of tangled emotional reasons.

MIND READER?

The sitting itself was extraordinary for the wealth of detail that Doris Stokes produced about my colleague, some of which plainly embarrassed him because of my presence. But she told him nothing that he did not know already – nothing that he did not, then cr later, confirm from his own knowledge. This is interesting because at about the same time the staff of the weekly magazine *The Unexplained* reported that they had invited Doris Stokes to a sitting that - reading between the lines – followed a curiously similar pattern. Settling on a young lady member of the staff whose grandmother had recently died, Doris Stokes found herself in communication with the old lady herself, but almost everything she had to communicate was already known to the girl.

No explicit conclusion was drawn from this significant fact in the magazine's report of the encounter, but in an assessment of the occasion written some years later, the editor of the magazine had this to say:

'When asked… whether she had considered the possibility that she was, in fact, reading the (unconscious) minds of her sitters, Doris Stokes replied that she would refuse to carry on her work if she felt she had been doing any such thing. "That would be an invasion of privacy," she said. "I don't think God would allow that." Nonetheless, the possibility remains that Doris Stokes is… highly telepathic, picking up memories from the mind of someone who knew the dead person [that is, of course, the sitter him- or herself). These memories are then dramatized by Mrs Stokes's own subconscious, and come to her in the form of voices…

'Presumably the reasons for this are two fold. In the first place, Doris Stokes has [a] very strong resistance to the notion that she is invading other people's most private space – the mind. And [in the second place]... she has been utterly convinced that we do survive death. She cannot prevent her talent manifesting itself, and so has rationalized it in a way that has brought her, and thousands of people who have sat with her, great comfort.'

SERIOUS QUESTION MARKS

This seems a very fair and logical deduction: Doris Stokes was not – as she undoubtedly, most sincerely, believed – in touch with the dead, but she was in touch with the minds of her sitters. But she was also, it seems, guilty of a quite different kind of touch – simple, basic fraud.

In *The After Death Experience*, published in 1987, author Ian Wilson described how he found out that Doris Stokes packed her public appearances with people (whom she placed in reserved seats at the front of the auditorium) whose personal details were, he and other researchers discovered, no secret to her. And the most impressive 'readings' at those appearances were, of course, for the people she had specially invited and with whose particular, intimate details she was already familiar.

Having attended such a demonstration – which followed exactly the pattern Wilson describes in his book – I can only agree with his conclusion: that at this stage in her career Doris Stokes was 'not all she seemed, and the most serious question marks hang over her'. In the same paragraph, Wilson generously suggests that Doris Stokes might 'really have been a genuine medium... rigging her shows through sheer fear of facing a huge audience' lest no 'otherworldly messages' came through. That is possible, but Wilson seems not to have taken one further factor into account.

When he saw Doris Stokes at the London Palladium – and discovered how she seemed so accurate in her readings – on 16 November 1986, Doris Stokes was dying of cancer, and she knew it. She actually 'passed over', as she would have put it, less than six months later, on 8 May 1987. The evidence that she rigged her

Doris Stokes takes a rest between sessions at a public demonstration in 1984. In the last few years before her death in May 1987 suspicions grew that her shows were not all that they seemed.

last big public demonstrations is difficult to refute, but by then Doris Stokes had become part of show business – whose brave and tragic motto is 'The show must go on'. My own experience of Doris in less clouded and painful days suggests that she did have a genuine talent, and my experience of her later suggests that her last illness at least (there may have been other reasons) combined with a sad and mistaken sense of loyalty to her audience to override her own honesty and integrity.

The real question for students of the paranormal is whether, at the height of her power, Doris Stokes communicated with the dead, or simply made contact with the minds of her sitters. We know her own answer to that question. We do not know the real answer.

LIVING ART FROM A DEAD HAND

The teenager took up psychic art in the hope of ridding his family home of the destructive poltergeist, but as his pen and paintbrush re-created the masterpieces of the great artists, he found the demands made on him both baffling and exhausting.

There are two kinds of 'psychic artist'. There are those whose paintings, drawings, writings or musical compositions are guided by long-dead artists. And there is a handful of visual artists who draw or paint portraits of those they see 'in spirit'. What kind of evidence does the work of these two quite different groups of artists offer for life after death?

To some extent the answer to the question depends on the art involved. In the early 1970s, the British healer Matthew Manning – then still a teenager – began what became a huge collection of paintings, drawings and sketches that were created 'through' him by artists as diverse as Leonardo da Vinci, Claude Monet, Aubrey Beardsley, Beatrix Potter, Paul Klee and Pablo Picasso. Manning did not go into trance to produce the pictures; he simply concentrated on the artist while sitting in front of a sketching block with pen, pencil or paintbrush at the ready.

In his book *The Link*, Manning admitted to being baffled by what was happening when he painted or drew these pictures. He commented: 'How do I ask Albrecht Dürer to draw through me… ?… The fact that the person I wish to communicate with does not speak English is apparently no barrier.'

Strangely, what did prove a problem for many of these long-gone artists was how to use colour (Picasso was a notable exception). But this difficulty, paradoxically enough, may be a sign that the communication between Manning and the artists was genuine.

One is reminded of the frustration expressed by psychical researcher Frederic W.H. Myers (through a medium's automatic writing) five years after his death in 1901: 'I appear to be standing behind a sheet of frosted glass – which blurs sight and deadens sounds – dictating feebly to a reluctant and somewhat obtuse secretary.' At least the problem shows that Manning, if not in trance, was not in his normal state of consciousness. A reasonably talented painter in his own right, he had won prizes for art while at school, and should not have had any difficulty in using colour if he had been in full conscious control of his materials.

PSYCHIC COLLABORATION

Some of the pictures produced like this were very close to those created by the artists in their lifetimes. Manning – or the Renaissance artist himself – made a remarkably accurate reproduction of a sketch of a hanged man by Leonardo. Another such 'copy' was of Beardsley's famous drawing of Salome. In themselves, of course, these pictures prove nothing at all about survival. Manning speculated on this point: 'The only explanation I have is that the artist appears to be making a point of identifying himself beyond a shadow of doubt by reproducing something with which he is already known to be associated.'

Beardsley, however, was apparently also prone to make mistakes and to change his mind – as any living artist might – when working through Manning. 'More than any other… Beardsley made many mistakes while drawing,' said Manning, 'but instead of covering them over with paper, which obviously he could not do, he

Matthew Manning claimed to have had a special connection with Pablo Picasso.

inked over them and changed them into something different.'

These works were often finished very fast – most in an hour or two, and without any preliminary sketching – far quicker and more spontaneously than a working artist would expect to complete a picture. This did not make the process easy, however. Picasso was a particularly demanding taskmaster: 'No other communicator tires me out as much as Picasso does,' wrote Manning. 'After only a few minutes, the time it takes him to do one drawing, I feel worn out and cannot continue for at least 24 hours.'

The Manning collection of psychic art seems authentic enough: but was it really produced by artists in the afterlife, using Manning as a medium? In *The Link* Manning states clearly of his psychic collaboration with Picasso: 'The first work from him came in July 1973, three months after he died. I specifically asked Picasso to produce a drawing for me.' But an equally valid interpretation is that Manning was unconsciously trying out – or trying on – a number of identities through his artistic efforts. He took up 'psychic art' and automatic writing, after all, in the hope of channelling his own inner conflict into less destructive paths than the particularly unruly poltergeist that had plagued him and his family for some years.

Manning in fact later distanced himself as far as he could from the idea that he was in touch with the spirits of the dead. In the early 1980s, he said, 'I have never [sic] claimed my drawings to have been communications from the spirits of deceased artists… I feel that I was merely attuning myself to the continuing inspirational force created in the first place by the artist. That is why many of my drawings are only copies, sometimes not very good, of drawings already made by the artist.'

PROLIFIC OUTPUT

Such a statement, complete with its economy with the truth, amounts to recantation. Such qualms have never had to cross the mind of London medium Coral Polge, but she does not even pretend to be continuing the work of famous dead artists. Her speciality is drawing portraits of quite ordinary people who have died – and she draws them not from photographs, nor from any other kind of image, but from feeling their presence 'in spirit'.

'I know exactly what to draw,' she has said, 'without thinking about it. It's involuntary, like breathing or walking.'

Coral Polge did actually train as an artist, although ironically she was 'hopeless' at portraits as a student in the 1940s; in any case her real interest then was in textile designs. But she was interested in spiritualism, and became a medium herself in due course. When another medium suggested she had a future as a psychic artist, she responded first by producing portraits of the spirit guides – those in the afterlife who, according to spiritualists, act as individual 'guardian angels' for every one of us – of her sitters.

But many people (including Coral Polge) found these unsatisfactory, since they so frequently could not be identified easily from the historical records. They were often Red Indians, nuns, monks, Chinese sages or even Zulus, often from distant epochs. They were not the easiest people to track down in their earthly existences. Gradually she moved on to drawing portraits of the dead relatives, friends and loved ones of her sitters.

She cannot produce portraits of the dead on demand, however. 'It creates barriers when people come expecting or wanting me to draw someone in particular,' she has said. 'I draw whoever comes through.'

Spiritualists often claim that each of us has an individual guardian angel.

In doing that - without any visual stimulus at all – she has been both prolific and extraordinarily accurate. It has been estimated that between 1950 and 1970 she drew nearly 1,800 portraits a year. Three out of the thousands of sittings that Coral Polge has taken over the years will show how precise her psychic vision can be.

AMAZING ACCURACY

One of her sitters was writing a book about the former UN Secretary-General Dag Hammarskjold, who had been killed in a mysterious aircraft crash in 1961. The visitor made no bones about her hope that Coral Polge would produce a portrait of the dead diplomat. Coral Polge did not feel able to oblige – as she says, such a demand 'creates barriers' – and her sitter was disappointed when Coral's pencil began to sketch the outline of what seemed to be a little girl with flowing blonde hair.

Coral's sitter in fact felt doubly disappointed, for she had been told by Hammarskjold through another medium that she would have a portrait of him from a psychic artist. At first it seemed that it was not to be this psychic artist – until Coral Polge had all but finished, and her sitter realized that she had drawn not a portrait of Hammarskjold as an adult statesman, but as a child. In Coral Polge's drawing she recognized Hammarskjold as she had seen him in a photograph taken when he was aged only two – complete with long fair locks, not unusual in small children in 1907.

Another had a double confirmation of Coral Polge's abilities as an all-round medium as well as psychic artist at a public meeting at which Coral was producing drawings as they came to her, and then asking the audience if any of them recognized the resulting portraits. Mrs Phyllis Timms, from Salisbury, Wiltshire, was sure that one such picture, showing an elderly man with a drooping, bushy white moustache, was of her late maternal grandfather, Herbert Light. No one else in the auditorium made any move to claim it.

But Mrs Timms wanted some further sign that the picture was indeed intended for her. Coral Polge, picking up some further psychic impression about the man she had drawn, suggested the portrait might be for someone in a green dress. Mrs Timms was wearing blue. Coral Polge insisted that green was the key link between the man in her portrait and someone in the here and now.

It was only at this point that Mrs Timms stopped thinking about colours and realized the significance of the word 'green'. Her maiden name, which she had not used for years, was Green. She claimed the picture.

These cases could be 'explained' by suggesting that Coral Polge had picked up her knowledge of her subjects' looks from the sitters – for it was the sitters she depended on to recognize whose likeness she had drawn. But in some cases the connection between sitter and portrait is not as direct or clear as that, and only later has the accuracy of Coral Polge's drawing come to light.

Singers Grace Brooks and Deirdre Dehn met when they were both working on the film of Lionel Bart's *Oliver!* Deirdre, it turned out, had a talent for automatic writing. Through her scripts, another singer, who first identified herself as Maria Garcia, communicated with Grace. Later 'Maria' gave her surname as Malibran. Intrigued, Deirdre went to work to find out if this was indeed a historical person, and her research discovered that Maria Malibran had been born Maria Garcia in Paris in 1808. She made her debut as an opera singer in London in 1825, and died tragically at the age of 28 in Manchester, England, as the result of falling from a horse.

Maria Malibran was a real enough person, then. In due course, Deirdre Dehn went home to Australia, and that seemed to be the end of Grace Brooks's contact with Maria. Then she went to a sitting with Coral Polge. Coral drew a portrait of a young woman with a hairstyle that was definitely not in any modern style. All Coral Polge could tell Grace Brooks was that This is a Spanish singer named Maria.'

Grace Brooks had no idea what Maria Garcia Malibran looked like, but she did know how to find out. Research in the British Museum turned up an engraving of a contemporary portrait of Maria Malibran. The likeness between this picture from life, and Coral Polge's psychically received likeness is uncanny. It seems hardly likely that Coral Polge, producing more than 30 portraits a week, would have had time to research this one case in order to make an impression on Grace Brooks. And she certainly could not have been relying on telepathy to give her the image in Grace Brooks's mind.

THE STORY OF DOC TESTER

While Coral Polge gave up drawing portraits of spirit guides, there is a fascinating story concerning one portrait of a spirit guide that deserves to be retold. The picture involved so many different people in its long wait for its rightful home that it speaks for a real and mysterious consistency between psychics, and strongly suggests that there is a truth of some guides – and in the survival of the individual identity after death.

In medium Tom Fox's consulting room in his house in Copthorne, West Sussex, hangs the portrait in oils of a rough-and-ready character who might have ridden the frontier in the days of Wild Bill Hickok and Doc Holiday. The tale of how this picture came to be on Tom Fox's wall is told here in his own words, taken from his autobiography *Medium Rare*:

'In the late Sixties I went for a private reading with a very well-known and respected medium, Billy Elton, the founder of the Spiritualist church in Aylesbury, Buckinghamshire. Among other

Coral Polge with one of her portraits of a dead person, drawn through her awareness of their presence.

181

things he told me that one of my spirit guides was an Australian doctor, whose name, he said, was Dr Tester. Now I'd never heard, seen, or sensed such a person at all, let alone known that I had such a character as a spirit guide. But I made a note of the name in my diary, as I always do put down details of a reading, imagining as I did so that this was some kind of fresh-faced modern colonial type – white coat, blond hair, maybe with glasses, and a cheerful and cheering manner for his rounds of the hospital wards.

'About a year or two later (during which there was no sign of Dr Tester in any shape or form) I was doing trance work in a development circle run by my old and dear friend Hilda Kirby. Among the members was another great friend, Jack Toyer. Just before we started one meeting – I remember he was sitting opposite me in the circle – Jack said, in a somewhat disapproving voice: "Tom… There's a spirit form, of a dirty old Mexican, standing behind you, you know."

'"Oh, is there?" I said. "Well, he's welcome. I don't know who he is, but he's welcome."

'I didn't give this "visitor" any more thought after that, because I soon went into trance. Blue Star, my Zulu guide, came through, and for some time was speaking through me about spiritual development and the world of Spirit. When he had finished Blue Star said, rather sternly, to Jack: "The man in the big black hat would like to talk to you."

Narciso Bressanello, a mediumistic artist who used to be a ship repairer, in his studio on a boat in Venice.

'With that, he gave everyone a blessing and left, and I then started to come out of trance. I was nearly "round" when I suddenly went under again, under a very strong influence indeed. The person who'd taken control of me this time said - without any preamble, polite introductions, or anything: "Who the bloody hell d'ye think you're calling a dirty old Mexican? I'm no dirty old Mexican, mate. My name's Doc Tester."

'That caused a bit of stir in our polite gathering since nobody had any idea who that was, and I was in no position to tell them. Cutting right across the chatter, the blunt Doc just told them all to stop making so much noise and, in so many words, to shut up. Then he launched into quite a long talk about healing – and very lucid, very informative and, in fact, entertaining he was.

'Doc Tester is a very powerful character, but he's not intolerant: he gently and jovially mocks people, though, if he thinks they're not living up to the best in themselves. So that first appearance was also peppered with wisecracks at people who, he thought, were speaking without thinking, or asking him silly questions. And then, just as Blue Star had done, he offered everyone a blessing and, with a promise to return another time, departed.

'After the meeting, as usual, we had a cup of tea all round. I needed it: I kept thinking that that couldn't be the Dr Tester that Billy Elton had mentioned.

'I said to Jack: "Are you really sure he had black hair?"

'"Absolutely," he said. "And the black hat. He was a scruffy old thing."

'I still couldn't believe it. This wasn't exactly the clean-cut young man that, for some reason, I persisted in thinking "my" Dr Tester had to be. And, as it happened, I personally heard no more from, or about, Doc Tester for a long time – about four or five years, in fact.

'In the early Seventies, I went to the Spiritualist church at Aylesbury one Sunday – just as an ordinary member of the congregation – and sat down at the back. During the service I became aware of a couple sitting in front of me – for, standing between them, with his arms around them – cuddling them, in fact – was the very strong visible presence of a teenage boy. He was about fifteen, I'd say, slimly built, and quite tall.

'The lady of the couple was, it turned out, an officer of the church, and after the service she made a point of speaking to the new faces, like me, who'd come to the church for the first time that day. I told her about the boy I'd seen with his arms around her and her husband. She called her husband over at once, and had me repeat the description. "That's our son," they agreed. "He died experimenting with a plastic bag - pulled it over his head and died of asphyxiation. We know it wasn't suicide. Just a hideous accident."

'We had quite a conversation after that. Their names, I discovered, were Vic and Pam Bradford. The next thing I knew I was being invited to tea with them for the following weekend.

'When I arrived at their house, the first thing I saw on their living-room wall was an oil painting of a man dressed in black, with black hair, and a big black hat. At once I asked the lady of the house who he was.

'"You tell me," she said.

'"His name's Doc Tester, he's Australian, and he worked in the outback," I heard myself saying without thinking. "And that's all I know."

'"Then he's yours," she said. "He's been waiting here three years for you."I was completely amazed. How could anyone else know about Doc Tester – especially when even I had doubted that he actually looked like that? How had anyone been able to paint this picture, or be sure that I would get to know about it?

'Then Pam told me the story.

'For her and Vic it began a couple of years after Doc – unknown to them, of course – had surprised our development circle. In Northampton there was a medium called Jack Burrell. He was also a psychic artist, who specialized in pictures of the family, friends, and spirit guides of people who came to him for readings. There were two unusual things about his art. He would paint only people who were dead, whom he had never seen in the flesh or in photographs, and he always painted with his eyes closed, because he worked in a state of trance.

'Among the pictures of spirit guides he painted was a portrait in oils of a blackhaired man, who was wearing a black hat. Looking rather like a character from a Western, actually, except that in the background of the picture there are sheep, not long-horn steers.

'When Burrell had completed this picture, he gave it to his friends Pam and Vic Bradford.

'"It's not yours," he explained, "and it's not for you. But I want you to keep it. Hang it on your living-room wall. This is an Australian doctor, and he's somebody's healer in Spirit. Someone will be along eventually to collect it. But that's all I can tell you."

'And there I was, looking at that painting, and knowing that this really was Doc Tester. The painting hangs on the wall of my consulting room now, a reminder and an inspiration to me always. I think Doc would be one of my favourite people, with his blunt speech, rambunctious style, and dry style of humour, and I treasure his picture.

'I've found out a bit more about him since – from himself and from others in Spirit. He was an ordinary, country doctor, working out in the Australian outback in the Twenties. He'd spend weeks at a time riding from station to station and settlement to settlement on horseback – which is why his clothes are always so scruffy: they're old, travelling clothes, and they're covered in dust from his journeys in the bush.

'To tell the truth, Doc has done more talking to people in development circles and the like than he has made himself felt by doing healing through me. On the few occasions that I have done healing I've known he's there, but he tends to stay in the background.'

PROOF AT LAST?

The authors of the Reader's Digest volume *Unsolved Mysteries of the Past* comment aptly on this singular example of psychic art: 'The most remarkable part of this story is that three mediums besides Fox himself independently either saw or were aware of Doc Tester, two of them before Fox had [learned] anything about his spirit guide; and the man who painted Tester's picture was someone whom Fox had never met.'

Whether or not they amount to proof of life after death, cases like this, and others – like Coral Polge's portrait of Maria Malibran – certainly confront us with a more than ordinary mystery.

VISIONS OF AN AFTERLIFE

After a routine operation, something went frighteningly wrong. The doctors brought Iris Lemov back to life within minutes – but she was no longer the same woman.

When Mrs Iris Lemov went into hospital for a routine operation neither she nor her doctors expected anything unusual to occur. What actually happened was to change her outlook on life – and death – altogether.

'I was brought back to my room after surgery,' she recalled in a journal article in November 1979, 'and was speaking to my nurse, when a strange separated feeling between my body and my brain occurred. High above my body I floated wondering why so many doctors were around my bed…'

Mrs Lemov had slipped suddenly and unexpectedly into a coma. But the abrupt dislocation of her consciousness and her body was not to be any ordinary out-of-the-body experience. For while she watched from above, she went deeper into coma and her heart stopped beating. To Mrs Lemov, looking down on the scene, it appeared only that her face had gone terribly pale. And then everything went suddenly dark.

She found herself sucked into a long black tunnel. Light glowed at the end of it. 'I felt frightened and excited as I neared the end of the tunnel,' she said. 'I felt peace, without pain, and free. The light at the end of the tunnel was bright but easy on my eyes.'

When she came out into the light, Iris Lemov found herself in a verdant, peaceful valley, which was 'a sight to behold. There was velvety green grass and calmness. Music coming from nowhere made me feel comfortable and I began to feel as if I belonged. I saw figures of people dressed in shrouds coming toward me and [they] called me by name. This man with a white beard told me to go back – your family still needs you – enjoy your life. This beautiful man was my grandfather who died two years before I was born…

'If we could all have the opportunity of seeing my valley during the course of our lifetime, how much more purposeful our lives would be.'

THROUGH THE MISTS

Iris Lemov's experience is typical of many who have clinically died, have been resuscitated and, in the brief period that they have been technically dead, have briefly visited the hereafter. Such people have, it seems, been vouchsafed a glimpse of the life after death. It is not surprising that the experience radically changes the attitude of most of these survivors toward death. For them, it no longer holds any fear, and, like Mrs Lemov's, their present lives are enriched as a result.

It is only with recent advances in medical technology – both drugs and equipment – that these 'near-death' experiences have been reported with any frequency – for the simple reason that they have allowed so many more people than ever before to be rescued from the very brink of death. But the truly striking thing about the reports of these brief sorties to the next world is their consistency. They may vary in detail, but the pattern of them is astonishingly uniform. Examples of other first-person accounts of such experiences will make this plain:

'I got up and walked into the hall to go get a drink, and it was at that point, as they found out later, that my appendix ruptured. I became very weak, and I fell down.

'I began to feel a sort of drifting, a movement of my real being in and out of my body, and to hear beautiful music. I floated on down the hall and out the door onto the screened-in porch. There, it almost seemed that clouds, a pink mist really, began to gather around me, and then I floated right straight on through the screen, just as though it weren't there, and up into this pure crystal clear light, an illuminating white light...

'It's not any kind of light you can describe on earth. I didn't actually see a person in this light, and yet it has a special identity ... It is a light of perfect understanding and perfect love.

'The thought came to my mind, "Thou lovest me?"' This was not exactly in the form of a question, but I guess the connotation of what the light said was, "If you do love me, go back and complete what you began in your life." And all the time, I felt as though I were surrounded by an overwhelming love and compassion.'

A woman who collapsed from a heart attack reported:

'I found myself in a black void, and I knew I had left my physical body behind. I knew I was dying, and I thought, "God, I did the best I knew how at the time I did it. Please help me."

'Immediately, I was moved out of that blackness, through a pale grey, and I just went on, gliding and moving swiftly, and in front of me, in the distance, I could see a grey mist, and I was rushing toward it. It seemed that I just couldn't get to it fast enough... Beyond the mist, I could see people... and I could also see something which one could take to be buildings. The whole thing was permeated with the most gorgeous light – a living, golden yellow glow… 'As I approached more closely, I felt certain I was going through that mist. It was such a wonderful, joyous feeling… Yet, it wasn't my time to go through the mist, because instantly from the other side appeared my uncle Carl, who had died many years earlier. 'He blocked my path, saying, "Go back. Your work on earth has not been completed. Go back now." I didn't want to go back, but I had no choice, and immediately I was back in my body. I felt that horrible pain in my chest, and I heard my little boy crying, "God, bring my mummy back to me."'

When near death some people have reported seeing divine messengers as they slip out of contact with this life, as shown in the engraving above.

THERE AND BACK AGAIN

Those who have spent years collecting reports like these – the chief researchers include Drs Raymond Moody, Kenneth Ring, Margot Grey, Michael Rawlings and Michael Sabom – have compiled, from their analyses of hundreds of examples, a typical pattern of events that occur to people who are briefly clinically dead. They call this the 'core experience', on which almost every individual near-death experience is a variation.

This essential sequence of the journey from life to death and back is as follows:

as people begin to die, they feel a blissful sensation;

as clinical death occurs, they have an out-of-the-body experience, floating above the scene in which their body is lying;

they go into a misty, or more often a dark area, and most see this transformed into a long tunnel with light at the end;

they hurtle with increasing speed down the tunnel;

as they emerge into the light, they are greeted by a relative or by a recognised religious leader such as Jesus of Nazareth;

the scenery at the end of the tunnel is often pastoral – a pleasant rural scene, or a beautiful garden;

soothing or 'heavenly' music is playing, though often its source is invisible;

sometimes, scenes from their earthly life pass before them, as if in a movie. These may also occur earlier in the sequence, before or during the passage through the tunnel;

a disembodied voice from 'the light', or the relative or other figure who greeted them, tells them to 'go back';

the return from this celestial scene is usually instantaneous. At once, the body feels normal sensations – usually the pain from their injury or from the efforts of those trying to revive them;

as a result of the experience, people no longer fear death. They also tend to express a reduced interest in material things, and a heightened interest in spiritual matters, although conventional religions often lose much of any former attraction they may have had.

A PSYCHOLOGICAL TRICK?

The very consistency of the near-death experience argues for its truth: that there is a place we go when we die, and our loved ones are there to greet us and ease us past the shock of the transition from this life to the next. But that very same consistency can be interpreted in a quite different way.

For example, the highly regarded parapsychologist Dr Susan Blackmore has suggested that one near-death experience is so like another not because we all experience the same actual, objective reality at the point of death, but because our brains are essentially built in the same way – just as we all have noses above our mouths, and eyes to watch over both, and ears one each side of our heads. As our physical system collapses, the shards of consciousness interpret these symptoms of death in the best possible light, calling on the failing memory to create a marvellously benign and reassuring, but essentially fantastic, mental environment. Dr Blackmore concludes that 'what is generally now called the near-death experience is a psychological trick, played by the dying brain on the consciousness in order to lessen the trauma of dying. Essentially, this type of experience is the brain's last fling.'

Indeed it may be. But there are several aspects of near-death experiences as reported that don't fit with this analysis and that suggest there may be an objective reality to these accounts of what happens when we die. The very first problem with the sceptical view of near-death experiences is of its own making. What possible biological reason can there be for the mind (or brain) to have evolved a 'trick' to make dying easier to bear? How did the mind discover that it needed to learn this trick? How could anyone - other than through reincarnation, in which one suspects Dr Blackmore does not believe – inherit it?

Even if there is a materialist explanation for the near-death experience, this strange formula is hardly the best way to express it.

'GREETING FIGURES'

There are further facets of reported near-death experiences that indicate that something real lies behind them.

First, there is the figure who greets the migrating soul, or consciousness, on its arrival in the 'other' world. It would be interesting to know more about what distinguishes those who have been greeted on the 'other side' by standard religious figures such as Jesus, St Peter or the archangel Gabriel, from those who have been met only with a seemingly sentient, all-embracing, 'clear white light', and from those who have had close relations and loved ones there to meet them. While prior expectations may create what (or whom) one perceives at this point, the figure (or lack of it) that people see may depend on their earthly circumstances.

It would be peculiar indeed if someone who had had a lifetime of almighty conflicts with relatives were suddenly to be greeted with boundless love and cosmic wisdom by the very same wicked grandad who had beaten them as children. It would be equally startling if an agnostic, who had never been averse to the existence of a Great Creator but had long suspected the prophet of Nazareth to be a con man, were to find that the figure welcoming him to the paradisaical garden was none other than a smiling Jesus Christ himself - who would then add injury to insult by telling him to go back and finish his business on Earth.

Besides, there is a long and hardy tradition – within close-knit families, at least – of dead relatives coming to 'collect' a dying person and usher them into the next world. And from time to time these bailiffs of the grim reaper have been seen by people quite separate from the person who is dying.

D. Scott Rogo, in *The Return from Silence*, cites a fine instance of such an event from the memoirs of the New York nurse Margaret Moser:

'In the winter of 1948-9 I nursed a very sick old lady, Mrs Rosa B… She was residing at that time at the Savoy Plaza Hotel on Fifth Avenue, and up to the last she was mentally competent.

'Early one afternoon… Mrs B. had been asleep, but suddenly I saw her sit up and wave happily, her face all smiles. I turned my head toward the door, thinking one of her daughters had come in; but much to my surprise it was an elderly lady I had never seen before. She had a striking resemblance to my patient – the same light blue eyes, but a longer nose and a heavier chin. I could see her very clearly for it was bright daylight; the window shades were only slightly lowered. The visitor walked toward my patient, bent down, and… they kissed each other. But then, as I got up and walked toward the bed, she was gone.

'Mrs B. looked very pleased. She took my hand and said, "It is my sister!" Then she slept peacefully again. I saw the same apparition twice later on, but never as clearly and always from another room. But every time she came the patient was obviously elated.'

Ms Moser later had corroborative evidence from her patient's sister's son that the apparition she and Mrs B. had both seen at the same time indeed resembled Mrs B.'s sister in all respects. Scott

Rogo commented that 'this story... points to the objective existence of the "greeting figures" commonly seen by people having [near-death experiences]... We obviously need to collect more stories of this calibre...'

D. Scott Rogo, sadly, is himself now dead, but here is a small contribution to this needed literature, which was reported to the author of this book by a member of the family involved. (In the interest of privacy certain personal details have been changed.)

In 1979 an exiled Iranian princess lay terminally ill from cancer in her house in London, England. Her husband was a doctor with a busy practice, and care of the dying woman fell largely to her elder daughter, Imrana, who was then aged about 14. She was with her mother in her final hours. At some point during that time, when it was obvious that no recovery was possible, the dying princess announced that her own father and an uncle, both long since dead, had arrived in her room.

In a more peaceful representation in a French 12th-century manuscript, Christ is shown as supreme judge.

She actually went so far as to introduce her daughter to the pair, although to Imrana they remained steadfastly invisible. Despite her feebleness, the fading woman then told them to go away, since she wasn't 'ready for them' yet. Apparently they did, for she soon ceased to be troubled by their presence. She next gave her daughter a long lecture on her future duties to the family. This responsibility discharged, she settled herself to wait for her 'guides' to come back to collect her. Her daughter saw her greet them before she finally gave up the ghost.

SWEET MELODIES

There is, then, some evidence that the 'greeting figures' reported by those who have had near-death experiences do have some objective existence. There is also evidence that the celestial music that dying people hear from, or in, the next world is not entirely of their own desperate imagining.

A close friend of a certain Mrs L. recorded the simultaneous experiences of several friends of the lady who, with her son, had gathered at her bedside shortly before she died in 1881. The report was given to Edmund Gurney, a senior member of the Society for Psychical Research in London, on 28 July that year, and it stated:

'Just after dear Mrs L.'s death between 2 and 3 a.m., I heard a most sweet and singular strain of singing outside the windows; it died away after passing the house. All [but one] in the room heard it, and the medical attendant, who was still with us, went to the window, as I did, and looked out, but there was nobody [outside]. It was a bright and beautiful night.

'It was as if several voices were singing in perfect unison a most sweet melody which died away in the distance. Two persons had gone from the room to fetch something and were coming upstairs at the back of the house and heard the singing... They could not, naturally, have heard any sound from outside the windows in the front of the house from where they were in the back.'

The only person who did not hear this sweet music was Mrs L.'s son, although the family doctor (the 'medical attendant') independently corroborated all the details of the first report, adding that the music consisted of 'a few bars... not unlike that from an aeolian harp – and it filled the air for a few seconds'. In his book quoted earlier, D. Scott Rogo remarked: 'The fact that the patient's son didn't hear the music implies that the sounds weren't from the street, but represented some form of psychic process.' He himself collected a number of reports of similar codas to people's lives, although they seemed to be rare in 20th-century experience.

Finally, the view that the near-death experience is imaginary, a 'trick' dictated by biology and designed to obscure the fact of death, falls down over a crucial phase in the core experience. In fact the sceptics do not even address this question. And that is: if the experience is essentially imaginary, how does the imagination manage to put the procedure so neatly into reverse, as it were, when resuscitation is successful, and produce a suitable figure to pronounce the words 'Go back – your business on Earth is not yet finished' (or phrases to that effect), time after time, in so many different people? This is a surprising and unexpected sub-routine to find in a biological programme supposedly designed to ease one into oblivion.

The light above the clouds. Some people who have had near-death experiences have felt they have risen above earthly things.

THE FINAL CURTAIN

It might be argued that near-death experiences must be imaginary because they are simply too good to be true: no doubt most people would like to find themselves in green pastures and pleasant company on the other side of death. But not everyone who has glimpsed beyond that final curtain has had such a comforting vision. Some have seen Hell.

'I found myself in a place surrounded by mist... There was a big pit with vapour coming out and there were arms and hands coming out trying to grab mine... I was terrified that these hands were going to claw hold of me and pull me into the pit,' one such unfortunate told researcher Dr Margot Grey.

Another told Dr Raymond Moody that, as he travelled toward the realm of light during his near-death experience, he passed a place of terrible desolation, full of 'washed out', only partly human forms with an 'absolute, crushed, hopeless demeanour', who 'seemed to be forever shuffling, moving around, not knowing where they were going, not knowing who to follow, or what to look for'.

Both these kinds of Hell have been reported by more than one witness. As Dr Michael Rawlings puts it, with black humour: 'It may not be safe to die.' Furthermore, the existence of the place of dreadful desolation has had some degree of objective verification.

A traditional Christian view of the way to the ultimate end of mankind is shown in this representation of the Last Judgement.

APPALLING SORROW

In 1961, when serving with the British Army in Germany, medium Tom Fox spent a night at the site of the former Nazi concentration camp, Bergen-Belsen. He dozed off, and then:

'I woke up, and something very like Hell itself flooded my mind.

'No more than five yards away, clearly visible, there was a man standing. He was pale and thin, and a sense of appalling sorrow was welling from him.

'It very soon became obvious that he was by no means alone. His was the only form I could see, but I rapidly became aware of the presence of a whole crowd of souls. Occasionally, at the edge of things, I would see their blurred or fleeting images, as if they were on the brink of becoming visible... But there was no doubting that they were there. For I could hear them clearly enough. I was being overwhelmed with the turmoil of their suffering and heartbreak. At first I tried to close myself off from the agonised clamour of those tormented spirits. They were speaking in their own languages, incomprehensible to me, but their anguish was unmistakable... Then, as I calmed down, I was able to distinguish personal voices and individual emotions.

'Some were consumed with the desire for vengeance; others asked only to be released from the nightmare of their experience, or to be freed from Belsen itself, the place to which they had become bound by their suffering. So many people had endured so many dreadful things in that camp, and in so short a time, that to those who had been there, it seemed that only those souls who had shared that terrible experience could possibly comprehend its enormity. Their time in Belsen had become their only reality. And so they had remained, tied to the place, to comfort one another.'

Fox prayed for them, and eventually the tormented host faded away. But, said Fox 'I have had learned more about human pain in those few hours at Belsen than many people do in a lifetime.' The near-death experience seems to offer the best evidence so far that there is a life beyond death – and that, as might be expected, it is as challenging in its own way as life on Earth.

ABRAHAM LINCOLN

The ghostly shape of Abraham Lincoln, America's 16th and most acclaimed president, is said to still walk the corridors of power inside the White House to this very day! The assassinated Lincoln is a particularly distinguished ghost.

While the settings for many hauntings often involve gloomy buildings, fog-shrouded nights and isolated surroundings, there are some ghosts that would seem to prefer a more crowded, more open environment.

Indeed, everyone from Winston Churchill to presidents and visiting heads of state have claimed to have seen the ghost of 'Honest Abe' at 1600 Pennsylvania Avenue. Former President Ronald Reagan's eldest daughter, Maureen, recalled just a few years ago that she, too, had seen it. 'I'm not kidding,' says Maureen. 'We've really seen it.' She and her husband, Dennis Revell, often slept in Lincoln's bedroom when they visited her parents in Washington, and claim to have seen the apparition, which sometimes glows a bright red, sometimes orange. Maureen and her husband claim that it is Lincoln's ghost. 'When I told my parents what I saw, they looked at me a little weirdly,' she admitted.

Eleanor Roosevelt, the wife of President Roosevelt, often thought she could feel Lincoln's presence when she was up late at night, writing in her diary. And President Harry Truman, who served from 1945 to 1952, also claimed to have heard Lincoln's ghost walking through the building.

The most detailed sighting, however, came from Dutch Queen Wilhelmina, who stayed as a guest at the Roosevelt White House. One night, after hearing footsteps outside her bedroom, she opened the door and, to her amazement, there stood Lincoln, complete with his trademark top hat. Queen Wilhelmina was so overcome by the sight, that she fainted to the floor with a heavy thud! With the exception of Maureen Reagan, there have been few sightings in recent years, though Nancy Reagan recalled that Rex, the family dog, would often sit outside the haunted bedroom and bark at the door for no apparent reason – and the pooch steadfastly refused ever to set paw in it.

In real life, Abraham Lincoln was a dedicated follower of the paranormal for much of his adult life, attending numerous seances, and several times he had chilling premonitions and nightmares of his own assassination. His wife, Mary Todd, whom he married in 1842, was also a firm believer in seances, and that same year Lincoln wrote to a friend explaining that 'I have always had a strong tendency to mysticism', and often felt that he was controlled 'by some other power than my own will'. However, it wasn't until the death of his favourite son, Willie, several years later, that he became a devotee of seances. He tried on many occasions to contact his dear departed son, but he never succeeded.

When he became President in 1860, he was often a guest at seances, and one medium, Cora Maynard, a friend of his wife, even claimed that she was responsible for Lincoln's landmark emancipation proclamation of 1 January 1863, which ordered the release of every slave in the United States! Mrs Maynard maintained that Lincoln issued the order after spirits told him to do so. While American historians doubt that a man of Lincoln's convictions would have issued so important an order simply to placate the spirit world, some agree that it might have bolstered his long-held belief that slavery was morally wrong.

It was a belief that would eventually cost him his life. On 14 April 1865, just three months into his second term of office and just five days after the southern Confederate forces surrendered to end the bloody Civil War, Lincoln attended the opening of a new play, *My American Cousin*, at the Ford Theater in Washington, DC, with his wife and several dignitaries. Shortly after the curtain went up, a

An artist's impression of President Abraham Lincoln's murder.

disgruntled Southerner, John Wilkes Booth, calmly walked into the presidential box and shot Lincoln in the head. He died the next morning.

Yet, incredibly, Lincoln had had numerous 'forewarnings' of his own death, and on the very day he was shot, he had remarked to his chief bodyguard that he had been having nightmares about his murder. His first premonition, however, came just prior to his election in 1860, when he saw a strange image of himself in a mirror. Next to his reflection was another image of himself, deathly pale in colour. When he tried to stare at it, it vanished. This was to happen several times during the course of his time in the White House, and wife Mary concluded that it meant he would serve two terms, but not survive the second!

Then, in the days leading up to his ill-fated trip to the Ford theater - which he had only attended because Mary had wanted to – he had a series of macabre, disturbing dreams. In his diary, he wrote about one of these vivid nightmares:

A DREAM OF DEATH

'I retired late. I soon began to dream. There seemed to be a death-like stillness about me. Then I heard subdued sobs, as if a number of people were weeping. I thought I had left my bed and wandered downstairs. There the silence was broken by the same pitiful sobbing, but the mourners were invisible. I went from room to room; no living person was in sight, but the same mournful sounds of distress met me as I passed. It was light in all the rooms; every object was familiar to me; but where were all the people who were grieving as if their hearts would break?

'I was puzzled and alarmed. What could be the meaning of all this? Determined to find the cause of a state of things so mysterious and so shocking, I kept on until I arrived at the East Room, which I entered. Before me was a catafalque, on which rested a corpse wrapped in funeral vestments. Around it were stationed soldiers who were acting as guards; and there was a throng of people, some gazing mournfully upon the corpse, whose face was covered, others weeping pitifully.

' "Who is dead in the White House?" ' I demanded of one of the soldiers. "The President," was his answer. "He was killed by an assassin." Then came a loud burst of grief from the crowd, which awoke me from my dream. I slept no more that night; and although it was only a dream, I have been strangely annoyed by it ever since.'

On the very day prior to his death, Lincoln even confided to one of his Cabinet members that he had had premonitions of the murder, and told his head bodyguard, W.H. Cook, that he had dreamed of his assassination for three straight nights. The startled guard begged the much loved President not to attend the opening, but Lincoln simply sighed and said he had promised Mary they would go. He never came out alive.

Following the state funeral service in Washington, Lincoln's body was transported by train to his home state of Illinois. But more than 100 years later, there are still some people who claim to have seen a phantom train, draped in black bunting, slowly wending its way along the same route to Illinois. Many years ago, an account of this sad phenomenon was recorded in an article carried in the *Evening Times*, a newspaper in Albany, New York:

'Regularly in the month of April, about midnight, the air on the tracks becomes very keen and cutting. On either side of the tracks, it is warm and still. Every watchman, when he feels the air, slips off the track and sits down to watch. Soon the pilot engine of Lincoln's

Visitors to the White House, including Winston Churchill, have claimed to have seen Lincoln's ghost.

funeral train passes along with long, black streamers and with a band of black instruments playing dirges, grinning skeletons all about.

'It passes noiselessly. If it is moonlight, clouds come over the moon as the phantom train goes by. After the pilot engine passes, the funeral train itself with flags and streamers rushes past. The track seems covered with black carpet, and the coffin is seen in the centre of the car, while all about it in the air and on the train behind are vast numbers of blue-coated men, some with coffins on their backs, others leaning upon them.'

STRANGE OCCURRENCES

'If a real train were passing, its noise would be hushed as if the phantom train rode over it. Clocks and watches always stop as the phantom train goes by and when looked at are five to eight minutes behind. Everywhere on the road about 27 April watches and clocks are suddenly found to be behind.'

It is also interesting to note that some months after the President was assassinated by Booth, his wife posed for a photographer – when the plate was developed, there was a foggy resemblance of Lincoln standing right there next to Mary.

For almost 60 years after Lincoln died, there were no known reports of his ghost inside the White House. But when Calvin Coolidge became the 29th President in 1923, following the death of Warren Harding, the ghost made its first known appearance. Coolidge's wife, Grace, recalled seeing Lincoln's shadow standing at the window inside the Oval Office, which is the presidential seat of power. It was only visible for a few seconds, and seemed to be looking forlornly towards the Potomac river, which wends its way into the distance. Incredibly, during Lincoln's term of office, he had once stood at that very same window, and was described by Army chaplain E.C. Bolles as looking thoroughly despondent. 'I think I never saw so sad a face in my life, and I have looked into many a mourner's face,' Bolles later recorded in his journal.

Following Grace Coolidge's experience, many other powerful and important people also claimed to have seen or heard the spectre of President Lincoln. But there have been no reported incidents since Maureen Reagan's encounter in the late 1980s. That is not to say, however, that Lincoln has finally given up the ghost on the White House! Maybe we will have to wait until George and Laura Bush leave office to know if they, too, heard or saw anything of Honest Abe.

HAMPTON COURT

Like President Lincoln, some other ghosts also prefer a more crowded environment than the traditional haunt. Such is the case with the spirits of Hampton Court, in Middlesex, which has been home to a series of unexplained events for centuries. Various ghosts have been sighted within its surrounds, including the puzzling case of the fair-haired boy. Before World War Two, the Old Court House, which was home to Sir Christopher Wren while he supervised renovations to the palace, was owned by a man called Norman Lamplugh. On a lovely summer's day, as guests mingled on the lawn, Norman's brother Ernest and another man, who were looking out across the gardens from a staircase, suddenly spotted a young boy aged about eight walking across the lawn. They looked at each other quizzically, for not only had Norman not invited any children to the garden party, but the fair-haired lad was clad in a page boy suit from the time of King Charles II, who died in 1685! His costume was authentic right down to the big silver buckles on his shoes!

The mysterious youngster then entered the house, and walked up the stairs right past the two startled guests. He said nothing, and seemed to not even notice them. He then walked down the hall, entering a room which had only one entrance, the one leading off the hall. The two men quickly followed the young guest into the room, but could find no trace of him!

But there are said to be ghosts at Hampton Court which pre-date even a 17th-century page boy. During the reign of Henry VIII, the king's third wife, Jane Seymour, gave birth to a son, in October 1537, at Hampton Court. Tragically, the baby died just seven days later. For hundreds of years ever since, people have reported seeing Queen Jane's ghost, clad all in white, gliding through the Court, her way lit by a taper, on the anniversary of the child's death.

Many have seen her presence come from a doorway in the Queen's Old Apartments, then wander silently down the stairway where she disappears into a gallery. Two servants who saw the apparition described her as 'a tall lady, with a long train and shining face'.

Then there was the case of the two Cavaliers who haunted Fountain Court. They were seen earlier last century by Lady Hildyard, who complained about their appearance and the strange noises she heard from her apartment which overlooked the Court. A short time later, a work crew was sent down to install new drains in the Court, and workers discovered the remains of two Cavaliers, buried just a few feet below the pavement. They were disinterred and given a proper burial, and that was the last anyone ever heard from them.

Not so the so-called White Lady of Hampton Court who was spotted by fishermen as recently as the 1960s. There are also said to be ghosts of the headless Archbishop Laud, who has been spotted walking quietly inside the hallowed halls of the Court, and

The palace has been home to ghosts for more than 400 years.

Mrs Sybil Penn, who was the nurse of Edward VI. Mrs Penn, a kindly soul who tended like a mother to the sickly young prince, and retired to an apartment inside Hampton Court after her service was done. She caught smallpox, and died in November 1568. She was buried at St Mary's Church, close to the Court, and remained there at rest for more than 250 years, until the church was struck by lightning and destroyed in 1829. Her tomb was taken to the site of the new church, but tragically her grave was vandalized and her remains scattered.

A short while later, her ghost was seen back at the apartment she had once lived in. At that time, a family was living there and they often heard the sound of a woman's voice and a spinning wheel. After making complaints, a team of workmen were brought in to check out the noises. They found a secret chamber leading off one of the rooms in the apartment – and inside, they found a spinning wheel, which was thought to be the one used by Mrs Penn some 300 years earlier! After the chamber was discovered, the ghost of Mrs Penn was itself seen for the first time. A guard on duty outside her apartment looked up one day to see a woman, dressed in a long robe and hood, coming from inside the rooms. The ghostly figure then vanished. He later claimed that the woman bore

King Henry VIII... several of his wives and servants are said to still call Hampton Court home!

a striking resemblance to the stone replica of Mrs Penn. Princess Frederica of Hanover, who had heard nothing about the ghost, also claimed to have seen Mrs Penn, this time in a long grey robe with a hood over her head. Since then, her ghost has been known as the Lady in Grey.

In the years since, many others have had brushes with the royal nurse. Servants have been woken in the dead of night by an icy hand touching their heads; they've heard footsteps and crashing sounds with no earthly explanation. Once, servants claimed they entered the vacant apartment and found it awash in 'a ghastly, lurid light'. But of all the ghosts said to inhabit Hampton Court, none has achieved the notoriety of the one believed to be the spirit of Lady Katherine Howard, Henry VIII's fifth wife, who was 19 when the King was first captivated by her charms. Lady Katherine was a tiny, waif-like girl, but no stranger to romance. She had had numerous suitors before she married Henry in July 1540, and continued her affairs even after she became his wife and Queen. Indeed, her love life was so hectic that enemies later chided her for living 'an abominable, base, carnal, voluptuous and vicious life', and branded her 'a harlot'.

She was eventually arrested on 12 November 1541, for her wayward lifestyle, but on the very night before she was taken away to the dreaded Tower of London for eventual execution by beheading, she begged Henry to spare her life. Her pleas fell on deaf ears, and Henry even watched in stony silence as she was dragged away by his sentries to meet her horrible fate. Over the centuries, her ghost is said to appear every 11 November running and screaming through what is today known as the Haunted Gallery. Numerous people have seen the ghastly apparition, and all describe it as a woman with long, flowing locks.

In the mid-1800s, the Haunted Gallery was closed and its space used for storing pictures. But a lady living in an apartment next door claimed that one night she was awoken from a sound sleep by a hideous scream which seemed to be coming from inside the Gallery. A short time later, a friend staying with her also heard the blood-curdling shriek.

But probably the most eerie story concerning Queen Katherine came after the Haunted Gallery was eventually reopened. An artist, who was doing a sketch of an old tapestry hanging on the wall, was stunned to see a disembodied hand appear right in front of it. The quick-thinking artist drew the free-floating hand, and the ring that it wore. Incredibly, the ring was later identified as one often worn by Katherine.

Yet another of Henry's wives, Anne Boleyn, is said to haunt Hampton Court. She was spotted about 100 years ago by a servant, who recognized her from her portrait. She was dressed completely in blue, and vanished within seconds. Her ghost has been spotted at several other sites around England, including the Tower, Hever Castle, Rochford Hall and Salle Church.

There have been other reports of hauntings at Hampton Court, though none of the ghosts could be identified. During World War Two, a policeman on duty saw 11 people on the palace grounds simply vanish into thin air, while stage actor Leslie Finch, who had just completed a play at the site, saw a Tudor-clad figure that vanished, leaving behind only a sudden iciness in the air. Similarly in 1966, a member of the audience viewing a light and sound display saw the ghost of Cardinal Thomas Wolsey, who gave the palace to Henry VIII, standing under one of the archways.

VERSAILLES

Although not as overrun by ghosts as Hampton Court, the great Palace of Versailles, just outside Paris, has some of the most intriguing tales of haunting ever recorded. In fact, this monument to the grandeur of pre-Revolutionary France was the site of a major investigation into psychic phenomena. Since 1870, there had been reports of 100-year-old apparitions not only of people, but also of buildings (!) within the Petit Trianon at Versailles, but it wasn't until 1902 that a painstaking analysis of the sightings was finally undertaken.

In 1762, Louis XV ordered the Petit Trianon built for his mistress, the beautiful Marquise de Pompadour, but she never lived to see its completion. However, when the house was finally finished in 1770, the King had by then taken another mistress, Madame Dubarry, who lived inside the estate occasionally. A carriageway led from the house to the King's farm at Versailles, called the Allée de la Managerie. Over the next few years, further work was carried out on the site. In 1773 a chapel was added, but its construction meant the carriageway had to be closed, and some of it was destroyed. Following Louis's death in 1774, the Petit Trianon was given to Marie Antoinette by the new king, Louis XVI, and she used it until the bloody Revolution ended the royal reign of the Bourbons (for the next 25 years).

Our story really begins on 10 August, 1901, when Eleanor Jourdain and Annie Moberly, both British scholars and the daughters of respected clergymen, were visiting the Palace of Versailles during a holiday stay in France. Although both were well educated, neither had any particular knowledge of the royal compound which could account for the stunning developments to come.

After wandering through the Grand Trianon where the Age of Kings has been resplendently captured in time, the two friends began walking towards the Petit Trianon. Given the vast size of Versailles, it is not surprising to learn that the two women soon found that they had become completely lost. However, they eventually came to the garden, which they entered. Moberly would later recall that when they did so, she felt 'an extraordinary depression'. Jourdain, too, was somehow aware of a strange feeling inside the garden, and both ladies felt a little ill at ease.

The Palace of Versailles – site of several paranormal events.

STRANGE FIGURES

Oddly, they later recounted, there had been a strong breeze blowing that day, and yet when they arrived at the Petit Trianon, the air had turned deathly still. Not a leaf moved. As they walked onwards, they suddenly noticed two strange-looking men. The women believed them to be gardeners, although they thought it a little odd that both men were dressed in 18th-century costumes, with greenish coats and tricorn hats. Later, Moberly recalled that 'I began to feel as if I were walking in my sleep; the heavy dreaminess was oppressive.'

Undaunted, the British holidaymakers asked the men for directions, and were told to continue their trek straight ahead. As they did, they saw a bridge and a kiosk. Sitting near the kiosk, they observed a curious-looking man in a slouch-hat and coat. Both women felt a little put off by his appearance. Suddenly, they heard footsteps behind them. They turned and a man with 'a curious smile' and strange accent gave them more directions. They believed him to be one of the gardeners they had just met. He vanished as suddenly as he had appeared.

As they neared the house, Moberly saw yet another figure, this time a woman, who was sitting on a small seat on the grass. She, too, was dressed in authentic period costume. A few seconds later, they watched as a young man, also smiling strangely, walked from the house using a solid door – a door they would later discover had been broken and left in ruins for many years. They also noticed the carriageway, which had been obliterated more than 130 years earlier!

The bizarre experience lasted for some 30 minutes, and afterwards both women concurred that the Petit Trianon had to be haunted. For the next ten years, these two well-educated ladies returned several times to the site in the hope that they could finally solve the mystery that had so disturbed them. Jourdain made a second visit a year later, and once more she felt the same oppressive atmosphere that seemed to hover over the area. As she crossed the small bridge that led to the former house of Marie Antoinette, she came across two workmen who wore the costumes of 18th century French labourers, right up to their pointed hoods. She also remembered hearing the sound of distant music.

However she was no closer to solving the mystery.

Moberly joined her for yet another visit, this time on 4 July 1904. Oddly, they could no longer find the paths they had taken earlier, and there was no sign of the kiosk or the bridge! Both had literally vanished into thin air. Moreover, the spot where they had seen the woman sitting was now occupied by an old bush, which had been obviously growing there for many, many years.

A CAPTIVATING RIDDLE

The two women were by now completely enthralled by the riddle of the Petit Trianon, and for the next six years, they researched its entire history, firmly believing they had somehow 'seen' the site as it had appeared in the late 1700s. Upon completing their research, they wrote a book, *An Adventure*, in which they came to deduce that the woman they had seen sitting on the grass had in fact been Marie Antoinette herself! They came to this conclusion when they discovered that that particular spot had been a favourite of hers.

They also identified the two gardeners as the Bersey brothers, who had been employed to work on the estate by the Queen. Despite their years of research, however, the women were treated with scorn and derision upon the release of their book. However, the book was a popular success, and it prompted other holiday-makers to come forward with similar bizarre tales of Versailles.

One such visitor was Englishman John Crooke who had taken his wife and young son to Versailles in the summer of 1908. However, their ghostly encounter came in the Grand Trianon, where they saw a woman sketching on some paper. She wore a long, cream skirt and a white hat. Crooke recalled that she paid no attention to them until he tried to get a peek at what she was drawing so intently. She grabbed her sketch so he couldn't see it, and then shot him an angry look. Suddenly, she disappeared. A short time later, the Crooke family saw two more strangely dressed people, who similarly vanished into thin air.

There were many other sightings to come over the years, some as recently as 1955. In 1928, two women, Clare Burrow and Ann Lambert, both English, went on a trip to Versailles. Neither had read the book written by Moberly and Jourdain, and yet they reportedly had a similar adventure. As they walked towards the Petit Trianon, Burrow, like Moberly 27 years earlier, suddenly felt an eerie languor. As they got closer, they saw an elderly, sinister-looking man, dressed in an 18th-century uniform. Despite his appearance, they asked him for directions, but ran off when he began shouting at them in guttural French. When they looked back at him, he had vanished. Throughout the course of the afternoon, they saw several other people all dressed in period clothes.

Ten years later, Elizabeth Hatton was strolling alone through the same grounds when from out of nowhere a man and woman, dressed like peasants, walked past her, pulling a wooden cart. When she turned to watch them, they slowly vanished before her very eyes. Many others have had similar experiences with vanishing people. In October 1949, Jack Wilkinson, his wife Clara,

Marie Antoinette, whose ghost was spotted at Versailles.

and their young son were touring the Grand Trianon. They noticed a woman, in 18th-century attire, holding an umbrella on the steps of the Grand Trianon. A few seconds later, she was gone.

One of the last recorded sightings came in May 1955, when a British lawyer and his wife walked towards the Petit Trianon. Like others before her, the woman felt a sudden depression, and then she and her husband spotted two men and a woman. Each was clad in the clothing suitable for French aristocracy before the Revolution. The men wore knee-length coats, black breeches, black shoes with silver buckles and black hats. The woman looked dazzling in a long yellow dress. Like other apparitions seen over the decades, they vanished into thin air without a trace to mark their appearance.

Sightings like these prompted much speculation about the existence of ghosts and other phenomena at Versailles. Many were sceptical, espousing the belief that all the startled visitors had simply seen people clad in the often-unfamiliar costumes of their native lands! Later, French writer Philippe Jullian would also claim that there was nothing sinister at all about the sightings. He said the poet Robert de Montesquiou and his friends would often dress up in period costume when they visited the Petit Trianon around the turn of the century. Yet Jullian's theory does not explain why there were sightings well into the second half of the 20th century, or how Montesquiou and his party could simply vanish without a trace.

Famed psychic researcher G.W. Lambert, who later wrote a book on the Versailles hauntings, believed in their validity. Using historical data available on Versailles, he concluded that the two gardeners first seen by Moberly and Jourdain were not brothers, but a father and son, Claude Richard and Antoine. However, he felt that the two English women had somehow seen Versailles as it would have appeared in 1770, and therefore the woman they saw sitting on the grass could not have been Marie Antoinette. Of course, the actual date is of little significance. After all, seeing something literally from out of the past is still incredibly bizarre, whether it dates back to 1770 or post-1774 when Marie Antoinette first came to the Petit Trianon.

In the final analysis, the hauntings of Versailles must be considered a puzzling mystery to this day.

HAUNTED HOUSES

Few ghost stories are more terrifying or bone-chilling than those of spooky addresses… because a ghost in the house can strike anyone at anytime. Even now, some of the most notorious haunted houses in history remain legendary.

Today, the site at 50 Berkeley Square is not unlike other buildings in that fashionable area of inner London. Now a bookstore, with its stately elegance intact, it was once a grand old home, and even the residence of short-term Prime Minister George Canning, who owned it until his death in 1827. But 100 years ago, young children would cross the street to avoid it. Women, and even men, would walk quickly past it, lest some unseen force somehow reach out onto the street and grab them. All over the capital, people feared and loathed the site as a place of evil and malevolence.

Fifty Berkeley Square, you see, was said to be haunted! And not just by some ghostly apparition that occasionally moaned or rattled the pots and pans, but by a real evil – a murderous malevolence so ghastly that as many as four people were said to have been literally scared to death by the very sight of it, while others were driven to total insanity, unable to ever fully explain what had so terrified them.

The story of 50 Berkeley Square begins in 1859, when a Mr Myers took over the house. According to reports at the time, the poor man was left standing at the altar by his one true love and from that day on he shunned society and turned into a bitter, cynical recluse, rarely seen in public or even outside the house. The story goes that he moved all his belongings into a cramped, tiny room in the garret, and would see no one except his manservant who brought him his daily meals. At night, however, while the rest of London slept or partied into the late hours, Mr Myers would mournfully walk the cobwebbed corridors of the house, his way lit by a single candle. Over the years, as he became even more eccentric, the once-proud house fell into disrepair, its windows caked with thick black dust and grime.

In 1873, when Mr Myers failed to pay his local taxes, he was summoned to appear before the city council. But the weird loner steadfastly refused to even answer it. Despite his refusal, however, local officials decided not to take the matter any further – because they had heard the house was haunted and felt sympathy for the wretched man so unhinged by his unrequited love. Matters grew steadily worse for Mr Myers and within six years the house had become so notorious that London newspapers began writing articles on it and its strange legend. After Myers' death, terrified neighbours claimed they could still hear loud thumps, moans and sobbing coming from inside, and some reports claimed that even pieces of furniture would inexplicably move around the house.

One of the many tales surrounding the origins of the 50 Berkeley Square haunting tells of a young child who was either tortured or frightened to death in the house's nursery. The tot's forlorn ghost, still sobbing and wearing a plaid skirt, is said to make periodic appearances. Another story claims that the ghost is actually that of a young woman, who shared the house with her lascivious, miscreant uncle. In a final, desperate attempt to at last free herself of his immoral advances, the young woman is said to have thrown herself from a window on the top floor to her death. For some time afterwards, people in the neighbourhood claimed to have seen her ghost, hanging on to the ledge, screaming for help. Eventually, there were so many sightings of various phenomena that the house actually became a tourist spot, so widespread was its infamy!

One of the most evil ghosts ever recorded in the annals of the paranormal lay in wait at number 50 Berkeley Square.

A CLUB OF SCEPTICS

But not everyone was ready to concede that it was haunted by unseen forces, and many believed that the cause of all the commotion could definitely be explained. Sir Robert Warboys was one such sceptic and, on a challenge from some fellow members of his club, he reportedly offered to spend a night inside the vacant house to prove that the bizarre tales of ghosts and evil were complete rubbish.

But the owner at this time, a Mr Benson, was reluctant to allow the bet to go ahead unless Sir Robert promised to take some precautions, including arming himself. Warboys good-naturedly agreed, and also took with him a bell Mr Benson had given him, which he could ring if anything went awry. Still, Sir Robert thought it all one big joke, and as he bade his friends good night, he scoffed at Benson nevertheless: 'My dear fellow,' he said, 'I am here to disprove the bunkum of a ghost, so your little alarm will be of no use. I bid you good night.'

With that, Sir Robert went upstairs. It was the last time anyone ever saw him alive. According to the story, all was well for the next 45 minutes. But suddenly, the little bell began to ring furiously from inside the bedroom. Then a shot was heard. People dashed up the creaky stairs, thrust open the bedroom door and found the limp body of Sir Robert sprawled across the bed. He had not been shot, but rather he is believed to have been literally frightened to death. His death mask was a face of sheer horror. His eyes bulged, and his mouth was frozen in twisted terror. His death only fuelled speculation that an intense evil lurked inside the house.

GUARANTEED PROTECTION

Not surprisingly then, the old house remained closed for some time afterwards until, in 1878, another well-heeled citizen, Lord Lyttleton, decided to follow in Sir Robert's footsteps by also daring to spend a night inside the haunted house. He, too, vowed to get to the bottom of the mystery and won permission from the new owner to spend a night in the very bedroom where Warboys had died some time before. But as a precaution, he took along with him two rifles which he had loaded with buckshot and silver sixpences, which folklore dictated would guarantee protection against whatever evil dwelt inside the room. During the course of that long, lonely night, Lyttleton got very little sleep as he tossed and turned, but once he did drift off he was suddenly awoken by a mysterious, grotesque shape that lunged at him from out of the dark. He managed to get off one shot at the apparition, which then vanished right before his startled eyes. Lyttleton was clearly shaken by his macabre experience, and wrote about his encounter in a book, *Notes and Queries*, which was published the following year.

SUPERNATURALLY FATAL

In it, the former sceptic conceded that 50 Berkeley Square was 'supernaturally fatal to mind and body'. For years afterwards, the aristocrat devoted much of his spare time to researching the macabre history of the house, and eventually located a woman who he said was driven insane after spending just one night inside the place. However, like so many others, Lyttleton could not determine why the ghost was so evil or what caused it to appear in such a hideous manner.

Another victim of that house of horrors was a new maid, whose terrifying ordeal was reported in *Mayfair* magazine. One night, after the household had long ago retired to bed, the owners were startled from their sleep by the maid's terrifying screams. They scrambled upstairs and entered her room, where they found her standing in the middle of her bedroom, 'rigid as a corpse, with hideously glaring eyes'. The poor girl was so overcome with terror, that she could not even utter a single word. She was taken to St George's Hospital, where doctors examined her and then asked her what had scared her so horribly. But the poor creature was too overcome to reply, and steadfastly refused to discuss the events of the previous night, saying only it was 'just too horrible' to describe. Her doctors never did get her to talk – because she died the very next day!

Yet another horrifying story of Berkeley Square concerns the macabre tale of two sailors, Edward Blunden and Robert Martin, who came to London on shore leave from the frigate HMS *Penelope*. It was Christmas Eve, and they had much trouble finding a room for the night. Freezing from the cold they eventually came upon 50 Berkeley Square, which was vacant at the time, so the seamen forced open a window and decided to sleep there. They came across a bedroom, which had been at the centre of all the previous sightings, and unwittingly bedded down for the night.

Blunden, however, had trouble falling asleep. He was nervous that someone might discover that they had broken into the house and summon the police to arrest them. He thought his fears had come true when he soon heard footsteps coming up the stairs. He was beside himself with panic, fearing that a policeman must have discovered the forced window and that he would be spending the night in a cold, damp jail cell.

He quickly woke Martin, and both heard the footsteps moving ever closer to the bedroom door. Then, the door opened, and both saw a hideous spectre coming towards them. Blunden quickly leaped to his feet, and made a grab for a heavy object resting on the nearby mantelpiece. He wasn't quick enough, however, and the ghost moved to stop him. As it did, Martin made his escape, running down the stairs and fleeing into the street. He was later found unconscious on the footpath, and after he was revived he told a passing policeman that he had seen an apparition, which he described as that of a white-faced man, his mouth agape in evil.

PANICKED INTO DEATH

The policeman was highly sceptical about the sailor's claims, but agreed to accompany Martin into the house to find his friend. When they arrived, they found Blunden's broken body sprawled on the basement stairs. His neck had been broken, and his eyes bulged in eternal horror. Apparently he had been so panicked by whatever he had seen that he had fallen down the stairs to his death. In the years since, many people have tried to explain the events inside 50 Berkeley Square, but no one has yet been able to offer convincing proof that the disasters that befell Warboys, the maid, Lord Lyttleton, the sailors and the others were not the work of some supernatural force.

In 1924, however, author Charles Harper wrote in his book, *Haunted Houses*, that one of the owners of the house, a Mr Du Pre, kept his mentally retarded brother imprisoned in the house. Mr Harper claims that the wretched lunatic was terribly violent, and given to frenzied bouts of sobbing and anger, in which he would throw objects about and scream with rage.

Borley Rectory is rightly called the most haunted house in England. Over the years, many residents have fled from it in mortal fear.

However, Harper's theory does not explain why the witnesses were never able to fully describe the monstrosity they had all seen. Nor does it explain why the house was so often put up for let. After all, who in their right mind would move into a house that came complete with a demented madman as a permanent guest in the upstairs room? Moreover, if both Sir Robert and Lord Lyttleton had shot at this insane prisoner, why was no blood ever found, let alone a body? And lastly, could any human being, no matter how deranged, literally frighten to death a knight of the realm and two of Her Majesty's servicemen? One can only answer with a resounding, 'No'.

Whatever strange disturbances occurred inside 50 Berkeley Square is a mystery which lasts to this very day. Fortunately for the new tenants, there have been no supernatural incidents reported at the site for many years.

BORLEY RECTORY

That is not the case with the Borley Rectory, with good reason called 'the most haunted house in England'. The Rectory, which lies some 60 miles north-east of London in the county of Essex, is a grotesque-looking building, isolated from surrounding houses by a lonely country road. The house, a gloomy red-brick monstrosity, has always had an eerie aura about it, and many visitors down through the years have remarked on its cold, forlorn appearance.

The Rectory was said to have been haunted from the very time it was built, in 1863, and down through the passing decades everyone who ever lived in the house and hundreds of visitors have all claimed that some supernatural force is at work inside.

A HAUNTED SITE

The first occupants were the Revd Henry Bull, who built it, and his wife and family. Even when they moved in, all were aware of the local legend that a monastery had once occupied the site, and that a monk had tried to elope with a nun from a nearby convent at Bures. According to the story, the ill-fated lovers were captured soon after they fled. The monk was hanged, and the poor nun bricked up alive inside one of the walls. Every 28 July, it was said, the lonely figure of a nun could be seen almost gliding along a path, forever searching for her long-dead lover. All four of the reverend's daughters saw the nun-like figure on 28 July 1900, and tried to speak with her. The apparition simply vanished into thin air. Numerous other people, including a local headmaster, also claimed to have seen the nun.

When the Revd Bull died in 1892 the Rectory was taken over by his only son, the Revd Harry Bull, who had also seen the nun. But there were many other mysterious intruders besides her. On many occasions, Harry Bull heard bells ringing with no possible earthly explanation, and he claimed to have seen and heard a phantom coach with horses. Once, he claimed to have seen the vehicle driven by two headless horsemen! Before his death in 1927 he told many people that he had no doubts that the place was indeed haunted.

For almost 12 months following his death, the Rectory remained vacant, largely because no fewer than 12 clergymen turned down the post and local folks avoided it as soon as nightfall approached. It was not until the Revd Eric Smith and his wife, both avowed non-believers in the paranormal, moved in in 1928 that the lights burned again inside the Borley Rectory. But soon after they arrived, their resolve weakened. They, too, began to see and hear strange, unexplainable things: Mrs Smith reported seeing the phantom coach and horses; lights inside the house would flick off and on by themselves; bells rang out; mysterious footsteps were heard. And on one occasion, Revd Smith said he heard a woman groan, then listened as she exclaimed: 'Don't, Carlos, don't!'

The church at Borley is said to have been haunted from when it was built, 130 years ago.

BLACK SHAPES

They also claimed to have seen black shapes wandering about the rooms and, on one occasion, they said that they saw the ghost of Revd Harry Bull! This is an astounding fact because sometime before his death, Harry said if he was not happy with his successor, he would come back to haunt the place.

The frightened couple finally decided that they had better get some professional help in to investigate the spooky occurrences, and soon famed ghost hunter Harry Price arrived on the scene to examine the paranormal happenings. Price quickly found volumes of evidence to support the Smiths' claims, including unexplained footsteps in the snow, terrified animals, knocks on doors and walls, objects flying about the rooms. Despite his assurances – or maybe because of them – that they were not imagining things, the Smiths had finally endured enough. One year after the sceptical couple first moved in, they were gone. But the ghosts remained!

In 1930, Revd Lionel Foyster and his wife Marianne arrived at Borley Rectory, and for the next five years, until they too left in panic, the hauntings not only continued, but increased in dramatic frenzy. Eerie messages – begging for 'Mass' and 'Prayers' – were found scrawled on pieces of paper and walls; Marianne was savagely struck across the eye by some invisible force; their three-year- old daughter, Adelaide, was locked in a room that had no key; objects were tossed violently around the rooms; bottles materialized from thin air, then vanished as they had appeared. Many of these paranormal phenomena occurred in the presence of witnesses, including a Justice of the Peace, a military officer and numerous other reliable spectators.

CONTINUED INVESTIGATIONS

Like the others before them, the Foysters eventually moved out and the Rectory was again vacant until 1937, when Harry Price decided to lease the site for 12 months so that he could continue his investigation into the dramatic hauntings. During the first few nights, he and a companion, Ellic Howe, drew circles in chalk around the bases of many movable objects in the Rectory. Each morning, the objects had somehow moved!

Gradually, Price gathered together a large team of investigators – at one stage there were 40 in all – who set up various experiments to try and record the ghosts' movements. This was to no avail, but in subsequent seances, Harry Bull appeared and told medium S.H. Glanville that the bodies of the monk and the nun had been buried on the site. In March 1938, another medium was told that the Rectory would burn to the ground that very evening, and that the hauntings would cease. Nothing happened, but it's interesting to note that indeed the place was gutted by fire in February 1939. By that time, Captain W.H. Gregson had owned the house for just three months. He was going through some books when a stack of them accidentally fell over, knocking an oil lamp to the ground.

Ghost hunters and researchers have flocked to the site at Borley Rectory looking for evidence of the paranormal.

SPOOKY REMAINS

However, shortly before the disaster, Revd Canon W.J. Phythian-Adams, who had recently read Price's book about the Rectory, discovered that a young French woman had been murdered at the site and that her remains were buried there sometime in the 17th or 18th century. At his suggestion, Price and his team excavated the cellar and found the remains of a long-departed young woman!

Towards the end of 1939, Dr A.J. Robertson organized yet another team of investigators to pore over the burned out remains of the Rectory. For the next five years, he and his team recorded more strange occurrences including inexplicable noises and rappings, stones thrown by an invisible hand, temperature changes which could not be accounted for by the prevailing weather and sightings of an eerie, incandescent patch.

Similarly, in recent years other reliable witnesses, including a headmistress, another rector and a Sunday school teacher, have all reported seeing or hearing evidence of the paranormal at the site. Organ music has been heard by many coming from inside the church, which is empty and locked; the nun has been sighted several times. One witness, who saw a female apparition in 1951, described the woman as sad and wearing a black hood, a white collar, a gold bodice and a long black skirt. Another witness, Peter Rowe, a retired official from the Bank of England, saw the nun running past the gate towards the former garden. Sightings of her have come as recently as the 1970s.

PECULIAR SMELLS

Incredibly, even though the Rectory itself is no longer still standing, peculiar smells can still be noticed emanating from where it once sat and the sound of furniture being moved about can also be heard. Others have reported hearing plates being smashed, while others have heard voices. The ghosts of Borley Rectory, it seems, are still at play.

A GHOST IN FLIGHT

Most encounters with ghosts occur in haunted houses or castles, but there is one remarkable story concerning a haunted passenger plane. This state-of-the-art commercial jet flew for many months with a very unusual passenger on board.

The ghost of Tri-Star 318 is as bizarre an apparition as anything to be found in the fog-cloaked graveyards or Gothic castles of England and France. Indeed, even a US government agency was unable to solve the mystery or explain what it was that many experienced airline crews had seen and heard. The first warning that something was amiss aboard Tri-Star 318 came in 1973, when Fay Merryweather, a senior stewardess of several years' experience and a respected member of the flight crew, was walking back towards the rear of the Eastern Airlines plane to prepare the lunch for the 180 passengers fleeing the snow of New York for the sun-baked beaches of Florida. But as she walked back into the galley to begin heating the food, she remembers feeling something – or someone – watching her every movement. She remembers feeling a little uneasy, then suddenly, she turned her eyes and saw it – the reflection of a face staring at her from the tinted glass door of the in-flight oven.

Merryweather remembered being shocked, but when she looked closer at the vision, she was somehow not frightened. The face wasn't some grotesque, contorted image. Instead, it was the one that looked worried! Then, the mouth began to move, but no sound came. The stewardess got the impression that it was trying to warn her about something. Not knowing what to do, she quickly but calmly walked up the cabin aisle to the cockpit, carefully ensuring she did not arouse the suspicion of her passengers, and informed the flight engineer of the strange sighting.

Puzzled, because he knew Merryweather to be an experienced flier and not one prone to fanciful hallucinations, the officer left the cockpit and his bank of instruments and followed her back to the galley to take a look himself. When he looked into the oven door, not only was the disembodied face still there – but the startled engineer recognized it! It was Don Repo, a former colleague who had died 12 months earlier in a tragic plane crash that occurred over the Florida Everglades! As both stared at the image in disbelief, they heard it whisper: 'Beware! Beware! Fire in the jet!' Strangely, there was nothing amiss on board the Tri-Star that day, but the ominous warning was to come true three months later on another Eastern Airlines flight.

A PUZZLING APPARITION

The puzzling apparition forced officials and Eastern Airlines crew members to recall that devastating night some months earlier, when tragedy struck the airline. Rep, an engineer, and pilot Bob Loft were killed along with more than 100 passengers while on the same run between New York and Florida on the night of 29 December 1972. The plane was a new Lockheed L-1011, or Tri-Star, the pride of the Eastern fleet and one of the most sophisticated planes then plying the skies over America. It was the first of the new generation of wide-body 'jumbo jets' to crash. The death toll at the time was the highest of any one-plane accident in United States' civil aviation history, and its downing made headlines around the world.

According to the lengthy, official investigation into the horrible crash of Flight 401, the trip had been routine for most of the way. Indeed, with Miami in sight, Captain Loft had announced cheerfully to his passengers and crew: 'Welcome to sunny Miami', as the plane passed over the city. 'The temperature is in the low 70s, and it's beautiful out there tonight.'

But as Captain Loft made the remarks, Repo went through the pre-landing motions, activating the sign instructing passengers to fasten their seat belts, then flicking the switch which would lower the wheels. It was then that the cockpit crew noticed that the square green light on the control panel which should have indicated that the nose wheel was locked and secured into position had failed to come on.

Captain Loft immediately put the Tri-Star on automatic pilot to circle, while Repo scurried to an observation point to see whether or not the nose gear had activated. As he did, Loft then decided to see if the problem was not merely a faulty indicator light. The captain guessed, correctly as it turned out, that the nose wheel was all right and locked into position and that the light was faulty. However, he still called off the landing and flew away from other airport traffic to make certain. After that, everything seemed to go wrong. Tragically, Captain Loft somehow bumped the automatic pilot switch into the 'off' position while he continued to check his panel – and neither he nor Repo realized the error until the plane was plummeting into a swamp.

There was nothing they could do, because unavoidable disaster was just seconds away. The left wingtip hit first, and the jet ploughed into the murky waters of the Everglades, leaving 101 people dead, and 75 lucky survivors. Initially, both Repo and Loft survived the horrific crash. Unfortunately, Loft died about 60 minutes later, still trapped inside the doomed cockpit, while Repo, who paramedics say seemed terribly angry when they pulled him from the smoking wreckage, lingered for more than a day before finally succumbing to his extensive injuries.

An Eastern Airlines Tri-Star… identical to the one that became known as a ghost plane.

DEATH COMES CALLING

Angelo Donadeo, an Eastern Airlines technical specialist on L-1011 aircraft, was returning to Miami that night from a trouble-shooting assignment in New York and remembers it well. Although he was a passenger, he rode in the cockpit with Loft, Repo and co-pilot A. Stockstill, who was also killed. 'That wasn't my first brush with death,' Donadeo recalled many years later. 'I was wounded in World War Two when the ship I was on was hit by a kamikaze. I had first, second and third degree burns all over my body. That doesn't haunt me either. I don't see any reason to worry about what fate has brought. I don't question what the Lord does.' According to the records, Flight 401 flew into the ground just 18 minutes before midnight, crashing into the Everglades 18 miles north-west of the airport.

A survivor, Richard Micale, told local reporters that it had all happened so quickly. 'I remember thinking "Shit! The plane's crashing," and before I got finished thinking it, it was over. You could hear the cry of death. Funny how people scream for God at a time like that. I probably did too, I'm sure.'

STUNNING STORIES

Witnesses recall that there was a huge flash of flame as two fuel tanks burst open, sending burning bodies and debris flying into the air and into the alligator-infested waters. Richard Marquis, a carpet-layer, was out that night on his airboat catching frogs with a friend, Ray Dickens. They headed towards the flash, and saw the lights of rescue helicopters, circling and searching over the black lagoon.

The scattered wreckage of Flight 401 which went down on a landing approach outside Miami International Airport in December 1972: months later strange events began.

They were much too far to the east and south, Marquis recalled, so he began to wave his headlamp in circles, guiding the rescue pilots to the crash site. Afterwards, he and his friend spent most of the night taking doctors and paramedics to the injured, and the injured to the levee where the helicopters were landing to whisk them away to the nearest hospitals.

Following the lengthy investigation, which took several weeks, maintenance crews managed to salvage parts of the doomed airliner, which were then installed into other Tri-Star craft. The galley was installed into Tri-Star 318, where stewardess Merryweather and the flight engineer encountered Repo's ghost. Although his warning of a fire never eventuated on that flight to Florida, it did come true three months later, when the plane was forced to turn back with engine trouble on a trip from Mexico to New York.

Repairs were ordered and, when completed, the Tri-Star was sent up on a routine test flight to check the servicing. Just as the pilot edged the nose into the air, one of the engines suddenly burst into flames. The official report issued some weeks later found that if it had not been for the experience and professionalism of the crew, the plane would have crashed.

THE CAPTAIN'S GHOST

Later, on another flight, Captain Loft's ghost was sighted. The plane was filled with Eastern Airlines' staff, returning to their home base in Florida from various destinations around the United States. Among those aboard was an off-duty pilot and a senior airline executive, who sat next to each other. Not long into the flight, the two men began chatting, and when the executive turned to look at his fellow passenger, he recoiled in horror – for sitting next to him was Captain Loft, who had been dead for more than 12 months! (Oddly, the third member of the flight crew of flight 401, First Officer Stockstill, was never seen.) The executive let out a scream, and a host of fellow workers and stewardesses rushed to his aid. They found him ashen and shaking – and the seat next to him very much empty. A short while later on yet another flight, Captain Loft appeared again, still dressed in his captain's uniform, sitting in the first class section of the plane. A stewardess came over to him, and asked why he did not appear on her passenger list. When he didn't reply, she went to see the captain, who accompanied her back to the first class cabin. He immediately recognized Loft, who then suddenly vanished into thin air right before their eyes.

There were several more sightings of the doomed fliers. A stewardess on another flight saw Repo's face appear on a luggage locker, while another spotted Loft near the bulkhead. In all, there were more than 20 sightings. One of the last came in 1974, when a pilot was conducting his routine pre-take-off check for a flight to Georgia.

As he inspected the complex bank of dials before him, the face of Dan Repo appeared. But this time, there were no warnings of near-disasters. Instead, the face whispered that he had already made the inspection, then added: 'There will never be another crash on an L-1011. We will not let it happen.' The voice had used the Lockheed serial number of the Tri-Star jet.

Still others claim to have had eerie encounters with the dead aviators. Some say they heard Repo's voice coming in over the public address system, while a few passengers say they felt inexplicable sudden rushes of cold air. During one haunting, in which Repo appeared yet again in the galley, he repaired an oven that had a circuit dangerously close to overloading. When the engineer assigned to the flight came to investigate the problem, he told the stunned air stewardess that he was the only engineer on the plane. Later, she looked up Repo's photo from his employment file and positively identified him as the man who had fixed the errant oven.

By this time the rash of apparitions had begun to worry crew members, but Eastern Airlines executives remained sceptical. Also, they didn't want the ghost stories made public, for fear that they could seriously erode the airline's passenger business. Those who reported seeing or hearing either Repo or Captain Loft were often urged to see a company psychiatrist, which was seen as the stage before getting fired. Eventually, however, as the number of sightings grew, Eastern management, which had no idea what could be causing the hauntings, called in an employee with devout religious leanings, and asked his advice. The man knew there could be just one way to rid the Tri-Star of its high-flying ghosts – an exorcism, which he did by splashing holy water about the plane. It worked, because the ghosts of Repo and Loft were never seen again. They were finally at rest – or so it seemed. Shortly afterwards, details of the sightings were forwarded to the Flight Safety Foundation, which oversees airline safety in the United States. Its report, issued several weeks later, concluded: 'The reports were given by experienced and trustworthy pilots and crew. We consider them significant. The appearance of the dead flight engineer in the galley door was confirmed by the flight engineer. Later, records at the Federal Aviation Agency record the fire which broke out in that same aircraft. We published reports of the ghost sightings in our safety bulletin issued to airlines in 1974.'

But the Flight Safety Foundation never offered an explanation of the eerie apparitions, and to this day the hauntings remain a complete mystery.

Interestingly, some locals also claim to have seen the ghosts of some of those who died on Flight 401 roaming the Everglades late at night. Sadie Messina, whose husband was aboard the doomed craft, had a terrible premonition as she waited at the gate for the plane that would never arrive. 'My husband always had a distinctive little whistle, a code whistle,' she said.

'When I heard that whistle, I knew he was home. We were waiting at the gate, my two sons and I, and I heard his whistle. It sounded like he was right behind me. I turned around to look, but, of course, he wasn't there.' Sadie swears she heard the whistle at precisely the time Flight 401 crashed. Her husband, Rosario Messina, was among the dead.

Further, a secluded strip of land just outside Miami, which was once targeted to house the world's largest airport, is also said to be home to Don Repo's ghost. In 1969, it was envisioned as a massive hub for SSTs and 747s, but today it is a windswept piece of prairie, used for training airline pilots. But locals say that they have had several reports of his ghost in the area!

The bizarre hauntings remain a mystery to this very day.

HAUNTED U-BOAT

It was the ghost from which there was no escape, the ghost that had its victims trapped – the ghost of U-boat 65. For the submariners in the German navy, a posting onto that submarine was almost as terrifying as coming under attack from the enemy.

Almost two years into the Great War, the battlefields of France and Belgium were literally running red with blood. Hundreds of thousands of young men were dying, an entire generation consigned to the mud and mayhem of trench warfare along the Western Front. The conflagration was so evenly matched that victories were measured in mere yards. Neither side could muster the reserves for that one decisive thrust to punch through the other's defences, and the war developed into a grotesque stalemate – except that in this case, the pawns were the young men of England, Germany and France.

The only breakthrough in the war, it seemed, might come at sea where, by the summer of 1916, the Kaiser's navy, led by the wolf packs of U-boat submarines, was beginning to take a heavy toll on British shipping. Hundreds of thousands of tons were consigned to the bottom of the seas by the fast-moving U-boats. Particularly hard hit was the British merchant fleet, which carried supplies vital to the war effort in Europe.

The Kaiser and his navy warlords were convinced that this was the way to break the back of the British bulldog and so, with the war two years old, Germany was devoting much of its total war effort to producing more and more submarines to press the attack. That year, among the many U-boats which came down the assembly line ready for British blood was UB65, which would go down in naval lore as the host to at least one ghost, and the scene of many disturbing and tragic occurrences. Indeed, UB65 became so infamous, that even as the war raged on, its panic-stricken crew grew increasingly reluctant to sail on her.

Even before she was launched, the 'Iron Coffin' as she became known, seemed to attract disaster. She was built to join a fleet of submarines prowling off the Flemish coastline, gorging on the slow, heavily laden ships crossing back and forward across the English Channel. But it seemed that everything that could go wrong during construction, did.

A HORRIFYING END

Not even seven days into her construction, as the hull was being laid, the first tragedy struck. As workers poured over the site, a giant girder hovering overhead on chains suddenly broke free, plunging into the hull. A hapless worker was horribly crushed under its massive weight, and lay there, in agony, for over an hour while frantic mates tried to rescue him. Tragically, he died just as the huge weight was finally lifted off him. An inquiry into the accident found there had been no faults in the chains used to hoist the girder, and officials were mystified as to what could have caused it to snap free.

Less than two months later, there was a second, more alarming tragedy. Three engineers who were assigned to the U-boat's engine room to test the submarine's dry-cell batteries, were overcome by deadly chloride fumes. They died before anyone could rescue them and drag them into the fresh air. No one ever determined why the batteries leaked the toxic fumes.

Thankfully, there were no more mysterious incidents during the remaining construction and shortly afterwards UB65 set sail for sea trials. But whatever dogged the boat seemed to follow it out of port because it quickly ran into a fierce Channel storm, and one hapless sailor was washed overboard to his death when the vessel came up to test her stability on the surface during rough seas.

After the man went overboard, the captain ordered the U-boat to dive. As she did, a ballast tank sprang a leak, flooding the dry-cell batteries with sea water and filling the engine room with the same deadly gas that had already claimed three lives while the boat was still on the slipway. After 12 nerve-racking hours the crew finally managed to get the ship to surface, where they flung open the hatches and breathed clean air. Amazingly, no one was killed, and the bedevilled craft limped back to Germany for repairs.

After several days, the U-boat was again readied for sea and her first on-line patrol. But as a battery of torpedoes was being placed on board, a warhead suddenly exploded, killing the second officer and badly wounding several others. Yet again, an inquiry was conducted, but no explanation for the explosion was ever found. In the meantime, the second officer was buried, and another round of repairs made to the jinxed vessel. Her jittery crew, already worried about the U-boat's growing reputation for being accursed, were given a few days' much-needed shore leave to calm their shattered nerves before setting out on their first active patrol.

A GHASTLY APPARITION

Yet just moments before she was set to leave port, another bizarre incident occurred – this time, a panicked sailor swore he had seen the apparition of the dead second officer. 'Herr Kapitan!' he blurted. 'The dead officer is on board!' The captain, of course, refused to take the report seriously, believing the sailor had had too much to drink during his shore leave. However, even the stoic skipper was a little taken aback when a second member of his crew also claimed to have seen the ghost of the second officer coming casually up the gangplank! The seaman was sobbing from fear when he told the captain that the apparition had walked aboard, strolled up to the bow, then looked out at the inviting sea. He then vanished into thin air.

That two crew members had reported seeing the dead officer gave the captain some reason for pause, but nevertheless he knew his duty lay at sea and in sinking British ships. UB65 had some early successes on its maiden voyage, sinking three Allied merchant ships in quick succession. However, the rumours of the unwanted ghost had spread through the crew like wildfire, and their celebration over any direct hits was tempered by their belief that their vessel was haunted.

When the Great War became bogged down on bloody battlefields, the Germans deployed more of their dreaded U-Boats.

STARTLED SAILORS

Indeed, there was almost full-scale panic after UB65 recorded its second kill, when startled sailors in the engine room saw the dead officer observing the instrument panel as he had done in the trial voyage. By the time the submarine returned to base, rumours of its ghostly visitor were already spreading throughout the entire U-boat armada. The captain did his best to dispel the talk, claiming it was all poppycock, fearing that the ghost tales would only further erode the morale of the 34-man crew. But in their hearts, the men of UB65 knew something was terribly amiss with their craft.

Then in January 1918, as the war dragged ever closer to its inevitable conclusion, even the captain could no longer dismiss the sightings as the rantings of some foolhardy seamen – for he, too, saw the apparition! It came as the U-boat was prowling in the Channel off Portland Bill. Because the weather was so foul and the seas extremely rough, the captain ordered the craft to surface. After breaking the surface, a lookout stationed on the starboard side was scanning the stormy horizon. He turned to look to port, when suddenly he spotted an officer standing on the deck, which heaved under the growing fury of the waves. At first, the crewman

U-Boat 65 was forced to limp back to harbour after another mysterious disaster. The submarine was bedevilled by tragedy and death.

thought the officer foolhardy for taking such a risk, but then realized that all the hatches were still battened down, bar the one from which he himself had climbed onto the deck. He knew no one could have come up through there without him immediately spotting him.

ALL-OUT PANIC

Suddenly, the crewman got a full look at the officer – and his face went white as the blood drained from it. There standing in front of him was the second officer, who had been buried with full honours back at home base. When he finally summoned the courage to move, the terrified seamen screamed to his shipmates that the ghost was on the boat. Below deck, the crew was close to all-out panic, and the captain had to act immediately lest a hysterical sailor put all their lives in jeopardy. He raced up the ladder, fully expecting to see nothing save a panicked crewman, when he, too, saw his dead comrade, his face a grotesque distortion. Seconds later, the ghost vanished, as if blown into the raging swell by the strong winds.

By the time the U-boat returned to port, navy authorities were already waiting. They were determined to get to the bottom of the mystery, fearing that the morale of the crew was so low that another disaster was just waiting to happen. With intense secrecy, each and every man assigned to UB65 was interviewed by a panel of high ranking officers.

The reader must remember that U-boat crews were among the most reliable and hardiest in the navy. They were subjected to long periods of confinement deep below the ocean surface, and had to withstand hours of nerve-racking pursuit by Allied destroyers. It was a fact that a submariner had only a 50-50 chance of ever returning from his mission, and that on a man-for-man basis, the U-boat force suffered the highest casualties of the war. So when these brave, innately fearless men, told navy officials that they were terrified of returning to their craft because of ghosts, then their story could not simply be dismissed as irrational rantings. And it wasn't. Although the Kaiser's sea lords could never admit to having a haunted ship – one could imagine the widespread effect on morale that would have on their other crews – they found the stories about the ghost of the dead second officer too convincing to simply laugh off or dismiss as the talk of overwrought sailors. Instead, they decided to break up the crew of UB65, sending some to other submarines and others to destroyers.

But that still left the problem of what to do with the vessel itself. Eventually, the U-boat was decommissioned at the port of Bruges, in Belgium, and a Lutheran pastor was asked to perform the ancient Christian rite of exorcism! In surely what must be one of the most incredible wartime scenes ever, a Belgian civilian was taken on board while German officers watched with a mixture of fascination and dread. Once the exorcism was completed, everyone breathed a sigh of relief.

A new crew and captain were assigned to the 'cleansed' ship, and it was business as usual for the next few weeks. The new skipper, a stern disciplinarian who scoffed at the stories of dead men walking the ship, warned his crew that he would not tolerate any renewed tales of ghosts or goblins. For the next two missions, it appeared as if everything was back to normal. There had been no sightings and no inexplicable accidents. But in May 1918, the ghost appeared again.

During the long voyage, in which UB65 was ordered to patrol the sea lanes off the Spanish coast as well as the English Channel, the dead officer was seen no fewer than three times. One of those who saw the ghost was the petty officer, who swore to God that he saw the man walk through a solid iron bulkhead and pass into the engine room! Another man, a torpedo handler, claimed the ghost visited him several times at night. The terrified soul became so disorientated that when the submarine surfaced to recharge its batteries, he leaped off the deck to his death in the seas.

On its final voyage – during July 1918, just four months before the Armistice was signed and peace returned to a ravaged Europe – the UB65 was spotted by an American submarine resting like a sitting duck on the surface. No one knows why. It was 10 July. The American sailors, who couldn't believe their good fortune, quickly armed their torpedoes and prepared to fire. But just before they did, the UB65 suddenly exploded, sending the remains of metal and men spewing out over a wide range of ocean.

Within seconds, all that remained of the submarine and her crew was a heavy oil slick and scattered debris. No one aboard the

American submarine ever gave the order to fire, and the crew swears no one launched a torpedo. What happened? To this day, no one knows. But it seemed a fitting, if bloody, end to the story of the haunted ship, which took its most enigmatic secret with it to its watery grave.

Just four months before the Armistice was signed, U-Boat 65 suddenly exploded – killing everyone aboard.

GHOST SHIP

Nothing strikes fear into a sailor as much as the sighting of a dreaded ghost ship, condemned to sail the world's oceans for all eternity. And of all the tales of accursed ships, none has remained as mysterious or as terrifying as that of the Flying Dutchman.

The *Flying Dutchman*, which was immortalized by the German writer Heinrich Heine and composer Richard Wagner in his opera, *Der Fliegende Hollander*, many years later, was a 17th-century brig that plied the sea lanes between Holland and the East Indies, at the centre of the lucrative spice trade. The full story of the ship's tortured journey through time was first recounted by the French writer, Auguste Jal, in about 1832.

In his book, Jal wrote that the vessel was rounding the Cape of Good Hope on its way to the East Indies, when it was struck by a frightful storm. The Dutch sea captain, a greedy, ill-tempered tyrant who was infamous for his cruelty, refused to listen to the pleas of his panicked crew who begged him to turn back for home lest the ship sink. But the captain only laughed at them and their terror, and he began singing blasphemous songs and drinking beer. As the raging storm worsened, it tore the sails and snapped the masts, leaving the *Flying Dutchman* completely at its mercy. But still the captain, now further emboldened by drink, laughed and ridiculed his terrified crew.

Then suddenly, at the height of the tempest, the clouds began to part, and a ghostly presence, said in Jal's account to have been God himself, appeared on the quarter deck for all to see. The crew were stricken with fright, but the evil captain began to blaspheme the presence when it offered safety.

'Who wants a peaceful passage?' the captain shouted. 'I don't. I'm asking nothing from you, so clear out of this unless you want your brains blown out.'

According to Jal, the ghostly presence just shrugged its shoulders, so the captain grabbed a pistol and fired a bullet into the spectre. But instead, the gun misfired, injuring the captain's hand. Angrily, he rushed towards the apparition, and went to strike it. But his arm went limp, as if paralysed. In his wild rage, the Captain began to curse and blaspheme even more 'and called the presence all sorts of terrible names'.

By now, the apparition had had enough and spoke gravely: 'From now on, you are accursed, condemned to sail forever. For you shall be the evil spirit of the sea. You will be allowed no anchorage or port of any kind. You shall have neither beer nor tobacco. Gall shall be your drink and red hot iron your meat. Of your crew, your cabin boy alone shall remain with you; horns shall grow out of his forehead, and he shall have the muzzle of a tiger and skin tougher than that of a dogfish.

'It shall ever be your watch, and when you wish, you will not be able to sleep, for directly you close your eyes, a sword shall pierce your body. And since it is your delight to torment sailors, you shall torment them. For you shall be the evil spirit of the sea. You shall travel all latitudes without rest, and your ship shall bring misfortune to all who sight her... And on the day of atonement, the Devil shall claim you.'

Then the presence vanished, leaving the captain alone, save for his cabin boy, who by now had the horns and the face of a tiger. From that moment on, Jal wrote, the *Flying Dutchman* was the bane of the seven seas, forever doomed to its miserable existence.

AN INFAMOUS INDIVIDUAL

Strangely, Jal never names the malicious and heretical captain, but history indicates that it may have been Cornelius Vanderdecken, who apparently had the same vile temper and cruel demeanour as that attributed to the unnamed skipper. Moreover, Vanderdecken frequently sailed the seas off Africa, and was known to pass the Cape of Good Hope every four to six months. He was also notoriously greedy, and never let the safety of his crew stand in the way of making good time. And he was notorious for his blasphemous language.

Likewise, another Dutch captain, Bernard Fokke, has also been linked with the legend of the doomed ship. Like Vanderdecken, Fokke, too, was a foul-mouthed despot, who often made the passage between Holland and the East Indies in 90 days, regardless of the weather or the mutterings of his crew. Interestingly, Fokke was also accused of making a pact with the Devil to ensure his trips were speedy. Eventually, there was a falling out between the two, and Fokke was said to have been damned for all eternity.

Of course, it doesn't really matter which of the two brutes was at the helm of the *Fying Dutchman*. After all, say the sceptics, the very idea of a ship being condemned by God or the Devil is proof enough that the entire legend is nothing but a joke or a story to frighten young children. But upon further examination, it becomes clear that while Jal must have embellished the story, there is ample evidence to suggest that there is much more to the *Flying Dutchman* story than just myth. It cannot simply be dismissed - because a vessel matching its description has been seen by sailors all over the world, and many of those ships which have come into contact with it have been hit by a bizarre spate of mysterious mishaps.

Indeed, it was once even seen by the future King of England! In July 1881, Prince George, who would later become King George V, was serving as a midshipman aboard HMS *Inconstant*, a heavily armed frigate and one of Her Majesty's most modern ships.

On 11 July, his log would recount, the ship was sailing between Melbourne and Sydney when suddenly he and 12 other crew members noticed an eerie light coming from over the horizon.

In his private journal, the Prince wrote: 'At 4 a.m. the "Flying Dutchman" crossed our bows. A strange red light, as of a phantom ship all aglow, in the midst of which light the mast, spars and sails

The crew of a whaling ship, the **Orkney Belle,** *saw the* **Dutchman** *off the frigid seas of Iceland.*

of a brig two hundred yards distant stood out in strong relief as she come up on port bow. The look-out man on the forecastle reported her as close on the port bow, where also the officer of the watch from the bridge clearly saw her, as did the quarterdeck midshipman, who was sent forward at once to the forecastle; but on arriving there, no vestige nor any sign whatever of any material ship was to be seen either near or right away to the horizon, the night being clear and calm. Thirteen persons saw her.'

UNEXPLAINED TRAGEDIES

Incredibly, the so-called 'curse' of the *Flying Dutchman* soon followed. The seaman who had first reported seeing the vessel fell from the top mast to his death later that very same day. Then, a few days later, the Admiral of the Fleet also died, and many of the crewmen became gravely ill. It was never fully explained why.

There have been numerous other sightings recorded throughout the years. A full 15 years before the young Prince reported seeing the haunted ship, those aboard the American vessel, the *General Grant*, had an equally horrible encounter with the doomed Dutchman. In early May 1866, the *General Grant* left port in Melbourne for the long voyage to England. Everything seemed routine for the first two weeks, until the winds slackened, sending the *Grant* drifting helplessly away from the normal shipping lanes. On 13 May, the ship was pulled by the currents towards Auckland Island, a dismal, rocky outcrop in the middle of nowhere. The *Grant* was driven along the coastline until it was eventually forced into a huge cave. Its masts scraped along the top of the cavern, sending a shower of rocks crashing onto its deck. Almost miraculously, no-one was injured, but the seafarers' ordeal wasn't over yet.

Because of its position, the cave was subjected to sudden onrushes of waves, which forced the *Grant* deeper and deeper into its bowels. Eventually, the masts became so wedged that one of them was forced through the hull.

The *Grant* began to take on water and, in a panic, some of the 46 passengers dived overboard to their deaths.

Those who remained joined the crew in frantically lowering three lifeboats. Unfortunately, one of the lifeboats was then dashed against the rocks and broke up. All but three of the 40 people aboard were killed. Those in the other two boats, 14 in all, were luckier. They made it out of the cavern, and decided to row towards nearby Disappointment Island.

After a break, they continued their slow journey to the Auckland Islands, where they lived a desperate existence for more than 18 months until they were rescued by another vessel.

According to accounts of the time, the *General Grant* was actually lured to disaster by the spectre of the *Flying Dutchman*. As the ship drifted helplessly in the still winds another ship, said to be the *Dutchman*, suddenly appeared on the horizon and led the *Grant* to its watery grave.

The crew of the whaling steamer *Orkney Belle* also had an eerie experience. This one took place in January 1911, as the *Orkney Belle* ploughed through the frigid seas off the coast of Iceland.

A second mate later recounted the sighting to the London *Daily News*: 'The captain and I were on the bridge and a thin mist swirled over everything. Suddenly, this thin mist thinned out... to our mutual horror and surprise, a sailing vessel loomed up virtually head on.

'I rammed the helm hard aport and we seemed to escape the collision by a hair's breadth. Then, with startling suddenness, old Anderson, the carpenter, bawled out: 'The Flying Dutchman'.

'The captain and I scoffed at him, for we thought that oft-fabled ship existed in the minds of only superstitious sailors.

'As the strange vessel slowly slid alongside within a stone's throw, we noticed with amazement that her sails were billowing, yet there was no wind at all. She was a replica of a barque I once saw in a naval museum. Meantime, practically all the crew rushed to the ship's side, some in terror, but unable to resist their curiosity. Not a soul was to be seen aboard this strange vessel, not a ripple did her bows make.

'Then, like a silver bell, so sweet was the tone, three bells sounded, as if from the bows of the phantom ship, and as if in answer to a signal, the craft heeled to starboard and disappeared into the fog...'

A GHOSTLY APPARITION

The second mate's story echoes that of dozens of others, some of whom claim to have seen the ghostly ship well into the 20th century, still sailing aimlessly across the seven seas.

In January 1923, its apparition appeared off the Cape of Good Hope and was seen by at least four veteran seamen. One of them, N.K. Stone, later wrote of the encounter: 'At about 0.l5 a.m., we noticed a strange "light" on the port bow… it was a very dark night, overcast, with no moon. We looked at this through binoculars and the ship's telescope, and made out what appeared to be the hull of a sailing ship, luminous, with no distinct masts carrying bare yards, also luminous; no sails were visible, but there was a luminous haze between the masts.

'There were no navigation lights, and she appeared to be coming close to us and at the same speed as ourselves.

'When first sighted, she was about two to three miles away, and when she was about a half-mile of us, she suddenly disappeared. There were four witnesses of this spectacle, myself, the second officer, a cadet, the helmsman and myself. I shall never forget the second officer's startled expressions – "My God, Stone, it's a ghost ship".'

Later, during World War Two, there were numerous sightings, and even Germany's Grand Admiral Karl Donitz admitted 'that certain of my U-boat crews claimed they saw the *Flying Dutchman* or some other so-called phantom ship on their tours of duty east of Suez. When they returned to their base, the men said they preferred facing the combined strength of Allied warships in the North Atlantic to knowing the terror a second time of being confronted by a phantom vessel.' Even Hitler's 'supermen' were afraid of ghosts!

Incredibly, the *Flying Dutchman* has also been seen by people fortunate enough to be on dry land when the eerie apparition appeared. In 1939, more than 100 startled swimmers at South Africa's Glencairn Beach in False Bay, near the Cape of Good Hope, claimed to have seen the *Dutchman* at full sail gliding gently across the water, even though there was no discernible wind that day. The stunned bathers were mystified at the sight, but when it suddenly vanished, they were absolutely baffled.

Three years later, this time near Cape Town, a South African family was relaxing on the terrace of their ocean-front home when they watched as an old sailing ship passed by them. All four of them later said that they viewed the ship for more than 15 minutes, until it vanished, leaving behind only a bright glow in its wake.

Since then, there has been at least one more sighting. In 1957, again off the coastline of South Africa, a group of people reported seeing an old vessel drifting eerily across the horizon, only to disappear without trace.

Of course, not every claimed sighting of the *Dutchman* can be taken at face value. The oceans, particularly at night, can play tricks on tired eyes and nervous dispositions. But in the end, there are just too many credible sightings – many by respectable men like Prince George, other Royal Navy officers and German U-Boat commanders – to simply reject the story of the *Flying Dutchman* out of hand. The mystery, like the ghost ship itself, will most likely go on forever.

King George was just one of many distinguished persons who have come across the haunted vessel.

While the *Flying Dutchman* is the most notorious of all shipbound ghost stories, it is by no means the only one. Consider the case of the large American vessel, the *St Paul*, which was involved in two tragic accidents, including a disastrous collision with the British cruiser, HMS *Gladiator*. Even today, the story of the *St Paul* continues to mystify, and dozens of 'earthly explanations' have been dismissed.

It was Thursday, 25 April 1918. The Great War was still waging across Europe, and America, which by now had thrown its full military muscle into the all-out conflict against the Kaiser's Germany, was busy refitting its cruise line ships into troop transport vessels. One such ship was the *St Paul*, a massive steamer which had once been the pride of the America Fleet. Early that morning, when the lengthy conversion work had been completed, the vessel set steam from its mooring at the Brooklyn docks for the short sail to Pier 61 on the Hudson River, on the west side of Manhattan. As the ship swung into the Hudson, Captain A.R. Mills noticed she was listing slightly to her port side.

The ghost ship has been blamed for several bizarre mishaps over the years, including shipwrecks.

250

Even Hitler's 'supermen' were terrified of the **Flying Dutchman***.*

AN UNEXPLAINED INCIDENT

He gave it little thought, however, assuming the crew were still filling the ballast tanks. When the ship approached the pier, two cables leading from the bow and the stern were thrown to the dock and secured. But as the *St Paul's* giant winches began to pull in the cables, the vessel began to list further. Suddenly and inexplicably, tons of water began to pour into her lower decks, forcing the boat onto her side, her towering masts scraping along the pier. Men began pouring over the sides, but fortunately, several tugs and a number of barges were close by, and rescued hundreds as they scrambled to safety. The incident could have been a major disaster if not for that stroke of good luck, and as a result, just four of the 400 men aboard were lost.

Initially, the investigation into the accident centred on German sabotage, but it was quickly ruled out. So, too, were dozens of other theories offered by everyone from old salts to the local newspapers. The real cause, however, was a shocker – when divers were sent into the river, they found that one of the ash ports close to the water line had not been closed! Every member of the crew was quizzed by the investigators, yet no-one was ever blamed for the error and to this day, the mystery of the open port has never been solved.

However, there was one other possibility – it might have been the sinister ghost of a dead sailor! To those who believe this to be the case, the timing of the disaster is the key. Because exactly ten years earlier – to the very day and to the very hour – the *St Paul* had been involved in a fatal collision with HMS *Gladiator*. Did a malevolent spirit choose that day, the tenth anniversary of the collision, to strike back? The accident involving the British cruiser occurred off the still waters of Southampton, when the *St Paul* was still a passenger liner.

The fog was so heavy that the two ships remained invisible to each other until they were less than half a mile apart. Once it was realized that a disaster was about to strike, Captain Walter Lumsden ordered evasive action, as did the pilot of the *St Paul*. Tragically, there was a miscalculation. Captain Lumsden ordered his ship hard-a-starboard, which left the *St Paul* heading directly towards her. A few minutes later, the inevitable occurred, as the mighty steamer ripped into the cruiser's starboard side. Twenty-seven of her crew were lost. At the inquiry that followed, Captain Lumsden was severely reprimanded by an Admiralty court martial, even though many considered his actions to have been the correct ones given the circumstances that day.

As we said earlier, ten years later to the hour of the disaster, an unseen hand opened the ash port aboard the *St Paul*, sending her to the bottom of the Hudson river. Mere coincidence?

POLTERGEISTS AND THE PARANORMAL

HEARTS ON FIRE

When John Heymer, a former detective with the Gwent police, entered the council house, he was sickened by the grisly scene that met his eyes. After conducting his investigations he was forced to a conclusion that risked making him a laughing stock…

In 1986, John Heymer, who had spent 25 years in the Gwent, Wales, police documenting minute details at the scenes of crimes, described the grisly scene that greeted him on 6 January 1980, when he investigated a mysterious death by fire in an Ebbw Vale council house:

'I opened the door [to the living room] and stepped into... a steamy, sauna-like heat... orange light emanated from a bare light bulb which was coated in a sticky, orange substance, as was the window... Heat had cracked one of the window panes.

'...On the floor, about one metre from the hearth, was a pile of ashes. On the perimeter of the ashes, furthest from the hearth, was a partially burnt armchair. Emerging from the ashes were a pair of human feet clothed in socks. The feet were attached to short lengths of lower leg, encased in trouser leg bottoms. The feet and socks were undamaged. Protruding from what was left of the trousers were calcined leg bones which merged into the ashes. The ashes were the incinerated remains of a man.

'Of the torso and arms nothing remained but ash. Opposite the feet was a blackened skull. Though the rug and carpet below the ashes were burned, the damage did not extend more than a few centimetres beyond the perimeter of the ashes. Less than a metre away, a settee, fitted with loose covers, was not even scorched. Plastic tiles which covered the floor beneath the carpet were undamaged.'

Heymer called in forensic scientists to confirm his suspicion that the victim had combusted spontaneously. They dismissed his proposal 'with knowing smiles', and suggested instead that the dead man had fallen into the coal fire in the room and ignited himself there. Heymer commented:

'Amazingly, the scientists saw nothing wrong in a man falling headfirst into a fire grate, igniting like a wax candle, then somehow picking himself out of the grate and sitting in his armchair to burn himself and most of his armchair to ash... the grate was tidy. It certainly did not indicate that anyone had fallen into the fire.'

A few weeks after this account appeared in the *New Scientist*, the journal published a letter from Dr Sidney Alford, who probably knows more about explosives than anyone else in the UK, and who offered a possible explanation of such cases of spontaneous human combustion:

'Anaerobic fermentation within the gut... produces sometimes prodigious quantities of inflammable gas; consumption of eggs, for example, which are especially rich in phospholipids, might well add to the normal methane and hydrogen significant amounts of phosphine, and, worse, phosphorus dihydride, thereby imparting to the gas the property of spontaneous inflammability – the dreaded phosphinic fart. (How many of your readers have attributed singed underpants and burning thighs to mere frustration or, while strolling on a warm summer night after a second soufflé, have observed their breath glowing?)'

Alford's conclusion was clear enough: the right combination of circumstances and body chemistry 'might explain the precocious burning away which John Heymer describes'.

BURNT TO CINDERS

The terrifying recurrence of spontaneous human combustion (SHC) – the hair-raising phenomenon in which a living person bursts into flames without warning or any sign of external ignition and is reduced to little more than a heap of ashes – has been the subject of fierce scientific debate for at least 300 years. Most scientists have regarded the very idea of SHC as ridiculous, and most medical textbooks omit any mention of it.

Yet hundreds of cases of mysteriously burned bodies have convinced the professionals on the spot – the firefighters and police – that nothing but spontaneous combustion could have caused the effects they have seen. Coroners are less easily persuaded, and many instances of SHC have been veiled by open verdicts. SHC is much more common than the official record would lead us to believe. Pathologist Dr David Price stated recently that he encountered a case roughly every four years.

Matters were not always so hedged about by fear of ridicule, as the literary record shows. There are nine famous allusions to SHC in pre-1900 fiction by distinguished authors, and there may well be more hidden in less celebrated works. The subject is mentioned in Washington Irving's *Knickerbocker History of New York* (1809); in Thomas de Quincey's 1856 revised edition of *Confessions of an Opium Eater*; and in Mark Twain's *Life on the Mississippi* (1883). Characters in Charles Brockden Brown's *Wieland* (1798) and Hermann Melville's *Redburn* (1849) succumb to a 'burning fiery death' without SHC being mentioned explicitly. SHC also features in Honoré de Balzac's *Le*

Cousin Pons (1847) and Emile Zola's *Le Docteur Pascal* (1893).

But the most detailed and revealing literary descriptions are based on real-life cases. Frederick Marryat used a London *Times* report of 1832 as the basis for his description of the death of the hero's mother, who is reduced to 'a sort of unctuous pitchy cinder', in *Jacob Faithful* (1833). The medical profession – when it deigned to notice SHC - regarded Marryat's description as a classic one, thanks to five 'typical' features: the victim was an elderly female; the victim was a chronic alcoholic; there was a lamp which might have started the fire; combustible materials in contact with the body were hardly burnt; and there was a residue of greasy ashes.

In *Bleak House* (1853), Charles Dickens killed off the sinister, alcoholic 'chancellor of the rag-and-bone department', Krook, by SHC. This fictional death echoes details of an inquest that Dickens attended 20 years earlier when he was a young reporter for the *Morning Chronicle*. Dickens was convinced of the reality of the phenomenon: in his preface, he bolsters his case for the plausibility of Krook's death by citing 30 press reports of death from SHC.

Charles Dickens, the 19th-century novelist, whose descriptions of spontaneous human combustion were based on real-life cases.

ACCUSED OF MURDER

The first medical writer to consider SHC was Thomas Bartholin, in *Acta*, published in Copenhagen in 1673. Then, in 1725, Nicole Millet was found burned to death in Rheims, in an armchair that remained unscathed by flames. Her husband was accused and convicted of her murder, but on appeal the court was persuaded that the death was a case of SHC. This inspired the scholar Jonas Dupont to gather together all the available evidence for SHC. His *De Incendiis Corporis Humani Spontaneis* was published in Leyden in 1763.

By the 19th century, Victorian moralists had concluded that SHC victims were invariably drunkards who had saturated their bodies with spirits – which were the source of the retributive flagration. Unfortunately, this theory is nonsense: such an unrestrained drinker would die of alcohol poisoning long before becoming flammable. As the sceptical investigator Joe Nickell puts it, 'alcohol may have indeed been a contributory factor [in deaths apparently due to SHC], although not in the way some nineteenth-century theorists imagined. A drunken person would be more likely to be careless with fire and less able to properly respond to an accident.'

The remains of a 65-year-old pensioner who died in a hayloft in Aberdeen, Scotland, possibly from spontaneous combustion.

But, as it happens, one of the first cases of apparent SHC, reported in the *Gentleman's Magazine* in 1746 and rehashed many times since, was of a woman not known for any close acquaintance with the bottle. She was the 62-year-old Countess Bandi, who burned to death near Verona in 1731. The sober noblewoman was reduced to a heap of ashes, though her legs and arms were untouched by fire. Despite the wealth of cases to choose from, the Bandi case, along with a handful of others (such as Grace Pett in 1744, Wilhelmina Dewar in 1908, Phyllis Newcombe in 1938 and Dr J. Irving Bentley in 1966), are repeated in nearly all the books and articles on SHC.

SELECTIVE DESTRUCTION

A strange feature of SHC deaths is the extraordinary speed with which the corpse – or what little may be left of it – decomposes once the flames have done their work. Another curiosity of such cases is the way that normally highly combustible furniture, linen and even clothing remains untouched by fire even though the victim's body – and the human body is one of the least flammable objects, consisting of about 75 per cent water – has been for the most part utterly destroyed.

This selective destruction is all the more mysterious given the intensity of heat needed to burn a human body. A crematorium furnace, for example, maintains temperatures of at least 1706°F in a forced draught. A temperature of around 3,000°F has to be maintained for several hours if there is no forced draught. But even a body burned in a crematorium fire at 2,000°F for over eight hours will still leave recognizable bones, whereas the bones of many SHC victims are reduced entirely to ashes. Furthermore, crematorium fires are fed by copious external supplies of fuel. What can fuel the burning of a human body in a case of SHC?

Sceptical investigators say that the progressive release of body fat, soaking clothing or bedding, acts like the wick of an oil-lamp to provide the fuel for the fire. Pathologist Dr David Gee of Leeds University showed in the mid-1980s how this process might occur. He coated a test tube with human fat, wrapped in human skin, to form a 'candle' 7–8 in long. He then wrapped cloth around it to simulate clothing. It took about a minute for a bunsen burner to ignite the 'candle', which then took about one hour to burn, the flame moving along the 'candle' against the direction of a draught from an extractor fan. But this demonstration proves nothing about cases in which people have apparently been burned to death when there is no external source of ignition, nor does it explain why they do not simply wake up early on in this grim process.

Researchers Vincent H. Gaddis (author of *Mysterious Fires and Lights*, 1967) and Ivan T. Sanderson (in *Investigating the Unexplained*, 1972) outline a possible sequence of events that might lead to SHC. This begins with loneliness, illness, or some similar emotional affliction that leads to a negative state of mind. This in turn affects the victim's metabolism in such a way that phosphagens, especially the vitamin B 10, build up in his or her muscle tissue. (Phosphagen is a compound like nitroglycerine, and is extremely combustible in certain circumstances.) Electricity generated by intense sunspots, magnetic storms – or, later researchers have suggested, electrical energies produced by geological activity – then triggers the combustion.

Research by Livingston Gearhart, published in the journal *Pursuit* in 1975, showed that a significant number of SHC events coincided with local peaks in the Earth's magnetism. It is possible that high geomagnetism contributes to the formation of ball lightning, which in turn can generate short radio waves similar to those used in microwave ovens and radar equipment. (The reason warning notices and high fences surround radar aerials sited in places accessible to the public is simply that if you get in the way of a powerful radar array while it is scanning, it will cook your liver while you wait. External burns take some time to appear.) Some SHC victims appear to have burnt from the inside outwards, as if they had been subjected to this kind of microwave radiation.

A less materialistic theory is that SHC is caused by the Manipura chakra (the body's 'fire centre', which oriental medicine and acupuncture locate in the solar plexus) somehow running out of control. An advanced yoga adept can stimulate this chakra so that he literally glows in the dark. In the Tibetan practice of tumo, adepts have been known to generate so much internal heat while in a state of trance that snow melts around them. And it has often been noted that SHC victims seldom cry out or struggle, as if they were in a trance.

ORDEAL BY FIRE

Sceptics have striven mightily – and sometimes with success – to provide rational explanations for cases of death by SHC, but such reasoning after an event that itself lacked witnesses is easier than accounting for the occasions when people have burst into flames and survived.

On 15 November 1974, travelling clothes-salesman Jack Angel stopped for the night in his mobile home at the Ramada Inn in Savannah, Georgia. He awoke the next day to find his right hand burned and blistered, and further burns on his chest, leg, groin, ankles and back. Despite this damage he had felt no pain, and his sheets and clothes were unmarked. He staggered into the motel

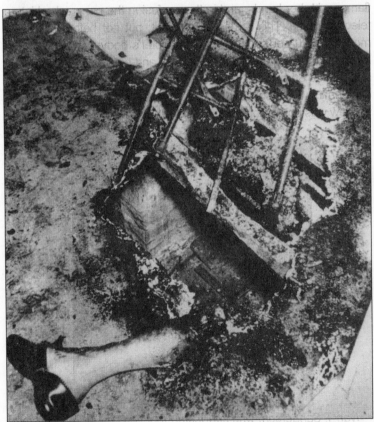

The remains of Dr John Irving Bentley, retired physician, who died on 5 December 1966 in northern Pennsylvannia, USA.

261

building and collapsed. When he woke again, he was in extreme pain, and in hospital. Doctors said the burns had begun inside his body, but did not explain how. As a result of his injury, Angel's burned hand and lower forearm had to be amputated. A Georgia law firm renowned for its success in product liability suits sued the makers of Angel's mobile home for $3 million damages – but after more than two years' investigation the cause of the fire remained elusive, even though the mobile home was dismantled down to its wheelbase in the search.

On 9 October 1980, Jeanna Winchester, then serving as an airwoman in the US Navy, was driving with a friend, Leslie Scott, along Seaboard Avenue in Jacksonville, Florida. Suddenly, yellow flames burst from Ms Winchester. Ms Scott tried to beat out the flames with her hands, and in the confusion the car crashed into a telegraph pole. The flames did die out, but not before scorching more than 20 per cent of Ms Winchester's body: burns disfigured her right shoulder and arm, neck, side and back, and her stomach and breast. She said later: 'At first I thought there had to be a logical explanation, but I couldn't find any, I wasn't smoking anything. The window was up, so somebody couldn't have thrown anything in. The

Ivan T. Sanderson, who suggested that SHC might result from an accumulation of certain extremely combustible compounds within the body, triggered by sunspots or magnetic storms.

car didn't burn.' Nor had gasoline been spilled inside the car, police had confirmed. 'I finally thought about spontaneous human combustion when I couldn't find anything else.'

In the spring of 1978, the all too aptly – named investigative journalist Harry Ashbrook had just visited the Royal Free Hospital in London's Hampstead to have a leg injury treated. He then went to the local Haverstock Arms to meet fellow-journalist Peter Kinsley for a drink. While they were sitting in the pub, Ashbrook suddenly let out a scream of pain and almost passed out. Smoke was pouring from his bandaged leg. Kinsley helped him to return to the Royal Free, this time to the emergency room, where baffled doctors found that although the bandage was untouched, something had burned a hole in Ashbrook's leg down to the bone. But for the victim's account, they said, they would have assumed that only a red-hot iron or a point-blank gunflash could have caused such damage.

Nineteen-year-old computer operator Paul Hayes, also a non-smoker, ignited without warning in the street in Stepney Green, east London, late at night on 25 May 1985. 'It was', he said, 'like being plunged into the heart of a furnace. My arms felt as though they were being prodded by red-hot pokers from my shoulders to my wrists. My cheeks were red-hot, my ears were numb. My chest felt like boiling water had been poured over it. I thought I could hear my brains bubbling. I tried to run, stupidly thinking I could race ahead of the flames.'

In the end, he lay on the ground and curled up in a ball. Half a minute later, the flames subsided as quickly as they had burst out. Hayes stumbled to the London Hospital, a few streets away, where he was treated for burns.

BLAZING ROWS

Spontaneous fires do not have solely human victims, although they may be associated with individual people. These cases are apparently a fiery form of poltergeist. In these, the focus of the outbreaks (often, but not always, a child) lives through a phase – often mercifully brief – during which they have the power to set nearby objects on fire. Some such cases lead one to think that there really is a cosmic punster at work behind the world's multifarious scenes. 'Blazing rows' seem to have marked a series of outbreaks associated with a Mrs Barbara Booley – who seems to have had a fiery temper – between 1971 and 1975. The first fire flared in August 1971 at the Berkeley Vale Hotel in Stone, Gloucestershire, after Mrs Booley had been sacked from her job as cook. The next broke out the following November, in a dormitory of St Hilda's School in Bridgwater, Somerset, where Mrs Booley was working, and had had a row 'with management' the day before. The third fire happened over Easter 1973 at Bath High School for Girls, Somerset. Mrs Booley said: 'Because I'd had a few words with a housemistress the previous day, police tried to pin the fire on me.' Fires numbers four, five and six erupted at the Swan Hotel, Tewkesbury, Gloucestershire, in August 1973. A parked car burst into flames in the hotel yard, and two days later flames broke out in a furniture storeroom. Mrs Booley left the hotel, and another fire broke out. The last reported incident was at the Torbay Hotel in Sidmouth, Devon. In early October 1975 Mrs Booley got the sack; the next day some bedding mysteriously caught light on a stair. Mrs Booley helped douse the flames, but was questioned once more by the police. She admitted that each blaze was preceded by an argument, but swore she did not set the fires. 'I wish I had been charged,' she said. 'Then I would be able to clear my name.'

Not all poltergeist-like fires are necessarily centred on anger. The talent, or affliction, of Benedetto Supino in this respect suddenly came to light in 1982. The son of a carpenter in Formia near Rome, Benedetto, then aged nine, was reading a comic in a dentist's waiting room when, unexpectedly and without visible assistance, it caught fire. One morning soon after this, Benedetto awoke to find his bedclothes on fire, and he was painfully burned. A plastic object held by his uncle burst into flames as Benedetto stared at it. Everywhere he went, furniture, fittings and objects smouldered.

Along with the fires came odd electromagnetic effects. Electrical equipment near Benedetto would function erratically and the power supply in his house failed several times. Top physicians and academics examined the boy without coming to any conclusions, while Archbishop Vincenzo Fagiolo pronounced the phenomenon 'not malign', to the relief of Benedetto's parents.

Another 'fire boy' made headlines in the Russian newspaper *Izvestia* in May 1987. In the presence of 13-year-old Sascha K, from Yenakiyevo in the Donets Basin of the Ukraine, clothes, furniture, carpets and electrical equipment had a tendency to burst into flames. The outbreaks, which resulted in over 100 fires, began in November 1986. He was taken to hospital for observation, and the clothing of a boy who shared his room suddenly caught fire. When Sascha was about, objects also flew in the air, and light bulbs would explode.

Lightning. Sceptics implausibly claim this to be the cause of some SHC cases.

Perhaps the most famous 'fire-prone' person of recent years is the Scottish nanny Carole Compton, tried in Italy in 1983 for arson. On 2 August 1982, Carole, then aged 20, from Aberdeen, was arrested and held in jail in Livorno accused of trying to murder Agnese Cecchini, the three-year-old Italian child for whom she was employed as nanny, by setting fire to her cot. There had been a similar fire the previous night in the girl's grandfather's bedroom. On both occasions Carole was dining with the family, well away from the source of the fires. The girl's superstitious grandmother accused Carole of starting fires by using the 'Evil Eye'.

The trial opened in Livorno on 12 December 1983. Mrs Ricci, who had previously employed Carole, spoke of the nanny's obvious unhappiness both in her work and in her love affair with an Italian conscript. There had been unexplained fires in the household, and she said that her maid Rosa had complained of Madonnas falling off walls, an electric meter spinning while Carole was near it, and vases smashing off tables. Mrs Ricci's two-year-old son used to cry out that Carole was burning him whenever she touched him. All these are classic symptoms of poltergeist activity.

Nonetheless, Carole was found guilty of arson and attempted murder, and was sentenced to two and a half years in jail. She was, however, released immediately as she had already spent 16 months inside awaiting trial. She was back in Aberdeen the next day. The verdict was perhaps inevitable; it avoided the embarrassment of locking up a woman for witchcraft or of admitting her paranormal ability to start fires.

Fire damaged this building in Brazil at the height of a spate of poltergeist activity there.

REPRESSED SEXUAL TENSION

There are numerous cases in the records of houses becoming affected by apparently spontaneous fires. On 6 August 1979, the Lahore family saw smoke pouring from an abandoned farmhouse on their property in Seron, in the Hautes-Pyrénées, France. The fire was put out but, within two hours, two more broke out, this time in the family's modern farmhouse, which stands opposite the old one. In the month that followed, there were about 90 mystery fires in the house. For a while, 20 gendarmes camped near the farm but, despite a round-the-clock vigil, they neither saw nor apprehended any arsonists. One day, 32 separate fires sprang up within the house, burning towels, sheets, clothes and furniture. First there would be the smell of smoke; then an object would be found with a circular charred spot, which would burst into flames before being rushed out to be doused with buckets of water.

The Lahore family comprised father Edouard, 59, and his wife Marie-Louise, their sons Roger, 29, and Jean-Marc, 24, and a foster daughter, Michelle, 19, who had come to live with the family six years previously. Repressed sexual tension figures in many poltergeist cases, as do spontaneous fiery outbreaks, but it is idle to speculate about this case without more information. The prefect of police, an investigating judge, and Gregoire Kaplan, head of the Laboratory for Physical Analysis in the town of Pau, failed to establish how the fires were started. Like Carole Compton, two young scapegoats were jailed, tried and convicted (in that order), with no evidence, no witnesses and no apparent motive. But this satisfied the authorities' honour, and the pair were soon pardoned and freed.

But in some cases, no poltergeist focus or any other apparent natural or paranormal cause can be found for the visitation of the flames.

On a cold January morning in 1932, Charles Williamson of Bladenboro, North Carolina, heard his wife scream for help. He and his daughter rushed upstairs to find Mrs Williamson on fire. They quickly ripped off her burning cotton dress. The woman had not been standing near a flame, nor had her dress been in contact with a flammable substance. Two days later, a bed caught fire in the same bedroom, as did the curtains in an unoccupied room. Soon after that, a pair of Mr Williamson's trousers hanging in the wardrobe burst into flames. The bizarre series of 'spot' fires broke out over a five-day period. Arson experts investigated, but the results were inconclusive.

In 1990, a spate of unexplained fires hit the entire village of San Gottardo in the Berici Hills of northern Italy. Electrical equipment went haywire and objects of all sorts caught fire. Inhabitants complained of sickness, stomach pains and skin inflammation, all of which resisted medication. Animals were restless and off their food. People blamed UFOs, Martians and the 'excess of electricity produced by high power generators at a nearby US communications base'. An army of investigators descended, but found no answers.

In that, they were hardly alone among those who have tried to discover the mechanism behind spontaneous fires of all kinds.

POLTERGEISTS

Blood was everywhere. It spurted from the walls, drenching pots and pans, clothing and the doors. When the horrified occupants fled from room to room, their feet made bloody footprints on the floor.

268

On 12 March 1985, the occupants of a house in Aboro, a district of the city of Abidjan (which was once the capital of the Ivory Coast in West Africa), had the horrific experience of seeing blood spurt from their walls. It drenched articles of clothing, pots and pans in the kitchen, the shower, and some of the doors. Even more grotesque, when the occupants moved around inside the house, they made bloody footprints. Not a single person in the place, however, was wounded or injured.

In September 1987, a middle-aged couple, Mr William Winston and his wife, were subjected to extremely disconcerting flows of blood, apparently from nowhere, in their home in Atlanta, Georgia. The blood somehow splashed itself on the floors and walls of several rooms in the house; on one particularly grim occasion, Mrs Winston climbed out of her bath to find the bathroom floor covered in blood. 'I'm not bleeding, my wife's not bleeding. Nobody else was here,' said Mr Winston. Backing the truth of the story is the fact that the mysterious blood was analysed, and found to be human, type O. Mr Winston and his wife have type A blood, although they are undoubtedly human. So where did these grisly emanations come from?

SEXUAL DISTURBANCE

These poltergeist attacks contradict the stereotyped image of what a poltergeist does and what, so to speak, causes it.

The typical poltergeist throws things about, makes disembodied 'bumps in the night', hides everyday objects, and (these days) plays tricks with the telephone, TV and video. Sometimes it plays with fire. But, as we shall see, the range of mischief of which poltergeists are capable is far wider than this: so wide, in fact, that it has been truly said that no case is quite like another. Among other weird effects in the poltergeist's startling repertoire are apports – objects appearing out of thin air; teleports – things moving by unknown means from place to place, sometimes seemingly through solid walls or locked doors; sudden inexplicable chills; disembodied voices; levitation of people and things; and disgusting smells with no apparent source.

As for where poltergeists 'come from', the true answer to that question remains a mystery. The word 'poltergeist' is German in origin, and simply means 'noisy spirit' – from its traditional manifestation as bumps, raps and bangs. Whether or not a spirit or some so-far undefined reaction between someone's state of mind or emotions and the recognized 'scientific' forms of energy is involved, the blunt truth is that no one knows how poltergeists work or why one person sets them off while another, with perhaps identical stresses or problems, does not. Nor does anyone know whether their effects come directly from an individual, or if the affected person conjures up (or 'calls in') a separate entity that does the mischief on his or her behalf. Recognizing their own ignorance on this question, psychic researchers now use the neutral if somewhat tooth-jarring term 'repetitive spontaneous psychokinesis' (RSPK) to describe poltergeist cases. Itself translated, it means, essentially, that physical effects occur with a psychic cause, more than once, and without deliberate intention on anyone's part.

The work of a poltergeist at a house in Dodleston, Chester, in the spring of 1985. During the time it was active, a computer in the house received messages from a man who claimed to be living in the 16th century.

But it is true that poltergeist activity has often centred on adolescent children, especially around puberty. Few people do not experience turmoil at that time, and in some cases the inner disturbance spills over into the external world – with sometimes distressing results for those in the immediate vicinity. But by no means all poltergeists can be explained (as far as they can be explained at all) by the presence of pubescent children, especially when there are none around to point the finger at.

There are plenty of cases on record, however, that suggest that sexual disturbance of some kind is at the root of many poltergeist infestations. Some occur around women who are going through the menopause – which may, given the obvious symbolism of the blood involved, have had something to do with the Winston case in Atlanta, Georgia.

Grown men may also generate poltergeists. In the 1980s, researcher Andrew Green reported a case of 'psychic disturbances of all kinds' acting upon an outwardly happy and normal family of four in Somerset, England. The two children were in their teens and at first glance it seemed most likely that they were the focus of the disturbances. In the event, it turned out that it was the 49-year-old father of the family who was at the centre of the disruption. Under huge pressure at work, he had developed insomnia and then become impotent; he was near breakdown when the poltergeist outbreak began. Once he had proper medical attention and support, the disturbances stopped.

In many cases, it is not people but the place they live that is at the heart of the matter, and the most common class of place that encourages poltergeists is council or public housing projects. One British analysis put the figure involving people in council houses as high as 86 per cent of all poltergeist incidents. This isn't necessarily to say that the families involved were faking the phenomena to improve their standard of living. Not all public housing is irresistibly attractive. A combination of the stress of moving, individual emotional conflicts within a family, and disappointment or even repugnance at the new home or its surroundings – and a house is, after all, the answer to a fundamental human need – may result in paranormal outbreaks.

LEWD PRESENCE

Some of the more bizarre poltergeist cases involve the apparent presence of discarnate spirits, and some of these are capable of extremely unexpected behaviour.

In early 1979, for instance, a poltergeist began shifting bottles and ornaments at the Whitchurch Inn, near Tavistock, Devon, but then stepped up the oddity of its attacks. While the landlady's family was out one night, a vase of flowers was upset, but the water in the vase 'simply disappeared'. The climax came when landlady Sheila Jones received a warm hug, apparently from someone behind her: she thought it was a customer getting forward, and turned around to retaliate – only to find herself looking into thin air.

Another lascivious poltergeist, also associated with a pub, has plagued the Albion Hotel in Bolton, Lancashire – drying up the beer in the pumps or making beer flow incessantly from a bar-tap, as the whim takes it, and turning off gas-taps to the beer kegs in the cellar. One night in July 1979, landlady Barbara Barnes was getting into her bath when she felt a hand caressing her bottom. Thinking it was her husband, she didn't object: only when she turned around to see the bathroom door closed and no one there besides herself did her hair begin to rise. Just to make certain he wasn't playing tricks, she went to look for her husband – who was still in the bar, and had been all the time.

While some poltergeists appear to enjoy sex, others apparently disapprove. What they do in either case may well reflect the unconscious or repressed – unadmitted – fascinations and longings, or fears, or even feelings of revulsion on the part of those involved.

Wedding nights can reveal all of these and, especially for the inexperienced, can in any case be times of extreme tension. Add a very young bride – 17-year-old Debbie Mikloz, in this case – and a flat that was new to her, and it's just possible something strange will happen to spoil the initial joys of married life.

In November 1978 Debbie and her new husband, Steve Mikloz, went to spend their very first night together in their new flat in Raunds, Northamptonshire, and took themselves to bed. Debbie suddenly had the alarming feeling that they were not alone – and then Steve felt something grab him by the throat and haul him out of bed, struggling for breath. But there was no one else in the room besides the nuptial couple.

With all amorous thoughts banished, the couple hurriedly got dressed and left. Since the assailant was invisible, the immediate assumption would be that this was the work of some kind of (jealous? puritanical? anyway, violent) ghost, but the landlords insisted that the flat had no history of haunting. Given the particular circumstances, a poltergeist remains the only plausible candidate. Whether the Miklozes were forcibly separated on any other occasion is, unfortunately for psychical research at least, not known. With some libidinous phantasms it is difficult to sort out whether a species of poltergeist or a straightforward haunting is at work. When a council house is the setting, one might be forgiven for suspecting poltergeists, real or imagined; and there are other factors in the following case that make certain tensions at least possible. But the 'symptoms' of the case could just as easily apply to a haunting. But to say that is only to replace one unknown with another.

In 1978 the Hardie family – mother Bessie, then 57, her son Bob, 24, and her daughters Valerie, 20, and Margaret, 19 – had been living in a council house in Stockton, Teesside, for some time. They had been disturbed by odd noises coming from the loft, but these were as nothing compared to the events that occurred after the council had made some repairs to the house. One night shortly after this work was finished, Margaret was lying in bed when she heard a huge thumping coming from the landing outside her bedroom. Next, the bedroom door opened of its own accord. Margaret's bed began to shake. To her terror, her bedclothes were then slowly lifted up and what felt like a human hand slid from her shoulders down the front of her nightie and came to rest on her legs. Margaret was now paralysed with fright, unable to move.

It seems it was only at this stage that she was actually able to see her assailant, who appeared as a bald-headed man, wearing a Victorian cape; he kept his head down, so she could not see his face. But she did hear the apparition say 'Come to the bathroom, Margaret' – and he repeated this strikingly unromantic invitation three or four times. At this point, Margaret managed to let loose a loud shriek. Her mother rushed in to find Margaret drenched with sweat but no one else in the room. The teenager took to sleeping downstairs, but the apparition pursued her there as well. Others in the family began to catch sight of the entity, but it did not molest them. The family decided to have the house exorcised to rid themselves of the lewd presence.

273

ELEMENTAL SYMBOLS

Without knowing a great deal more about the relationships between the individuals in the Hardie family, or the emotional history of the main victim, Margaret, it is impossible even to speculate on what might have lain behind these attacks – if, indeed, a revenant spirit was not at work, as seems quite possible. Psychic researcher Joe Cooper made the same point about the importance of seeking out the nature of a psychic victim's relationships, in his report of a particularly idiosyncratic poltergeist that persecuted an elderly gentleman living on his own in a hotel in Yorkshire in the late 1980s.

He was afflicted by phenomena as varied as his clothes spontaneously igniting while hanging in a wardrobe, objects whizzing about under their own steam in the hotel lounge, and a pair of scissors that (also by itself) scratched crosses on the lid of a piano. But the most distressing, yet weirdly slapstick, aspect of the infestation was a deluge of water that repeatedly poured from thin air to drench the old man as he lay in bed reading.

Various attempts to get to the bottom of the mystery came to dead ends. Exorcism had no effect. A medium pronounced that at a certain spot in the hotel hallway a young soldier had slit the throat of a servant during World War One, but neither the local newspaper archives nor older residents confirmed the story. Besides, even if they had existed, why would either of these characters soak an innocent old man in another part of the building with water, or set fire to his clothes? On a simple symbolic level it makes no sense unless, say, there had been some curious punning connection between their names. One could imagine such a link between a Private Waters, a waiter called Match and an old man called Box but, as the soldier and the servant were both figments of the medium's imagination, which did not stretch to the matter of anyone's names, even that devious path is a dead end.

Cooper suggested a change of room for the old man, which seemed to stop the mysterious fires but did not entirely prevent the inconvenient floods of water. And the scissors persisted in vandalizing the hotel piano.

About a month after this change of accommodation, news came that the elderly gentleman's wife had died. She had been in a coma

John Glynn examines his wrecked bedroom during a poltergeist outbreak at his home in Runcorn, Cheshire, in 1952.

in hospital all the while – a fact that, it appears, neither the old man nor anyone else had imparted to the investigators, exorcists, mediums and so on who had become interested in the case. The poltergeist had started its mischievous work not long after the wife had been taken unconscious to hospital, however, and came to an abrupt and permanent halt when she died.

One can only wonder what kind of relationship the couple had had. He seems to have said nothing about her to anyone, let alone visited her. She visited elemental symbols of fire and water upon him (and, perhaps, symbols of death – graveyard crosses – that may also have been symbols of faith). That may be too grandiose an interpretation. Perhaps she was still burning with love for him: hence the fires. Perhaps he was not only indifferent (as he plainly was), but didn't wash often enough for her liking – hence the trials by water. Who can say? If the old man had only mentioned his wife and her coma, however, the investigators might have been able to learn a little about the relationship – and we might all be a little the wiser about the ways of poltergeists.

A CRY FOR ATTENTION

The renowned psychic researcher Harry Price characterized poltergeists in terms that were hardly complimentary, if accurate: 'mischievous, destructive, noisy, cruel, erratic, thievish, demonstrative, purposeless, cunning, unhelpful, malicious, audacious, teasing, ill-disposed, spiteful, ruthless, resourceful and vampiric'. The list reads like something from a thesaurus conceived in Bedlam. And for the vast majority of poltergeists, it remains an accurate description.

The literature of poltergeist infestations reads like a grotesque roll-call of the most mean-minded, petty and spiteful acts that human malice can devise. Looked at another way, such behaviour in human beings almost always erupts as a result of anger and rage – at oneself, at injustice, at emotional blackmail, at the impossible position (the double-bind) one has been shoved into mercilessly by others. It is irrelevant whether such an assessment is accurate, honest, truthful, or objective: indeed such a depth of emotion is rarely touched by people capable of a disinterested and impartial outlook. But scratch anyone, and – however rational they are – if there is one place in their lives about which they will reveal (and in some cases admit) such depths of feeling, that place will be their own family. There is nothing quite like the human family for creating massive, uncontrollable feelings of rage. And it seems to be on rage – the kind of crazed, lacerating destructiveness exhibited by a cornered animal – that poltergeists thrive.

And yet they can sometimes be kindly.

For more than a year, Derek Newman's family put up with a classic low-life poltergeist. It threw ornaments about, made a mess in the kitchen, and advertised itself importantly with bumps and thumps and bangs in their flat in Sheffield, Yorkshire. One night in January 1982, the usual commotion began, waking the family. Derek Newman said that the racket was 'like someone running round the lounge with a hammer'. He, however, had had enough, and decided to answer the poltergeist in kind. He picked up a hammer and opened his bedroom door. Dense, choking smoke poured in. Derek realized that his flat was on fire and dialled 999. As their flat went up in flames, firemen rescued the Newman family from their balcony.

Derek Newman has said that, were it not for the poltergeist, he and his family would have died in the blaze. But what started the fire in the first place? Was it the poltergeist – whatever that may be, or whatever it was expressing - or was it an accidental blaze that awoke the poltergeist because it threatened it with the worst fate any egotistical spirit could fear – namely, loss of attention?

This way of looking at poltergeists may not help explain the mechanics of the phenomenon, but it may illuminate one of its aspects. Put baldly, poltergeists seem sometimes, and perhaps more often than not, to be a way of crying out for attention. Harry Price's description of a poltergeist could as well be the characterisation of a juvenile delinquent. Whether we can forgive such behaviour or not, it is not very difficult to

An illustration of the poltergeist that has come to be known as the demon drummer of Tidworth, from Saducismus Triumphatus (1961) by Joseph Glanvill, chaplin to Charles II and Fellow of the Royal Society.

understand. Few of us are not confused adolescents under our thin veneer of adult maturity – anxious for acceptance to the point of unconditional love, while demanding the room and a licence to be entirely, independently, and with splendid selfishness, ourselves.

There is a kindlier way of looking at the poltergeist, and that is to see it as the manifestation of the human spirit driven to extremes when its identity is under threat. While many children may regard the physical and emotional changes of puberty as an adventure and a source of pride, others may surely see them as a threat, fearing the loss of childhood simplicity (the besieged identity) and the sometimes alarming, often messy, onset of the unknown and the responsibilities it brings. If a child senses a risk of dubious sexual interest from a parent or sibling at this time, the whole turbulent process will be still less welcome.

Children are not alone in suffering crises of identity. Adults may feel trapped in a relationship, or stifled by their jobs or colleagues at work; a man suffering a bout of impotence, for whatever cause, may feel literally emasculated. Desperation is not the exclusive property of adolescents (although it often suits them to think so), and neither are poltergeists. In many cases, investigators are hampered in finding the roots of a poltergeist attack because they cannot bring themselves to enquire about intimate details of personal or family life, or because (not surprisingly) those involved are ashamed or afraid to reveal them to anyone, let alone comparative strangers.

At about this point, the usual objection rings out from the sceptics. But, they cry, if all that is true, why don't we all generate poltergeists when we're under stress?

This is really as pointless a question as 'Why do some people hate Beethoven?', or 'Why doesn't everyone breed racing pigeons?' Temperament, disposition, talent, environment, heredity – all or any of these may be involved. Some people have short tempers, others the patience of a saint. Some people work off their tensions, confusions, or rage by playing squash, listening to old Gong albums, drinking whisky, or even robbing banks. Some become comedians. Some produce poltergeists.

ROYAL OMENS

The link between a threat to the identity and poltergeist outbreaks is particularly plain in some cases.

In *The Paranormal*, scholar and historian of the paranormal Dr Brian Inglis relates how, on 28 January 1936, the funeral procession of the late King George V of England wound its way through the streets of London from St James's Palace. Among the regalia borne with the relics of the King was the Imperial State Crown. At one point, the Maltese Cross that tops the crown fell off. At this unexpected and somewhat undignified event the new king, Edward VIII, reportedly exclaimed: 'Christ! What's going to happen next?' He was overheard by the then Minister of Agriculture, Walter Elliott, who commented wryly to his companion Lord Boothby: 'That will be the motto of the new reign.'

Given the care with which the priceless British Crown Jewels are tended, such an occurrence would be unusual in any circumstances. But Edward VIII's identity was in question from

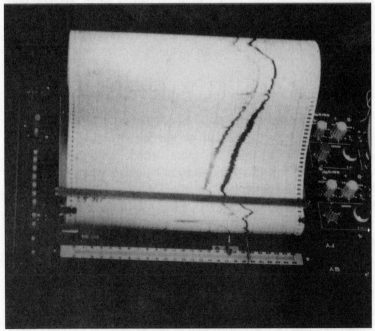

Equipment installed at Mulhouse recorded inexplicable, sudden drops in temperature – a characteristic of poltergeist haunting.

several directions: apart from assuming the identity of the monarchy (and having to give up his notorious social life for duties of state), he knew he would shortly have to choose between remaining king and marrying the divorcee Mrs Wallis Simpson – and their liaison indeed threatened the institution of the monarchy itself. Edward VIII's personal status and that of his royal office were thus in jeopardy. In the fraught emotional conditions of that particular royal funeral, then, it would not be surprising if a brief spasm from a poltergeist, centred on the new king, was responsible for distressing the major, most visible and most gorgeous of the symbols of monarchy on view that day. In the event, Edward VIII abdicated after just 325 days on the throne.

Dr Inglis cites another curious incident involving the British Crown. When the former King James II entered Dublin in 1689 with the intention of raising the Catholic Irish against the new Protestant King William III, who had ousted him, his mace-bearer stumbled and fell. The cross on the crown of the mace lodged between two paving stones. James, who was to fail entirely in his attempts to regain the throne, was deeply troubled by the omen. We can only speculate on whether it was caused by psychokinesis from James's own subconscious recognition that his cause was lost, or whether it was no more than an ominous coincidence.

SAINTLY PRICE

Religion, for those who enjoy its certainties, is a powerful force in a believer's sense of his or her identity, and it's likewise unsurprising to find that the more ardent adherents of many religions have been surrounded by poltergeists when their beliefs were threatened. When they set about medieval Christian zealots, the poltergeists were invariably labelled 'demons' that were taken to be testing the victim's strength of faith – or simply setting about them with special vigour just because they were especially saintly and, therefore, a thorn in the side of the forces of darkness.

This may well have been the case, but it is worth remembering the psychologists' truism that people who profess an absolute, unbending belief in anything (from the joys of capital punishment to the flatness of the Earth) that is not amenable to direct proof must spend a great deal of energy repressing their awareness that they might possibly be wrong. It is a platitude that converts are particularly prone to intolerance of their former sins when they find them in others, and it takes no great psychologist to see that they are really resisting the temptation to backslide – in other words, they are projecting what is in fact an internal battle. So we may speculate with some justification that the poltergeists that beset the holy men and women of the Middle Ages were not precisely demons, but the projections of inner struggles. Scratches, pinching, showers of filth, and the usual harassment with loud noises were all part of the price the saintly paid for their faith.

Such outbreaks are not, however, confined to Christians. Dr Inglis cites the case of a Bishop Weston, who was determined to show some native tribes people in Zanzibar that the local demons could not faze a good Christian. He went into a reputedly haunted hut, only to stagger out covered in clods of earth that the 'demons' had plucked from the walls of the hut and liberally showered about when he stepped in. In this case, one might presume that behind the attack lay the faith of the local people, who might justifiably be incensed that their demons should not be accorded a proper respect.

Yet even the most assiduous psychological analysis of such idiosyncratic poltergeists can explain no more than the conditions that call them forth. It does not explain the mechanism of the poltergeist – how it picks things up and throws them about, or sets fire to someone's skirts, or speaks in gruff but disembodied voices. We are left somewhat in the position of someone who knows that buying an airplane ticket and boarding the aircraft will get them to the land of their choice – but from whom all knowledge of jet engines, aerodynamics or even the existence of the pilot has been kept hidden. The temptation to think that the ticket is the cause, and not the condition, of the journey is plain enough.

HUMAN ENIGMAS

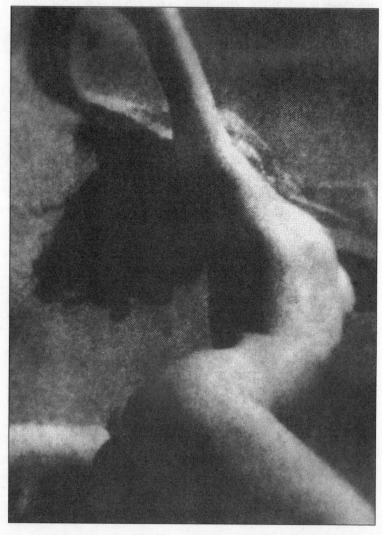

At four, Zheng Xiangling could see glowing auras surrounding people; at six, she could accurately predict the sex of unborn babies; by the time she was 24 she had developed an X-ray vision which the leaders of the People's Republic of China found extremely useful.

When the Beatles chanted 'I'm looking throu-ou-ough yooou' on their 1965 album 'Rubber Soul' they were giving a new twist to a common enough figure of speech. The unfortunate creature addressed by the foursome was so empty of interest that she was transparent. The following year, Pete Townshend of The Who used the metaphor in more traditional vein in 'I Can See for Miles', as he described how he could see into a certain lady's mind, heart and questionable motives with ease.

Being able to 'see through' other people's motives is a talent some are blessed with more than others, but a few rare individuals can apparently go further than that: they can see through human flesh.

Adepts of the ancient Chinese discipline of qigong have from time to time claimed to have developed X-ray vision, which they say is two-dimensional and limited to black and white imagery, by using a regime of breathing exercises to control their qi, or 'life-energy', as it flows through their bodies. But one modern adept has surpassed even that ability.

Reports of the wild talent of Miss Zheng Xiangling first surfaced in the West in 1988, when she was 24. A doctor who then worked at the General Staff headquarters of the People's Liberation Army in Beijing, Miss Zheng can see her patients' bones, veins and internal organs in three dimensions and full colour – and can presumably see anyone else's as well, when and if she chooses. Her ability is not limited to human flesh: she can read words written - out of her sight – on paper that has then been tightly folded, for instance, and is reported to be able to will goldfish to die.

In her lifesaving role, Miss Zheng usually diagnoses her patients, who remain fully clothed, in the dark. She is particularly good at detecting cancers, heart disease, arthritis and respiratory problems, and with greater accuracy than standard hospital equipment. The process however is exhausting, and she sees patients only twice a week – and they, according to her friends, are a veritable 'Who's Who of the Chinese leadership'.

Miss Zheng believes she has inherited her extraordinary ability from her grandfather, whose reputation as a diagnostician in his native Shaanxi province was unsurpassed. The first sign of unusual powers came when she was aged four, when she discerned glowing auras around people. Within two years she was accurately predicting the sex of children carried by her pregnant relatives. Her brother, too, has similar powers, and is said to be employed by the police occasionally to spy on suspected criminals – by looking through the walls of their houses.

While Zheng Xiangling developed her ability through rigorous discipline, it can emerge spontaneously. In March 1978, 37-year-old crane driver Mrs Yuliya Vorobyeva was working in a mine near Donetsk in the Ukraine when she ran into an electricity line and received a massive 380-volt jolt. She was pronounced dead, and lay in the local mortuary for two days before a post-mortem was held. But no sooner had scalpel sliced skin than the 'corpse' began to bleed – and to shake uncontrollably. After that uncomfortable awakening, Mrs Vorobyeva did not sleep for six months. Finally, she succumbed to a long, deep sleep – which refreshed her in an extraordinary way.

'One morning,' she told the newspaper *Izvestia* in June 1987, 'I went out to buy bread. I got to the bus stop and a woman was standing there. I went up to her and suddenly I was paralysed with horror. I could see her intestines and straight through her as if she were a picture on a television set.'

One of Margaret Fleming's 'thoughtographs'. The ability to project images onto film or paper by mental energy alone.

Investigated by a Dr Yeizhertin at Donetsk hospital, she told him – correctly – within seconds of their meeting that his hearing was better in one ear than the other, and that his left eye was stronger than his right. In similar forthright fashion she correctly told the reporter from *Izvestia* that he had a red liquid in his stomach – which had once been a jelly. Ms Vorobyeva now specializes in diagnosing rare diseases and, according to doctors at Donetsk, 'has never made a single mistake'.

THOUGHTOGRAPHY

Among the more exotic human talents, being able to see through solid matter has its unlikely parallel in the ability to produce images, as it were from nowhere, on film – without actually pointing the camera at the object it photographs.

The great exponent of thoughtography in modern times was former merchant sailor and Chicago bellhop Ted Serios. He was last reported, in the mid-1980s, to be living in obscurity in a slightly ramshackle house at the end of a dirt road near Mendon, Illinois, on the border with Missouri, and working as little as possible. 'If you gotta work and be poor,' he told visitors, 'you might as well not work and be good 'n' poor.' But for a time in the 1960s and 1970s, Serios was famous.

He worked with a Polaroid camera, which at least proved that his effects were not the result of chicanery in the darkroom. And very strange effects they were, on occasion. Equally extraordinary was the lather into which Serios threw himself to get those effects. Much of his work was documented by psychologist Dr Jule Eisenbud, in Denver, Colorado – some distance from Chicago, to which city Serios would sometimes capriciously return without warning in the midst of a session. The sessions themselves were chaotic, as Eisenbud often had to pursue Serios around town and, even when settled, Serios himself would psyche himself up (he was never able to produce 'thoughtographs' to order) with copious amounts of beer, becoming ever more dictatorial and temperamental as he went on drinking.

Newscaster Bob Palmer described Serios's style: 'Ted would bolt out of his chair and charge the... camera. There, he would grunt, purr, curse, and squint, and with an incantation that would do a diceroller proud, he'd wind up and let go. On the downhill side of these incidents he'd whirl round and demand, "Did you see anything? Did you see anything?"'

Nonetheless Serios did on many occasions produce photographs. Sometimes staring into the camera lens, sometimes in another room from the camera, sometimes with the camera pointing into empty space as he raged around it, Serios somehow managed to get images of distant locations onto the film. Sometimes they were pictures of specific targets that Eisenbud had asked him to 'thoughtograph', but they were often quite random images – and often strange in themselves.

In May 1965 Serios produced a string of pictures of a storefront rather strangely named the Wld Gold Store. This turned out to be the former Old Gold Store in Central City, Colorado. The curiosity was that when Serios 'took' his pictures, the store's name had been changed to the Old Wells Fargo Store. The 'W' in Serios's pictures, and on the storefront, was placed exactly where the letter 'O' had once been. Eisenbud was also unable to find any source that Serios might have used to fake the photograph. Another location in Central City that Serios 'thoughtographed' was Williams's Livery Stable. The oddity here was that his picture showed the building's windows bricked up, and the material of the facade was different from that of the actual building.

Central City is some 40 miles west of Denver, set in the mountains a little north of US Highway 40. It is conceivable that Serios went there on his unannounced departures from sessions with Eisenbud, or that he went there before the sessions, and he may have taken photographs of the place. What is clear enough is that he had no way of physically getting into the Polaroid cameras used in the experiments – they were in any case sealed and marked against interference – to plant these curious pictures. Still less likely is it that Serios – not, by all accounts, the most solvent or careful character on Earth – would have bothered to make a journey to Canada to fake up a picture of a building on an airstrip belonging to the Royal Canadian Mounted Police. And that photograph, too, has its internal anomaly. The word 'Canadian' is strangely misspelt, which it certainly is not on the actual building.

Serios is not alone in projecting thoughts onto film, nor are his necessarily the strangest results in the field. *Fate* magazine of

June 1976 published two astonishing photographs obtained in a psychic experiment by Margaret Fleming. The first showed a leaping nude, which Ms Fleming had psychically projected onto film negative. A few days later she took another print from the same negative – but the image had subtly altered, as if it had continued to move. Nor was Serios the first to produce mental pictures on physical film. Japanese psychic Tenshin Takeuchi, working with investigator Dr Fukurai, produced numerous 'thoughtographs' in 1915. On one occasion he projected three pictograms, precisely those requested by Fukurai, onto a photographic plate; on another, he reproduced a whole sentence from a book.

MAGNETIC PERSONALITIES

Factory worker Leonid Tenkaev, of Saratov, Russia, is a very attractive man when he wants to be. His wife, his daughter, and his grandson are equally attractive. All four have the uncanny ability to make metal objects stick to their bodies at will.

According to Dr Valeri Lepilov, professor of physics at Saratov State University, the four have only to 'concentrate and think about generating heat inside their bodies' to turn on their magnetic ability. 'In a few moments objects can be attached to them.' The force these members of the Tenkaev family exert is considerable. Leonid, who was born in 1928, has made as much as 52 lb of ferrous metal stick to his person. Removing the objects, says Dr kpilov, can be hard work – 'like dragging a metal object off a real magnet'.

The Tenkaevs say they have become aware of their strange talent only since 1987 – a year after the Chernobyl disaster. Certainly they are not the only Russians, or even Eastern Europeans, whose odd magnetic gifts have been in the news since then – but it is a moot point whether the cause of their fame has anything to do with the after-effects of a nuclear accident, or more to do with the greater freedom of the press in formerly communist countries.

Fifty-five-year-old militia patrolman Nikolai Suvorov, for example, was reported by Russia's *Soviet Weekly* in June 1990 as also being able to generate a magnetic force at will, so that things made of metal stick to his skin; while Bulgaria's Sofia press agency reported in 1991 that no fewer than 300 'magnetic' people turned up at a contest to see who could keep metal objects on their bodies the longest.

But what creates this ability is a mystery, as is the ability such people have to turn it on and off whenever they want. Even stranger, it is not always strictly a magnetic effect. Unlike an ordinary iron magnet, the human magnet's powers are not limited to ferrous metals. Militiaman Suvorov, for instance, can attract plastic and glass as well as metal to his body. Inga Gaidochenko, from Grodno, Belarus, has been known to make a 9 lb sledgehammer stick to her, despite her youth (she was born in 1979), and can also attract plastic, wood and paper – but not glass. Something rather more like gravity than electricity or magnetism seems to be at work here – but why should glass be immune to it?

There are many such cases on record. In 1889, Frank McKinstry of Joplin, Missouri, was reported to feel himself becoming 'charged' early each morning, and then he had to keep walking – otherwise, his feet would stick to the ground, immobilizing him. If another person lifted his feet – as sometimes they had to – the effect would dissipate with a small, faint flash. McKinstry, interestingly, also had the reputation of being a good dowser.

In 1890 the Massachusetts College of Pharmacy studied the case of 16-year-old student Louis Hamburger, who made mincemeat of scientific preconception by lifting a glass jar full of iron filings, weighing about 5 lb, with the tips of three fingers. To do this, his fingertips had to be dry – a peculiarity because water is an excellent conductor of electricity, and children are constantly warned not to switch lights on and off with wet fingers. Hamburger's favourite demonstration was to draw his fingers up the outside of a glass beaker full of iron filings, so that they could be seen rising to follow the movement of his hands. In a more recent case, in 1938, Mrs Antoine Timmer demonstrated to a meeting of the Universal Council for Psychic Research in New York how her personal magnetism caused cutlery to stick to her hands; they could be removed only with a sharp tug.

A SHOCKING STATE OF AFFAIRS

For some, their weird electrical abilities are more of a curse than a blessing. Oxford don Dr Michael Shallis discovered that Mrs Jacqueline Priestman, of Sale, Manchester, had more than 10 times the usual amount of static electricity in her body, which may explain her disruptive influence on household equipment, which began - for no discernible reason – when she was 22 years old. No fewer than 30 vacuum cleaners, five electric irons and two washing machines have succumbed to Mrs Priestman's electric personality, while her electric cooker cuts out when she tries to use it and her TV set changes channels at her approach.

Dr Shallis says: 'It's not certain what causes this severe build-up of static. Such people seem to be able to transmit miniature bolts of lightning that break down the insulation of some electrical appliances.'

He cannot explain why this build-up of electricity started when Mrs Priestman was 22, or why the effects are limited to her own

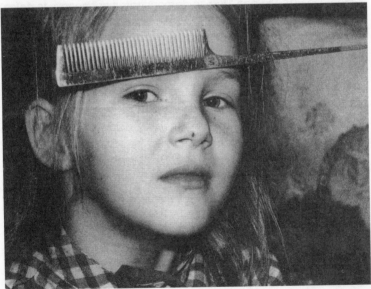

Eight-year-old Svetlana Glyko displays her extraordinary powers of attraction. Svetlana, from the Commonwealth of Independent States, can hold combs, teaspoons and other small objects on her forehead.

home. However, by an irony, her husband Paul is an electrical technician. Is this perhaps some kind of real-life pun on the part of a poltergeist? More information about the Priestmans' domestic life might clarify matters, but in the circumstances they would probably prefer simply to be rid of their electrical plague than help develop the esoteric theories of psychic investigators.

The sudden onset of personal electrical power is not unusual, it seems, in cases of the kind – if anything about them can be called 'not unusual' in any sense. Xue Dibo, a 36-year-old boilermaker from Urumqi, in China's Xinjiang province, felt 'strange sensations' at the beginning of 1988, and then found that whenever he touched people he was giving them an electric shock that was strong enough to knock them over.

REPELLENT

Not everyone who has such bizarre abilities is disturbed by them. Teenager Lulu Hurst was known as the 'Georgia Wonder' and at her parents' instigation appeared on stage between 1883 (when she was 15) and 1885 to demonstrate her capacity to defeat the usual laws of physics. She could draw all kinds of objects to her, metallic or not – even a straw hat – at will. With equal facility she could repel ordinary physical force: a favourite device was to line up a group of burly men at the end of a billiard cue, and invite them to push her over. Lulu Hurst could resist their combined force, just as she could resist any attempt to lift her against her will.

Still more famous was the similarly dubbed 'Little Georgia Magnet', Annie May Abbott, who toured the world in the late 1880s and 1890s. She weighed only 98 lb but even Sumo wrestlers could not shift her from where she sat in a chair – which gave her no opportunity to exert a sideways deflecting force. She could also make objects immovable, simply by resting her fingers on them.

More recently, Welshman Brian Williams of Cardiff made the news in 1952, when he was photographed holding an electric lightbulb between finger and thumb – with the bulb glowing brightly from the electricity in his body.

Another human torch appeared at the Asian Games in Beijing in September 1990 to entertain visitors to the Olympic Hotel. Chun Tianzhao plugged himself into the mains and put a screwdriver to his temple until the tool glowed. Then he held hands with various members of the audience, apparently controlling the flow of electricity through his body so that they felt sensations ranging from mild tingling to a jolt that made them scream.

Like Miss Zheng mentioned above, Li Qinghong is a qigong master, and works in medicine – in his case, at the Railways Ministry Hospital in Beijing. The first unusual result of his training in qigong was his discovery that he could adjust the volume of his radio as he wanted it, without having to touch the dials. Li progressed to the point of soaking himself in water, standing in a puddle, and wiring himself into the 220-volt mains electricity supply. Having survived that experiment, he now acts as a human transformer in his healing work. He seems not only to be immune to electricity but to be able to augment current and voltage from the mains supply. He has been seen to 'put frozen fish on a pair of electric spits – which failed to cook the fish until Li took hold of them, whereupon the fish began to 'smoke, hiss and crackle'. Li's hands remained not merely unaffected, but quite cool throughout the operation.

Some paranormal electrical abilities can seriously disrupt domestic life. One woman found that all manner of household equipment – washing machines, vacuum cleaners, cookers, televisions – refused to work in her presence.

INNER POWER

There is nothing strange about electricity in the human body: without minute electrical charges making connections between the synapses in the brain, we would not be able even to think, let alone wonder how strange are the ways of the world. And some animals can store and discharge electricity – electric eels can deliver a jolt of up to 500 volts, enough to kill the average would-be predator, and certainly enough to stun a human being. The existence of the electric eel suggests that electric people, if relatively few and far between, are not necessarily breaking the laws of nature, even if what brings about their unusual ability is little understood.

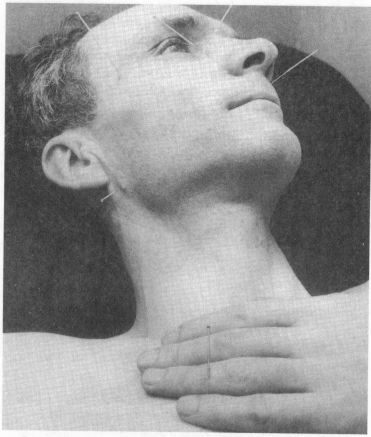

Practitioners of acupuncture use needles to stimulate qi, the universal life source that flows through the body.

There may be another kind of explanation – or at any rate clue – to this kind of phenomenon in the notion of qi (often transliterated ch'i) energy cited and seemingly brought under control by Dr Zheng and other adepts. The concept of qi is not an easy one: writing in *Fortean Times* No. 2 researcher Steve Moore noted that it is 'difficult of definition in any sort of everyday or scientific terms: it is at once "breath" spirit, non-muscular energy, or "inner power". It is that energy which flows along the acupuncture meridians. It is also the energy developed by practitioners of the "Internal schools" of the martial arts, the most well-known of which is T'ai Chi Chuan.'

The electrical and magnetic powers that some Westerners exhibit or acquire by chance or accident are frequently reported among qi masters. Moore quotes a number of accounts of such talents that had been deliberately fostered through mental and spiritual discipline.

When, for instance, a female student of a martial arts master tried to attack him on one occasion, 'she found a force propelling her backwards, and then she started bouncing up and down until her feet began to hurt'. Another master, walking in the street with a friend, was hit in the back by a pedicab, which rebounded 10 ft and tipped over. The master, without a break in the conversation, walked on as if nothing had happened. One particular instance is highly reminiscent of the 19th-century 'wonder girls' and their talents. The master Yang Ch'eng-fu 'could magnetise or attract his opponent's arm so that it stuck to his own as he moved'.

Western sages have yet to explain acupuncture in their own scientific terms. How they might come to grips with the whole concept of qi is a challenge few seem willing to take up. The broader lesson is that we all could probably learn much about other paranormal phenomena if scientists would but accept that the bizarre and inexplicable is not therefore impossible. Indeed, because such things as electric people or poltergeists are inexplicable, they are all the more worthy of investigation. But to most scientists, probably for no better reason than their own preference for the quiet safety of conformity, such promising, tantalizing fields of research remain out of bounds.

UNEXPLAINED
ARRIVALS

*The amputated human finger materialized out of thin air.
The police combed the city's hospitals but no one claimed
the missing digit. A clue to a grisly murder – or something
far more horrific?*

In March 1986, a respectable citizen of what was then West Berlin, Germany, was climbing into his car in the Tegel district of the city when he heard something land with a thud on the vehicle's roof. He looked out to see what had made the noise, and saw a human finger roll off the top of his car and into the gutter. He prudently left the grisly object where it was, drove off, and reported what he had seen to the police. On checking, the police found there was no mistake: there was an unmistakably human finger lying by the roadside. A search of the city's hospitals was ordered for its owner, but no one was found with a missing digit.

The finger seems to have had no earthly owner in the immediate neighbourhood: so did it come from further afield, or did it come from some unearthly realm?

The same question applies with even greater force to a small white bull that appeared apparently from thin air in a locked cowshed belonging to farmer Derek Steedman, on the Isle of Wight. One moming in January 1984, Steedman found that his herd of 12 Hereford calves had been joined by a two-week-old white Charolais crossbred. It had no identification, and ten months after its arrival no one had claimed it, despite wide local publicity.

THROUGH LOCKED DOORS

The term 'apport' originally meant anything, either inanimate or alive, which materialized in the presence of a medium. The phenomenon was first reported by a Dr Billot in 1839. He described a seance he witnessed in 1819, during which a packet containing three small pieces of bone apparently appeared from nowhere on the floor in his presence. There are innumerable accounts of such things happening in the seance rooms of the 19th century, and parapsychologists have made a definite distinction between materializations that psychic mediums produce apparently out of thin air, and apports as such, which seem to have been transported from one place to another, sometimes through solid walls with locked doors and windows, by some paranormal means. In practice, it is extremely difficult to tell which is which, unless the mysteriously appearing objects are already known to the people they appear before. This has happened: the pioneering 19th-century scientist and psychical investigator Sir William Crookes had one such experience.

In a locked seance room, he thought he heard a handbell ringing, as if someone were carrying it around the room. Then it fell beside him. It was indeed a bell – which, he later discovered, one of his sons had been playing with while the seance was taking place. There was no way the bell could have been brought into the locked room by any normal means.

On 3 December 1908 the citizens of Sydney, Australia, were no doubt amused to read in that day's *Morning Herald* newspaper that the Melbourne millionaire Thomas Welton Stanford, brother of the American railroad magnate and former US Senator Leland Stanford, had been visited by a customs official who suspected that the gentleman owed import duty on several certain small items.

But the reason Stanford had not paid taxes on the curious assortment of dead singing birds, Babylonian clay tablets, ancient coins and other bric-a-brac was simple enough: they had been 'imported' through the agency of a Dr Whitcomb, a former general practitioner of Melbourne, but who had died in England, aged 47, in 1878. Dr Whitcomb was the spirit guide for the medium Charles Bailey, and Bailey had produced these and dozens of other objects as apports in seances.

No more was heard about the officious customs inspector, but many of the apports produced by Bailey are still in the keeping of Stanford University, California, founded by Senator Leland Stanford. His brother Thomas, an ardent spiritualist who employed Charles Bailey as his private medium between 1902 and 1914, also donated $500,000 to the university to establish a fellowship in psychical research.

Bailey's ability to produce apports was prodigious and spectacular. In March 1903, he was put to the test by Dr Charles McCarthy, an eminent Sydney physician, who sewed him into a stout, double-stitched canvas bag, which was sealed at the openings for his head and hands. In the course of six seances, Bailey aported Babylonian clay tablets inscribed with cuneiform writing, coins, semi-precious stones, an Arabic newspaper, a number of live birds, a crab, and a foot-long shark.

In June 1903 Bailey underwent a second series of tests for McCarthy. Prior to the seances he was stripped and searched, made to wear boxing gloves and a fresh suit of clothes during the seance, and enclosed during it in a 'cage' made of mosquito netting. None of this appeared to daunt the medium or staunch the flow of exotic apports.

On other occasions, conducting seances for Thomas Welton Stanford, Bailey produced among other things many more live songbirds, nests with fresh eggs in, quantities of sand 'replete with aquatic fauna', a live turtle, live fish, a fishing net, ivory, beads, a human skull and leopard skin.

Researcher Ivan Sanderson once remarked of apports: 'We've got sound through matter, and sight through matter, why not matter through matter? Matter is 99 per cent holes anyway, and anyone can squirt a jet of water through a chicken wire fence.' Solving the problem may be a little more complex than that, and on a number of occasions medium Charles Bailey was caught out in circumstances that strongly suggested he had hidden his 'apports' about his person before entering the seance room. But he convinced many – and the things he brought into this world can still be seen in the library of Stanford University, California.

Charles Hoy Fort, renowed researcher into anomalous phenomena. Fort was particularly interested in the many accounts of inexplicable showers of fish.

OUT OF THIN AIR

Such events at seances have become less and less common since the end of World War One. This may be because mediums have concentrated on different kinds of spiritual manifestation – and is certainly partly explained by ever more rigorous tests designed to discourage frauds. What remains inexplicable are the hundreds of reports on record of objects that appear as if from nowhere in front of witnesses who are neither mediums nor even remotely interested in psychic matters of any kind. And in these cases it is impossible to say whether the objects involved have come from some other recognizable geographical location, or have materialized 'out of thin air'.

By far the most common apport met today is what Ivan T. Sanderson has called 'Fafrotskies': these are things that are alleged to FALL FROM THE SKIES.

FAFROTSKIES

Fafrotskies have been recorded since the earliest written records began in Sumeria about 5,500 years ago. Then, anything that fell from the sky was thought to have a divine origin. Falls of rain, ice, meteorites – let alone small creatures or artefacts – were seen as equally baffling and were believed to be the gift of the gods. The very idea of water suspended in the air, which was deemed to be empty space, must have seemed as unnatural as the idea that fish or fingers could be waiting in the sky to fall to Earth.

This kind of logic remains potent even in scientific circles in modern times, long after we have ceased to think that a thunderstorm is a sign of the wrath of God. In essence, this sceptical attitude says: 'If science can't explain something, that something can't exist.' Science, as the famed researcher into anomalous phenomena Charles Hoy Fort pointed out, is as much a faith in its own way as the most extreme religion; to reinforce the point, he called anything rejected or ignored by science 'the damned', and wrote a large book detailing how many and how various such 'damned' phenomena really are.

This prejudice of science was nowhere better demonstrated

than in 1772, when a committee of the Académic Française, which included the famous chemist Lavoisier, investigated a stone that had dropped with a loud explosion on Luce in Maine, France, on 13 September 1768. The committee concluded that, as there are no stones in the sky, no stones can fall from the sky. (Unlike the ancient Sumerians, however, they were too inhibited to call the stone a gift of God.) Reports of meteorites – which was what the stone actually was – were due to either peasant superstition or faulty reasoning. Astronomers quietly abandoned this position in the 19th century, but more exotic fafrotskies remained, and still remain, among the 'damned' in orthodox scientific eyes.

TORRENTS OF STONES

In 1860, R.P. Greg published a report on meteorites in the Report of the British Association. It listed almost 2,000 items, complete with dates, reaching back to AD 2. Besides the large amount of most unmeteoric behaviour that Greg documented – 'meteorites' that bounced along, hovered or made angular turns – there were many items said to have 'come down' with meteorites, such as delicately undefined 'gelatinous substances' and even, less delicately, blood.

Stones, whether meteorites or not, have dropped out of nowhere in the most curious circumstances. Two fishermen at a lake in Skaneatles, New York, had their sport interrupted on the evening of 27 October 1973 when three stones, of ever larger size, fell into the lake in front of them. They looked around to find who had thrown them but, finding no one, went back to their rods – only to be battered by a rain of pebbles, which seemed to follow them as they abandoned their fishing and ran for their car. When they stopped to change their clothes, more pebbles fell on them, and on emerging from a bar to which they had repaired to recover, they were yet again showered with stones. When, at last, they parted outside the home of one of the pair, they were assaulted by 'torrents' of still more stones.

Yet more bizarre was the case, reported in 1957, of the young Aborigine farmworker of Pumphrey, Western Australia, around whom stones fell even when he was indoors. Two witnesses swore that on one occasion stones fell at their feet when they were with the young man inside a closed tent (whose material also lacked holes). Scientists claimed, somewhat implausibly, that 'freak winds' were responsible, but did not explain how they collected the stones or why they should deposit their cargo exclusively around one individual.

SHREDS OF MEAT

Fortunately for those unconvinced by the claim that science has all the answers to everything all the time, Charles Hoy Fort produced a treasury of fafrotski reports in his books. In *The Book of the Damned* (1919) in particular, he bombarded the open-minded reader with data of falling ice, ashes, mud, sulphur, hot water, bricks, cinders, stone axes, nails, iron chains, snakes, eels, ants, worms, periwinkles (on the city of Worcester, England, on 28 May 1881), 'butter' (actually a foul-smelling dark-yellow substance that fell over large areas of southern Ireland in 1696), seeds, nuts,

The gigantic meteor crater near the Grand Canyon, Arizona. Reports of meteorites falling from the skies were long dismissed as absurd by the scientific establishment – until the 19th century, when the evidence for their existence became irrefutable.

jelly, and more – including those most frequently reported mysterious apports, showers of fish and frogs – as well as rather more horrid apports of blood and meat.

On 20 July 1851, in the middle of a routine parade at the Benicia army base in San Francisco, California, troops were showered with blood and pieces of what seemed to be beef. Eighteen years later, on 1 August 1869, two acres of the farm owned by a Mr J. Hudson, of Los Nietos, California, were covered with a fall of blood, hair and shreds and strips of meat, some of them 6 in long. The day was clear and windless. This weird phenomenon was still going strong in 1968, when on 27 August blood and flesh fell for about five minutes on an area roughly 1,000 yds square between the towns of Cacapava and São Jose dos Campos in Brazil, and it has been reported many times since.

SNOWED UNDER

When falls of lumps of ice occur, at least rationalists and sceptics can pull a more or less plausible explanation out of the hat: falls of ice are usually blamed on faulty aircraft de-icing equipment and leaking airborne lavatories. But in one study by atmospheric physicist James McDonald, the scientist found that only two out of 30 selected ice falls in the 1950s could be blamed on aircraft.

Inexplicable ice falls have been recorded throughout history. Even if planes had existed at the time to drop these ice bombs, many were so huge that they would have stopped the planes taking off in the first place. For example, a lump with a volume of 18 cubic feet fell on Hungary in 1802, and one measuring about 20 ft around, 'of proportionate thickness', and weighing about half a ton fell on Ord, in the Isle of Skye, Scotland, in 1849. And mysterious lumps of ice continue to fall from the sky.

A 'volleyball-sized' chunk crashed through a roof in Portland, Oregon, on 25 April 1989. It was milky-white in colour and smelled slightly of sulphur. (Other apports have been reported as smelling of sulphur, and some are positively hot when they first appear.)

A 70 kilo block of blue-green ice fell from a cloudless sky on a field near Belgrade in August 1989. A chunk of ice the size of a football fell from a cloudless sky into a garden near Lake Vattem in Sweden in April 1990. It was 'milky' with shades of grey, brown and lilac. A Swedish TV report mentioned several pieces falling over a limited area, and showed several impact craters.

A 20 lb block of ice smashed through the roof of a house in Batley, West Yorkshire, on 11 October 1991. It fell into the kitchen, shortly after the occupant, Mrs Mavis Anderson, had left the room with a cup of tea.

When Mrs Pauline Reidy of Burbank, Illinois, went out to check her car one September evening in 1982, she was astonished to find a small 3 ft by 3 ft snowdrift lying on her front steps. Although it was a cool evening, snow was not expected; and indeed this was the only snow in sight. There was no indication that it had been dumped by a prankster.

BEANFEAST

But what can science make of showers of fruit and nuts, or even beans? In early March 1983, Rita Gibson of Topsham, near Exeter, found a scattering of strange pink beans in her back garden. They were larger than rice grains and smaller than orange pips. 'They could not have been thrown,' she said, 'because our house is surrounded by three walls around a courtyard.' Though they were out of season, they were quite fresh. This was not an isolated example of a bean fall – in September 1945, a lady from St Louis, Missouri, querulously telephoned the local weather bureau to ask if the world was about to end after a shower of beans had fallen around her house.

During the night of 8–9 November 1984, East Crescent, Accrington, in Lancashire, was bombarded with apples – best quality Bramleys and Coxes. Derek and Adrienne Haythornwhite found at least 300 on their back lawn, on the path and in the hedges, and more were found in nearby gardens. The couple were woken up in the night by a thunderous noise on the roof. According to Adrienne Haythornwhite, 'They kept on falling for an hour or longer.'

There was nothing new about this bizarre event, in a way. In 1687, the seeds of ivy berries were found inside hailstones that fell on Wiltshire, England, while on 9 May 1867, Dublin policemen were bombarded with 'nuts or berries' (some may have been hazelnuts) that rained down on them 'in great quantities and with great force'.

RAINING SPRATS AND FROGS

On the night of 27–28 May 1984, there was a fall of fishes in the borough of Newham, east London. Four had been found at the house of Ron Langton and his wife in Central Park Road, East Ham; three in the yard and one on the roof. Mrs Langton said that she had seen another fish on the same day, in a house gutter about half a mile away. The Natural History Museum in London identified the fish as flounders and smelts.

That day, too, a man in neighbouring Canning Town found 30 fish in his garden; his house is about one and a half miles east of the Langtons' house. Another Canning Town resident had found four fish. No one saw any fish fall; all were found in conditions suggesting they fell from above. It had rained heavily and thunderously during the night. All locations were within two miles of the River Thames, and the Natural History Museum suggested that the fish had been transported by a waterspout; but there had been no reports of waterspouts in the Thames that night, though flounders are found in the Thames Estuary.

Small freshwater fish, identified as thread fin shad, fell around Mr and Mrs Ellmers, and their neighbour Walter Davies, in Bonita, California, on the evening of 10 August 1984. They came down with 'harsh wet splats' from a cloudless sky. There was a population of these fish in the Sweetwater Reservoir about two miles away but no funnel cloud capable of lifting the fish had been seen. Nor had anyone seen the flight of pelicans that one wag suggested had caught and then (for reasons that remained unexplained) had dropped the fish.

On the evening of 21 April 1985, there was a heavy rainstorm in the area of St Cloud, Minnesota. One couple noticed 'a white thing with five legs' in their backyard, which on closer inspection turned out to be a starfish. Turning on their outside lights, the couple saw more starfish on their lawn. There was one on the roof of a neighbouring garage roof and more in another garden. The starfish were ocean dwellers that were found only off the coast of Florida. The implausible explanation offered was that the creatures had been flung from a tall building at St Cloud State University a mile away as a joke by students, and then blown by strong winds before falling to the ground.

Many thousands of dead sardines fell 'like a sheet of silver rain' around the house of Harold and Debra Degen of Rosewood, near Ipswich, Queensland, Australia, on 6 February 1989. The Degens gathered a bowlful, some for their cat to appreciate and some to keep as souvenirs. The rest were 'gobbled by kookaburras'. According to the local police, the fall was confined to an area of only two acres.

After fish that fall from the sky, showers of frogs are the classic example of the inexplicable apport from the sky. Tiny – frogs that fall are always tiny, it seems – rose-coloured albino frogs fell in the neighbourhood of Stroud in the west of England during torrential rain some time in October 1987. Two similar falls had been observed in nearby Cirencester two weeks earlier, about the time Britain was dusted with 'Sahara' sand. There was a fourth incident in the Charlton Kings area of Cheltenham, Gloucestershire. According to one witness, the frogs bounced off umbrellas and pavements and hopped off in their hundreds to nearby streams and gardens. The Gloucester Trust for Nature Conservancy investigated the possibility that the frogs had arrived with the sand, possibly 'carried in atmospheric globules of water across land and sea'. The pink frogs seem to have settled in; they were observed in the area as late as the following June.

These recent reports form part of a tradition that reaches back at least as far as the second century AD, when the ancient Greek historian Athenaeus recorded a fall of fish that lasted for three days.

Evidence of a fish fall in East Ham, London, in 1984. There was no doubt that the fish were real, but where they came from – and how – remains a mystery.

PENNIES FROM HEAVEN

If some of the things that fall from the sky are fairly revolting – like the tissue from the lungs of 'a human infant or horse' that fell from a cloudless sky on Bath County, Kentucky, on 3 March 1876 – some have been altogether sweeter in nature. Parts of Lake County, California, were showered with candy during the nights of 2 and 11 September 1857, and some of the local ladies made syrup from the crystals. Still sweeter, to some, are falls of money. Several thousand silver coins fell near the city of Gorky in Russia on 17 June 1940; pennies fell in droves – along with lumps of coal, just to confuse the issue – in 1927 and 1928 in Battersea, London; a single, mint-fresh 2-franc French piece fell into a garden in North Carolina in October 1958; 18 months earlier, however, 'thousands' of 1,000-franc notes rained down on Bourges, France, although no one ever reported losing the huge sum involved. In December 1975, precisely $588 was handed to police by honest citizens of La Salle Street, Chicago, after a shower of dollar bills - though how much was kept by less upright folk is anyone's guess.

Some falls of coins seem to cluster in particular places (and occasionally around a particular individual). Visitors to the graveyard of St Mary's Church, Kenardington, England, have more than once been showered with hot coins. In 1989, David and Sophie Gough witnessed just such a fall; the coins were dated between 1902 and 1953 – 'old' money in Britain, which changed its currency in 1971, and therefore no longer legal tender. Where had it been in the intervening years? The Goughs' comment that 'no aircraft were flying overhead' at the time seems hardly relevant: no one expects aircraft to scatter coins wherever they go, let alone money that has been useless for many years

AN ILL WIND?

The standard explanation for mysterious apports like these is the innocent tornado. Since Jerome Cardan first put the argument forward in the 16th century, sceptics have fallen back on the claim that a whirlwind or waterspout has lifted up the fish, frogs, nuts or whatever else is involved, and deposited them at a distance.

As wind speeds of 280 mph have been measured in tornadoes, there is nothing surprising in the idea that they can lift heavy objects and dump them far away from their original location. A 'moderately devastating' tornado – called T6 on the conventional scale – is characterised thus: 'heavy motor vehicle levitated; strong houses lose entire roofs and perhaps also a wall... less strong buildings collapse'. Tornado damage is well-known for being highly localized and weirdly capricious. One tornado in Iowa destroyed one half of a house and left the other half intact, even leaving a clock ticking on the chimney piece. A baby was plucked from its mother's arms at Louisville in 1890 and set down unharmed six blocks away. In Oklahoma in 1905, a tornado removed all the shoes from the people it struck and killed in its path. In 1911, a schoolgirl in Bradford, England, was lifted 20 ft into the air by a gust of wind and was dashed to the ground and killed. In 1943, in Lansing, Michigan, a tornado stripped a row of 30 chickens bare of their feathers.

The result of a tornado at Arreton, Isle of Wight, on 19 June 1985: dagger-sharp pieces of glass, 9–12 in long, lie deeply embedded in aluminium.

Tornadoes (and waterspouts and freak winds) no doubt do account for some unexplained arrivals, and falling fish are the most obvious candidates; it's most likely that the waterspout responsible won't be seen, especially at sea or at night. The trouble with the tornado hypothesis when applied to other objects is that one never seems to hear of the corresponding loss of a harvest of apples, or nuts, or dollar bills – these showers of money, after all, can't all be ill-gotten gains, snatched by the winds of poetic justice from the hands of thieves, who might suffer further by admitting the loss. And tornadoes do not deposit calves in cowsheds with such care that they remember to lock the doors behind them afterwards.

Still less likely is it that tornadoes, or any other unusual weather conditions, would not only select coins to drop on the unsuspecting, but select one person upon whom to drop nothing but coins. A man who happened to come in the way of falls of frogs one month, fish the next, and coins a year later is not to be expected according to the laws of chance, probability and averages. Someone, like Albert Williamson of Ramsgate, Kent, who in 1989 admitted he had been showered with coins (and nothing else except God's own rain) on and off for six years, is not likely to believe, any more than anyone else, that anything as unpredictable as the weather was responsible.

Besides, these things keep falling from clear blue skies; in Chesterfield County, South Carolina, even rain fell for about 12 days out of a sunny cloudless sky in October 1886. Fish, frogs and toads in such falls are more often than not alive – a likely story if they have been suspended in the chill upper atmosphere for days on end. And how tornadoes find blood, meat and other grim organic matter to drop in highly selective areas is not easily explained, either.

Charles Hoy Fort suggested that such things came from a 'Super-Sargasso' sea in the sky. The notion is, to say the least, fanciful – but perhaps no more ridiculous, in the final analysis, than the all-embracing application of the explanation that tornadoes, waterspouts and 'freak winds' account for every one of such events. To anyone with an open mind – that is, to anyone with a genuinely sceptical outlook – where falls, or apports, of these things ultimately come from, remains as much a mystery as it ever was.

VANISHINGS

The stage magician discovered his astonishing ability by accident, but he was unable to control it. Then one evening, in front of a startled audience, his body started to become translucent.

Stage magicians can create extraordinary illusions when it comes to making people and things – even a pair of live leopards – seem to disappear, but none has matched the trick performed at least three times by Dr William Neff in the 1960s. On those occasions he became invisible, literally disappearing into thin air in front of witnesses.

The first time this happened was during his stage act while he was performing in Chicago. The second time, he was at home, when he vanished without warning – 'casually', as he put it – and reappeared in front of his wife, who was apparently not amused.

The third occasion was again during his stage show, at New York's Paramount Theater. This time, radio broadcaster 'Long John' Knebel was in the audience – as reliable a witness as anyone could wish for, as Knebel was well known for his hostility to claims of the paranormal. In his book *The Way Out World* Knebel says he saw Neff's form 'becoming minutely translucent' until 'you could see the traveler curtain clearly behind his translucent figure'. Yet more bizarre was that Neff's voice was unaffected by his invisibility, although it's unlikely, in the circumstances, that any of those present paid much attention to what he was saying. Knebel described Neff's reappearance like this: 'Gradually a rather faint outline, like a very faint pencil sketch… appeared again.'

The irony was that Neff himself was unaware of his own ability. He did not know when he had become invisible and had no way to control the phenomenon.

DISAPPEARING TRICKS

The case of Dr Neff throws a huge spanner in the works of anyone trying to explain (or explain away) what happens when people 'mysteriously disappear'. We are not here considering cases in which the victims have simply dropped out of sight for their own reasons or almost certainly been the victims of crime. These are cases in which people vanish within minutes or seconds, and of whom no trace has been found despite immediate and intense searches, and who neither had any apparent wish or need to disappear, nor were snatched away by any natural agency.

If no natural cause can be found, the presumption is usually that such people have been translated into some 'other dimension';

once, people would have said they had been stolen away by the fairies. (In some cases, they may be taken through some other dimension to land up in another place on this Earth; these are known as 'teleportations'.) Perhaps that does happen; but in Neff's case since his voice could still be heard by his astonished audience the process was, at best, only partly begun – let alone completed – and reversed itself shortly thereafter. On the other hand, maybe disappearing people do what Neff did, but more thoroughly if no more willingly, and without the privilege of being allowed to be heard or to reappear. Perhaps we are surrounded by invisible people.

Whatever the mechanism of such events, the following cases leave one boggling at the speed and arbitrariness with which people (and occasionally things) are seemingly snatched from this existence – and, unlike many such stories in the literature of the paranormal, they are genuinely mysterious.

INTRIGUING CAVE PAINTINGS

In 1847, the German explorer Ludwig Leichardt set out to cross the Great Australian Desert from east to west, having already crossed the continent from Moreton Bay, Queensland, to Port Essington, Northern Territory, between 1844 and 1845. Nobel Prizewinner Patrick White based his novel *Voss* on Leichardt's next expedition, which took 50 bullocks, 20 mules and 7 horses with them when they set out for Perth from the Darling Downs, west of Brisbane. Somewhere along the Cogoon river, the entire party vanished. Repeated searches found absolutely no trace of man, beast or equipment. A disappearance in the Australian outback is perhaps not inexplicable, but the story has a curious sequel.

In January 1975, Zacharias Mathias, a 40-year-old wildlife ranger, arrived in Darwin with photographs of a series of intriguing Aboriginal cave paintings. They depicted a pipe-smoking white man riding a horse, with a second white man on foot but carrying a saddle. A group of Aborigines was shown carrying a third white man. The President of the Northern Territory Historical Society immediately made plans to send an expedition, guided by Mathias, to investigate the paintings, which 'would give us the first positive clue to the disappearance... of Ludwig Leichardt'. But then Mathias himself vanished, and was never seen or heard from again.

DEEP TROUBLE

In June 1872, the Mississippi riverboat *Iron Mountain* (not Iron Maiden as some accounts have it) left Vicksburg, Mississippi, with 52 passengers plus a deck cargo of cotton bales and towing a string of barges laden with cotton and molasses. Some hours later, another riverboat, the *Iroquois Chief*, rounded a bend just outside Vicksburg and nearly ran into a haphazard, leaderless fleet of barges. They turned out to be from the *Iron Mountain*, and their tow-rope had been cut - a sure sign that the riverboat had been in deep trouble.

The only difficulty was that there was no sign of the *Iron Mountain*, nor had there been any since she had rounded the bend in the river and gone out of sight of Vicksburg. This is truly bizarre for, if the ship had sunk, her deck cargo at least would have been seen floating by someone on the busy river, and it is hardly likely that all 52 passengers (let alone the crew) would have drowned, let alone in such a way that not one of their bodies would float. No one heard an explosion – which would have scattered debris very

In earlier times, a person's sudden disappearance would be explained as the work of the fairies, who lived in a parallel world that could rarely be perceived by mere mortals.

obviously and very wide, for the *Iron Mountain* was one of the queens of the Mississippi – over 180 ft long, with a beam of 35 ft, and with five boilers to power her massive paddles. But searchers found nothing: no passengers, no crew – alive or dead – and no cargo or wreckage. The *Iron Mountain* had simply vanished.

THE LADY VANISHES

On 12 December 1910, socialite Dorothy Arnold, the 25-year-old niece of the US Supreme Court judge Rufus L. Peckham, left her family's fashionable home at 108 East 79th Street at about 11 a.m. and went shopping for an evening dress. At about 2 p.m., she met a friend, Gladys King, on Fifth Avenue. They chatted for a while and parted, Miss Arnold giving her friend a cheery goodbye wave. Dorothy Arnold was never seen again. If she was kidnapped, no ransom was demanded. She had no cause to commit suicide or flee her comfortable and carefree existence as one of New York's elite. She just… disappeared.

In February 1975, Mr Jackson Wright was driving his wife Martha from New Jersey to mid-town Manhattan. It was snowing heavily and once they had entered the Lincoln Tunnel at Weehawken and were free of the weather, Wright drew up to clear the snow from his car and improve visibility. Martha, aged 36, began to clear the rear window, while Wright dealt with the windshield. When he had finished, Jackson Wright looked up to speak to his wife. She was nowhere to be seen.

On Saturday, 14 July 1990, an outing organized by the Orkney Heritage Society and the Royal Society for the Protection of Birds landed 88 ferry passengers on Eynhallow, a small uninhabited island off Rousay, for a short visit. Only 86 intrepid birdwatchers returned. Police and coastguards searched the island and the mainland coastline for the missing visitors, and a rescue helicopter with heat-seeking equipment scanned the area for signs of life. Nothing was found.

According to local tradition, Eynhallow is a sinister place. It is said that no mice, rats or cats can survive there, and that blood will flow from any corn cut after sunset. One legend has it that Eynhallow is a 'vanishing isle', appearing and reappearing as it will. To complicate matters concerning the missing pair, some believers in

Orcadian folklore suggested that the two missing 'tourists' might actually be mermen or mermaids, returning to their ancestral home. The Fin Folk, as they are known in Orkney, are supposed to look much like humans. Their scales appear simply as clothing, the female tail as a shining skirt – although none of the other visitors to the island seem to have noticed anything so distinctive about their companions. Nor is it clear why merfolk should book their passage on a boat rather than make the journey in their natural element.

Another related (but no less far-fetched) solution to the mystery was put forward: that the two humans had been kidnapped by mermaids. The reason: mermaids, although beautiful when young, grow repulsively ugly as they age, unless they can secure a human husband.

Sometime after midnight on 26 February 1985, Richard Brownell, aged 27, and his 25-year-old fiancée Sandra O'Grady left a bar in Newport Beach, California, with another man after they had told friends that they had paid him to fly them to Las Vegas for a spot of gambling. An hour later, a single-engine Cessna 152 light aircraft crashed into the Pacific Ocean off Newport Beach. The bodies of Brownell and O'Grady were found strapped to their seats inside. No engine faults were found, and three searches of the surrounding ocean failed to find another body.

When two birdwatchers went missing from Eynhallow in Scotland's Orkneys, in 1990, local people offered two extraordinary explanations: either the missing pair had been abducted by mermaids, or they were themselves merfolk and had returned to their ancestral home.

Neither of the dead couple could fly a plane, so a third party, the pilot, had to have been on board. A car belonging to the plane's owner was found near the plane's tie-down spot at John Wayne Airport, but his whereabouts were unknown. The dead pair had had about $3,000 on them when they set out, but only small change was found on their bodies. Did the pilot who offered them a lift rob them, then bail out, leaving them to die? Or did something more bizarre occur?

At 5 a.m. on 17 January 1989, Graham Marsden, 45, a businessman from Poole, Dorset, filled up his red Volkswagen Polo at the Rownhams service area on the M27 motorway near Southampton, Hampshire. After paying his bill, he asked the way to the men's room. He was last seen walking towards it. His car stood unattended for an hour, and finally the worried cashier went to look for him. There was no sign of the man, and the police were called. They searched the surrounding woods with tracker dogs, but found nothing.

Self-professed witness Carlos Allende claimed that an application of the theory of relativity by Albert Einstein enabled a ship to be teleported from one dock to another.

Marsden appeared to have no personal or financial worries - no reason, in fact, to want to disappear. 'If he planned to disappear,' a police spokesman commented, 'why did he fill his car with petrol first and leave it at the pumps? And why choose a service station miles from anywhere? We are mystified.'

A Venezuelan DC-9 jet took off from Maracaibo International Airport, 350 miles from Caracas, at 3.55 p.m. on 5 March 1991. It was on a routine flight, and was due to land at Santa Barbara el Zulia, another oil city in western Venezuela 135 miles away, 35 minutes later. Radio contact with the ground ceased after 25 minutes, although air traffic controllers on the ground received no distress signals. The official Venezuelan news agency, Venpres, released a list of the 38 people on board, including one child and five crew. A plane and a helicopter flew in daylight over the normal route the jet would have taken – a plains area on the rim of Maracaibo Lake – but found no sign of wreckage.

TOP-SECRET EXPERIMENTS

These disappearances have every sign of being random and inexplicable. There is no reason why the people involved should have vanished, unless, by some extraordinary coincidence, every one of them (all 52 passengers of a Mississippi riverboat – and all 38 people on board a Venezuelan airliner?) had for instance a mole on their right arm that made them of irresistible if, to us, unfathomable interest to whatever powers took them away. And there may be perfectly prosaic explanations for all of them, although there seems not to be, according to our current knowledge. But unlike these random cases of mysterious disappearance, others attract the suspicion that some kind of determined intelligence lies behind the vanishings.

In one notorious instance, the agency responsible has been unequivocally identified: and there is nothing mysterious or paranormal about it. It is the US Navy.

The story goes that a top-secret experiment by the US Navy in 1943 first made a warship invisible and then, later, teleported it from one dock to another. The only evidence for this is the testimony of

Carlos Miguel Allende (who also called himself Carl M. Allende), who first gave his version of what happened in two rambling letters to scientist and UFO writer Morris K. Jessup in 1956.

According to Allende, a US government scientist, Dr Franklin Reno, had developed an application of Einstein's relativity theory that enabled the US Navy to render the destroyer USS *Eldridge* and her crew invisible. This experiment was conducted at sea in October 1943 and was witnessed by Allende from aboard the steamer SS *Andrew Furuseth*. (The records show that Allende was indeed on this boat at this time.) Allende alleged that the *Eldridge* was bathed in a strange force field, which extended 'one hundred yards out from each beam of the ship'. The experiment was a success, except for side effects on the crew: some died, some went insane, and some continued to lapse into invisibility. Allende said the incident was reported in a Philadelphia paper sometime between 1944 and 1946.

This report has never been traced. Charles Berlitz and William Moore, who wrote a bestseller called *The Philadelphia Experiment*, reproduce an alleged news report about a brawl in a tavern near the Navy docks in Philadelphia, which says that during the mayhem two sailors vanished into thin air. This report came from an anonymous source and was a photocopy, not the original clipping, and shows neither the newspaper's name nor its date. It has not been proved authentic. It does not even look like an item from the Philadelphia newspapers of the time, all of which printed their news in narrower columns than the clipping that Berlitz and Moore reproduce.

Allende also said that, in a further experiment, the USS *Eldridge* was teleported from its Philadelphia dock to a dock in the Newport News area of Virginia, and back again. He was not a witness, but saw a report in a Philadelphia paper, which 'may have been in 1956'. This report has never been found either.

The US Navy has always denied the story, and said that the technology required does not exist. Dr Franklin Reno is untraceable, although Berlitz and Moore claimed that Franklin Reno is a pseudonym, and that they had talked to him. All he told them was that he had provided figures for a discussion on a project using electromagnetic fields to deflect torpedoes and mines. This hardly constitutes corroboration of Allende's story.

None of the crew of the *Furuseth* has ever made any statement about the alleged experiment. Even Berlitz and Moore admit that the Navy is unlikely to have conducted a top-secret experiment in open seas and in full view of merchant ships like the *Furuseth*. In any case, records of the two ships' movements rule out October as the month for the experiment; the only possible date is 16 August, and there is no direct evidence that either ship was near the other on this date.

If there is any doubt that the entire 'Philadelphia Experiment' story existed from start to finish purely in the mind of Carlos Miguel Allende (give or take a few writers), an extract from his original letter to Morris Jessup should allay it. Social workers and psychologists will instantly recognize the style:

' "Results" of My friend Dr Franklin Reno, Were used... The Result was & stands today as Proof that The Unified Field Theory to a certain extent is correct... The "result" was complete invisibility of a ship, Destroyer type, and all of its crew. While at Sea. (Oct. 1943) The Field Was effective in an oblate spheroidal shape,

British troops in Gallipoli in 1915. According to three witnesses, a whole regiment of men was abducted, apparently in a mysterious clound, during the ill-fated Gallipoli campaign.

extending one Hundred yards (More or Less, due to Lunar position & latitude) out from each beam of the ship. Any Person Within that sphere became vague in form BUT He too observed those Persons aboard that ship as though they too were of the same state, yet, were walking upon nothing. Any person without that sphere could see Nothing save the clearly Defined shape of the Ships Hull in the Water...

'There are only a very few of the original Experimental D-E's Crew Left by Now, Sir. Most went insane, one just walked "throo" His quarters Wall in sight of His Wife & Child & 2 other crew Members (WAS NEVER SEEN AGAIN), two "Went into 'The Flame'", i.e. They "Froze" & caught fire, while carrying common Small-Boat Compasses... THEY BURNED FOR 18 DAYS... The experiment Was a Complete Success. The Men Were Complete Failures.'

INEXPLICABLE LOSSES

Another highly dubious disappearing act, which was first made public in 1965, is the one involving an entire regiment of British troops, the First-Fourth Norfolks, who allegedly vanished into a cloud (which may have been a UFO) in the midst of the battle for Hill 60 in Suvla Bay, Gallipoli, Turkey, on 21 August 1915. According to three eyewitnesses, who were serving with the New Zealand Army, manning an observation post in a neighbouring sector, that day was cloudless and bright but for a group of clouds that, oddly, did not move despite a breeze blowing at about 4–5 mph. One cloud – an 'absolutely dense, solid-looking structure' – seemed to be resting on the ground across a creek near Hill 60. The New Zealanders, whose post overlooked Hill 60 by some 300 ft, then observed:

'A British regiment, the First-Fourth Norfolk... marching up this sunken road or creek towards Hill 60. However, when they arrived at this cloud, they marched straight into it, with no hesitation, but no one ever came out to deploy and fight at Hill 60. About an hour later, after the last of the file had disappeared into it, this cloud very unobtrusively lifted off the ground and, like any cloud or fog would, rose slowly until it joined the other similar clouds which were mentioned at the beginning of this account. On viewing them again, they all looked alike "as peas in a pod". . . as soon as the singular cloud had risen to their level, they all moved away northwards... In a matter of about three quarters of an hour they had all disappeared from view.

'The regiment mentioned is posted as missing or "wiped out" and on Turkey surrendering in 1918, the first thing Britain demanded of Turkey was the return of this regiment. Turkey replied that she had neither captured this regiment, nor made contact with it, and did not know it existed... Those who observed this incident can vouch for the fact that Turkey never captured that regiment, nor made contact with it.'

This story has been repeated time and again in books and broadcasts about 'unexplained mysteries', but there are plenty of proven errors in this account, as researcher Paul Begg divulged in 1979, in his meticulously researched book *Into Thin Air*. The first mistake should have been obvious to anyone with any acquaintance with British Army organisation, let alone to those who fought alongside the British in Gallipoli: the First-Fourth Norfolks is the first battalion of the Fourth Norfolk Regiment, not a regiment in its own right. Second, that particular battalion did not disappear that day or any other, but went on to fight with distinction in Gallipoli until the end of 1915, when it was relieved and posted elsewhere. However, on 12 (not 21) August, the First Battalion of the Fifth Norfolk Regiment's Colonel, 16 officers and 250 men did vanish. On that day, they were in hot pursuit of the enemy when night fell; the next day, there was no trace of them. But they were operating 4 and a half miles from the position of the New Zealanders, and nowhere near Hill 60.

Sir Ian Hamilton, the general commanding the operation, described the disappearance of the First-Fifth Norfolks in despatches as 'a very mysterious thing', but it has to be remembered that the Gallipoli campaign was one of the most disastrously mismanaged of World War One: conditions both in and out of combat were appalling, confused and lethal, and of the 34,000 British and allied troops who died there, no fewer than 27,000 have no known grave. That less than 1 per cent of this number vanished without explanation in the heat of battle – and at night - in one small incident is not so surprising.

Why should three New Zealand veterans make up such an

outlandish tale? Perhaps the answer is that they did not. Begg suggests that they simply fused together their 50-year-old memories of August 1915 and two separate accounts in an official account of the Gallipoli expedition, 'The Final Report Of The Dardanelles Commission'. The two accounts are on facing pages in the report.

The first describes the disappearance of the First-Fifth Norfolks on 12 August. The second describes the peculiar weather conditions of 21 August, when a combined Australian and New Zealand force attacked Hill 60: 'By some freak of nature Suvla Bay and Plain were wrapped in a strange mist on the afternoon of 21 August.' On that day, too, the Sherwood Rangers attacked Hill 60 and were wiped out; it is possible that the old soldiers confused the disappearance of the Norfolks with the carnage, and unusual weather, that they witnessed around Hill 60.

Significantly, the report was published in full only in 1965 – the year the three New Zealanders published their curiously conflated account of these two incidents (and dates), and which was the 50th anniversary of the battle – making it all the more likely that the 'witnesses' would have read it. Simple human error would account for the creation of the 'kidnapping' of the Norfolks by a cloud. Wishful thinking, and a shortage of the kind of research that distinguishes Paul Begg's work, accounts for the story's repetition and acceptance at face value. The fate of 267 men from the First-Fifth Norfolks is still a mystery - but it is not a mystery that has any connection with the paranormal.

However, some very weird clouds do certainly exist, as a report in the *Philadelphia Inquirer* on 1 August 1904 testifies. The British SS *Mohican* had just berthed at Philadelphia, having arrived, the paper said, from Ibraila, Rumania (in fact, later research has established, it was on its way there). According to Captain Urquhart, the *Mohican's* master, the ship had been on a heading for the Delaware breakwater when a weird 'magnetic' cloud had descended around it at latitude 37° 16° North, longitude 72' 48' West. For half an hour it enveloped the ship and 'made everything glow'. The compass spun wildly, while iron chains on deck were magnetized, clinging together so powerfully that no one could move them. The cloud was grey, with glowing spots in it, and so dense that nothing could be seen beyond the decks. 'It appeared as if the whole world was a mass of glowing fire,' said Urquhart. 'The hair on our heads and in our beards stuck out like bristles on a pig… all the joints of the body seemed to stiffen… there was a great silence over everything that only added to the terror.' Then the cloud lifted and moved off over the sea.

The Mohican did not disappear, however, and neither did any of her crew. But there is no lack of ships that, if they themselves have remained untouched, have indeed suffered the inexplicable loss of their crews.

The sudden disappearance of the entire crew of the **Mary Celeste** *is one of the greatest mysteries. The ship was found adrift in the Atlantic in December 1872.*

A CARGO OF GOLD

The most celebrated of these cases is undoubtedly that of the *Mary Celeste*, which was found in the Atlantic Ocean on 5 December 1872 at latitude 38° 20° North, longitude 17° 50° West – about 400 miles west of Lisbon, Portugal - with her jib, fore topmast staysail and fore lower topsail set, her cargo intact, and in sound condition. The only things missing were the ship's boat, and her entire crew of seven. Stories that sailors from the *Dei Gratia*, the ship that found her, went aboard to find the captain's beakfast laid and the food still warm upon the plates are fiction, but there is no doubt that the *Mary Celeste* was in almost perfect order and that no satisfactory explanation has ever been found for the peculiar disappearance of her crew. There is equally no doubt that the *Mary Celeste* was a jinxed ship; what forces were really at work, whether normal or paranormal, about this boat, is anyone's guess.

But the *Mary Celeste* is by no means the only ship to have lost its crew for reasons that remain unexplained. Paul Begg cites the following in his invaluable book *Into Thin Air*.

On 28 February 1855, the barquentine *James B. Chester* was sighted about 600 miles south-west of the Azores, in the Atlantic Ocean, 'yawing back and forth and [apparently] sailing with no one at the wheel'. That, indeed, proved to be the case, nor was anyone else on board. The boarding party, from the *Marathon*, found signs that the ship had been abandoned in a hurry, but the evidence could as well point to the crew being kidnapped, for drawers had been rifled, and none of the ship's lifeboats had been launched. On the other hand, the ship's compass and papers were missing, indicating a deliberate and calculated departure by officers and men. To confuse the issue further, the ship was completely sound, and the cargo intact.

One of the most tantalising tales of lost ships is that of the wool clipper *Marlborough*, which sailed for England from New Zealand in 1890. She was carrying a cargo of gold bullion, even then worth perhaps as much as £2 million; a temptation, perhaps, for someone in the know, for she was never seen again. But, nearly a quarter of a century later, the Wellington (New Zealand) *Evening Post* of 13 November 1913 reported that the crew of the British ship *Johnson* had made a curious discovery off the coast of Chile that year. (The standard New Zealand–England voyage in those days was first to Iquique, Chile, then round Cape Horn and across the Atlantic to Cape Town, South Africa, with a final leg up the Atlantic, often calling at Hamburg before finally dropping anchor in the Pool of London.) The *Johnson's* crew had come across a derelict ship, its sails mouldy and in tatters, its timbers rotten, and with a score of skeletons as its only crew. The ruined hulk's prow bore, in faded letters, the name *Marlborough*. The report does not say whether or not the ship's fabled cargo of gold was still aboard, or even if anyone looked for it - perhaps for the simple reason that by then the *Marlborough* and her gold had been forgotten. In October 1917, the *Zebrina* set sail in fair weather from Falmouth, Cornwall, for Brieux, France. Two days later she was found with no crew but in perfectly good condition. There was no clue as to why she had been abandoned – or her crew abducted, if that is what happened. In July 1941, the French cutter *Belle Isle* was found drifting with her sails set near the Gulf of Lyon. She was perfectly seaworthy but for the lack of her crew. There were no signs of violence on board.

NORMAL OCCURRENCES?

Mysterious disappearances do occur, but only when someone like the dematerializing Dr William Neff returns from such a vanishing to describe the experience will we be sure that something paranormal is afoot. Which does not mean that something paranormal is not afoot in these cases – it only means that we have no evidence for it. But then we have no evidence that anything 'normal' occurred, either.

CURSES

The pregnant serving maid, cruelly abandoned by her
aristocratic seducer, put a curse on the noble family. Even
when his brother committed suicide at the age of 26, the
young 8th Earl of Craven refused to believe in the curse.
He was proved fatally wrong.

At 2 a.m. on 30 August 1990, 28-year-old Simon Craven was driving to his home, Peelings Manor, near Pevensey, Sussex; he was cruising along the seafront in Eastbourne, Sussex, when his car collided with parked vehicles. Craven died in the ambulance that rushed him to hospital. This was no ordinary traffic accident, however: the dead man had been the 8th Earl of Craven, and his death appeared to fulfil a 350-year-old curse on his family. The late Lord Craven's grandfather, the 5th Earl, died aged 35 during a wild party aboard a yacht. The 6th Earl died of leukaemia at 47. Simon Craven succeeded to the title in 1983 when his elder brother Thomas, the 7th Earl, shot himself in a fit of depression at the age of 26. Apart from the original Earl Craven – who was granted the title by King Charles II in 1664, and died aged 91 in 1697 – it is said that no one who has held the earldom has lived beyond the age of 57.

The curse is in fact supposed to hang over the Cravens' ancestral home, Morewood House in Hamstead Marshall, Berkshire – the first peerage to be granted the family was the Barony of Hamstead Marshall – and, according to tradition, was laid on the family by a servant girl, whom one of the dynasty's sons had made pregnant and abandoned. The house was sold after the 7th Earl's suicide, but the sale seems neither to have saved the 8th Earl from an untimely end, nor to have left the house. Only a week before Simon Craven's death, a verdict of suicide was recorded on Morewood's latest owner, Dr Robert Reid. (The double tragedy is not necessarily a result of the curse being somehow confused: 'house' and 'family' are often used synonymously of great families, as in 'the House of Windsor' for the present British Royal Family, so the curse would presumably affect both.) Despite this grim history, the Cravens' lawyer maintained that none of the family believes in the curse.

If not quite a curse, something very similar afflicted the family of Doreen Squires of Riverdale, Devon, for several generations. She felt she had reason to worry when her son Martin, aged 25, had a piece of steel fly into his right eye while working in a saw mill in nearby Totnes. Her father, grandfather and great-grandfather had all lost their right eyes in accidents. Jim Chapple, a stone cracker, lost his eye to a stone chipping. His son Jim, a blacksmith, lost his to a piece of steel while making a horseshoe, and his son Adrian,

Doreen's father, lost his in a quarry blast. All had been born on 29 September, which is the birthday of the British naval hero Horatio, Lord Nelson. He lost his right eye during the blockade of Corsica in 1794: he was in the way of a bit of gravel that was sent flying when an enemy cannonball landed near him. Martin Squires, however, recovered from his accident with no lasting damage to his sight. But he was not born on 29 September.

A GRISLY MONSTER

Curses on families and their succeeding generations are by no means new. The second of the ten commandments given to Moses on Sinai contains the threat of just such a retribution should the Hebrews fall into idolatry; Exodus 20, verse 5, says plainly: 'for I the LORD thy God am a jealous God, visiting the iniquity of the fathers upon the children unto the third and fourth generation of them that hate me'.

The ancient Greeks took curses seriously. Not even animals were exempt. The reason, according to Greek myth, that crows are black is entirely due to the wrath of the goddess Athene; once, they were pure white, and were her favourite birds besides. The tale goes that the god Hephaistos was besotted with Athene, and tried to rape her, but he bungled the dreadful business, so that his sperm fell on Mother Earth and made her pregnant instead. The result was a grisly monster, part boy, part serpent. Athene felt a curious obligation to look after this strange creature, but (in the way of goddesses) delegated the task to the daughters of King Kekrops of her patron city, Athens.

Athene secreted the hideous child in a basket, and insisted the princesses never look inside it. Naturally, they peeped, and were so disgusted at what they saw that they promptly threw themselves off the Acropolis. This is where a crow, whose identity has never been established, made a fundamental error of judgement. Thinking he was doing Athene a good turn, he told the goddess what had happened. Athene was outraged, and rewarded the crow, and all his kind, by turning his feathers black. The truth of this story is plain to anyone who has seen the hooded crows of Greece: a sad reminder of their former brilliant whiteness is preserved in the dull grey-pink plumage on their bodies – while all the rest is deep black.

Rough copies of the allegedly Celtic heads that were found in a garden in Hexham, Northumberland, and indentified as ritual sculptures dating from the 2nd century AD.

THE MUMMY'S CURSE

A good curse, like a diamond, it seems, is forever. The most famous ancient curse is probably the one allegedly uttered by those who buried the Egyptian boy king, Tutankhamun, who died at the age of 18 in approximately 1340 BC.

Rumours that tampering with Tutankhamun's grave were fraught with psychic danger began with the death of the 5th Earl of Carnarvon in 1923. This happened just a few months after the discovery of the boy Pharaoh's tomb, and Carnarvon had sponsored the dig that uncovered it. Carnarvon had first employed the English archaeologist Howard Carter, who found Tutankhamun's last resting place, to search for antiquities in Egypt in 1907. By 1922, Carter had unearthed a number of tombs and made some interesting finds, but in Carnarvon's eyes the expense involved, by now some £40,000, was beginning to seem onerous in view of his meagre returns – archaeology then being largely a matter of digging up what treasures one could, and selling them to the highest bidder: essentially, it was grave-robbing made respectable by the interest of aristocratic European gentlemen and a dash of accompanying scholarship.

In October 1922, Carter persuaded Carnarvon to keep financing his searches for one more season and, perhaps to celebrate his continued employment, bought himself a yellow canary. His Egyptian workers said it would bring him luck. On 26 November 1922, Carter, literally, struck gold: he broke into the grave of Tutankhamun, along with Carnarvon, his daughter Lady Evelyn, and Carter's assistant, Arthur Callender. Four days later, Carnarvon received a prophecy of his death in Egypt which the noted mystic, Count Hamon, had received by automatic writing.

The front of the decorated head-dress on the mummy's golden mask bore the image of Wadjet, the cobra goddess who protected Egyptian royalty; when Carter's canary was gobbled up by a cobra, the Egyptian workers on the site were convinced a human death would shortly, and surely, follow. It did.

By the end of February Carnarvon was ill; his teeth were falling out, and he was racked by fever. He went into a coma – the cause was diagnosed as blood poisoning – and he died, aged only 57, on 4 April 1923. At the same time, it is said, his pet fox terrier Susan howled, and died with her master.

At this point the notion began that the Pharaoh's tomb was cursed. The first to fuel the flames of the 'Curse of the Pharaohs' were, of course, the hacks of Fleet Street, who with red-rimmed eyes reported that carved above the entrance to Tutankhamun's tomb were the words 'Death shall come to him who touches the tomb' – or perhaps they were 'Death will slay with wings whoever disturbs the peace of the pharaohs', depending on the reporter.

Such protective threats certainly were written on some royal tombs in Egypt. One states bluntly that anyone disturbing the sanctity of the last royal resting place 'shall hunger, thirst, faint, and sicken', but Howard Carter resolutely maintained that no such curse was attached to Tutankhamun's grave. In the early 1980s, Richard Adamson, a former military policeman who had worked as a guard on the dig, stated that the rumour of a curse had been started by Carnarvon himself – simply to keep thieves away from what he knew was a fabulous treasure.

Nevertheless, there have been other sudden and not altogether explicable deaths among those who have visited the tomb or come in contact with its riches. A Professor La Fleur died the very evening of the day he visited the tomb; the American millionaire George Jay-Gould died after developing a fever on the day he went; A.C. Mace, one of Carter's assistants, resigned in 1924 after persistent bouts of fever and died in 1928; Richard Bethell, another assistant, died at the age of 45. Arthur Weighall, a third, died of an unknown fever. Of those who were associated with the find, he was claimed as the 21st victim, after Carnarvon's half-brother, who killed himself.

Howard Carter, however, not only led the team who broke into the grave but removed a number of treasures from the tomb for his personal collection; he was surely the prime candidate for supernatural vengeance, but he lived another 17 years without mishap and died unspectacularly, aged 65, in 1939.

The latest theory to explain the apparent curse is that some mummies are radioactive. In January 1992, a Cairo University professor was reported in *New Scientist* as suggesting that Carnarvon and others may have died from radiation sickness. But Howard Carter, it seems, was immune even to that.

A WEREWOLF

In February 1972, brothers Colin and Leslie Robson were clearing weeds in the garden of their council house at Hexham, about 20 miles from Newcastle upon Tyne, Northumberland, when they found two carved stone heads, each about the size of a tennis ball. One, which the Robsons called 'the boy', was greenish-grey, glinting with quartz crystals, and very heavy; the other was of rougher material, and its witchlike appearance made the Robsons dub it 'the girl'. The brothers took the heads inside, but then odd things began to happen: the heads turned around spontaneously, a mirror frame was found shattered in a frying pan, mysterious whiplash sounds were heard and one of the Robson daughters had her mattress showered with glass.

The effects were not limited to the Robsons' household while the heads were in their house. One night the next-door neighbour's ten-year-old son thought something was touching him in the dark as he was trying to sleep. His mother told him not to be silly, and was promptly horrified to see a 'half-human, half-sheep' shape come towards her, touch her, and slink out of the room on all fours. The Robson boys said, too, that a luminous flower had grown one Christmas at the place where the heads were found, and a mysterious light was seen hovering above the spot one night while the heads were in the house.

When, later in 1972, the heads were borrowed for study by Celtic scholar Dr Anne Ross, an archaeologist at Southampton University, the Robsons' house was troubled no more by unpleasant and unearthly events. Initially, Dr Ross identified the heads as typical Celtic sculptures, about 1,800 years old. She kept them in a box in her study. A few nights later, she woke up cold and frightened, and saw a tall figure in her bedroom doorway:

'It was about six feet high, slightly stooping, and it was black against the white door... The upper part I would have said was wolf and the lower part was human. It was covered with a kind of black, very dark fur. It went out and I just saw it clearly and then it disappeared and something made me run after it – a thing I wouldn't normally have done, but I felt compelled to run after it... I could hear it going down the stairs. Then it disappeared toward the back of the house. When I got to the bottom of the stairs I was terrified.'

Dr Ross then returned to wake her husband. A search revealed nothing.

A few days after this, Dr Ross's teenage daughter Berenice came home from school and saw a large entity – which she described as 'as near a werewolf as anything' – rush down the

In response to Iraq's missile attacks on Israel during the Gulf war, an extremist Jewish group performed the rare Rod of Light ceremony, in which a death curse was pronounced on Iraqi president Saddam

stairs towards her. It vaulted over the banisters and landed on the floor with a 'kind of plop'. Like her mother, Berenice felt compelled to follow the thing as it padded away, and it vanished by the door of the Rosses' music room. Subsequently, Dr Ross occasionally felt a cold presence in the house, and heard the thing's footsteps. Her study door would fly open on its own.

The entity, although described as a 'werewolf', bore some resemblance to the wulver – half-man, half-sheep, of Northern European myths, which has been sighted several times this century in the Shetlands. The wulver is reputedly well-disposed towards people unless it is provoked, although visitors to the Rosses' house said the air of evil was palpable as long as the heads were there.

Even after she had removed the heads from her house, Dr Ross was still periodically aware of the entity in her house. She said it was as if it had been 'locked in' to the other Celtic heads in her possession. Eventually, she disposed of the whole collection and had the house exorcized.

Dr Ross assumed that the ancient heads – which were cult objects among the Celts, who would also place severed human heads over their doors to ward off evil – still held the magic powers invested in them nearly 2,000 years before. But then, later in 1972, the previous occupant of the Robsons' house, truck-driver Desmond Craigie, revealed that he had made the heads with cement in about 1956 for his daughter, and that they had been thrown in the garden where they were later found.

Dr Ross countered that the heads were indisputably Celtic in appearance, at least, and noted that spectrographic analysis had shown no sign of calcium silicate, the major component of cement. But she also remarked that: 'no matter when and by whom these heads were fashioned, the phenomena they engendered… seem at least irrefutable, if inexplicable… I do not maintain that the heads are Celtic in origin; but that they have in some way drawn to themselves powers such as were attributed to real [i.e. severed human] or manufactured heads in the pre-Christian world.'

There is, of course, another interpretation. It is worth remembering that in the three households apparently affected by the heads, there were adolescent children – who are frequently the focus of weird psychic manifestations if there is a poltergeist about.

(They may indeed 'manufacture' the poltergeist at some strange interface between mind, emotion, energy and matter.) Did adolescent turmoil and ancient magic meet to produce the singularly disturbing entities that disrupted the Robsons, their neighbours, and the Rosses?

A woman selling amulets at a witch doctors' market in La Paz, Bolivia.

LASH OF FIRE

The Celtic heads of Hexham may have been the bearers of an ancient Druidic curse. Perhaps, surprisingly, curses are still cast by the priests of the world's major religions, even today. The story of the jackdaw of Rheims, against whom the bishop pronounced an anathema 'with bell, book and candle' is well known.

Even the traditionally rather mild Church of England has its Service of Commination, which first appeared in the 1662 *Book of Common Prayer*. The service contains 12 curses – some of them for what today seem rather minor offences: 'Cursed is he' for example, 'that removeth his neighbour's landmark', while others are obscure to the modern ear: 'Cursed is he that smiteth his neighbour secretly.' Slander and drunkenness, too, lay one open to being 'cast into utter darkness'. The service leaves room for other sinners and their wickedness to be cursed, and was used against church thieves as recently as 1981 – by the Revd Robert Nesham of Down Ampney.

Judaism has its pulsa de nura (Aramaic for 'lash of fire'), also known as the Rod of Light ceremony. This is held in a room lit by black candles where a minyan (at least ten righteous men) has gathered to recite cabbalistic incantations and burn a paper inscribed with the names of the one to be accursed and his or her mother; during the service the shofar (ram's horn) is blown to dispel shedim (evil spirits).

In September 1981, Rabbi Moshe Hirsch threatened to invoke the Rod of Light against archaeologist Yigal Shilo, whose excavations of a part of ancient Jerusalem apparently threatened to disturb a medieval Jewish cemetery. 'This ceremony is an absolute last resort,' said the Rabbi, adding: 'It has been invoked only twice in the last 30 years, both times with horrible consequences. There are many ways of dying, some less pleasant than others.' Shilo denied that the 'threatened' cemetery existed, and in the end escaped unscathed, as Rabbi Hirsch was unable to discover the name of the archaeologist's mother.

In January 1991, during the Second Gulf War (Operation Desert Storm), the ultraorthodox Eda Haredit group in Israel did indeed perform the ceremony, and pronounced a death curse on President Saddam Hussein of Iraq. At the time of writing, he was still alive.

The entire state of California was once placed under a ritual curse of sorts, and by a judge – for even the secular law, it seems, can pronounce anathemas. In the case of US District Judge Samuel King, his order of the court had perhaps a more profound effect than he expected. Annoyed because jurors could not attend his San Francisco court because of heavy rains, Judge King declared in 1986: 'I hereby order that it cease raining by Tuesday.' Five years of severe drought promptly afflicted California. Once he was reminded of his motion, Judge King proclaimed: 'I hereby rescind my order of February 18, 1986, and order that rain shall fall in California beginning February 27, 1991.' Later that day – well within the deadline set by the judge – a fierce Pacific storm drenched California with more than 4 in of rain, the state's heaviest rainfall in ten years. The judge, apparently unimpressed by the coincidence, said this was 'proof positive that we are a nation governed by laws'.

AN ANTI-CURSE

Chiang Mai, Thailand's second largest city, suffered a far more complex fate in 1991. That summer, a story began to circulate that the town was cursed.

The origins of the trouble went back to 1986. Then, a construction firm proposed building a cable railway to the holy mountain, behind the city, which was the seat of an ancient temple. The monks at the temple were enraged by the plan; students gathered a 20,000-signature petition against the project. Feelings among both people and monks were obviously rising, for Royal Thai Air Force pilots who flew over the city reported seeing monks sitting on clouds in the lotus position. But, attracted by the prospect of the railways, construction companies began to build modern apartment blocks and hotels around it. This, said popular opinion, was upsetting the geomantic harmony of the city.

When building started for a 24-storey apartment block next to an old temple on the banks of the River Ping, and the citizens of the Old City realized there was nothing they could do to stop it, they decided to invoke evil spirits against the developers.

There was a large demonstration in August 1989. To arouse the spirits, people carried various symbols of disharmony, such as broken plates, and women mocked the holy sutras. At the climax of the ceremony, the sky darkened and there were three dramatic lightning flashes. Three days later, the city was shaken by an almighty earthquake. The people had no doubt that evil spirits had been aroused.

In April 1991, a strong wind uprooted the oldest holy Bodhi tree at the Suan Dork Temple. At the beginning of May, when the rainy season normally starts, the paddy fields continued to be parched. The property market collapsed. New projects were cancelled. The governor promised a stop to high-rise building. At the end of May, a Lauda Air Boeing crashed killing 13 VIPs, including the governor and his wife. Four days later, the abbot of one of Chiang Mai's most important Buddhist monasteries died.

People started to desert the ill-starred city in droves. The only thing to do was to bring the evil spirits abroad back under control. 'The evil spirits are so powerful that only an extra-strong anti-curse can drive them away,' explained Mani Pajomjong, Professor of Pedagogy at Chiang Mai University, and a former monk. The city council appointed him Master of Ceremonies for the spirit cleansing.

At sunrise on 8 June 1991, women arrived at the main gate of the city with trays of offerings, which were then laid out in seven different corners of Chiang Mai. The offerings had been paid for by banks and construction companies and consisted of fish, raw meat, bamboo shoots, fruit, sugar cane and cheroots laid out on banana leaves. The largest offering was reverently placed at a crossroads where the founder of the city, King Meng Rai, had been struck down by lightning in AD 1311. 'We invite the spirits to a feast and ask them to leave the city,' announced Professor Mani enticingly. At 5 p.m., 108 monks began chanting a sutra to break the spirits' power.

'This has nothing to do with superstition; it's about our relationship with Nature,' said a professor at the university. 'With all this modernization we are losing our roots. The curse has forced us to think about the environment.'

The monks had just finished their chant when a light rain fell. As the offerings were taken to the river to be thrown in, the sky opened and the sun shone on the city. 'If people are angry with the new high-rise buildings,' said Professor Mani afterwards, 'they can always invite the evil spirits back.'

A SHIP OF ILL FORTUNE

The *Mary Celeste* is one of the most famous ships in maritime history; her discovery some 400 miles east of the Azores on 5 December 1872, her sails set, and all in order aboard – but for the minor detail that not one of her crew was present, and not one has been seen, dead or alive, since – has made her the supreme example of the mystery ship.

But the mysterious disappearance of the *Mary Celeste's* crew is only the high point in the story of a ship that seems to have been doomed from the start – and whose ill luck did not cease on that eerie winter day in the north-east Atlantic.

Sailors have long held that to change a ship's name will bring her bad luck. The *Mary Celeste* was launched in 1861 as the *Amazon*, from the shipyard of Joshua Dewis on Spencer's Island, Nova Scotia. She was a brigantine, a two-masted vessel square-rigged and with three jibs on the foremast, with a gaff-rigged mainsail, a staysail and four foresails on the mainmast. She measured 99 ft 4 in from stem to stern, with a beam of 25 ft 6 in, and her gross weight was 198.42 tons. Her maiden voyage had not even begun when her first designated skipper, Robert McLellan, fell ill and died. A new master, John Nutting Parker, took the *Amazon* out on her maiden voyage but, somewhere off the coast of Maine, she ran into a fishing weir – a set of stakes driven into the seabed to trap fish – and gashed her side. While she was being repaired ashore, a fire broke out. Captain Parker lost his job.

The *Amazon* acquired a third skipper, who took her across the Atlantic. In the Straits of Dover she collided with a brig, which sank. While the *Amazon* was being repaired, her master resigned his command to find another berth.

Matters now become a little vague, but it seems that the *Amazon* went back across the Atlantic after her repairs in England – only to run aground off Cape Breton Island, Nova Scotia. She was probably then sold to an Alexander McBean, who may actually

Medium Marvello Creti and members of his Societa Ergoniana.

have salvaged her; he spent $16,000 repairing and enlarging the vessel, and in the process he may have changed her name to *Mary Celeste*. True to her nature, the ship bankrupted McBean, and she then went through a succession of owners until finally being bought by a New York consortium, J.H. Winchester & Co. On 7 November 1872, under her new name, she set out on the voyage that was to make her name a byword. She was carrying 1,701 barrels of commercial alcohol, insured for $36,943, to Genoa, Italy.

Twenty-eight days later she was discovered by the British brigantine *Dei Gratia* in perfect order but with no one on board. After a lengthy legal wrangle as to salvage rights in the ship, ownership of the *Mary Celeste* was restored to the Winchester company in New York, and in March 1873 she finally delivered her cargo to Genoa. Winchester then promptly sold her - and she changed hands 17 times in the next dozen years.

No-one, it seems, had any luck with the *Mary Celeste*. She had an incorrigible and depressing tendency to lose her cargo, her sails, and on some occasions her sailors, to run aground, and to catch fire. In the end a notorious old salt named Oilman C. Parker bought her late in 1884. Parker has been called 'undoubtedly guilty of every maritime crime short of piracy', and he clearly had no intention of trying to make an honest penny out of the *Mary Celeste*. He loaded her with a cargo insured for $30,000 but worth at most $500, and sailed her from Boston to Haiti, where he deliberately ran her aground in the Gulf of Gonave on 3 January 1885. He unloaded the cargo, and then set the ship alight.

The insurance companies involved smelled a rat as well as a sinking ship, and soon discovered the truth. Parker and his associates were arrested, and would have been tried for barratry - maritime insurance fraud – which then carried the death penalty. They walked free thanks to a legal technicality, but were not yet free of the jinx of the *Mary Celeste*. Parker himself soon went bankrupt, and died in penniless obscurity. One of his associates went mad; another committed suicide. The *Mary Celeste*, it seems, brought ill fotune to all who sailed in her.

SLIPS IN TIME

Lost in foul weather and piloting a poorly equipped plane, Victor Goddard knew that his life depended on him finding the right direction. What he didn't expect to do was to fly into the future…

In 1934, Victor Goddard (later Air Marshal Sir Victor Goddard) of the Royal New Zealand Air Force had to fly a Hawker Hart biplane bomber from Scotland to England. On the way, he ran into bad weather and then had the nasty experience of going into a tailspin. After getting out of that scrape, he realized he was no longer sure where he was. The aircraft lacked sophisticated instruments and he was navigating by sight – and in that weather there was not much to be seen.

Goddard knew he ought to be within a few miles of Drem, an airfield that had been in use in World War One but had since been abandoned. Not long before, he had actually visited the place by car, just to find out if it was still possible to land there. He had found instead that the airstrip had been turned over to farmland, and that the former hangars were now being used as barns. But from the air he would certainly recognize Drem, and if he could find it, he could get himself back on course. Goddard lost height, flew under the cloud, and went to look for the disused airfield.

He found it. The first odd thing about the place was that it was bathed in sunlight, despite the inclement weather he had just encountered. Still more surprising – despite what he had seen just a few days previously – the airfield was now fully operational. The hangars had been repaired, and on the freshly laid tarmac apron sat four aircraft – one of them a monoplane fighter of a type he had never seen before. The final touch of strangeness was that these aircraft were painted yellow, and the ground crew around them were wearing blue uniforms.

It was weird enough to find an abandoned airfield suddenly in tip-top working order, but there were no aircraft in the RAF painted yellow, and in any case all RAF fighters in service at that time were biplanes: the first monoplane, the Hurricane, did not even fly until 1935. And RAF technicians wore khaki denim uniforms. What had suddenly happened at Drem? The place was real enough: Goddard took new bearings and completed his flight safely.

Reporting what he had seen to his wing commander, he was told unhelpfully but unambiguously to 'lay off the Scotch'. In 1938, Drem was reopened as a flight training station. By then, the first Hurricanes were entering RAF service, and training aircraft were routinely painted yellow to distinguish them from operational aircraft. Ground crew, too, were issued new working uniforms –

denims in a dark shade of RAF blue. When he eventually discovered and put together all these bits of the jigsaw, Goddard realized that he had seen Drem not as it actually was on that intemperate day in 1934, but as it was to be in the not too distant future. He had even managed to slip in time to a day when the weather was fine – helping him find his way home.

Goddard seems to have been a man with a charmed life when it came to narrow shaves in aircraft – later in his career he escaped a crash landing that should have devastated the aircraft he was in, and that he had been forewarned would result in his death. But there is a key difference between the premonitory vision that warned Goddard of that crash and what he experienced directly in 1934. For the premonitory vision was just that: a mental image of the future. In this case, Goddard – and his aircraft! – actually seem to have shifted, both together, from a foul-weather day in 1934 to a fair-weather day sometime after 1938. Goddard had experienced what psychical researchers call a timeslip.

TIME TRAVELLER

Goddard's experience was relatively unusual – but by no means unique – in being a slip forward in time. It is, for some reason, more common for those who have been subjected to timeslips to find themselves walking into the past. Joan Forman, who has researched and described a formidable range of these experiences (and on whose work any discussion of the phenomenon must rely very heavily), reported in her book *The Mask of Time* the intriguing case of an elderly man she called Mr Squirrel – who, like Goddard, slipped across time in pursuit of a particular personal need.

Squirrel was an enthusiastic amateur numismatist, a coin-collector, from Norfolk, England. Sometime in 1973 he found he needed some envelopes in which to store his coins, and he went to nearby Great Yarmouth, a resort on the coast, to find some. He had heard that there was a stationer's shop there that stocked exactly the thing he needed. Squirrel had never been to the shop before, but he did know how to reach it.

When he got there, he noticed that the street was still laid in old-fashioned cobbles, but that the shop itself looked bright, new, and

An Edwardian shop with the kind of fittings and decor that greeted the Norfolk numismatist in his timeslip in 1973.

freshly painted. When he went into the shop he found it empty, and glanced around at the place: the till was an old-fashioned box type; there was a frame full of walking-sticks for sale; decorated frames for photographs were on display. Then a young assistant approached him, wearing a long black skirt and a blouse with 'mutton-chop' sleeves; her hair was piled on top of her head.

Squirrel told her what he wanted, and she produced a brown box full of small, transparent envelopes. He commented that they had a surprising amount in stock. The girl explained that fishermen bought them all the time, to keep hooks in. She told him the price of his purchases was a shilling: he gave her a new 5p piece, which was then the same size, colour, weight and – most important – the same value as the old shilling coin. Then he left the shop. All the time he had been in it, there was no sound from outside and inside there had been absolute quiet apart from his conversation with the girl.

Squirrel thought little of these details at the time: many girls were wearing clothes with a Victorian or Edwardian flavour in 1973, and doing their hair to match; decimal coinage had been introduced only two years before, and he (like many people, especially the elderly) still thought of prices in the old money. The shop assistant apparently looked at the coin he gave her with some surprise, although she said nothing about it. However, the details of that visit did come to mind with some force when Squirrel went back to the shop a week later for more envelopes for his coin collection.

This time, there were no cobbles in the street, but ordinary modern paving stones. The shop facade now looked weathered, not bright. Inside, too, the details had changed. The mature lady who served him denied any knowledge of a young girl assistant, and then said the shop not only had none of the envelopes Squirrel wanted - but had never stocked them!

This experience would have been uncanny enough; what makes it especially so was the fact that Squirrel still had the envelopes that he had bought in his brief visit to another age – and could not have bought them in 1973. Joan Forman tracked down their makers, who confirmed that they were sold in the 1920s, although they were first made before 1914.

Without the envelopes, it is reasonable to suggest that the elderly Mr Squirrel's experience, on its own, had been some kind of hallucination, or at any rate a purely mental journey across time. However, it is not possible to describe the set of new transparent envelopes that followed Squirrel back into 1973 as some kind of portable phantasm. This disconcerting detail raises even more questions about the nature of timeslips than does the apparent ability of Victor Goddard's very solid aircraft to travel with him into the future.

GHOSTLY MONKS

Two other intriguing instances reported by Joan Forman show a quite different facet of this mysterious phenomenon – and give yet another twist to the problem of what actually happens in a timeslip. Both timeslips happened to the same person, a Mrs Turrell-Clarke, who experienced them when she was living in the quaintly named village of Wisley-cum-Pyrford in Surrey. And both suggest that her timeslips, at least, were indeed a journey of the mind, or possibly even of the soul. In the first of these strange events, Mrs Turrell-Clarke was cycling from her home to the village church, where she was going to the evensong service. Suddenly, the modern road under her turned into a path across a field; her bicycle vanished, and she found herself on foot. Approaching her was a man dressed like a 13th-century peasant. She herself, she felt, was wearing a nun's habit. The man stood aside to let her go by. Within seconds the scene shifted again, and the mystified Mrs Turrell-Clarke found herself back on her bicycle in the middle of the 20th century.

Her second experience came a month later. This time she was actually in the church at Pyrford at a service. She was joining in the singing of a plainsong chant when the church – which dates back to the 13th century – apparently regressed in front of her eyes to its original state. The floor was of plain earth, the altar of stone; and in the centre of the church a group of monks in brown habits were in procession, singing the same plainsong chant that Mrs Tunirrell- Clarke had joined in singing just a few minutes before - or, to put it another way, some 700 years later!

The most curious part of the experience, however, was that Mrs Turrell-Clarke felt that, during the few moments it lasted, she was viewing this scene as 'one of a small group of people at the back of the church, taking little part in the proceedings'.

Pyrford church was originally a chapel belonging to nearby Newark Abbey. The monks there wore black habits, but Mrs Turrell-Clarke discovered that in 1293 the monks of Westminster Abbey had used the chapel – and they wore brown habits. Presumably it was members of this order that she had seen; at least the information gave some credibility to her odd experience.

But what kind of experience was it, really? Both these timeslips could be regarded as in some sense imaginary, however authentic the details. Yet if in both these cases Mrs Turrell-Clarke did slip through time for a few minutes, who was she, and where was she, while she visited the Surrey of the 13th century? Were these simply very elaborate forms of ghosts that she saw – phantoms of the Surrey landscape and the Pyrford church, complete with inhabitants?

This seems unlikely, for she saw these things through someone else's eyes. In her first timeslip, she felt she was wearing nun's robes. But who was the nun? Mrs Turrell-Clarke in a previous incarnation? An innocent religious whose consciousness was briefly taken over by this migrant from the future? Or was some kind of long-distance, time-travelling telepathy involved, so that she saw the past through someone else's mind, but without taking it over? And was she still seeing through the eyes of the nun in her second timeslip, or through another person's? And for what purpose did they occur? No special information was passed on to the witness; no problem was solved – far from it: every aspect of these cases bristles with problems.

However, an especially interesting question is raised by the possibility that these visions were telepathic in nature. Did the person, or people, through whom she had these experiences in turn see into the future, while she looked into the past? The question 'Where was Mrs Turrell-Clarke during her timeslip?' becomes more and more intriguing – and more and more difficult to answer – if they did use her mind as a window onto times to come.

PHANTOM OMNIBUS

One interpretation of timeslips, as mentioned above, is that they are forms of haunting. If there is anything to this speculation, the 'ghosts' involved are not purely spirits, or spiritual representations, of dead people in the way we usually take ghosts to be. That spectres of inanimate objects do apparently exist is nothing new in the annals of psychical research: a famous example is the phantom No. 7 omnibus belonging to London Transport that on various occasions in the 1930s was seen powering down Cambridge Gardens in Notting Hill, causing at least one motorist to plough into parked cars in an attempt to avoid it.

Even if one accepts that a phantom path can haunt its descendant, a modern road, or that the past life of a church can cloak its modern interior, the timeslips experienced by Mr Squirrel and Mrs Turrell-Clarke were singular in that both the witnesses interacted with the so-called ghosts: a peasant stood to one side to let Mrs Turrell- Clarke go by; Mr Squirrel not only had a whole conversation with a phantom shopgirl in a phantom shop, he bought a set of phantom envelopes that nevertheless remained strikingly physical and material even when Squirrel himself had 'come out' of his timeslip.

The experience of Victor Goddard (and, as we shall see, others who have found themselves briefly inhabiting the future) also, rather comprehensively, disposes of the 'haunting' interpretation of timeslips. A complete collection of all the reports of hauntings from the future would make a very thin book indeed. The text would be something of an anticlimax, too. It would consist of three words: 'None so far.'

A London omnibus of the 1930s – like the one that occasionally haunted Cambridge Gardens in London's Notting Hill district.

'GHOULE OF TOMORROW'

This does not mean that on his strange flight into the future Goddard and his aircraft might not have seemed spectral to anyone on the ground, had they bothered to look up. And perhaps a 13th-century Surrey peasant went home one night to tell the story of the nun he had seen unexpectedly appear on the path, and stood aside for, and seen vanish before his eyes... Something like this may be reported in the distant future by a family living in what is now Germany. In the early 1980s a British family was travelling on one of the former West Germany's autobahns. The road wasn't busy, and their attention was taken by a lone vehicle approaching very fast on the other side of the divided highway. It looked like no car they had ever seen – in fact it looked more like a UFO. It had no wheels visible, and was cylindrical in shape. There were four round porthole-like windows. As it flashed by, they saw four 'very frightened faces' staring at them out of the windows. If the British family saw a phantom from the future, it was clear the phantoms were equally astonished and alarmed to be seeing a ghostly

345

were equally astonished and alarmed to be seeing a ghostly automobile from what to them was the distant past – no doubt a sight as disconcerting as that of a spectral Roman chariot rattling down a modern autostrada would be today.

The British healer and psychic Matthew Manning experienced a bizarre series of episodes in his adolescence that bear out the notion that if there is an interaction with figures from the past or future during a timeslip, the other party involved will see the present-day witness as some kind of 'ghost'.

In 1971 Manning met an apparition of a man, walking with the help of two sticks, on the stairs of his parents' house – which dated back to the 17th and 18th centuries. The ghost was no translucent spectre, however: it was apparently solid, and Manning at first took it to be a living man – not least because he spoke to him. Rather matter-of-factly the man apologized for alarming Manning, and explained that he was taking exercise for the sake of his legs, which were bothering him. The entity claimed to be one Robert Webbe, who had in fact owned the house and had parts of it built. It was then that Manning realized he had encountered a ghost. Webbe appeared many times after that. The apparition became almost part of the family, even playing pranks on them. At other times Manning communicated with Webbe through automatic writing. At one point in such a dialogue he asked Webbe if there were a ghost in the house. Webbe indignantly denied it: if there were, he would 'chase it away'. He added that he thought Manning was merely trying to frighten him.

Manning then asked Webbe whom he thought he was talking to. Webbe gave the following fascinating reply: 'I think sometimes I am going mad. I hear a voyce in myne head which I hear talking to me. But tell no one else they locke me away.'

Manning then explained why he was asking these questions. As far as he was concerned, he himself was in the here and now and solid flesh; Webbe, to him, was a ghost. At this, Webbe reportedly became distressed and unable to believe what he was being told. He ended by insisting that Manning must be a 'ghoule of tomorrow'.

What seems to have happened in this case – especially given the notable solidity of Webbe's form, and his ability to have otherwise ordinary two-way conversations when he was actually visible – is a kind of cross-haunting – or a two-way timeslip. Both parties involved thought they were being haunted. It is as if two segments of time were interlocking – rather as if the circles of light from two spotlights were overlapping. But how this happens remains as mysterious as any other aspect of any other kind of timeslip.

STRANGE BLACKOUT

Timeslips may involve more than people and places. In at least two instances, they have featured radio transmissions from the distant past.

Alan Holmes, First Radio Officer of the Cunard liner *Queen Elizabeth 2,* was on watch in the radio shack aboard the ship during a transatlantic voyage some time in 1978, listening for messages on the frequency reserved for radio-telephone (RT) communications, when he received a message in Morse code: 'GKS GBTT QSX AREA 1A'.

There were several things wrong with this message. First, what was a Morse message doing on the RT voice frequency? Next, the message, once translated from Morse, was still using a code for ship-to-shore messages that had gone out of use years before. Third, the message appeared at first glance to be coming from the QE2 herself, whose call sign is GBTT, or 'Golf Bravo Tango Tango'.

Holmes said: 'It was uncanny... The radio procedure used was dropped years ago... it came from another age. I can't believe it was sent by a ghost.'

If it was not a ghost, then the next most reasonable explanation seems to be that a timeslip had occurred. For the call sign GBTT was also used by the old Cunarder *Queen Mary* – and she had been taken out of service in 1967, and sold to the City of Long Beach, California, where she was turned into a floating hotel and conference centre. And the form of the transmission was exactly the one that was in use when the *Queen Mary* was at sea. Holmes deciphered the anachronistic message as a routine position check from the old liner *Queen Mary* to the international shipping radio station Portishead, which is at Burnham in Somerset.

It's coincidence enough that the QE2 had inherited the call sign from the *Queen Mary* before the code was discontinued; it is quite bizarre that the new ship, with that same call sign, should have picked up a message sent out at least 11 years previously.

Holmes suggested an explanation: 'Sometimes radio signals bounce off the moon and "turn up" in Australia. This message could have bounced out into space more than ten years ago and just zipped around until it found its way back to Earth, so we picked it up.' He suggested that the signal might have bounced off something at least five light years away in space and, by an extraordinary freak, come back to Earth in such a way that the QE2 had been in the way of the returning signal. The odds against that happening are, however, literally astronomical or 'inconceivable', as a spokesman for Portishead put it.

When Donald Mulholland, the station manager for Portishead, was interviewed about the affair in the Autumn 1978 edition of *Hello World*, the magazine of the Post Office External Telecommunications Executive, he suggested that the whole thing was a hoax. Holmes retorted by saying he was fed up with justifying the event: 'If I'd been alone on watch, I'd never have mentioned it. I was not alone in the radio shack at the time, and the message really did come in.' If it was a hoax, he went on, it would be difficult to lay on and hardly worth the bother. 'The hoaxer would have had to know exactly what frequency we were listening out on and when.'

BBC TV's report on 11 August 1978 about the bizarre message revealed a further curious detail: shortly after the QE2 received the message, 'a mysterious blackout silenced all messages to and from Atlantic shipping for a time'.

Another strange case of a timeslipping radio message was also reported in 1978. After Mrs Helen Griffith wrote to the London *Daily Express* describing how she had heard the sounds of a World War 2 battle as she crossed the English Channel in 1977, a Mr A.J. Peterson wrote to the newspaper in response (the letter was printed in the 22 August editions), with another story of an inexplicable radio message that had somehow slipped in time. While his son was serving with the Green Howards in Borneo in 1968, his patrol picked up a radio message they couldn't decipher. 'Back at base they handed the message to intelligence who found that it was in a long-discarded code... [It turned out to be] a message sent during an action in the last war.'

ECHOES OF THE PAST

The sounds of battle are sometimes heard again years after the event. The most famous such case is that of two women who, while on holiday in Puys, near Dieppe, on 4 August 1951, claimed to have heard a blow-by-blow rerun of the assault on Dieppe by an Allied amphibious force on 19 August 1942. That battle left 3,623 killed or wounded. The ladies' account seemed to tally with the military records, and investigators for the Society for Psychical Research stated their belief that it was 'a genuine psychic experience'. But whether this was a timeslip, a mass phantom, or a simple delusion, is open to question. It has also come to light that the ladies' oft-cited claim to have known nothing about the military details of the Dieppe raid may well be false.

The most recent such account maintains that sounds from World War Two sea battles can still be heard echoing around the North Atlantic. The US Navy has a network of super-sensitive hydrophones called SOSUS (Sound Surveillance System) buried on the ocean floor to detect enemy submarine traffic. Armies of listeners compare the incoming sounds with vast computerized libraries of natural sounds and the known engine noises ('sound signatures') of vessels in the world's submarine navies. According to the magazine *US News and World Report*, sounds like distant explosions and cannon fire have been picked up ever since SOSUS was installed in 1952.

It has been suggested that the sounds were perpetuated by freak conditions that made the sea act like a superconductor. One expert in underwater surveillance thought the cause might be deep undersea channels, which do indeed exist, that 'act like huge natural telephone cables. Sound seems to be able to travel along them without deterioration in the signal. The sound goes back and forth, losing hardly any of its strength.' But, he said, 'not all sounds are "stored" in this way for years. The sounds apparently have to have occurred at the right place... but how [they] get into this system remains a mystery.'

Some apparent timeslips may, then, have a natural explanation, but most, it is absolutely clear, do not. The answer to the mysteries they present is buried somewhere in the extraordinary, and barely understood, capacities of the human mind.

THE SORRAT STORY

Some considered Neihardt a charlatan and a fraud; others reserved judgement, but only the Oglala Sioux knew the truth about his astonishing powers. He founded the controversial society that set out to prove that pens write by themselves and metal rings could interlink without a single break.

In a basement in Rolla, Missouri, a pen sits up by itself and at lightning speed scribbles a message on a piece of paper. Two seamless leather rings shuffle toward each other. Without a break appearing in either of them, one ring connects with the other, and they interlink. Then they flip apart. Still, neither is broken. A letter, addressed to a person in another country, is left in a sealed container without stamps on it. It disappears – and turns up a few days later at the correct address bearing a US postmark but Equadorian, not US Mail, stamps...

And so it goes on. The catalogue of major psychokinetic events that have taken place as a result of the work of the Society for Research into Rapport and Telekinesis (SORRAT), based in Rolla, is now enormous. The group has been working together since 1961, and was established with the deliberate intention of bringing forth, once again, some of the more spectacular psychokinetic manifestations that amazed and graced the seance rooms of the Victorian era. Needless to say, SORRAT has met with its share and more of controversy in the years since 1961.

The arch-sceptic James Randi has said that he cannot believe anyone would take SORRAT's work seriously, and that it is 'not any more worth refuting than the Santa Claus myth'. Others have reserved judgement on the group's claims, but acknowledge that it has established a method of investigating psychokinesis that should be a model for all researchers. Others acclaim the films and stills of the phenomena as a brilliant record, a more than reasonable proof, of the reality of psychokinesis. Meanwhile, SORRAT, unmoved, continue their work, and stand by their story.

What is that story?

PARANORMAL RAPPINGS

SORRAT was founded by Dr John G. Neihardt who, apart from being Professor of English Literature at the University of Missouri at Columbia, MO., and poet laureate of his native state of Nebraska, was the author of *Black Elk Speaks*. This extraordinary narrative, written in the 1930s, was the product of Neihardt's long and close friendship with the Oglala Sioux shaman Black Elk, and has been recognized as of enormous anthropological importance. The Oglala Sioux appreciated Neihardt enough to honour him with honorary membership of their tribe. Of more importance to psychical research, however, may be what Neihardt did not put in that book.

There is some evidence that Neihardt was himself initiated as a shaman, which implies that he had unusual mental, emotional and psychic strength – and physical stamina as well. Part of the shaman's task as a spiritual hub of the tribe is to make direct contact with the spirit world, which may be done through using hallucinogenic or psychotropic drugs; through drumming, dance and song, or ascetic, yoga-like exercises of self-deprivation; and often all of these together.

Whether the climactic shamanic 'flight' into the Otherworld to bring its wisdom back to the world of mortals is a real spiritual journey, an out-of-the-body experience, or an elaborate mystical illusion, no one who has not undertaken it can even begin to guess. But, whether or not Neihardt himself made this journey, his friend Black Elk certainly had, and the poet from Nebraska developed both a stern respect for the world of the spirit and a fascination for the paranormal. What particularly intrigued Neihardt was the fact that people with a powerful belief in a world of spirit could generate - or perhaps it was attract – psychokinetic effects. SORRAT was founded in part to explore that relationship.

In its early years SORRAT met every Friday evening at Neihardt's home at Skyrim Farm near Columbia. There was no solemn ritual involved; the group – the hard core numbered between 15 and 20 – simply sat about talking and joking and waiting for something to happen. Everyone recognized that months might pass before anything occurred; but the notion of 'rapport' among the members of the group, without which nothing would happen, was central to the SORRAT philosophy.

The first noticeable phenomenon was a peculiar coldness that surrounded objects left on a table during the sessions. Measurements showed them to be as much as 5°F colder than the surrounding room temperature. Within a few months, paranormal rappings began.

The raps were, it soon transpired, undoubtedly disembodied. They moved around the room on request, when everyone's hands and feet were visible, and even continued to sound outside the house, when they seemed to come from under the ground. Next, the group set up a code to communicate with the 'agency' - their carefully chosen neutral term for whatever was causing the sounds. Using the code they gradually encouraged the 'agency' to graduate to carry out simple 'tasks' – and to complete them would require some manifestation of psychokinesis.

By 1966 the SORRAT group had managed to levitate a massive oak table weighing 82 lb, and keep a light metal tray in the air – with no one touching it – for a full three minutes. Other effects were beginning to emerge, as well: mysterious lights appeared, objects appeared in the midst of the group as if from nowhere, others moved paranormally from place to place. Once, a life like apparition materialized on the lawn outside Skyrim Farm, and was photographed. The 'agency' maintained that this was 'Myra', who had died over a century before.

FRAUD DETECTIVE

In 1969 there was a new development. Dr J.B. Rhine, Professor of Psychology and Director of the Parapsychology Laboratory at Duke University, Durham, North Carolina, had long been interested in Neihardt's work with SORRAT, and now suggested that the phenomena were so persistent and on such a scale that some professional help might be useful in gathering proof that they were indeed occurring. He offered the services of William E. Cox, his chief field investigator into psychokinesis. Cox had some 20 years' experience in researching psychokinesis, and was also a trained magician. Not only was he therefore well qualified to detect fraud, he also, as a result, knew how to prevent it.

One obvious solution to the problem of fraud – or even accusations of fraud – was a locked container in which the 'agency' could be invited to do its work. Neihardt built a huge transparent chamber for the purpose, but the results were poor. Cox decided to take a leaf out of the original SORRAT book, and work gradually towards a fully sealed and equipped container. He decided to start with shallow wooden boxes, with transparent lids and simple seals, in which relatively minor psychokinetic effects could occur and be photographed.

These became known in the annals of SORRAT as 'coffee boxes', because more often than not the bottom of these sealed trays was lightly and evenly covered in coffee grounds to track any movement of the objects inside. The coffee grounds also helped prevent the movement being effected by tilting the box, since they would reveal what had happened – by simply heaping up at one side or one end. A typical experiment was to put two dice in the box and ask the 'agency' to move only one – which it did successfully, and left tracks in the coffee grounds. Again, tilting the box would have made both dice move, and obscured any tracks.

Other boxes held nothing but carbon paper and a stylus. The 'agency' was invited to leave written messages by pressing the stylus on the carbon paper, so marking the pale wooden floor of the box. The results varied from meaningless scrawls to whole words. These early 'direct writing' experiments, though successful in their way, were to develop into something far more remarkable and elaborate in the years to come.

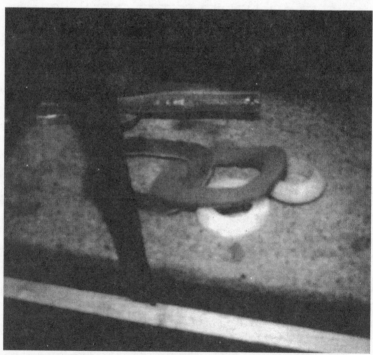

A set of rings, put separately into the Rolla mini-lab, link spontaneously and without a break in the material.

354

In 1973, SORRAT's founder, John G. Neihardt, died. As a result of that loss the group at Skyrim wavered somewhat in its purpose, but already a new and astonishing phenomenon was emerging with a few individuals. As a consequence, no doubt, of a dozen years' practice in letting psychokinetic events come forth, two of the founder members of SORRAT, Dr John Thomas Richards and Joseph Mangini were beginning to experience spontaneous psychokinesis in their everyday lives.

William Cox retired from the Parapsychology Laboratory at Duke in 1977, and settled in Rolla to monitor the psychokinesis that was occurring around Richards. Cox had made the extraordinary discovery that psychokinesis was possible even without the encouragement of the group when checking the state of the 'coffee boxes' at Skyrim, and – most astonishing of all – that psychokinesis would occur even when no one was even thinking about the boxes, SORRAT, or the group, let alone psychokinesis as such.

SEALED AND PADLOCKED

It was now time to put the achievements of SORRAT on record, and in a way that would, as far as possible, show that the psychokinetic effects they were able to produce were genuine.

(For those already convinced of the reality of psychic phenomena, SORRAT's greatest creation, out of infinite patience and dedication, was the circumstances in which spontaneous psychokinesis could occur at all. For psychical researchers, the invention of the mini-lab that followed as a direct consequence was an equally important accomplishment, if not more so. Here was a tool that could be deployed and adapted in a seemingly endless variety of ways not simply to test for psychokinesis, but to prove that it had occurred.)

The means Cox hit upon for this purpose was the 'mini-lab' – an elaboration on the original transparent chamber constructed by Neihardt. The first was a lidless Perspex box that was inverted to stand with its open side sealed against a heavy wooden base by steel strips and two heavy duty padlocks. Inside it, Cox placed a number of objects, which the 'agency' was asked to manipulate in various ways. This spent some time at Skyrim before being moved to Dr Richards's home in Rolla, near Columbia.

Interesting things happened there. On one occasion Cox had set the mini-lab up in Dr Richards's sitting room. Inside the container were (among other things) a pencil and paper, dried peas that had been dyed white and blue, a small glass tumbler, some leather rings, pipe cleaners, and six cotton spools strung on a wire that was twisted at the ends to hold them together. Dr Richards and a number of friends simply sat down in the room, turned out the light, and waited. In due course, noises came from the sealed mini-lab, and eventually stopped. When the light was turned on again, things inside the container were not quite as they had been – although the seals were unbroken and the locks still secure.

One of the six cotton spools had apparently vanished. The wire on which it had been strung had been retwisted. The glass tumbler now held 30 blue dried peas. The leather rings had moved. Two pipe cleaners had been twisted into rings that were linked together.

The obvious difficulty about this event as evidence was that the only testimony to its truth was from those who had taken part in the session – and from Cox, who had arrived towards the end of the apparent movements inside the mini-lab. It was obvious that some kind of independent recording of what went on in the mini-lab, as it was happening, was necessary. Cox found a collaborator in a Mr S. Calvin, who helped to design and build a mini-lab that would provide the kind of evidence Cox wanted.

ASTOUNDING EVENTS

The new mini-labs were once again made of a transparent tank, upturned and capable of being sealed against a hefty base with strips of steel and heavy padlocks once the 'target' objects were set up inside. A rubber gasket sealed off the narrow gap between the baseboard and the container to prevent anything being slid inside it. The ends of the steel strips were tied together with plastic string, which was then melted. Cox impressed the warm plastic with the seal on a notary's ring, and then covered this with adhesive tape. Any 'break-in' to the mini-lab would thus be more than obvious.

A key difference between the old and new mini-labs lay in how the objects inside were set up. They were now placed on, or linked to, highly sensitive microswitches that would operate immediately if anything attached to them moved. These switches triggered lights and an 8 mm movie camera, which was linked to a timing device so that it would take 30 seconds of film every time a switch flipped on. A digital clock stood in front of the mini-lab to record when the events took place.

Two of these carefully prepared devices were put in the basement of Dr Richards' home in Rolla during the spring of 1979. It was here that the most remarkable of the SORRAT evidence for psychokinesis has been filmed, with reactions ranging from dismissiveness or rage on the part sceptics, to undisguised and unadulterated delight on the part of believers.

The list of astounding events that have occurred since then in the mini-labs would fill many pages. But even a brief summary could not exclude the following:

• Spontaneous combustions
Film exists showing a candle igniting of its own accord inside the sealed mini-lab. As a result the glass container cracked. Film also shows paper bursting into flames by itself – either effect would be difficult to achieve as a 'special effect', or in cruder terms, as a deliberate hoax.

• Metal bending
Spoons, forks and plain strips of metal left inside the mini-lab have been distorted by psychokinesis and the process has been recorded on film.

• Spontaneous inflations
Balloons have often inflated themselves inside the mini-lab. One such occasion was independently filmed by the production crew of the Yorkshire Television series *Arthur C. Clarke's World of Mysterious Powers* on Labour Day 1983.

• Direct writing
There are many instances on record of pens taking it upon themselves to write messages without the intervention of any

human agency, and at extraordinary speed. William E. Cox estimates that direct writing occurs at twice the average human writing speed at least. The quality of the messages received varies from the banal through the metaphysical to the unashamedly jokey in rhyming verse.

On Easter Sunday 1991 an exceptional result was had from an experiment proposed by Dr Berthold Schwarz and set up in a plastic box with a cardboard liner at Skyrim Farm. In the container were a pencil stub and a block of marble, plus a note from Dr Schwarz requesting the 'agency' to give the initials of the person to whom the marble block was important. The box was left in the Skyrim study while a group of SORRAT members waited in the living room. Nothing happened for over an hour, and the group was ready to decide that nothing would, when the phone rang.

On the line was Maria Hanna, a SORRAT member living in Barstow, California; she had just had a series of paranormal raps in her home that, using the usual code, had said that a poem had appeared at Skyrim. Ms Hanna had had no idea that a SORRAT meeting was in session until she called. The group headed as one for the study to check the box. Inside, written in pencil on the cardboard liner, were the following lines:

I am you and you are I! When the world is cherished most, You shall hear my haunting cry, See me rising like a ghost. I am all that you have been, Are not now, but soon shall be! Thralled a while by dust and din – Brother, Brother, follow me!

This, says Dr Richards, is a stanza from Dr Neihardt's poem 'The Ghostly Brother'. Yet more astonishing was what had happened to Berthold Schwarz's block of marble. Carved into it were the letters 'CM'. When told of this, Dr Schwarz confirmed that these were the initials he had been hoping to have communicated (and that he had been keeping) to himself. He then revealed that the marble came from the face of a building that had been named in memory of 'C.M.', who had been a close friend of Dr Schwarz and was now dead.

• Linking rings

It has long been a goal of parapsychological researchers to prove the successful working of psychokinesis by achieving the permanent interlinking of two separate rings of some seamless material – wood, leather, or metal, for instance. SORRAT films show momentary interlinking of leather rings (each cut from a single piece of hide). Messages from Cox and Richards to the 'agency' had persistently requested this achievement, but to no avail. One directly written response said testily: 'We've tried, but can't make the damn leather rings stay linked – sorry.' Another time, the 'agency' answered: 'When the psi energy is sufficient, we shall try to do this for you. However, do not expect to overcome the envious prejudice of your inferiors...' However, in 1985, a metallurgist known only as Donald C. created two rings of a unique metal alloy whose formula only he knew. During an experiment at Skyrim Farm, the rings linked – and stayed that way. According to Dr Richards, 'Careful laboratory analysis shows that there is no cut or break in the metal of either ring.'

• Levitations and extractions

Film has shown the leather rings that are usually installed in the mini-lab, as well as numerous other objects, rising into the air of their own accord. Film has also shown letters being extracted from – and through – the envelopes that contain them, although the envelopes (and, of course, the mini-lab) have clearly remained sealed as the paper has come forth.

•Psychokinetic sortings

The original mini-lab event has been repeated more than once, with dyed dried peas that have been left in the mini-lab in a mixed assortment of colours sorting themselves into single-colour groups.

• Card calling

Sealed sets of Zener cards, fresh from the makers and packed in random order, have been left in the mini-lab, and the 'agency' has been asked to call the order of the cards. Responses have been acquired through paranormal rapping, direct writing, and other means, and in about one attempt in three have been absolutely accurate for the whole run of the pack. In one unusual experiment conducted in 1991, Cox placed a blank audio tape next to a sealed pack of ordinary playing cards, which are always sold shuffled in random order. When the audio tape was taken from the mini-lab it was found to have on it a recording of a 'soft, feminine voice with an Arabic accent', correctly calling the order of the entire 52 cards in the deck – which remained sealed.

• Apports

Film exists of a piece of typewriting appearing from nowhere in front of the mini-lab. Other, mundane objects have also appeared inside the mini-lab.

A Florida cockroach that was left inside the mini-lab with a plain lightbulb has been apported into the lightbulb – along with paper and white powder that, according to a message from the 'agencies' behind the event, was necessary 'to prevent breakage'.

• Teleports

Possibly the most controversial of all SORRAT's claims is that objects have been placed inside the sealed mini-lab and then appeared elsewhere with no human intervention. The first time this occurred was in May 1979, when Cox secured a green felt-tipped pen inside the container – and later found it on the floor of Dr Richards' basement, although the mini-lab remained untouched. Materials as varied as pipe-cleaners, water, matchbooks, peas, mica sheets, string, jewellery, film, and paper have transported themselves in or out of mini-labs. Films show such items appearing and disappearing and, yet more astonishing, actually passing through the glass of the sealed container. These events led the experimenters to leave sealed, addressed, but unstamped letters inside the mini-lab to discover whether or not they would find their way to their intended destinations. They did. Often the letters have been adorned with unusual postage stamps – South American, Italian and even Australian ones have been attached to the envelopes – although they have all reached their destinations by way of the US Mail Office in Rolla and bear the Rolla postmark.

A number of psychical researchers around the world have received such letters, and during the Yorkshire TV filming mentioned previously, the production team left one – sealed but unstamped – in the mini-lab for paranormal posting to Arthur C. Clarke, along with several quarters (25-cent pieces), which were not in the envelope. Two weeks later, the letter and one of the quarters disappeared from the mini-lab. Both - with the missing quarter now in the envelope, which had somehow acquired stamps to the correct value for airmail - turned up at Clarke's residence in Sri Lanka shortly afterwards.

One of the more startling teleports that the mini-lab achieved involved a living creature. In January 1992, psychiatrist and parapsychologist Dr Berthold E. Schwarz provided SORRAT with a large Florida cockroach from his home state and an ordinary clear lightbulb, with the request to the 'agency' behind the mini-lab to put the roach into the lightbulb. According to Dr Richards' testimony, 'the cockroach, some white packing powder, and two slips of paper with notes paranormally written on them entered the sealed bulb'. One of the notes was written paranormally by the 'agency' to a SORRAT member, Eilly Fithian. The lightbulb remained unbroken and sealed to its base connector.

• Paranormal sounds

In another experiment using audio tape, Cox pre-recorded a cassette from beginning to end with the sound of a clock ticking. He left this tape in the mini-lab, again without a recorder. When it was retrieved and played, the tape also now held the sound of a series of paranormal raps – but the sound of the ticking clock had not been erased.

CONTROLLING SPIRIT

Who, or what, is responsible for the psychokinesis in the mini-labs and other SORRAT experiments? What is the 'agency'?

Opinions differ on this among SORRAT members themselves. Some believe the 'agency' is a product of members of the group's own subconscious. Some, including Dr Richards, prefer to think of the 'agency' as a group of spirits. The 'agency' itself has not always been consistent on this point. It has referred to itself by name, but at least once insisted that this particular personality resided in 'the fifth level of the subconscious' of one of the SORRAT members.

In the very first rapping experiments at Skyrim in the 1960s, the group asked whatever was behind the raps to identify itself. The answer was 'John King', the name of a spirit control (and long-dead pirate) who has allegedly acted as an intermediary between this world and the next for several mediums, including two of the most famous – and notorious – of the 19th century, Eusapia Palladino and Florence Cook. Since King announced 'himself' to SORRAT, a number of other names of alleged spirits or entities have cropped up in direct writing or through other communications. They have names like Explicator, Rector, Imperator, Mentor, Illxin, Eowald, and Expeditor – as well as, more mundanely, Sam, Mickey and Grady. Taken together these sound like the cast of some old-time spaceflight-and-sorcery radio serial. Whether they are genuinely disembodied entities (as they themselves claim) who happen to like slightly camp science fiction, or useful dramatization; from the collective unconscious of the SORRAT group, has to remain an open question.

Most psychical researchers would agree that the true answer to that question doesn't matter, for the time being at least. The value of the SORRAT work does not lie in any evidence it might contain for survival after physical death. The value of the independence of the alleged entities is that their manifestation removed any responsibility for producing paranormal effects from the members of the group. Apart from increasing the general relaxation of the meetings, so facilitating the 'rapport' that Neihardt believed to be crucial to producing psychokinesis, this lack of individual responsibility also meant that no particular member of the group would be deemed indispensable to the production of psychical phenomena. And it is the variety, depth and range of the psychokinetic effects that SORRAT has produced that is so impressive.

HOAX EXPOSED?

SORRAT's other great achievement is the invention of the mini-lab. It can, of course, be improved. Two cameras at right angles to each other, with a third giving a wide-angle, panoramic view of the whole ensemble and its background would vastly reduce the set-up's vulnerability to fraud, as would either enclosing the cameras within the chamber or sealing the room in which the lab is placed with as much attention as has been devoted to the mini-lab itself. A 24-hour digital clock showing local time to the second as well as the date would both pinpoint events in time and verify the accuracy of timing of the camera runs. Using video cameras rather than movie film would improve the quality of the 'proof' as well – if only by reducing the opportunities sceptics have of crying 'Hoax!' and producing hilarious, but pointless, stop-action home movies of their own that purport to 'expose' the SORRAT work as fraudulent.

SORRAT has produced two major breakthroughs in psychical research: spontaneous, large-scale and persistent psychokinetic phenomena; and the basis of a research tool that no serious parapsychologist interested in psychokinesis should be without. What will they do next?

HEALING TOUCH

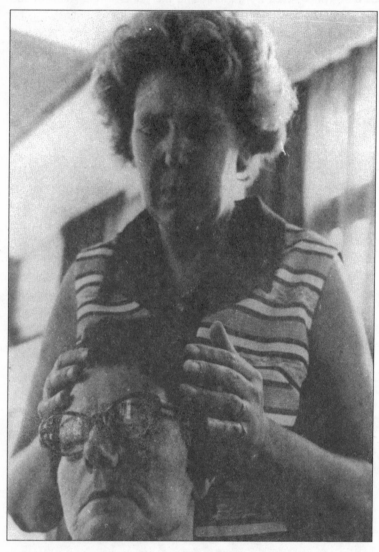

The sudden discovery that she was a healer brought Rose Gladden great joy. It was only later that she realized the gift could also be a burden that would drive her to the very edge of madness.

At the age of 19, in the 1940s, Rose Gladden discovered she was a healer.

'I had gone into a shop in London called Dyers and Chapman and found Mr Chapman, who had collapsed, lying under the counter. I asked him what was wrong and he said, "I'm in terrible pain. I have an ulcer."

'Now I didn't know where that ulcer was. All I thought was, "I wish I could help him," and I heard a voice say, "You can. Put your hand there."

' "But where?" I asked myself. "He hasn't told me where this ulcer is." With that I saw a little star, just as if it had fallen out of the night sky, floating over his left shoulder and, as I watched, the star floated down and stopped on the top half of the stomach.

'Mr Chapman confirmed that was where the ulcer was. As I put my hand there, I never saw but felt another hand come over mine and hold it steady. I felt my hand being filled with a tremendous heat. I couldn't move it away. It was as if it was glued to that part of the body. After a while, my hand was pulled like a magnet to his side and then away from his body.

'With that, he said, "That's gone, it's marvellous. Your fingers felt as if they were holding the pain and as you took your hand across, the pain went with it."

'I was absolutely overjoyed. I still didn't know you called it healing. I just knew I was beginning to realize why I was born and what I had to do was help people.'

THE PRICE TO BE PAID

Successful, unexpected and apparently simple as this discovery was, Rose Gladden did not find the process of becoming a full-time healer by any means easy. Since childhood she had seen 'forms and beings' that other people could not see; then, after her experience with Mr Chapman, during her twenties, she had a series of psychic experiences that were so intense and disturbing that she thought she might go mad. Today, she says she had to suffer in order to learn, and that without that distressing episode her work would be less effective. Although she is a psychic, not a 'spiritual' healer, and does not call on a spirit guide in her healing, she does believe that a spirit world exists and that it contains malignant as well as benign entities.

Rose Gladden has two ways of deciding how to go about treating a patient. She sometimes sees silver lines and spots mapped out on people's bodies, showing where the root of a particular complaint lies. She was at first mystified by the fact that these often showed in quite different places from where patients complained of suffering pain, although treating them (by laying her hands on the spot where the light showed) would effect a cure. It was years before she discovered that the lines and spots corresponded precisely with the lines and 'meridians' in the body identified by acupuncturists.

Rose Gladden is also one of those who claim to be able to see the human aura. This has been variously defined: as 'an envelope of vital energy, which apparently radiates from everything in nature' (from *Harper's Encyclopedia of Mystical and Paranormal Experience*); as 'a spiritual sphere surrounding everyone' (Swedenborg); as the physical body's 'etheric double' (Dr Walter J. Kilner, *The Human Aura*); some writers also identify the aura as the 'astral body' that is capable of leaving and returning to the physical

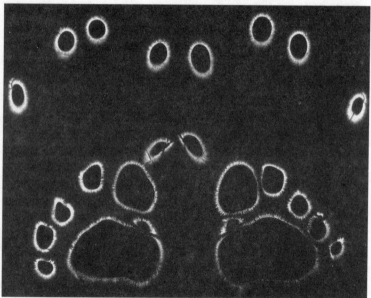

A Kirlian 'photograph' of fingertips and toes. The Kirlian technique detects static electricity on the surface of the skin – not, as some have claimed, the human aura that some psychics are apparently able to detect.

body. A curiosity of the aura is that no two psychics see it in the same way, and often differ in their interpretations of the various bands of colour they are able to see in it, but there is general agreement that any physical sickness is reflected as disturbances in the aura, and may show there long before pain or other symptoms appear in the body.

Rose Gladden interprets this in an interesting way. She maintains that physical maladies are the result of imbalances and blockages of energy in the aura, not that an 'unhealthy' aura is a symptom of physical illness. Consequently she concentrates her treatment on the aura, not on the affected part, if that is the way the ailment presents itself.

MAGIC BULLETS

Rose Gladden is one of but a handful of healers who do not depend on a spiritualist interpretation of their gift. However, the evidence suggests that whether or not the healer considers the effect to be mediated by the spirit world, or is directly from God (as with faith healers), or that he or she simply acts as a channel for a 'universal life-force', the effects are the same: a very high proportion of the people who take their ailments to healers are cured.

Whatever the explanation or the source for the healer's powers, this would suggest that the state of the patient's mind, at least, has a massive degree of control over the state of the body. Part of the healing process, in other words, seems to depend on the confidence and reassurance that people gain by putting themselves entirely in the healer's hands. In effect, they heal themselves, as responsibility for the affliction is taken out of their hands and placed in someone else's.

Yet something more than this seems to be happening with psychic healing, and anyone might reasonably object to such a line of argument, not least an orthodox general practitioner. By taking an illness to a doctor you are also putting yourself in someone else's hands, even though conventional medicine addresses physical problems with physical methods such as surgery, or with physical tools, such as drugs, which are aimed like 'magic bullets' at the physical causes of specific ailments.

There is no doubt that in most cases, given an accurate diagnosis, conventional medicine works. The patient has entrusted a specifically physical malady to the doctor, and the doctor finds the physical cure. To that extent, mind and body are as one. But the exclusively physical approach does not always work. Given the miraculous subtlety and complexity of the human body, and also the largely unfathomed intricacy of its relationship with the mind and with the emotions, this failure is not entirely surprising. Furthermore, conventional medicine traditionally regards symptoms as the clue to the underlying causes, and tackles those first.

If healers succeed where conventional medicine fails, it may be partly because the patients entrust something different – something not merely physical, and something more than the physical symptoms of disease – to the healer. By accepting the reality and the importance of the interplay among mind, spirit and the emotions, and the part they may be playing in the illness, the patients implicitly put their whole being in the hands of the healer. And the healer, unlike the family GP or the specialist consultant, knows how to respond.

SERIOUSLY DISTURBED

This line of argument still supposes that suggestion plays a large part in the healer's art. However, as noted a few sentences earlier, something more seems to be happening when psychic healing takes place. When Rose Gladden laid her hands on the place where a bright light told her Mr Chapman's ulcer was, there was no 'suggestion' involved: neither Chapman nor Rose Gladden herself knew that she had the power to heal. And one of the wonders of psychic healing is that it can often deal with diseases that are intractable to modern medicine, such as cancer or multiple sclerosis.

Walter J. Kilner observed that the human aura reflected a person's state of health, and noted that 'weak depleted auras suck off the auric energy of healthy, vigorous auras around them'. Unhealthy parts of the aura, or the spirit, or one's general sense of well-being, will feed on the more vigorous parts in exactly the same way; but the overall effect is to disturb the system. The same is true of all energy systems: power moves from areas of high energy into areas of low energy, in an eternal and perfectly natural struggle to create and maintain a balance in nature. You can see the same thing happening across the Earth's surface, nightly on the television weather forecast. Areas of low atmospheric pressure are fed by areas of high pressure in an attempt to even things out; the result in temperate climates is wind, cold fronts, rain... and the occasional spell of fine and balmy weather. An aura – or a person's psyche, or energy lines and meridians, or what you will – will constantly fluctuate in this way, but can, like the weather, become seriously disturbed. In meteorological terms, such a major disturbance in the balance of energies expresses itself as a storm or a drought; in terms of personal health, it means illness. And what, by all accounts, the healer does, is the equivalent of giving a troubled body an energy transfusion, which rights the balance – which, as it were, calms the storm or brings rain to the parched earth.

HIDDEN POWERS

The mystery in psychic healing is twofold. Exactly what that energy consists of is anyone's guess. And how it can work even when the healer may be thousands of miles from the sufferer is equally inexplicable.

The sensation that patients most often report feeling when they are touched by a healer is that of heat. Patients have also described tingling feelings, 'something like an electric shock', or even vivid impressions of colours before the eyes as the healer has touched them. At the same time, according to the *Harper's Encyclopedia* quoted earlier, healers have reported 'something of the consistency of heavy air' – whatever that may mean in practice - departing them, usually through the hands. The spiritualist healer Ambrose Worrall, in contrast, felt himself depleted of energy, indeed, but through the solar plexus.

These reports are both too various and too subjective to allow much of a guess as to what in fact has passed between the parties involved. And, intriguing and possibly helpful as they are, descriptions of what occurs in terms of the human aura really amount to explaining one mystery in terms of another. Only a relatively few people can see the aura, and they differ in their descriptions and analyses of it; it has stubbornly remained undetected by orthodox scientific means.

That something does pass between healer and healed seems to be beyond doubt, however. Dora van Gelder Kunz, a pioneer of a modern form of healing called Therapeutic Touch, has even gone so far as to suggest that there is actually a two-way interaction between healer and patient, and that in the process both are made more whole and healthy.

THE FINAL HEALING

The mystery of psychic healing is only deepened by the ability of certain healers to treat their patients at a distance – even without meeting them.

The most famous exponent of distant healing was probably Edgar Cayce. Born in Hopkinsville, Kentucky, in 1877, Cayce followed the pattern of many other healers in being able to discern non-physical forms, and the human aura, from an early age. Until he was 21 he worked as a salesman, but had to abandon his job because of a chronic and apparently incurable sore throat, made worse by bouts of laryngitis. In 1898, Cayce lost his voice completely and, as a last resort, went to hypnotist Al Layne in the hope of getting some relief from his distressing condition.

Layne concluded that Cayce was immune to post-hypnotic suggestion (a command given during hypnosis to be carried out in the normal waking state), so he put Cayce into trance and asked him to identify the cause of his illness, and to suggest a cure himself. The ploy worked: Cayce was able to speak again at the end of the session. Layne suggested that Cayce should take up diagnosis and healing himself, in partnership with Layne.

Cayce refused, and promptly lost his voice again. Taking this as a sign that healing others was to be his destiny, he began to give readings – diagnoses and cures while in trance – in 1901. A key factor in Cayce's gift was that whenever he used it against his own principles – and he was a devout Christian – or even gave up readings, he would lose his voice. In this respect, and like many other psychics, Cayce was not entirely in control of his strange talent. He did not direct it; rather, it seemed to use him as a channel.

Thanks to a newspaper article about him in 1903, Cayce found a large following, and this increased still further in 1911 when a feature on his work – and his successes – in the *New York Times* brought him to national attention. By this time he was working in partnership with Dr Wesley Ketchum, a homoeopath who carried out the treatment that Cayce prescribed.

Cayce had begun his work by being hypnotized in the presence of the patient; now he needed no more than the name and address of the patient, and to put himself into trance. The reading would begin when someone (often Cayce's wife) would tell him: 'You now have the body of [here the name and address was read out]. You will go over this body carefully, noting its condition and any parts that are ailing. You will give the cause of such ailments and suggest treatments to bring about a cure.'

Cayce believed that every single cell in the body was individually conscious, and maintained not only that during a reading he could see every nerve, gland, blood vessel and organ inside his patient's body, but that the cells themselves communicated their condition to his entranced mind. The treatments he prescribed ranged from orthodox drugs or surgery (Cayce had no objection to conventional medicine where it was appropriate), through massage,

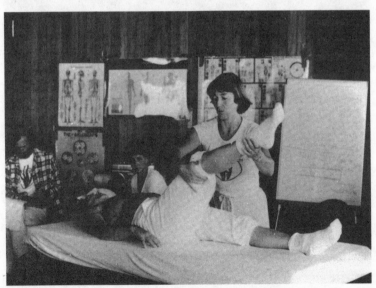

John F. Thie's technique, know as 'Touch for Health' uses direct manipulation as part of the therapy.

manipulation, osteopathy and electrotherapy, to herbal remedies (some of remarkable obscurity) and plain, simple exercise. The effectiveness of his prescriptions was vouched for by thousands of patients.

Many of Cayce's later ideas have been mocked – perhaps with some justice – for their outlandishness. For example, he came to believe that he himself was a reincarnation of one of the angels who inhabited the Earth even before Adam and Eve, and later was incarnated as an inhabitant of Atlantis. But as a healer he has had few equals.

The transfer of energy typical of healing took its toll on Cayce, who found the work exhausting. Warned that giving more than two readings a day would kill him, he nevertheless averaged four each day after 1942, in response to requests that flooded in as a result of the USA joining the war against Germany and Japan. In June 1943, he increased this to six a day; in August 1944 he collapsed from exhaustion, and was dead within five months. He had referred to his impending death as a 'healing'.

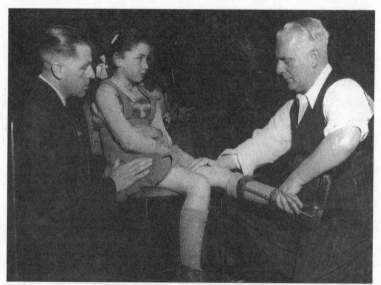

In the 1950s Harry Edwards was Britain's foremost healer, and his fame was so widespread that he was able to fill the 8,000-seat Royal Albert Hall to capacity for his demonstrations.

UNCANNY PRECISION

The most celebrated British clairvoyant healer was probably Harry Edwards, who died in 1976. During his prime in the 1950s he could fill London's giant Albert Hall with people anxious to receive his services. Edwards did not invoke spirit guides or use any ritual, whether healing at such a huge gathering or at home. He simply rolled up his sleeves and for a few moments put his hands on whatever part of the body was troubling the patient.

Astonishingly, Edwards took up healing virtually by chance. He seems to have had no inkling of any psychic capacities as a young man, and he was already in his forties when he made his first attempt at healing – and that was at a distance. This he did only after he had attended Spiritualist church services to please a friend. At these, he was told by a number of mediums that he had a latent ability as a healer, and that next time he knew someone who was ill, he should concentrate his thoughts on his or her recovery.

Edwards heard that a friend of a friend was terminally ill with tuberculosis, and decided to do what he could to help the man. He simply sat down and began to meditate. Then, images came into his mind of a hospital ward, and he found himself concentrating on the occupant of the last bed but one in the ward, as seen from the point of view in his mind. Edwards sent out a 'get well' message as powerfully as he could, although without great confidence in its likely efficacy.

However, when Edwards described the scene he had had in his mind to his friend, he found that he had 'imagined' the ward in the hospital and the circumstances of the TB victim with uncanny precision. Better still, the patient had reported feeling better almost immediately after Edwards had made his attempt at healing. Within a few weeks the man was up and about, and soon after that was back at work again – quite confounding his doctors, who had fully expected him to die.

The next encounter Edwards had with his paranormal gift - and it was one that lends some credence to the suspicion that the lives, let alone the talents, of healers are somehow beyond their control – came not long after this. Harry Edwards lived in Islington, London, and worked in a printing shop in the neighbourhood. One day a woman came into the shop, obviously distracted and, admitting she had no reason for bursting in, poured out her story to Harry. Her husband had lung cancer in an advanced degree: he was so far gone that he had been sent home from hospital – in short, to die.

Edwards personally believed there was little he could do to help (there was nothing he could do about the unfathomable way in which the distressed woman had found him), but made an effort nonetheless. Two days after her first visit, the woman dropped in to the printing shop again. Her husband, she said, had already begun to recover. And recover he did: he lived for a score more years. The curious irony of this case was that he himself never learned of the part that Harry Edwards may have had in his sudden return to normal life. His wife never told him of her strange impulse to walk into a printing shop in Islington, for fear he would mock her intuition.

If this whole episode was no more than a crazy coincidence, it was fortunate as well as fortuitous. Edwards' third attempt at healing was also unusual, for it was the first time he actually had physical contact with his patient, a young girl suffering from TB of the lung. What marked the occasion for Edwards was what happened when he put his hands on the girl's head. He had experienced nothing of the kind before: his entire body seemed to come alive, filled with energy, which flooded down his arms and out of his hands into the patient. When this extraordinary sensation ceased, he heard himself telling the girl's mother that her daughter would be up in three days. Indeed she was, and at her next medical examination was pronounced completely cured.

These three events convinced Edwards that he should devote himself to healing; in due course, he gave up his printing business and in 1946 established a sanctuary at Burrows Lea in Shere, Surrey, to carry on his work full-time. He was still working when he died in 1976. The sanctuary still thrives, run by a group of healers.

INEXPLICABLE PROOF

A number of healers have collaborated in tests to discover if there is any 'objective' element in what they do. The British healer Matthew Manning, for instance, has been involved in this research, attempting to influence the growth rate of seedling plants, to destroy cancer cells in the laboratory, and to increase the enzyme level in samples of blood. Testing on items like these removes the possibility that they may respond as a result of their own suggestibility – which may account for a healer's success with human patients.

Much work along these lines was done by the biochemist Bernard Grad of McGill University in Montreal, Canada, during the 1950s. His research with the retired Hungarian army colonel Oskar Estebany was particularly revealing. Estebany had discovered his own healing ability by working not with people, but with horses of the Hungarian cavalry.

Grad tested the healer's ability to influence the growth of barley seeds successfully, but he performed one crucial experiment with Estebany. One involved 'wounding' a number of laboratory mice (actually just a tiny sliver of skin was painlessly removed from each one). Sixteen of the 48 animals were given healing treatment by being held in Estebany's hands twice a day for 20 days. Another 16 were put in incubators heated to body temperature for the same period twice a day, to simulate the warmth the first group received from Estebany. A third group of 16 mice provided a final control: they were left to heal naturally.

By day 14 of the experiment, the size of the wounds of the control group had diminished as expected: about a third had reduced to less than half their original size, and the remainder were smaller yet. Of the 'heated' group, about half had reduced to about half their initial size; if anything, the group as a whole was healing more slowly than the control group – not surprisingly, since warmth encourages the multiplication of bacteria. Estebany's group had healed faster than either of the others: their three biggest wounds were smaller than one-seventh the size they had been initially; the rest were equal in size or (more often) smaller than those of the untreated control group.

Grad and Estebany were no nearer explaining the mechanism of the healer's art than anyone else, but they had shown that it had a real effect on live animals – who could not be accused of 'healing themselves' through auto-suggestion, faith, or any other psychosomatic means.

OUT OF THE BODY

The torture was agony but Ed Morrell refused to be broken. Even as his cruel jailers slowly squeezed him to the jaws of death, he found a way to escape.

Ed Morrell had the bad luck to be incarcerated in the Arizona State Penitentiary, rated one of the four most savage jails in the USA. One of the more refined methods of torture that Morrell suffered there was to be tied into not one but two strait-jackets; then water was poured over him, so that the jackets shrank. It was, he wrote in his book *The Twenty-Fifth Man*, like being 'slowly squeezed to death'. But, time and again, Morrell escaped from this agony: his consciousness – some would say his soul, others would call it his 'astral body' – left his body to suffer, and floated away, free from pain.

In this 'out-of-the-body' state, Morrell was able to travel not only around the immediate vicinity of the prison, but to other countries. He seems even to have been able to travel in time. On one disembodied journey he saw a woman that he later was to meet in the flesh – and many.

Out-of-the-body experiences (OBEs) are often associated with escape from extreme physical pain, as in Morrell's case; victims of road accidents, for instance, have often reported that their conscious self has floated free from their broken bodies, so that they survey themselves from a point above (and often slightly to one side of) their physical position.

The British secret agent Odette Hallowes positively looked forward to her OBEs when she was captured and tortured by the Gestapo during World War Two. When the pain reached a certain intensity, she would literally rise above it, leaving the sadists 'below' her to get on with their inhuman work while she, now free from any physical feelings, felt a profound sense of relief.

DRUG-INDUCED?

It is not necessary, however, to suffer extreme stress, shock or trauma in order to have an OBE. The experience can happen spontaneously and without warning to someone who is especially relaxed. One such episode was reported by a florist known only as Pat who, when she was 20, in April 1970, shared a flat in Canterbury, Kent, with her musician cousin.

'I [was] lying on the sofa for a few hours, listening to my cousin play the piano. I was completely relaxed and felt as if I were going to sleep,' she recalled. 'Suddenly I was aware that I had actually risen to ceiling height. I turned over and seemed to hover... I could see everything in the room quite clearly, even myself lying on the sofa... I suddenly found myself way up in the sky hovering over Canterbury. Only it wasn't April any more; it was a summery day.

'I didn't want to return, indeed I had a great sense of elation. But... what would happen if I travelled on into the unknown? As I was thinking about this I found myself staring down at my body again. I decided I couldn't do it... as soon as I had made my decision I was back in my body before you could say "Jack Flash".'

Others have reported having an OBE as a result of sheer boredom – one lady office worker claimed she found her mind frequently drifting into a reverie during particularly tedious meetings, and she would find herself wondering, 'What's on the other side of that wall?' Then, she would 'float' out of her body, out of the meeting-room and 'have a good look round'. Relaxation and a relatively idle, non-concentrating conscious mind seem essential to initiate this class of OBE. In 1971, psychologist Dr Charles Tart surveyed 150 regular smokers of marijuana and discovered that 44 per cent of them had had an OBE while using the drug. Other surveys have established that roughly one person in four has experienced an OBE at least once in their lives – suggesting that the state of fatuous euphoria typically associated with smoking dope increases the likelihood of you getting literally out of your head.

ASTRAL BODIES

These OBEs - brought on by intolerable physical stress or when the mind has, in effect, gone blank through relaxation or boredom - occur of their own accord; those who have them cannot control either their onset or, apparently, the way they end. But OBEs can be induced deliberately and enjoyed at will.

In their book *The Projection of the Astral Body* (1929), Sylvan Muldoon and Hereward Carrington describe several ways in which to achieve an OBE. All involve lying on your back in bed with the eyes closed. You might then concentrate on loosening the 'astral body' from the physical body, by rotating your point of view in the imagination around a central axis – so that you are looking at your own feet, for example, or at the length of your body. From these positions you should look at the ceiling, the wall on one side, the floor, and the wall on the other side.

Another suggestion is to hold the image and imaginary sensation of going up in a lift until you drift off to sleep, while telling yourself that you will wake up fully out of the body. A third method is to make sure you go to bed thirsty, and go to sleep while imagining going to the kitchen for a drink of water – and telling yourself to wake up, out of the body, at the sink. These methods do indeed work, although at first they take a great deal of concentration and will power.

The fact that an OBE can be deliberately induced has meant that the true nature of the experience can be explored through tests and experiments. The first question to be answered, naturally enough, is: does the consciousness really leave the body during an OBE and wander about at will?

The anecdotal evidence that this does actually happen is

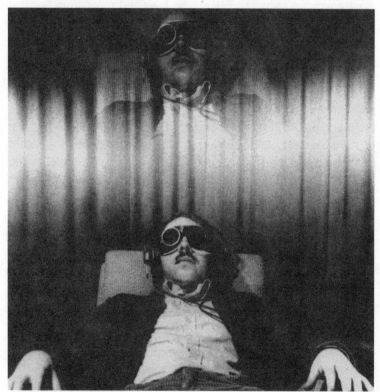

An attempt to induce an out-of-the-body experience using coloured eyeglasses and aural stimulation through headphones, conducted at the Freiburg Institute in Germany 1982.

conflicting. In Pat's OBE, cited earlier, it is curious that once out of her own basement flat and apparently high in the sky above Canterbury, the weather changed from that of a normal April day in England (which means it was raining) to that of a sunny, summer day. Dr Susan Blackmore, a world authority on OBEs, became intrigued by the subject because she had them herself. In one, she floated to the ceiling, through it and above the housetops of her neighbourhood. Looking down, she could see the red roofs and chimneys of the buildings below as she flew over them... In her down-to-earth analysis of the event, Dr Blackmore noted wryly that in fact the roofs she supposedly floated over were actually made of grey slate, and that none of the buildings in the district had chimneys like the ones she saw.

Dr Blackmore has also had an interesting response from an experiment set up with a friend who lives 200 miles from her and who claimed that he had OBEs regularly and could 'travel' long distances at will. To find out if he did travel in reality or in imagination, Dr Blackmore left three items on the top of a cupboard in her kitchen, out of sight of any casual visitor. They were a small object such as a comb or a piece of candy, a three-digit number, and a short word. The arrangement was that when her friend paid a flying visit during an OBE, he would check the top of the cupboard, note what was there, and send her a postcard describing what he had seen. Each week Dr Blackmore changed the three objects. She did this for five years. No postcard ever arrived.

TRAVELLING CLAIRVOYANCE

Others have reported entirely different experiences. The American medium Eileen Garrett, for example, tells in her autobiography how she carried out an experimental OBE at the request of a doctor who lived in Newfoundland. Garrett lived in New York, and had never been to the doctor's home. She projected herself from New York to the house in Newfoundland, and there saw the doctor, who was himself somewhat psychic and was apparently able to detect her arrival. She noted a number of objects laid out on the doctor's table, and also saw that he had a bandaged head. He told her, speaking out loud, that he had had an accident that morning. Next, he pulled a book from a shelf and opened it so that she could read the title page.

All this information and more about what Garrett had seen during her out-of the-body visit to Newfoundland was written down and mailed to the doctor the same day. Next day, he telegraphed a reply confirming everything Garrett had reported.

Here we have two diametrically different accounts of OBEs, both from people renowned for their honesty. How can we account for the apparent contradiction?

First, let's suppose that Dr Blackmore is correct in thinking an OBE is essentially an imaginary experience – a 'dramatized reconstruction of a memory of the physical world', in Prof. Arthur Ellison's words.

Second, Eileen Garrett was one of the most accomplished mediums of all time. It seems likely, then, that what she saw on her OBE to Newfoundland was correct not because she was spiritually or astrally there in person, but because she was there psychically. The modern term for what she was doing is 'remote viewing', a form of extrasensory perception that used to be called 'travelling clairvoyance'. Telepathy may have been involved too, for the doctor in the experiment was also psychic.

Third, it is well-known among psychical researchers that Dr Blackmore herself is distinctly un-psychic; she has remarked ruefully on the fact that she actually seems to inhibit extrasensory perception many times. Her own lack of psychic gifts and her tendency apparently to block others' extrasensory perception would not only explain the discrepancies between her view of her neighbourhood during her OBE and the actual facts about the place. It would also account for her friend's being unable to discover what she had put on the top of her kitchen cupboard – either she was blocking him from getting at the information telepathically, or he himself has no talent for extrasensory perception (or both).

We've seen from accounts of many other psychic phenomena that extrasensory perception (like an OBE) is often triggered by a crisis. It's also apparent that both extrasensory perception and OBEs can occur as a result of profound relaxation that amounts to a trance state. An OBE may not make someone without any latent psychic ability into a sensitive, but it may make a chink in his or her psychic armour; and to someone moderately sensitive who has many OBEs it may help their extrasensory perceptions develop. Thus Ed Morrell could see his future wife during one of his repeated OBEs. He was having a precognitive vision.

Even if OBEs are not literally journeys of the soul out of the body, but an extraordinary facet of the imagination, they are nonetheless replete with unsolved mysteries.

INTRIGUING EXPERIENCE

There are many reports of the curious effects experienced during OBEs – by both those undergoing them and those researching them. One such series of oddities was recounted by Dr Arthur Ellison, Professor of Electronic Engineering at the City University, London, until 1986 and at one time a president of the British Society for Psychical Research.

Ellison had himself induced his own OBEs as an experiment, but abandoned this line of research simply because he was exhausted by the lack of sleep it entailed. He did have one very curious experience during his second OBE, however. He had succeeded in floating out of his bedroom window and was aiming to drift down to the lawn below, where he intended to walk about. (It is, incidentally, a peculiar quality of OBEs that those who have them seem to travel about with a sense of having a body of some kind: hence the term 'astral body' used in many discussions of the phenomenon.) Ellison was starting his descent to the ground when: 'I had one of the most intriguing experiences to date. I felt two hands take my head, one hand over each ear, [and] move me... back into the bedroom and down into the body. I heard no sound, and saw nothing.'

Ellison felt, on balance, that it was more likely that an OBE was an imaginative reconstruction of reality and not an actual paranormal mode of travel. But there remained the problem of people who picked up undoubtedly genuine information during OBEs that they had no other apparent means of having acquired.

Ellison decided to test for the possibility that information of this kind was acquired telepathically.

For his experiments he had an electronic machine built. This would generate a random number and show it on a standard digital panel at the back. No one would see this number at any time during the experiment, except for the subject – and then only if they could read it during their OBE. On the front of the machine, a second display would record the number that the subjects claimed to see and show whether the claim was correct or not. It could also tell whether individual digits in the three-figure number had been read correctly. It still did not show the original number.

Ellison chose as his subjects people who could be hypnotized and would then have an OBE. The advantage of this system was that they could report from their physical state what their ostensibly disembodied selves were seeing. The machine could thus display runs of 20 or more numbers, giving the answers statistical validity.

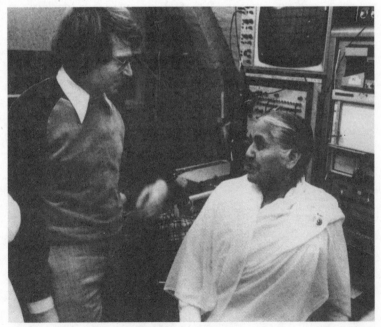

Indian yoga adept Pushal Behen about to undergo an analysis of her brain-wave patterns with an electro-encephalograph.

MACHINE
MALFUNCTION

There were two intriguing results of Ellison's experiments with this device. He first tested the machine with a female subject and, to speed up this initial informal trial, checked the psychic's claims by looking at the numbers at the back of the machine himself. She achieved a correct score of almost 100 per cent. But when a completely secure run of numbers was made, she scored zero, and made some rather feeble excuses about not being able to read the numbers properly because they were 'too small' – which, strange to say, had not been a problem before.

The obvious conclusion was that when no one was actually aware of the target figures, she could not see them. Or, to put it another way, she could identify the numbers only through someone else's awareness – that is, by telepathy.

On two further notable occasions Ellison tested well-known psychics with his machine. The first, an American, achieved a score of 8 correct numbers out of 20 without even going into an OBE – about eight times any score that one might expect by chance guessing. When Ellison tested the machine the following day, he himself – who makes no claim to psychic ability at all – achieved the same astonishingly high score. Checking the guts of the device revealed a fault in the circuitry.

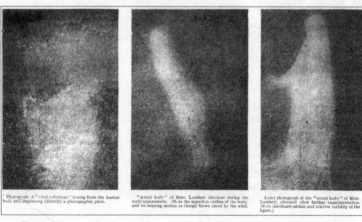

Photograph of "vital radiations" issuing from the human body and impressing (directly) a photographic plate.

"Astral body" of Mme. Lambert obtained during the early experiments. (Note the imperfect outline of the body, and its swaying motion as though blown about by the wind.

Later photograph of the "astral body" of Mme. Lambert, obtained after further experimentation. (Note the clearer outline and relative stability of the figure.)

These three photographs, published in the Occult Review of May 1916, purport to show the emergence of the astral body of one Madame Lambert from her physical form.

The British psychic came up with exactly the same high score. Then, in a control run, so did Ellison. Once again, apparently, the machine had malfunctioned. Ellison concluded: 'An experienced psychical researcher... might observe that this kind of thing often happens. It is as though the unconscious mind of the psychic, knowing that a high score was required, achieved this by the easiest available method – by using [psychokinesis] on the microcircuit rather than clairvoyance. But it is impossible to prove this contention: it merely remains a possibility.'

CRISIS APPARITIONS

No less mysterious are those rare cases in which subjects having an OBE actually appear in front of someone they are visiting in their disembodied state.

On 26 January 1957, just such an encounter took place between 26-year-old Martha Johnson and her mother. During an OBE, Martha 'floated' to her mother's house 926 miles away, in another time zone. When she arrived, she found her mother in the kitchen. Martha took a couple of steps toward her, but then came abruptly back to her body. She looked at her bedside clock: it read 2.10 a.m.

For her part, Martha's mother wrote to her at once to tell her own side of the story – and, when she did so, she had no idea that Martha had been having an OBE. She had noticed nothing at first, then gradually became aware of Martha standing in the kitchen in a typical posture: with her arms folded and her head slightly tilted to one side. She started to say something to her daughter – but then Martha abruptly vanished. She noted in her letter how good Martha's new hairstyle looked. The time she had seen her, she added, was 'ten after two, your time'.

There was no sense of crisis or foreboding in this experience; Martha's mother seems to have taken the whole episode in her stride. Only when both parties were about to put the situation to the test by communicating did it break down: as if psychic reality and the mundane world were incapable of coexisting.

Circumstances were to say the least slightly different when Mr W. Lee of Bridgnorth, Shropshire, visited his mother in what seems to have been an OBE, in 1963. Lee was doing his stint of national service in the British Army at the time, and did not like it. He rebelled from time to time, and found himself at the mercy of an old Regular Army sergeant. He, on this occasion, landed Lee and three other conscripts with a punishment known by the innocuous name of 'pack drill'. At that time a standard infantryman's pack, fully loaded, weighed about 40 lb. Much of the kit inside was spare clothing. The sergeant ordered the four to fill their capacious packs not with issue kit but with housebricks, and then sent them out on the parade ground to drill with these back-breaking loads at a cracking pace.

It was a very hot day. One of the four kept collapsing. Lee, determined not to be beaten by the sadistic punishment, kept on marching. 'I just kept on going while the commands being shouted at us grew dimmer and dimmer,' he wrote years later. 'In the end I could not hear them. My heart did not seem to be beating and I could not see. Somehow I kept turning and marching but I was no longer there. Eventually the torture ended…'

That was all there was to that particular event, Lee thought, until the next time he returned home on leave. His mother then told him a curious tale.

On the same day that Lee had become an automaton on the drill square, his mother and his younger brother had been out shopping. 'They were about 100 yards from the nearest bus stop to our home,' he wrote, 'when a bus stopped and I got off in my Army uniform. [My mother] called to me as I walked up the road but I did not answer or turn round. It would be about 300 yards to the corner of our road, and my mother and brother… ran to try and catch me up, because I was walking very quickly. I rounded the corner four or five seconds ahead of them and when they too came round the corner I had disappeared. There was only a postman to be seen.

'My mother asked [him] where had the soldier gone and he told her nobody had come round the corner.'

In cases like these, the distinctions become blurred between what is an OBE, what is a *doppelgänger* (the psychic double of a living person), and what is a 'crisis apparition' – the apparent ghost of someone who is, nonetheless, still alive. Even if most OBEs are the work of the imagination, incidents like these latter two show that we still only barely understand the phenomenon as a whole.

NOSTRADAMUS
AND VISIONS
OF THE FUTURE

NOSTRADAMUS

Nearly 500 years ago a medieval doctor retreated to his secret study, night after night, to journey into the future. The images that he saw were so terrifying that he concealed his prophecies in an elaborate code. Now that code has been broken, and history has confirmed the accuracy of many of his predictions – but are the final devastating prophecies about to come true?

History credits a man named Nostradamus as being the greatest seer who ever lived. His prophecies, cast nearly 500 years ago, have been interpreted by learned scholars, laymen and sceptics alike as the first – and accurate – drafts of great world events. Nostradamus correctly foretold the Great Fire of London and the coming of Adolf Hitler. He prophesized the death of Henri II of France, the triumph and death of Elizabeth I of England and the French Revolution. If his last prediction is right – that of a war to end all wars – then civilization as we know it could be destroyed. It is the one prophecy that all students of Nostradamus hope and pray is incorrect – but if his record is anything to go by, mankind should surely fear the worst.

Nostradamus was born Michel de Nostradame in St Remy de Provence on 14 December 1503. His father, James, was a lawyer, born into a Jewish family who had converted to the Catholic faith. Michel was a brilliant student who spent his time in between lessons reading books on fortune telling and the occult. His grandfather, who had a great influence over his schooling, also taught him the 'celestial sciences' – astronomy. After studying humanities at Avignon he went to the University of Montpellier where he read medicine and philosophy. Medicine was to be his first calling and he excelled as a physician. When he was 20 Nostradamus retreated from Montpellier as it was ravaged by the Great Plague laying waste to Europe's cities and villages, but returned two years later, after practising in Bordeaux and Narbonne, to complete his medical degree. It was at this time that he changed his name from Nostradame to Nostradamus, 'Man of Our Lady'.

He left Montpellier for Provence, his home region which was also being decimated by the plague. He soon earned a name for himself as a courageous physician who, regardless of his own safety, began venturing into the worst-stricken areas to aid the sick, but he refused to 'bleed' people, one of the most common – and cruellest – medical practices of the age. Older and more powerful physicians than Nostradamus expounded the virtues of this nonsensical practice, believing that the illness in an afflicted person's body flowed away with the blood. Instead Nostradamus set about making compounds and potions to relieve suffering and later noted their compositions in a book.

In 1534 after being invited by a prominent philosopher to stay with him at his home in Agen, Nostradamus met and married a beautiful noblewoman. He had a son and a daughter by her but soon the plague – a virulent strain called 'le charbon' because sufferers were stricken with great black pustules on their bodies – came to Agen and claimed the lives of his family. Heartbroken, Nostradamus wandered around France for several years; the prime purpose of his travels seems to have been the collection and study of potions and medicines from apothecaries and pharmacists across the land. He also travelled to Italy, where one of the legends about his mystical powers first grew. He saw a young monk leading a herd of swine down a narrow street; as the monk drew level with him Nostradamus bowed down on one knee and addressed him as 'Your Holiness'. Later, the humble swineherd, Felice Peretti, became Pope Sextus V, long after Nostradamus had died.

By 1554, when the plague was thought to be on the retreat, Nostradamus had settled in Marseilles, but that year there were massive floods and the swollen rivers, polluted with infected corpses, carried the disease to every part of the region. Once again Nostradamus found himself working around the clock to ease the suffering of the people. It was remarkable that in his close contact with so many sufferers he never succumbed to the disease himself.

The prophet lived in an ordered world where the divine right of kings reigned supreme. What mystical powers, then, did he tap into to foresee the French Revolution and with it the storming of the Bastille, where enemies of the state were held in appalling conditions?

In November 1554 he settled in Salon where he married Anne Ponsart Gemelle, a rich widow. Most of the treasures and rewards that grateful towns had heaped on Nostradamus for his care of plague victims had been given away to the poor, but a comfortable life now seemed a certainty thanks to his wise marriage which provided him with a daughter and three sons, a peaceful home life and no money worries. He converted the top room of his house into a study and began work on his immortal *Prophecies* – the foretelling of the future using all his wisdom, astronomical gifts and occult beliefs. In such an age, when the terror of the (church) Inquisition hung heavily over anyone deemed to be a heretic, Nostradamus was certainly taking chances in committing his predictions to paper. He initially composed the prophetic riddles – quatrains – for his own interest; it was only later that he decided to publish them. However, he made sure that they were extremely difficult to interpret, written as they were in a hotchpotch of high French, Provençal French, Italian, Greek and Latin, and riddled with symbolism. Their time sequence was deliberately mixed up so that their meaning and chronology 'would not be immediately discernible to the unwise'. The latter was probably a built-in safeguard in case the guardians of the rack and the branding iron in the Inquisition became displeased with him. In a section on Nostradamus in his book of seers entitled *They Saw Tomorrow*, Charles Neilson Gattey said: 'Even today, when one first reads the original French edition, one's initial reaction is of perplexed disillusion. The language is enigmatic, at times almost unintelligible, as if written in code. The verses are not in chronological order and jump about in time and subject. Strange soubriquets of Nostradamus' own coining are used for famous personalities. Everywhere we find mystifying puns and anagrams.' But ever since their publication the *Prophecies* have withstood the test of time and proved that Nostradamus was an incredible seer. By 1555 he had completed the first part of his life's work – an almanac of prophecies that were to chronicle world history from his time until the end of the world. The forecasts were called 'The Centuries'; the word 'centuries' had nothing to do with a span of 100 years – it was because there were 100 verses in each book, of which the author intended to write ten. In the preface to the first, Nostradamus wrote that he was afraid that he would be killed by an angry mob if he committed to paper the future which had been revealed to him in prophetic visions. 'That is why I have withheld my tongue from the vulgar and my pen from paper,' he said. 'But later on I thought I would for the common good describe the most important of the revolutionary changes I foresee, but so as not to upset my present readers I would do this in a cloudy manner with abstruse and twisted sentences rather than plainly prophetical.' Only some of the Centuries are dated – although Nostradamus claimed he could have given a date to all of them had he so wished. Regarding 1792, for instance, when the French Revolution was at its height, he wrote that the year would be 'marked by a far worse persecution of the Christian Church than ever was in Africa, and which everyone will think an innovation of the age'. That year, Madame Guillotine was at her bloody zenith across France.

At the beginning of his work he also gave the reader an insight into how he divined his prophecies, again in the form of a quatrain: 'Sitting alone at night in secret study; it is placed on the brass tripod. A slight flame comes out of the emptiness and makes successful that which should not be believed in vain.' He went on: 'The wand in the hand is placed in the middle of the tripod's legs. With water he sprinkles both the hem of his garment and his foot. A voice, fear; he trembles in his robes. Divine splendour; the god sits nearby.' According to Nostradamus expert Erika Cheetham in her authoritative work *The Prophecies of Nostradamus*, he touches the middle of the tripod with his wand and then moistens his robe and feet with the water placed on it. 'This is the same method as was used to obtain inspiration by the Apollonian prophetess at the oracles of Branchus in Classical times,' she said. 'Nostradamus is afraid of the power he evokes when it comes to him; he hears it as well as sees it; it appears to speak to him and he writes down the prophecies. He is unafraid once the gift has possessed him. This dual aspect of his vision is most important when interpreting the centuries.'

Nostradamus also relied heavily on the impressive library he had built up, containing many rare books and manuscripts on the occult. He was influenced by dark, magical texts which he later decided to burn when they came into conflict with his deep religious beliefs. He claimed that when they burned a 'subtle illumination' was cast over his house, acting as a catalyst for further divination and prophecy. He wrote: 'Many occult volumes, which have been hidden for centuries have come into my possession, but after reading them, dreading what might happen if they should fall into the wrong hands, I presented them to Vulcan, and as the fire devoured them, the flames licking the air shot forth an unaccustomed brightness, clearer than natural flame, like the flash from an explosive powder, casting a peculiar illumination all over the house, as if it were wrapped in sudden conflagration. So that you might not in the future be tempted to search for the perfect transmutation, lunar or solar, or for uncorruptible metals hidden under the earth or the sea, I reduced them to ashes.' While using his psychic, meditative and prophetic powers for the Centuries, he was also a firm believer in astrology, using many astrological charts, constellations, planets and signs, to date the quatrains. His implication in the introduction to the Centuries was that, while future events and their dates are determined by planetary movements, their description needed to be modified by the 'spirit of prophecy'.

He ends his introduction to the prophecies by stating that he is not 'vain' enough to call himself a prophet. He says he is a mortal man, 'the greatest sinner in the world, and heir to every human affliction, but, by being surprised sometimes by a prophetical mood, amid prolonged calculation, while engaged in nocturnal studies of sweet odour, I have composed books of prophecies, containing each one a hundred astronomical quatrains which I have joined obscurely and are perpetual vaticinations from now to the year 3797'.

At the end of 1555, the first three Centuries and part of the fourth were published and the fame of Nostradamus spread across Europe with all the speed of the plague that he had devoted his earlier life to conquering. Much of his celebrity spread by word of mouth, from village to village and city to city, as books were expensive and purely a luxury for the rich. But it was at the highest levels of French society where his prophecies aroused most interest, particularly at the court of the royal family. In a superstitious age, someone like Nostradamus was regarded with a mixture of both awe and fear.

Catherine de Medici, wife of Henri II of France, was an avowed occultist, who had entertained many fortune tellers, seers, prophets and charlatans as she tried to plot the course of her beloved husband's reign. She sent for Nostradamus shortly after the publication of the Centuries – both curious and concerned about several passages which, if they were realized, were ominous for the king. It was Quatrain 35 of the first Century which was most worrying, however, as it seemed to predict his death in battle. It read: 'The young lion will overcome the older one, in a field of combat in single fight; He will pierce his eyes in their golden cage; two wounds in one, then he dies a cruel death.' Nostradamus arrived in Paris on 15 August 1556 with specific instructions from Catherine de Medici to interpret it.

Catherine was certain of Nostradamus's powers from the first moment she saw him; an aura seemed to emanate from him, particularly from his eyes, and he was adorned with none of the charms and amulets so beloved of the 30,000-odd occultists who made Paris their home. Initially, she hedged around asking him to interpret the quatrains pertaining to the king, instead asking him advice on cosmetics and alternative healing practices. Curiosity, eventually, led her to seek an explanation of the king's death. Nostradamus explained as delicately as he could that he had no power over the visions he had, that he merely recorded events as they came to him. He was aware that a previous seer to the court, a man named Gaurico, had endured horrific torture for prophecies

Nostradamus commanded by Catherine, is depicted here with occult symbols such as the zodiac, a cat and skulls. He is engaged in summoning up pictures of future French kings in a mirror.

about the king's demise, but he told her anyway – that the king would die in a duel. In 1559 his prediction came true. In celebration of two royal weddings, jousts, tournaments and feasts spanning a three-day period were held in Paris. On the final day the king jousted with Captain Montgomery of the Scottish Guard, with both men wearing the emblem of a lion on their chests. When they rode against each other for a third time the splintered end of Montgomery's lance pierced first the king's throat and then knocked up his protective visor, piercing his eye. Mortally injured by the 'two wounds in one', he was carried from the field of combat to die in agony ten days later.

After this, Nostradamus drew up the horoscopes for the royal offspring – children for whom he had already predicted grim fates in the Centuries. Rather than piling on the agony, he diplomatically concentrated on the positive aspects of their lives, predicting that all Catherine's sons would be kings; only François died before he could ascend to the throne.

After his royal audiences he lived in Salon, continuing to work on the Centuries and, upon command, drawing up horoscopes for his many learned and wealthy visitors. In 1564 Catherine, now Queen Regent, went on a royal tour of France with 800 family members, courtiers and attendants. One of her first calls was on Nostradamus, whom she dined with and bestowed upon the

France's moment of shame: the sword of Alfred Dreyfus is ceremonially broken. Nostradamus foresaw the Dreyfus Affair of 1985, when trumped-up charges against Dreyfus bitterly divided the nation.

privileged title of Physician in Ordinary. It carried with it a small stipend and other benefits; more importantly, it silenced those justices and clergy who mumbled from time to time about heresy and witchcraft being practised by the old sage.

One interesting incident worth recording occurred during this royal visitation in Salon. Nostradamus, whose visions were the root of his prophecies, also occasionally foretold future events by looking at a person or touching them. He attached great importance to birthmarks upon a person's body, believing them portents of greatness. It was while the royal retinue was at Salon that he made a request to view the naked body of a young boy who was with them - ten-year-old Henri of Navarre – but the boy was shy and feared he would be beaten. The old seer crept into his bedchamber that night and examined the boy as he slept, and found the birthmark he was seeking. Catherine still had two sons in line to the throne but Nostradamus was adamant: the child would be king of France. His prophecy was true – Henri of Navarre became Henri IV of France.

After the royal visitation he worked on completing five more Centuries, bringing the total to eight in all, but the completed works were not off the printing press until 1568, two years after he died. Nostradamus made his will on 17 June 1566 and left a large sum of over 3,500 crowns. On 1 July he told his local priest to give him the last rites as he would not be seen alive again. Sure enough, he foretold his own death, with his body being discovered the next morning, a victim of virulent dropsy. He had penned a quatrain for the occasion: 'On returning from an embassy, the King's gift safely stored, No more will I labour, for I will have gone to God, by my close relations, friends and brothers, I shall be found dead, near my bed and the bench.' He lived for 62 years, 6 months and 17 days. His legacy is a work that, through the ages, has been as relevant for people as it was when he was alive. As a prophet, he had the satisfaction of both seeing his predictions come true in his own lifetime as well as having them quoted in the highest circles. Before his death his fame had spread to England where two of his almanacs were printed in London, but it wasn't until 1672 that *The True Prophecies or Prognostications of Michel Nostradamus*, Translated and Commentated by Theophilus de Garencieres, a doctor of the 'College of Physick' in London, were printed, spreading his prophecies to a much wider and altogether more learned audience.

His last request was to be buried upright – he couldn't bear the thought of people walking over him 'during my final sleep'. Placed into the wall of the Church of the Cordeliers in Salon, it was not to be his final grave. In Quatrain 7 of Century IX he had written that evil would come to any man who violated his resting place. It so happened that during the French Revolution the church was pillaged, with one of the looters desecrating his grave, ripping out his skull and using it for a drinking cup. Sure enough, the vagabond was shot dead as soon as he emerged from the crypt. Nostradamus was reinterred in the Church of St Laurent in 1813 where he has been allowed to rest in peace ever since. A tablet nearby says: 'Here lie the bones of the illustrious Michel Nostradamus, whose almost divine pen alone, in the judgement of all mortals, was worthy to record, under the influx of the stars, the future events of the whole world. He died at Salon in the year 1566. Posterity, disturb not his sweet rest! Anne Ponce Gemelle hopes for her husband true felicity.' It was written by his second wife.

Although Nostradamus enjoys fame long after his death, he does remain an enigma to many. In his scholarly work *Oracles of Nostradamus*, author Charles Ward wrote of him: 'It has been well said that the man and his works are an enigma. Everything in our author is ambiguous; the man, the thought, the style. We stumble at every step in the rough paths of his labyrinth. We try to interrogate, but grow silent before a man of emotionless nerve and of impenetrable mask. What are these centuries? What is Nostradamus? In them and him all may find something; but no man born of woman can find all. The Sphinx of France is here before us; a riddler, riddling of the fate of men; a man at once bold and timid; simple, yet who can plumb his depth? A superficial Christian, a pagan perhaps at heart; a man rewarded of kings; and yet, so far as one can see, furnishing no profitable hint to them that could make their life run smoother or remove a single peril from their path. Behold this Janus of a double face; his very breath is double; the essence of ambiguity lies wrapped incarnate in him and it moulds the man, the thought, the style.'

THE CENTURIES

Only by reading the prophecies – and the violent world events which they seem tailored to – can the enthusiast of Nostradamus really begin to grasp his astonishing powers. There follow some of the most remarkable events that this remarkable individual foresaw, together with interpretations as to their meanings. Some of his more foreboding prophecies, dealing with cataclysmic events yet to come, are left, appropriately, until the end.

CENTURY 1, QUATRAIN 7

Arrived too late, the act has been done. The wind was against them, letters intercepted on their way. The conspirators were fourteen of a party. By Rousseau shall these enterprises be undertaken.

TRANSLATION: This is widely regarded as Nostradamus's foretelling of the Dreyfus scandal which rocked France at the turn of 20th century. Alfred Dreyfus was a Jewish officer of the General Staff falsely accused of passing on vital military intelligence to the arch-enemy, Germany. Nostradamus mentions letters – and indeed, it was later learned, shortly before Dreyfus was pardoned and released from Devil's Island, that faked documents had smeared him in the first place. The term 'vent contraire' in the language of Nostradamus is interpreted by scholars as meaning political, anti-Semitic reasons for his false arrest. But by far the most interesting part of the quatrain is the mention of Rousseau in the last line. Waldeck Rousseau was perhaps the most virulent, violent Dreyfus accuser. And there were, it is believed, no less than 14 generals, staff officers and politicians involved in the conspiracy to brand Dreyfus a traitor.

CENTURY 1, QUATRAIN 18

Because of French discord and negligence an opening shall be given to the Mohammedans. The land and sea of Siena will be soaked in blood and the Port of Marseilles covered with ships and sails.

TRANSLATION: In these few words Nostradamus predicted the most cataclysmic event yet to befall mankind – World War Two. The discord is a reference to the chaos that France found herself in during 1940 which allowed the armies of Italy, allied with Hitler, to march into Africa, where their blood was spilled in the desert. The harbour at Marseilles was in German hands and remained a busy port throughout the war.

CENTURY I, QUATRAIN 26

The great man will be struck down in the day by a thunderbolt. An evil deed, foretold by the bearer of a petition. According to the prediction another falls at night time. Conflict at Reims, London and pestilence in Tuscany.

TRANSLATION: This is a prime example of the 'open to interpretation' tag that applies to so many of Nostradamus's predictions, but several historians believe that he is referring to the twin assassinations of the Kennedy brothers, John and Robert. Gunshots are the 'thunderbolts' with one dying during the day – JFK - and his brother being murdered five years later in June 1968. The petition mentioned could be a reference to the numerous death threats both received while in public life, and the mention of the three places refers to the anguish that swept the world at the news of the deaths.

CENTURY I, QUATRAIN 60

An Emperor will be born near Italy, who will cost the Empire very dearly. They will say, when they see his allies, that he is less a prince than a butcher.

TRANSLATION: Nostradamus predicted the arrival on Earth of Napoleon I, France's greatest warrior son who was indeed born closer to Italy than France upon the island of Corsica. A squanderer of men and resources in his endless campaigns, he cost France dearly in both – hence the additional reference to butchery. Nostradamus had great success in predictions about Napoleon and the Centuries are dotted with references to him.

CENTURY I, QUATRAIN 64

At night they will think they have seen the sun, when they see the halfpig man: Noise, screams, battles seen fought in the skies. The brute beasts will be heard to speak.

TRANSLATION: In this remarkable quatrain Nostradamus foresaw a battle in the skies, a totally unique and unknown experience in the times he came from. 'Sun' means searchlight, piercing the sky; pig-like man perfectly sums up the ghoulish appearance of an aviator in goggles and oxygen mask, distending his face like a pig. 'Brute beasts' are the men, speaking to each other over their voice microphones and the screams may be, according to Cheetham in her work on Nostradamus, the whine of bombs as they fall to Earth.

CENTURY I, QUATRAIN 97

That which neither weapon nor flame could accomplish will be achieved by a sweet speaking tongue in a council. Sleeping, in a dream, the king will see the enemy not in war or of military blood.

TRANSLATION: This relates to the death of Henri III of France in 1589, a monarch who did not die in combat or jousting, but who was assassinated by a monk who pretended he wanted to pass on a message to him. The reference to the dream means the victim will have a premonition of his death – as was the case. Henri III told his royal circle three nights before his murder that he had dreamed of his violent end.

The preceding quatrains give the reader an idea of the style that Nostradamus employed with his predictions. He ranged over the whole gamut of human affairs and emotions: peace and war, love and hate, religion and disbelief.

QUATRAINS ON ENGLAND

In the following sections more of his predictions are grouped according to individual subjects. England was a source of endless intrigue and curiosity for Nostradamus – he believed that the English were to be envied and closely watched at the same time. Perhaps that is why he foresaw so much of how British society would develop.

CENTURY I, QUATRAIN 23

In the third month, at sunrise, the Boar and the Leopard meet on the battlefield. The fatigued Leopard looks up to heaven and sees an eagle playing around the sun.

TRANSLATION: Nostradamus saw the end of Napoleon at Waterloo, the boar signifying the forces of Prussia which teamed up with those of the leopard – England, for Napoleon referred to the British lion on her armed forces' standards as the English Leopard – for the final crushing blow aimed at Boney's ambitions on the Continent. The eagles are those of Napoleon's standards, the Imperial Eagles. The English Leopard is indeed exhausted, but Napoleon knows the end is near.

CENTURY III, QUATRAIN 80
He who had the right to reign in England shall be driven from the throne, his counsellor abandoned to the fury of the populace. His adherents will follow so low a track that the usurper will come to be protector.

TRANSLATION: This prophecy foretold the fall of Charles I. Nothing could be clearer – the king was driven from his throne and his right-handman Strafford was beheaded. The Scots, his countrymen, sold the king back to Parliament in 1646 for a sum of £400,000 after which Cromwell – referred to in the French version as 'Le bâtard' – became Lord Protector, not the king.

Queen Victoria as she appeared in 1876, the empress of a mighty empire upon which the Sun never set. An avowed and ardent royalist, Nostradamus would no doubt have approved of this iron lady of her times.

CENTURY IX, QUATRAIN 49

Ghent and Brussels will march past Antwerp, the Senate at London will put their King to death; salt and wine will be applied contrariwise, so that they will set the whole kingdom in disarray.

TRANSLATION: This is the foretelling of the death of Charles I; ironically Quatrain 49, as the king was executed in 1649. Salt and wine was used as a metaphor by Nostradamus for force and wisdom, and is a good example of the vagueness attached to so many of his predictions. The references to the Netherland cities in the first line concerns a war in the Low Countries.

CENTURY VIII, QUATRAIN 76

A butcher more than king rules England. A man of no birth will seize the government by violence. Of loose morals, without faith or law, he will bleed the earth. The hour approaches me so near that I breathe with difficulty.

TRANSLATION: If the preceding quatrain was obscure, then this foretelling of the coming of Oliver Cromwell into English national life could not be clearer. Charles Ward in his work wrote: 'Here we have a most remarkable forecast. It puts into a clear light what view Nostradamus had formed of Cromwell. There appears to have been visually present to him the butcher-like face of Cromwell, with its fleshy conch and hideous warts. This seems to have struck him with such a sense of vividness and horror that he is willing to imagine that the time is very near at hand. A full century had, however, to elapse, but he sighs as with a present shudder, and the blood creeps.' It is a departure from the norm in the Centuries in that in it Nostradamus has imparted a sense of the genuine revulsion he felt, giving the reader an idea of how horror-stricken he was when the prophecy came upon him.

CENTURY X, QUATRAIN 100

England the Pempotam will rule the great empire of the waters for more than 300 years. Great armies will pass by sea and land; the Portuguese will not be satisfied.

TRANSLATION: This is the very last quatrain of the last Century but, as stated before, there was no order to the prophecies written down. Most scholars regard this as a statement on the greatness of the British Empire, stretching from Elizabethan times through to the reign of Queen Victoria, when indeed Pax Britannica ruled the waves and the world before modern times sharply reduced her power and influence. Portugal is mentioned because she is Britain's oldest ally in treaties that go back almost 1,000 years – although, of course, it was practically half that time ago when Nostradamus penned his prediction. Pempotam is a good illustration of the quasi-classical words that Nostradamus typically peppered his prophecies with – it derives from the Greek pan, meaning all, and the Latin potens, meaning powerful.

CENTURY IV, QUATRAIN 96

The elder sister of the British Isle shall be born 15 years before her brother; true to her intervening promise, she will succeed to the kingdom of the balance.

TRANSLATION: This means that Mary, elder sister of Edward VI, shall ascend the throne of England. Nostradamus got it slightly wrong here – she was 26, not 15, years older than her brother. She ascended to the throne with the aid of husband William of Orange. The phrase 'kingdom of balance' is one of those pithy comments that often laced the quatrains. In using it, Nostradamus draws attention to England's continual quest for a balance of power in Europe and the world, so that no state should outgrow another either militarily or politically and thus threaten stability.

CENTURY VI, QUATRAIN 74

The rejected one shall at last reach the throne, her enemies found to have been traitors. More than ever shall her period be triumphant. At seventy she shall go assuredly to death, in the third year of the century.

TRANSLATION: Elizabeth I was long withheld from the throne – and, of course, when she ascended to it she naturally regarded all those who had kept her from it as enemies and traitors. No reign was ever more triumphant than that of Elizabeth as she defied the might of the Catholic Church in Rome, destroyed the Spanish Armada and seized Spanish lands in the Americas. England flourished as she had never done before with righteous pride in great achievements. And, as Nostradamus predicted, Elizabeth died when she was 70.

Great Britain comprising England, will come to be inundated very forcibly by the waters. The new league in Italy will make war such that all band against any one of the cosignatories.

TRANSLATION: England became Great Britain when Scotland was united with her in 1603 at the accession of James I, who assumed the title 'King of Great Britain'. Historians believe the floods Nostradamus speaks of occurred around the end of January 1607, when the sea breached dykes in Somerset and overflowed the countryside. An old Latin book called *Rerum in Gallia, Belgia, Hispania et Anglia* gives details of the disaster, an almost apocalyptic event at the time.

Prince Charles, pictured here in polo outfit. The medieval sage was amazingly accurate when it came to describing the trials and tribulations of the House of Windsor.

The blood of the just shall be required of London, burnt by fireballs in thrice twenty and six; the ancient lady shall fall from its high place and many edifices of the same sort shall be destroyed.

Through many nights the earth shall tremble; in the spring two shocks follow each other: Corinth and Ephesus shall swim in the two seas, war arising between two combatants strong in battle.

The great plague of the maritime city shall not diminish till death is sated for the just blood, basely sold and condemned for no fault. The great Cathedral outraged by feigning saints.

TRANSLATION: Historians by tradition have grouped these three quatrains together when analysing their meaning. The first is an astonishingly accurate description of the Great Fire of London, which happened in 1666, the year Nostradamus predicted. St Paul's is, in the original, taken to be the 'Dame antique' which falls to the flames. The 'just blood' or blood of the just is a reference to the many innocents who died in their wooden homes as the fire, which started in a baker's shop, levelled the medieval city. Nostradamus was no republican; he believed in the divine right of kings and would have seen the fire visited upon London as a fit punishment for the execution of Charles I.

The second quatrain concentrates on the English war with the United Provinces of the Netherlands between 1665 and 1667. 'Cruising' within the narrow channel separating England from Europe, he draws a simile with Aegean waters – Corinth for England, Ephesus for Antwerp.

The third concerns the Black Death, or Great Plague, which devastated London in 1665. 'Maritime city' (due to its dependence on shipping and trade) was a common description of the English capital in use during Nostradamus's day. The outrage he refers to is most probably his own; a confirmed Catholic, he viewed with dismay the Protestantism which he foresaw arising in England against the Church he loved.

CENTURY IV, QUATRAIN 89

Thirty of London shall conspire secretly against their king; upon the bridge the plot shall be devised. These satellites shall taste of death. A fair-haired king shall be elected, native of Friesland.

TRANSLATION: In 1689 William III – a fair-haired native of

Friesland – became king of England after sailing from Holland. It is interesting to note that when Nostradamus was alive the possibility of a Dutchman taking over the throne of England was as likely as a Soviet politician taking over the White House! Experts estimate that between 30 and 50 opponents of James II conspired to get William on the throne – and that the satellites facing death are his supporters.

CENTURY III, QUATRAIN 57

Seven times you will see the British nation change, dyed in blood for two hundred and ninety years. Not at all free through German support, Aries fears for the protectorate of Poland.

TRANSLATION: The second part is easy enough – Britain going to war for the sake of Poland, as was the case in 1939. It is the first part which vexes historians, wondering when it is that the 290 years starts from. There are some who believe that it is a reference to Prince Charles. Erika Cheetham says: 'This may mean that Prince Charles will be the last King on the British throne.'

CENTURY VI, QUATRAIN 41

The second leader of the kingdom of Annemarc, through those of Frisia and the British Isles, will spend more than one hundred thousand marks, attempting in vain a voyage to Italy.

TRANSLATION: Perhaps rather tenuously, experts believe the reference to Annemarc pertains to Princess Anne and Captain Mark Phillips. At the time of writing England and Frisia had the same ruler – Philip of Spain, husband to Mary of England and ruler of the Netherlands. In Century IV, Quatrain 27, there is a reference to 'Dannemark' which may be construed as also being about the royal couple – a well-concealed Nostradamus riddle, and one that has yet to be fully understood.

CENTURY VIII, QUATRAIN 82

Thin, tall and dry like reeds, playing the good valet in the end will have nothing but his dismissal, sharp poison and letters in his collar, he will be caught escaping into danger.

TRANSLATION: Her Majesty Queen Elizabeth II was mortified – as was the nation – when the keeper of her royal art collection, Anthony Blunt, was exposed as one of the Oxbridge communist traitor ring which included such notorious agents as Kim Philby and Guy Burgess. He was a trusted official who betrayed his trust at the highest levels.

CENTURY X, QUATRAIN 19

The day she will be saluted as queen, the prayers coming the day after the blessing. The account is right and valid; once humble, there was never a woman so proud.

TRANSLATION: A reference to Queen Elizabeth I of England, after she succeeded her sister Mary Tudor to the throne. Humble in the days before she became monarch, she nevertheless made up for it with monumental pride during her reign.

CENTURY X, QUATRAIN 22

Not wanting to consent to divorce, afterwards recognized as unworthy, the king of the islands will be forced to flee, and one put in his place who has no sign of kingship.

TRANSLATION: As clear as a bell – the abdication of Edward VIII over his love affair with the divorced American woman, Wallis Simpson. He was forced to leave his homeland because of the establishment's disdainful view of the woman he loved. George VI, who was not in line for the throne, finally became king.

QUATRAINS ON NAPOLEON

Nostradamus gave many predictions for Napoleon, the soldier-statesman who took France to undreamed-of heights in his wars of conquest. An avowed royalist, perhaps the prophet saw in him some of the greatness which he believed France lost after the Revolution of 1789 - something he also foretold. There follows Nostradamus's most amazing predictions on Napoleonic rule – quatrains which, no matter which way they are interpreted, leave no room for misunderstanding about this great warrior-statesman whose arrival he predicted.

CENTURY III, QUATRAIN 35

In the Southern extremity of Western Europe, a child shall be born of poor parents, who by his tongue shall seduce the French army; his reputation shall extend to the Kingdom of the East.

TRANSLATION: Napoleon's birthplace was Corsica, his parents poor and his proclamations of greatness ('la gloire') for France and her warriors electrified the troops under his command. The last line may refer to his famous expedition to Egypt or his designs upon the throne of Imperial Russia, which ended in defeat and misery in the winter campaign of 1812.

CENTURY IX, QUATRAIN 33

Hercules, King of Rome and Denmark, surnamed the triple giant of France, shall make Italy tremble and the wave of St Mark, first in renown of all monarchs.

TRANSLATION: In his book, Ward argues that Nostradamus in this quatrain not only predicts the arrival of Napoleon but also the whole Napoleonic dynasty. He says: 'There was a Celtic Hercules fabled to draw men by their ears, but this Hercules means the Napoleonic dynasty. As to King of Rome, Napoleon actually assumed that title, and later on he conferred it upon his son by Marie Louise.'

CENTURY V, QUATRAIN 60

It will have chosen badly in the cropped one, its strength will be sapped badly by him. So great will be the fury and violence that they will say that he is butchering his countrymen with fire and sword.

TRANSLATION: Traces of the bitterness and disenchantment which the French began to feel about Napoleon, after the euphoria of his earlier victories had worn off. Here there is none of the elan, the glory: merely a sense of bitterness and recrimination as Frenchmen die on battlefields all across Europe.

CENTURY X, QUATRAIN 24

The vanquished prince is exiled in Italy, escaped by sea sailing past Genoa and Marseilles. He is then crushed by a massive concentration of foreign armies. Though he escapes the fire the bees will be drained to extinction.

TRANSLATION: Following his flight from Elba, Napoleon landed in the south of France, near Marseilles, where he rallied troops for the final showdown with foreign armies on French soil. It took place, of course, at Waterloo, where the massed legions of Britain and Prussia decimated him. The bees 'drained to extinction' is a clever touch. The bees being Napoleon's emblem, Nostradamus shows that his ambitions have been thwarted, his power spent, yet he is not dead.

CENTURY VII, QUATRAIN 61

Never shall he in broad daylight, reach to the symbol of sceptre-bearing rule. Of all his possessions none will be of a settled permanency, conferring of the Gallic cock a gift of the armed legion.

TRANSLATION: This is taken to mean that the Emperor Napoleon will never enjoy a settled seat of firmly established government, but he does bequeath a unique gift to France, one which changed the way nations recruited their forces and the way they fought wars. Until Napoleon's time, armies consisted of professional recruits or mercenaries. Napoleon conscripted huge national armies which effectively made Europe an armed camp – the 'armed legion' of the last line of the quatrain. Some believe there may be a hint in the quatrain in 'settled permanency' to the graveyards of Spain and Portugal where so many of his brave soldiers fell fighting for him.

The warrior son of France, Napoleon, featured extensively in the predictions.

CENTURY IV QUATRAIN 26

The great swarm of bees shall rise, that none can tell from whence they came. Night's ambush; the jay beneath the tiles. City betrayed by five tongues not naked.

TRANSLATION: The bees in question stand for the massed ranks of the Napoleonic army, and also his personal emblem which was woven on to embroideries which he carried into battle. Ward believes that the meaning of 'none can tell from whence they came' is a reference to the bonhomie and brotherly love engendered by the Revolution – that men are no longer distinct classes, but a single unit united in a common cause. The second part of the quatrain refers to a five-man committee that literally handed Paris over to Napoleon during the coup of 9 November 1797, who were bribed to give way to his consular officers. The coup was planned the night before. In the French, Nostradamus cites the word 'treilhos' which most interpret as the Tuileries, which became Napoleon's headquarters. Students of Nostradamus are intrigued by this quatrain as it is the only one he wrote in a purely Provençal dialect.

CENTURY VII, QUATRAIN 13

The short-haired man shall assume authority, in maritime Toulon, tributary to the enemy; he will afterwards dismiss as sordid all who oppose him; and for fourteen years direct a tyrant.

TRANSLATION: The English had seized Toulon in the name of Louis XVII and held it for a few months until Napoleon retook it. He overturned its government and suppressed free speech in a tyranny which lasted until his overthrow after the battle of Waterloo – a 14-year period. 'Sordid' is generally believed to be a reference to the English, whom Nostradamus believed never had any right to be in France at any time in history.

CENTURY VIII, QUATRAIN 57

From a simple soldier he will rise to the empire, from the short robe he will attain the long. Able in arms, in church government he shows less skill; he raises or depresses the priests as water a sponge.

TRANSLATION: Napoleon was a plain soldier in 1785, consul for life in 1799 and emperor from 1804 until 1814. He changed the formal consular short robe for longer ones. Valiant in battle, he was less skilled in ecclesiastical affairs; nevertheless, he vexed the priests and penetrated into every nook and cranny of their office.

CENTURY I, QUATRAIN 88

He shall have married a woman just before the divine wrath falleth on the great prince; and his support shall dwindle in a sudden atrophy; Counsel shall perish from this shaven head.

TRANSLATION: This is a reference to his infidelity to Marie-Louise of Austria – his wife – with Josephine Beauhamais, his mistress. The shaven head is regarded as an unmistakable reference to Napoleon by Nostradamus experts, relating to the former's close-cropped hair. Counsel perishing from his shaven head alludes to good judgement fleeing Napoleon – perhaps as the result of epilepsy.

CENTURY I, Quatrain 4

Throughout the universe a monarch shall arise, who will not be long in peace nor life; the bark of St Peter will then lose itself, being directed to its greatest detriment.

TRANSLATION: This is the Emperor Napoleon reviving his pretensions and ambitions to the Holy Roman Empire, but as Nostradamus says, he was doomed to enjoy neither peace, nor life as an emperor, for long. Pope Pius VII first crowned Napoleon as emperor and then became his prisoner when the dictator annexed the Papal States to France in 1809. Religious anarchy existed in France during this time.

CENTURY II, QUATRAIN 44

The eagle, drifting in her cloud of flags, by other circling birds is beaten home. Till war's hoarse trumpet and the clarion shrill, recall her senses to the insensate dame.

TRANSLATION: The eagle – the Napoleonic eagle carried by his legions – is in full retreat from the gates of Moscow in the 1812 winter campaign which decimated his legions. The other birds are a reference to the imperial eagles of Russia, Prussia and Austria chasing it all the way back to Paris. The martial music and devastating defeat bring France back to its senses and end in the ultimate defeat of Napoleon.

Journey's end for the warrior is Elba – his ultimate exile where spartan living and few home comforts are an unpleasant change from the lifestyle he enjoyed as emperor.

CENTURY X, QUATRAIN 86

Like a griffon the King of Europe will come, accompanied with those of the north. Of red and white there will be a great number, and they will go against the King of Babylon.

TRANSLATION: The King of Europe is Louis XVII, coming like the mythical griffon, marching with legions dressed in red and white – Austrian and British troops – who will enter Paris, here described as Babylon.

CENTURY VI, QUATRAIN 89

Between two prisons, bound hand and foot, with his face anointed with honey and fed with milk, exposed to wasps and flies, and tormented with the love of his child, his cupbearer will false the cup that aims at suicide.

TRANSLATION: Napoleon, after being consecrated by Pius VII, and anointed with honey and milk, is then imprisoned in Elba and St Helena. The wasps are a reference again to the imperial bees. The two prisons are also taken to mean two wretched states he alternated between after he destroyed his family with his philandering.

CENTURY II, QUATRAIN 99

Roman land as interpreted by the augurs will be greatly molested by the French nation. But the French will come to dread the time of the North wind having driven their fleet too far.

TRANSLATION: In 1812 the ambitions of Napoleon were broken upon the snow-covered steppes of Russia in the campaign that decimated his Imperial Army and his hopes for glory. 'Having driven their fleet too far' is a clear indication that Napoleon had over-extended his forces in his drive on Moscow, the mistake which would be made by that other 'bird of prey', Hitler, nearly a century and a half later. The first part of the quatrain refers to the Vatican States which had been absorbed into the Napoleonic empire in 1810.

CENTURY II, QUATRAIN 29

The oriental will quit his post, to cross the Apennines and see after Gaul. He will transfix the heaven, the mountain ice and snows, striking each of them with his huge magic wand.

TRANSLATION: 'The oriental' is a reference to Napoleon returning to France after his Egyptian expedition, via the Apennines and Alps. Napoleon built marvellous roads through the mountains using his troops, hence the reference to heaven, ice and snows – elements that he kept at bay. His magic wand is nothing more than a huge riding switch that he habitually carried.

CENTURY IV, QUATRAIN 54

Of a name that never belonged to a Gallic king. Never was there so terrible a thunderbolt. He made Italy tremble, Spain and the English. He wooed a foreign lady with assiduity.

TRANSLATION: A simple foretelling – one of several – of the coming of Napoleon, a man with no name like any other. The foreign lady referred to in the last line is believed to be a reference to Marie-Louise of Austria.

CENTURY VIII, QUATRAIN 53

In Boulogne he would make up for his shortcomings, but cannot penetrate the temple of the Sun. He hastens away to perform the very highest things. In the hierarchy he never had an equal.

TRANSLATION: Over the French seaport of Boulogne towers a column dedicated to Napoleon. From its summit on a clear day visitors can see England – and that is all Boney managed to do, even though he intended to launch his invasion from the shores of Boulogne. Westminster Abbey was built on the site of a pagan Sun temple – the high English church which Napoleon never managed to enter. The 'very highest things' he sought to perform included his vanquishing of the Papal States and his attempted conquest of Russia. And he was without equal in his lifetime.

CENTURY IX, QUATRAIN 86

From Bourg la Reine they shall not come straight to Chartres. They shall camp close to Pont Anthony: seven chiefs for peace, wary as martens, shall enter Paris cut off from its army.

TRANSLATION: After the battle of Waterloo and the final defeat

Napoleon at Fontainebleau, from the painting by Paul Delaroche in the Museum of Leipzig.

414

of Napoleon, seven nations were drawn to make peace treaties in which it was hoped Europe could live without war and fear. Austria, England, Prussia, Portugal, Sweden, Spain and Russia – the allied nations against Napoleon – entered Paris on 3 July 1815. The city was stripped of its garrison which was sent to Chartres.

CENTURY I, QUATRAIN 98
The general who led infinite hosts, will end his life far from where he was born. Among five thousand people of strange custom upon a chalk island in the sea.

TRANSLATION: Having mapped out his life – his affairs, his battles, his victories and his defeats – Nostradamus successfully foretold the end for France's greatest warrior son. Death came to him far, far from home, upon the island of St Helena, amid people he neither knew nor whose customs he understood.

Iranian royal family. The Shah and his queen in the glory days before the Iranian revolution banished the Pahlavi dynasty from the world stage.

QUATRAINS ON GREAT WORLD EVENTS

Nostradamus also gave numerous predictions on Napoleonic successors including Louis XVIII and Louis-Philippe, but it is perhaps his predictions on great world events, events that have shaped the world we inhabit, that arouse the most interest in him. Some are obscure, others could not be plainer. There follows a cross-section of some of his more incredible, perceptive prophecies.

CENTURY I, QUATRAIN 77

A promontory that stands between two seas; a man who will die later by the bit of a horse; Neptune unfurls a black sail for his man; the fleet near Gibraltar and the Rocheval.

TRANSLATION: Standing between the Mediterranean and the Atlantic is the promontory of rock called Gibraltar. Rocheval is an old French word for Cape Roche. It was between Cape Roche and Gibraltar that the greatest British victory at sea, which determined British policy for a number of years to come, occurred in 1805. In that engagement Lord Nelson, deploying superior skills, destroyed the French fleet. A year later Admiral Villeneuve, one of the French commanders on the day, was strangled at a remote French country inn by someone using the bridle of a horse as a weapon. The black sail unfurled on the day of the battle was aboard HMS *Victory*, Nelson's flagship, to commemorate the loss of the commander-in-chief.

CENTURY I, QUATRAIN 70

Rain, famine and war will not cease in Persia; too great a trust will betray the monarch. The actions started in France will end there, a secret sign for one to be sparing.

TRANSLATION: It is bitterly ironic to think that the intelligence agencies of the Western world, including the mighty CIA and KGB, could not predict the end of the Peacock Throne in Iran whereas a man who died half a millennium ago could. In this remarkable vision, Nostradamus saw events unfolding centuries beyond his own time that seemed impossible right up to the time they happened. It was a disbelieving world which watched the Shah of Iran being toppled by the religious leader, the Ayatollah Khomeini, in 1979. Rain, famine and war – and all their ensuing misery – partly caused the Shah to be overthrown, but it was in France that the exiled Ayatollah plotted for years for the religious fundamentalist state to take over from the Pahlavi dynasty. The 'sparing' referred to at the end is interpreted as 'spartan' – certainly a fitting description for the new order which currently reigns in Iran.

CENTURY I, QUATRAIN 34

The bird of prey, flying to the left, before battle is joined with the French, he makes preparations. Some will regard him as good, others bad or uncertain. The weaker party will regard him as a good omen.

TRANSLATION: Throughout the centuries there are several references to World War Two and to Adolf Hitler, but this is the first clear portent of the fate to come for mankind. The bird of prey is used by Nostradamus to describe both Napoleon and Hitler – both conquerors of different ages. His reference to the bird flying to the left is a clever one; to the left of France are the Low Countries, through which Hitler launched his mechanized armies in an entirely new form of warfare, the Blitzkrieg, in 1940. The references to the good, bad and uncertain are interpreted as descriptions of the weak and divided French governments in the final days of the Third Republic.

The bomb-ravaged streets surrounding St Paul's in London. Nostradamus was tragically correct in his prophecy of a new kind of war from the air.

CENTURY II, QUATRAIN 100

In the islands shall be such horrible tumult, that nothing shall be heard except a warlike surprise. So great shall be the attack of the raiders, that everyone shall shelter himself under the great line.

TRANSLATION: This suggests the use of incendiaries and other air-dropped bombs being used on great cities, particularly London, in World War Two, where the inhabitants sheltered from the nightly firestorms in the underground rail system.

CENTURY I, QUATRAIN 47

The speeches of Lake Lemon will become angered, the days will drag out into weeks, then months, then years, then all will fail. The authorities will condemn their useless powers.

TRANSLATION: At the end of World War One – which, incidentally, Nostradamus also correctly predicted – the combatant nations came together in the belief that a new family of countries was necessary, to bind itself to the aims of perpetual peace instead of future possible wars. The League of Nations first met in Geneva in 1920 – the city which sits on the shores of Lake Leman. With penetrating insight in a few short lines, Nostradamus seems to sum up the futility, the bickering and squabbling which defined the League in its few short years of operation before it dissolved in acrimony before the onset of World War Two. In Quatrain 85 of Century V, Nostradamus further cements his vision of a failed league when he writes: 'Through the Swiss and surrounding areas they will war because of the clouds. A swarm of marine locusts and gnats, the faults of Geneva laid quite bare.'

CENTURY II, QUATRAIN 38

There will be a great number of condemned people when the monarchs are reconciled. But one of them will be so unfortunate that they will hardly be able to remain allied.

TRANSLATION: Shortly before the outbreak of World War Two, a pact was struck between Hitler and Stalin which pledged that each would not attack the other. It was a devastating pact with enormous implications for world peace. No one believed that the architects of the two great totalitarian states, one fascist one communist, could work together. However, Nostradamus clearly saw this reconciliation of modern-day monarchs – and the great

418

number of innocents who were murdered on both sides. Finally, the partners in crime fell out in 1942 with Hitler's massive attack on the USSR – his avowed quest since the earliest days of the Nazi party.

CENTURY II, QUATRAIN 24

Beasts wild with hunger will cross the rivers, the greater part of the battlefield will be against Hister. He will drag the leader in a cage of iron, when the child of Germany observes no law.

TRANSLATION: This is the German who observed no law – Adolf Hitler. It was he who loosed his beasts 'wild with hunger' across the river boundaries of Europe and the USSR, pillaging, murdering and destroying everything in his path. Dragging leaders in a cage of iron is a reference to old medieval practices of humiliating defeated rulers. Hitler humiliated the conquered lands under his swastika in a more sophisticated manner. Critics have argued among themselves over the years whether Nostradamus actually meant a man called Hister or whether he knew he was

The bright, shining hope of the Western world on his inauguration day in 1961. Nostradamus saw his coming – and his tragic departure.

419

called Hitler and disguised his true identity, as he was wont to do in so many of his predictions. One thing is certain: the Führer himself was convinced that Nostradamus meant him and great propaganda was made from this quatrain in the years before he embarked on his crusade which would end in millions of deaths.

CENTURY II, QUATRAIN 1

Towards Aquitaine, by British assaults, and by them also great incursions. Rains and frost make the terrain unsafe, against Port Selin they will make mighty invasions.

TRANSLATION: In 1915, utilizing a plan drawn up by Winston Churchill, the Allies embarked on a perilous expedition which, had it succeeded, could well have shortened World War One, with all its misery and death, by several years. The Allies launched an assault on Turkey – the port of Constantinople was known as Selin in the time of Nostradamus – hoping to bypass the Western Front, with all its misery of frost, rain and snow. Again, this is a remarkable example of the powers of Nostradamus. The plan was scoffed at by the high command – even more so in hindsight when the bloodied remnants of the British and empire forces retreated after being held at bay by the Turks at the Dardanelles straits.

A Russian soldier sits in the fetid, waterlogged bunker that was the last headquarters – and the suicide location – of Adolf Hitler in May 1945. But Nostradamus suggests that Der Führer may have lived after the collapse of his Third Reich.

CENTURY II, QUATRAINS 56,57

One whom neither plague nor sword could kill will die on the top of a hill, struck from the sky. The abbot will die when he sees the ruin of the people in the shipwreck trying to hold on to the reef. Before the battle the great man will fall, the great one to death, death too sudden and lamented. Born imperfect, it will go the greater part of the way; near the river of blood, the ground is stained.

TRANSLATION: Historians and enthusiasts of the occult have pored over these two quatrains for many years. Most concur that they refer to the killing of John F. Kennedy, although opinion is divided. Nostradamus chronicler Erika Cheetham says: ' "Mort trop subite" in the original probably implies an assassination and "nay imparfaict" a person born with a physical deformity. Senator Kennedy was born with a congenital illness. Many of John F. Kennedy's critics agree that he had a great deal of charisma but wonder whether his political judgement would have been sound had he lived to serve another term of office. "It will go the greater part of the way" may well refer to Kennedy's stand against Khrushchev's attempt to set up missile bases in Cuba. The Russian fleet did, after all, get the greater part of the way from Russia. It was after this confrontation that Kennedy was killed at Dallas.'

CENTURY III, QUATRAIN 58 and CENTURY IX, QUATRAIN 90

Near the Rhine from the Noricum Mountains will be born a great man of the people, born too late. He will defend Poland and Hungary and they will never know what became of him.

A leader of Great Germanies who will come to give help which is only counterfeit. He will stretch the borders of Germany, and will cause France to be divided into two parts. Living fire and death hidden in globes will be loosed, horrible and terrible, by night the enemy will reduce cities to dust.

TRANSLATION: In these two quatrains Nostradamus again gives clear, undisguised warnings of the advent of Adolf Hitler and the terrible revenge he will exact on mankind. The globes he refers to are obviously a reference to bombs falling on cities like London and Berlin, the product of his vicious war. Defending Poland and

Hungary – he actually attacked them – could be part of Nostradamus's usual trick of trying to be cryptic about actual events. The final line is interesting in the first quatrain, it could imply that Hitler LIVED after the fall of Berlin. Certainly there has been much dispute about whether or not he and mistress Eva Braun died in the ruins of the bunker as the Russians closed in.

CENTURY III, QUATRAIN 71

Those besieged in the islands for a long time will take strong measures against their enemies. Those outside, overcome, will die of hunger, by such starvation as has never occurred before.

TRANSLATION: This is Nostradamus's way of painting a portrait of embattled Britain at war, blockaded by the U-boats as she builds up her war machine and the resolve of the leaders and the people for total victory over the Axis powers grows stronger. The references to those outside and the starvation they suffer is seen as a twofold thing: the starvation and deprivation in conquered Europe and in the concentration camps, and also the starvation of the soul, deprived as it was of love, compassion and religious beliefs under the edicts of the Third Reich.

The mighty Rhine, the 'Great River' which Nostradamus referred to in his prophecy about the French Maginot Line.

CENTURY III, QUATRAIN 75

Pau, Verona, Vicenza, Saragossa, swords dripping with blood from distant lands. A very great plague will come with the great shell, relief near but the remedies far away.

TRANSLATION: In 1976 in Seveso, Italy, occurred one of the worst man-made disasters in history. A massive chemical plant explosion destroyed wildlife, contaminated drinking water and agricultural land and caused women to give birth to deformed babies. The cloud of gas drifted across a large section of Italy – but, interestingly enough, the towns that Nostradamus wrote about were not affected, nor was the plan to combat the disaster formulated in them. Much of the land is still unusable, proving that the remedies are indeed still far away.

CENTURY III, QUATRAIN 100

The man least honoured among the French will be victorious over his enemy. Strength and lands he explored in action, when suddenly the jealous party dies from a shot.

TRANSLATION: Recognizing the coming of Charles de Gaulle, a man virtually unknown in France before the collapse of the Third Republic, was a remarkable feat. Strength, in terms of political power and prestige, was gathered during his years in exile as the war raged in various countries, and the envious one dying from a shot is thought to be the traitorous appeaser of the Germans, Admiral Dadan, killed on 24 December 1942. Like Hitler and Napoleon, the quatrains are peppered with references to De Gaulle, supporting many believers' contentions that Nostradamus excelled in prophesying the coming of great men upon the world stage.

CENTURY III, QUATRAIN 97

A new law will occupy a new land around Syria, Judaea and Palestine. The great barbarian empire will crumble before the century of the Sun is finished.

TRANSLATION: No one could have foretold in the 20th century, let alone in his day, the creation of the state of Israel in exactly the spot where it would eventually be born in the wake of World War Two, but that is precisely what Nostradamus accomplished. However, part of the prophecy remains unfinished. Nostradamus tags the Arab countries around Israel as 'barbarian' and warns that they will be finished by the end of the 20th century – the century of the Sun.

CENTURY IV, QUATRAIN 32

In those times and areas where the flesh gives way to fish, the common law will be made in opposition. The old order will hold strong then be removed from the scene entirely, all things common among friends put far behind.

TRANSLATION: Communism falls. Nostradamus did not specify in which country, but it is interesting that the system has effectively collapsed in the USSR. Dried fish, as opposed to fresh meat, was a staple of the grumbling peasants under the communist regime. 'All things common among friends' – i.e., communism and the community spirit it was intended to engender among the proletariat – are broken. In other quatrains Nostradamus foretells an alliance that Russia will make, possibly with the USA. Some already believe that this has happened, interpreting 'alliance' as the business deals that are now taking place due to the fall of the old order.

CENTURY IV, QUATRAIN 61

The old man, mocked and deprived of his position by the foreigner who will suborn him. The hands of his sons are devoured before his face, he will betray his brother at Chartres, Orleans and Rouen.

TRANSLATION: With this quatrain Nostradamus paints one of his clear pictures – about Marshal Petain, the former hero of Verdun who disgraced his nation in World War Two by becoming the puppet head of Vichy France, the vassal state of Nazi Germany. During his time as premier he was referred to contemptuously by his subjects as 'The Old Man'. The three French cities mentioned were all liberated by the Allies on the same day, and held strong connections with the old France of Nostradamus's times. Interestingly, each one is the site of some of France's most celebrated and mystical cathedrals, all of which were visited by Nostradamus during his travels and from where he drew divine inspiration for the prophecies.

CENTURY IV, QUATRAIN 80

Near the great river, a great trench, earth excavated, the water will be divided into fifteen parts. The city taken, fire, blood, cries and battle given, the greater part concerned with the collision.

TRANSLATION: Before World War Two France poured the greatest part of her military resources, and her national faith, into a static defence line named after a World War One engineer called André Maginot. The line stretched from near the Rhine – 'the great river' – across her north-eastern borders, petering out at the start of the Ardennes forest, which the French high command deemed too thick for armour or artillery to operate in. Ironically, in an earlier quatrain, Nostradamus had already predicted this by pointing out that France's enemies would advance through countries to her left - i.e. the low countries of the Netherlands and Belgium. The collision he refers to is the clash of armies throughout the war.

CENTURY IV, QUATRAIN 100

Fire will fall from the sky on to the royal building when the light of war is weakened. For seven months a great war, people dead through evil, Rouen and Evreux will not fail the king.

TRANSLATION: Nostradamus here predicted the Franco-Prussian War of 1870–71 which sowed the seeds of permanent bitterness between the peoples of France and Germany. The war lasted PRECISELY seven months, during which time a fierce siege of Paris laid waste to many royal buildings. The reference to the Normandy towns of Rouen and Evreux is because they did not become republican along with the rest of France after the war, preferring instead to support a restored monarchy.

The ruins of Paris after the Commune uprising of 1871. The city Nostradamus loved was virtually destroyed.

CENTURY V, QUATRAIN 45

The great empire will soon be desolate, transformed near the forest of the Ardennes. The bastards will be beheaded by the oldest, Aenodarb will rule, the hawknosed one.

TRANSLATION: This foretells the fall of France in 1940, coming as it did via the German advance through the Ardennes forest which the French generals perceived as impenetrable. The bastards are believed to be the two senior French commanders who thoroughly botched battlefield attempts to stem the onrushing tide of German armour, although they were not beheaded, merely captured. The hawknosed one is a reference to General de Gaulle, although no one has found a satisfactory explanation for the classical name Aenodarb.

CENTURY V, QUATRAIN 94

He will change into the Greater Germany, Brabant and Flanders, Ghent, Bruges and Boulogne. The truce feigned, the great Duke of Armenia will assault Vienna and Cologne.

TRANSLATION: Again, this is a quatrain concerning Hitler and, more specifically, his designs of conquest upon the world. The 'feigned truce' is seen as the lame excuse he gave to the world upon his invasion of Poland – that he was merely aiding 'ethnic Germans' persecuted by the Poles. The Duke of Armenia is seen as the Russians who, towards the end of the war, invaded Germany from the south and east.

CENTURY V, QUATRAIN 72

Through feigned fury of a divine emotion the wife of the great one will be badly violated. The judges wishing to condemn such a doctrine, the victim is sacrificed to the ignorant people.

TRANSLATION: In this Nostradamus has summed up the plight of the Czarina Alexandra, wife of Czar Nicholas, who became spellbound by the evil monk Rasputin. Rasputin exerted a terrible grip on the Russian court, and thereby Russian life, due to his hocus-pocus about her son's haemophilia which she believed. The 'ignorant people' are the masses with whom the Romanov family were so utterly and so completely out of touch, which led to the Russian Revolution, their downfall and murder.

CENTURY VI, QUATRAIN 31

The king will find that which he desires so greatly; when the Prelate will be wrongfully taken. The reply to the Duce will make him angry; in Milan he will put several to death.

TRANSLATION: The foretelling of the rise to power of Mussolini – together with the title of Duce which he conferred upon himself. In Milan several of Mussolini's opponents were exiled while the Prelate, taken to be the Pope, finds himself in a Catholic country surrounded by the forces of the anti-Christ.

The Great Dictator, Benito Mussolini. His brand of Fascism would lead Italy into ruinous, bloody war.

CENTURY VIII, QUATRAIN 80

The blood of innocents, widow and virgin, with many evils committed by the Great Red One, holy images placed over burning candles, terrified by fear, none will be seen to move.

TRANSLATION: In 1917 the Romanov dynasty, which had ruled Holy Russia, was swept away in a great revolution that used the colour red for its flag. The blood of innocents could pertain to the children of the royal household, who were massacred along with the czar and czarina, or the many millions that died in the ensuing terror after the Bolsheviks took power. Organized religion, bedrock of the czarist regime, was also outlawed in the new order as prescribed by the followers of Lenin. Some interpret the last line as being about the massacre of the royal family at Ekaterinburg in 1917. 'None will be seen to move' may mean that Nostradamus saw that all were murdered, giving the lie to a woman who, for years afterwards until her death in the late 1980s, claimed she was the Princess Anastasia who escaped from the execution site.

CENTURY IX, QUATRAIN 16

From Castel Franco will bring out the assembly, the ambassadors will not agree and cause a schism. The people of Riviera will be in the crowd, and the great man will be denied entry to the great Gulf.

TRANSLATION: This is another of those extraordinarily perceptive prophecies in which the master makes no attempt at disguising his portent for the future. In this he warns of the coming of Franco and the Spanish Civil War. The reference to 'the great man being denied entry' refers to Franco's inability to cross the Mediterranean when he was exiled to Morocco. Gattey writes: 'Ingenious commentators have surmised that the personages named are the late General Franco and his predecessor, the dictator Primo de Rivera and that the verse also refers to the struggle for power between the two men. The last line alludes to Franco's exile in Morocco, or to his meeting on 12th February 1941 with Mussolini on the Riviera, when he refused to permit the troops of the Axis to pass through Spain and attack Gibraltar. The "great Gulf" is the Mediterranean.' Nostradamus foresaw the Spanish Civil War and Franco's dictatorship in the earlier Quatrain 54 of Century III. He wrote: One of the great ones shall fly into Spain which will then bleed with a long round. Armies will pass by the high mountains, destroying all, after which he will reign in peace.

CENTURY IX, QUATRAIN 11

They will come to put the just man wrongfully to death, publicly in the midst he is extinguished. So great a plague will be born in this place that the judges will be forced to flee.

TRANSLATION: This tells of the execution of Charles I of England – while giving an insight again into Nostradamus's belief in the divine right of kings. Charles was beheaded in 1649. The second part of the quatrain is the Great Plague of London which came in 1665. Nostradamus believed that the plague was God's retribution against the men who had overthrown the king.

CENTURY IX, QUATRAIN 55
The dreadful war which is prepared in the west, the following year pestilence will come, so horrible that neither young, nor old, nor animal will survive. Blood, fire, Mercury, Mars, Jupiter in France.

TRANSLATION: Another two-in-one quatrain in which he successfully foretells World War One – the war in the west, or Western Front - and the massive influenza outbreak across Europe that followed it, which claimed more lives than the fighting. The planetary references refer to their position at the time the prediction would come true – again, correctly.

CENTURY IX, QUATRAIN 77
The kingdom is taken, the king will plot while the lady is taken to death by these sworn by lot. They will refuse life to the queen's son and the mistress suffers the same fate as the wife.

Divining new methods of war in all their grotesque horror seemed to be a special gift belonging to Nostradamus. Here are men of the East Lancashire Regiment in a trench at Givenchy in World War One.

TRANSLATION: Erika Cheetham believes this to be one of his more 'impressive' quatrains. She writes: 'After the [French] royal family's imprisonment, Louis XVI was executed in January 1793. He was condemned by the convention who elected these powers to itself. However, the queen, who was not executed until the following October, had a newly created Revolutionary tribunal elected to judge her, which was selected by lot. This was an institution unknown to France in Nostradamus's day. The third line tells the fate of Louis XVII. Whether he died or lived abroad is irrelevant; his kingdom was denied to him. Finally, the most interesting line of all. While the queen was imprisoned in the Conciergerie, the old mistress of Louis XV, Mademoiselle du Barry, was taken for a while to the prison of Sainte Pelagie.'

Halley's Comet, the extraterrestrial orb which Nostradamus refers to in several quatrains through the Centuries.

CENTURY IX, QUATRAIN 100

A naval engagement will be overcome by night; fire in the ruined ships of the west. A new code, the great coloured ship, anger to the vanquished and victory in a mist.

TRANSLATION: This describes the attack on Pearl Harbor, 7 December 1941, in which the greater portion of the American Pacific Fleet was destroyed in a surprise attack launched before dawn by a Japanese carrier-borne force. The new coding is believed to refer to aircraft launched from ships, a new kind of war which eventually led to the Allies' victory over Japan.

THE SHAPE OF THINGS TO COME

What does the future hold for us, as defined in the writings of Nostradamus? Even the most hardened sceptic must concede that the old sage has had some remarkable successes in interpreting the ages. There follows a selection of some prophecies yet to be realized – culminating in those which could spell doom for mankind if the sleeping seer of Salon got them right.

CENTURY II, QUATRAIN 91

At sunrise a great fire will be seen, noise and light extending to the north. Within the globe death and cries are heard, death awaiting them through weapons, fire and famine.

TRANSLATION: Erika Cheetham believes this to be the portent of a great war between Russia and the USA. Although the threat of nuclear confrontation has abated since the fall of the Berlin Wall and the collapse of communism, many observers think that the situation is still too volatile to predict lasting peace. If this can be linked with Century II, Quatrain 46, it is ominous indeed. That one states:

After great misery for mankind an even greater approaches when the great cycle of the centuries is renewed. It will rain blood, milk, famine, war and disease. In the sky will be seen a fire, dragging a great trail of sparks.

TRANSLATION: Halley's Comet is obviously the fire in the sky with the sparks trailing behind. It too appeared again at the end of the 20th century – without the rain of 'blood, milk, famine, war and disease', which some thought could be a third world war.

The Statue of Liberty at the entrance to New York harbour. If Nostradamus has got it right the Big Apple will one day burn under a massive aerial bombardment.

CENTURY IV, QUATRAIN 99

The brave, elder son of a king's daughter will drive the Celts back far. He will use thunderbolts, so many and in such an array, few and distant, then deep into the west.

TRANSLATION: Celts are taken to mean the French. Not being part of NATO, does Nostradamus predict a new tyrant within Europe ready to use thunderbolts – possibly nuclear or chemical missiles – to seize the unprepared French?

CENTURY V, QUATRAIN 90

In the Cyclades, in Perinthus and Larissa, in Sparta and all of the Peloponnesus, a very great famine, plague through false dust. It will last nine months throughout the whole peninsula.

TRANSLATION: Nostradamus is usually very specific about plagues or famines. Here he talks of 'false dust', i.e. possibly man-made, which has led many to believe that this could be a reference to chemical or biological warfare. The Balkans have long been a troublespot in the world – World War One was sparked off over them and, more recently, the bloody civil war between Bosnia and Serbia has been fought over parts of the area.

CENTURY VI, QUATRAIN 5

A great famine, the result of a pestilence that will extend its long rain the length of the Arctic pole. Samarobrin one hundred leagues from the hemisphere; they will live without law, exempt from politics.

TRANSLATION: Samarobrin has yet to be defined, but most analysts concur that Nostradamus is back to his theme of a chemical fallout on the Earth, possibly emanating from far out in space. Some argue that he foresees a manned space station, where people will indeed live without politics and normal laws, and whose use is corrupted to rain down death on the people below.

CENTURY VI, QUATRAIN 97

The sky will burn at forty-five degrees, fire approaches the great New City. Immediately a huge, scattered flame leaps up when they want to have proof of the Normans.

TRANSLATION: If this one is true then New Yorkers must fear a massive aerial bombing at some point which will destroy most of the metropolis. New York County actually lies between the 40° and

45° parallel in the USA. The last line is typically muddled and no one seems to have come up with a satisfactory explanation of his reference to 'the Normans'.

CENTURY VI, QUATRAIN 24

Mars and the Sceptre will be in conjunction, a calamitous war under Cancer. A short time afterwards a new king will be anointed who will bring peace to the earth for a long time.

TRANSLATION: Seen by most as another reference to war towards the end of the 20th century – but this one more hopeful, with the promise of a new peacemaker to give Earth some respite.

CENTURY VIII, QUATRAIN 9

While the eagle is in unison with the cockerel at Savona, the eastern sea and Hungary. The army at Naples, Palermo, the marches of Ancona, Rome and Venice a great outcry by the Barbarian.

TRANSLATION: Here Nostradamus warns of a Moslem invasion of Italy, naming key Italian cities as targets for the hordes. Italy, home to the Church of Rome, would make a key target for religious fundamentalists seeking to exert domination over the Christian Church. And with the rise of Islamic fundamentalism around the world it is not too far-fetched a prophecy.

CENTURY VIII, QUATRAIN 81

The new empire in desolation will be changed from the Northern pole. From Sicily will come such trouble that it will bother the enterprise tributary to Philip.

TRANSLATION: This tells of a civilization moving southwards, shifting the centre of power in a world region – possibly North America – leading some to believe it will occur after a nuclear holocaust as people look for new life and sustenance in unaffected zones. The references to Sicily and Philip imply that the war might emanate from there or Spain – once ruled by King Philip. This might link up with Century VIII, Quatrain 9, concerning the Moslem invasion of Italy. If Moslem fundamentalists rule this part of Europe perhaps Nostradamus is implying that nuclear war may be triggered in the future.

Perhaps more than any other symbol of our age, the mushroom cloud explosion of an atomic bomb has burned itself into mankind's collective soul.

CENTURY IX, QUATRAIN 83

The Sun in twenty degrees of Taurus, there will be a great earthquake; the great theatre full up will be ruined. Darkness and trouble in the air, on sky and land, when the infidel calls upon God and the saints.

TRANSLATION: Twenty days after the Sun moves into Taurus is 10 April, so Nostradamus gives us the date of a catastrophic earthquake – one which modern-day scientists believe must apply to the San Andreas fault, and more specifically to the destruction of San Francisco, which all experts say MUST happen – it is merely a question of when.

CENTURY X, QUATRAIN 67

A very great trembling in the month of May, Saturn in Capricorn, Jupiter and Mercury in Taurus. Venus also in Cancer, Mars and Virgo, then hail will fall greater than an egg.

TRANSLATION: Nostradamus displays his extensive knowledge of the planets in this quatrain, describing a rare event in the heavenly bodies when all fall into place in a set pattern. Astrologers say the planets will not be in conjunction in this manner until May 3755. Then the world can expect massive earthquakes, followed by enormous hailstones.

CENTURY X, QUATRAIN 72

In the year 1999 and seven months there will come from the skies the Great King of Terror. He will bring back to life the great King of the Mongols. Before and after war reigns happily.

TRANSLATION: It is perhaps fitting – if not sombre – to end a study of Nostradamus upon his most melancholy, unfulfilled prophecy. He tells of an Asian anti-Christ, steeped in the traditions of the warrior hordes of the Mongols, visiting death and destruction upon the face of the globe. Most experts believe that this new demon will be an anti-Christ, committed to tearing down the values of Judaeo-Christian society as we know them. If Napoleon and Hitler were the two other anti-Christ figures that Nostradamus draws in some of his prophecies, then this will be the third and final one.

He makes a further reference to this in Century VIII, Quatrain 77. In that he writes:

436

The anti-Christ very soon annihilates the three, seven and twenty years his war will last. The unbelievers are dead, captive, exiled: with blood, human bodies, water and red hail covering the earth.

This implies that the third anti-Christ, after Napoleon and Hitler – the one yet to come – will be annihilated, but that it will take 27 years of fearsome war to do so. The reference to red hail could mean atomic fallout, such as that which blanketed the Japanese cities of Hiroshima and Nagasaki after the dropping of the atom bombs towards the close of World War Two. Although Nostradamus signals the end of civilization as we know it, there could be hope still. In Century I, Quatrain 48, he gives the actual end of the world as much later. He writes:

Twenty-seven years after the reign of the moon passes, seven thousand years another will hold his monarchy. When the sun shall resume his days past, then is my prophecy accomplished and ended.

Erika Cheetham translates his prophecy thus: 'According to Roussat the cycle of the Moon lasted from 1535–1889, which places the date of the first line as 1555, the publication date of the first part of the Centuries. Nostradamus seems to envisage another 7,000 years from that date to the cycle of the sun when all will be accomplished. It is as though Nostradamus believes the Centuries are written at the start of a new era lasting 7,000 years.'

Even after the third anti-Christ, then, there is still hope for humanity.

VISIONS OF THE FUTURE

Prophets, Psychics and Seers

THE ORACLE OF DELPHI

The great scholar Homer, seen here meditating upon the Iliad. He was one of the great chroniclers of the Oracle of Delphi.

For 1,000 years mankind sought guidance from the gods of Olympus at the shrine of Apollo at Delphi.

Oracles are shrines where gods are said to speak with mortals through the mouths of priests – and none is more famous than that of the Pythia of Delphi, a shrine constructed by the ancient Greeks in homage to the god Apollo. Here was the most influential oracle of the classical world, built on the slopes of Mount Parnassus, north of the Gulf of Corinth, where people came to commune with their gods and be guided by their wisdom.

The cult of Apollo spread rapidly throughout the ancient world – he was regarded as the best and brightest of the ancient Greek gods, as the deity of music, archery, prophecy, healing and animals, and he was identified with the Sun. Legend has it that Jupiter, seeking dominance over the central point of the Earth, despatched two eagles to fly in opposite directions over the globe and they met at Delphi, which the gods then called the Navel of the Earth. Fumes were seen issuing from a cave near the site, laying the foundations for the idea that the spot was mystical and linked with the gods in Olympus. It acquired its Pythian forename from the legend of Apollo slaying the Python, a snake-like dragon.

The oracle was run by priests who interpreted the incoherent ramblings of the Pythia, a middle-aged woman dressed as a young maiden who sat on a tripod inhaling fumes of chopped herbs and spiced oil. It's not known why a certain woman was chosen, but she became the conduit between the priests and the gods, with citizens of Greece paying for the privilege of learning their fortunes. It lasted for 1,000 years: after the Greeks, the Romans and even conquerors from the Orient believed in its mystical properties. Socrates, the great philosopher, wrote of the profound changes that overcame pilgrims who journeyed to it.

In the 5th and 4th centuries BC it cost an Athenian two days' wages to ask the oracle questions. Mediums – there was always a minimum of three working a shift system – were on hand to work morning to night on the allotted days that consultations with the gods were allowed. Knowledge seekers made written requests to the Pythia and she went into a trance-like state after inhaling the herb and oil mixture. When the incoherent mutterings spewed forth, they were interpreted by the priests for the customer. Apollo's influence over the ancient Greek world – a world of civility, moderation and conservatism – is regarded by historians as being particularly important. These values were passed on to the pilgrims at Delphi, making the shrine a moral as well as a metaphysical force for its believers. Carved in a pillar of a temple at Delphi are the maxims of the ancients who governed Greece: 'Know thyself', 'Nothing in excess', 'Go surely', and 'Ruin is at hand'.

Socrates, the philosopher, whose humanitarian and scholarly wisdom was embodied in a thousand years of Greek learning.

Historians believe the first seekers of truth at the oracle wanted merely to learn if their hunting would be good the next day or if their crops would ripen. As time went on the oracle assumed an ever-larger role and the direction of the gods was sought in all the affairs of state. Answers were frequently ambiguous – which left them wide open to interpretation but guaranteed that they could never be accused of being wrong!

The summoning of Olympian guidance at Delphi lasted until well into the Christian epoch. Apollo is said to have delivered his last advice in the year AD 362 to the Emperor Julian who sought to restore pagan gods and worship to his Byzantine empire. Julian said that when he sought advice from Apollo the message came back: Tell the king that the curiously built temple has fallen to the ground, that bright Apollo no longer has a roof over his head, or prophetic laurel, or babbling spring. Yes, even the murmuring water has dried up.'

ST MALACHY
Predictor of Popes

Nine hundred years ago an Irish monk predicted the line of popes that would lead the Roman Catholic Church up to and beyond modern times.

Using symbolic titles, set down in Latin, Malachy O'Morgair – monk, bishop and later saint of the Catholic Church – bequeathed to the world an astonishing set of prophecies in which he successfully predicted the succession of Roman pontiffs from Celestine II in 1143 to the present day. A learned scholar, a man of outstanding wisdom, virtue and humanity, his stunning prophecies were not even discovered until 400 years after his death.

He was born in Ireland in 1094, and was given the Gaelic name Mael Maedoc ua Morgair. Ireland was a wild, dark place in those times, the only physical and spiritual havens being the monasteries which dotted her bleak landscape. His father, Mugron, was a professor at Armagh, the country's seat of piety and learning, and from his earliest days Malachy – the name which he adopted when he entered the Church – was drawn to Christianity. He studied under the Abbot of Armagh and in 1119 was ordained as a priest. He became Abbot of Bangor in 1123. With this rise in his status he embarked upon clerical reforms.

Ireland's ecclesiastical system was in a state of chaos. The Church was still basically a tribal hierarchy, based on the system set up by St Patrick. Paganism was rife in the countryside (mainly due to marauding Danes). The clergy was corrupt, the churches in disrepair, the people left in a state of religious limbo between heresy and Catholicism. Malachy made it his task to reform the Church. He was responsible for bringing in the Roman liturgy, Christian marriage rites and the Latin mass.

In 1140 he journeyed to Rome and, en route, stopped at a French monastery at Clairvaux, where he befriended Abbot Bernard – later St Bernard – who subsequently wrote a contemporary biography of Malachy's life. So impressed was Malachy with the Cistercian way of living, as practised by Bernard and his brothers, that he requested Pope Innocent II at the Vatican to relieve him of his bishopric to become a simple disciple at

Pope Innocent II, one of the greatest medieval figures. His ecclesiastical reforms were far-reaching.

Clairvaux. The pope refused, saying that there was much work for him still to do in Ireland. While he was in Rome the pope announced that Malachy was to be papal legate over all Ireland. Returning to his country with renewed vigour, Malachy brought paganism to an end and order to the Church.

Malachy was intrigued by mystical theology – as was St Bernard – and he demonstrated some amazing prophetical attributes. One story has it that he was able to foretell what he was to be given to eat on a given day three months hence. He even gave a grim prediction regarding himself: that he would die at Clairvaux on his next visit there. Sure enough, on 2 November 1148 while resting there, en route to Rome, he passed away surrounded by the entire community. In 1190 he was canonized by Pope Clement III, and became the first Irish-born saint.

His life was well chronicled by St Bernard, and other essays on his life and times have dealt with his good works and his teachings, but no contemporary mention was ever made of the prophecies. It wasn't until 1559, when the Benedictine historian Anrold Wion mentioned them in his work *Lignum Vitae*, that the world knew of their existence. In 1871 the Abbé Cucherat in France put forward his theory that Malachy had visions between 1139 and 1140 during his first papal visit. He said that he committed these visions to paper and handed the manuscript to Pope Innocent II. Innocent II then placed the manuscript in the archives where they remained undisturbed for four centuries. It is still not entirely clear how they eventually surfaced into the public domain. What is patently clear, however, is both their appeal and their accuracy.

Malachy did not come straight out and say 'so and so will become pontiff'. Instead he used a practice later made famous by Nostradamus, of wrapping up his visions with quirky Latin and secular images. His phrases were short – no more than four words – but within them, say the interpreters of the prophecies, lay the clues to the papal succession. The first, for instance, he called 'Ex Castro Tiberis', which translates into 'From a castle on the Tiber'. Guido de Castello (or 'castle') was the first pontiff who ruled from 1143 to 1144. The second he titled 'Inimicus Expulsus' or 'The enemy expelled' which translated into Lucius II, pontiff from 1144 to 1145. Lucius II was born Gerardo Caccianemici. 'Cacciare' in Italian means to expel and 'nemici' are the enemies. In his reign

Lucius II suffered severe head injuries as he attempted to expel a foreign army from Rome. The third pontiff was Eugene III, called 'Ex Magnitude Montis' by Malachy, meaning 'From the great mountain'. His place of birth was Montemagno and he ruled from 1145 to 1153.

The list of the popes as predicted by Malachy, with the descriptions he attached to each, continues with Anastasius IV, 'Abbot from Suburra' and Adrian IV, 'From a white country'. Adrian IV was born Nicholas Breakspear and was the only English pope to date; England was known as Albion, the white country.

A little research will reveal how Malachy's descriptions link with the popes who followed: Alexander III, 'From the guardian goose'; Victor IV, 'From the loathsome prison'; Paschal Transtiberina, 'The road beyond the Tiber'; Calixtus III, 'From the Hungary of Tuscia'; Lucius III, 'The light at the door'; Urban III, 'A sow in a sieve'; Gregory VIII, 'The sword of Lawrence'; Clement III, 'He shall go forth from the school'; Celestine III, 'From the Bovensian territory'; Innocent III, 'A signed count'; Honorius III, 'A canon from the side'; Gregory IX, 'The bird of Ostia'; Celestine IV, 'The Sabinian lion'; Innocent IV, 'Count Laurence'; Alexander IV, 'The standard of Ostia'; Urban IV, 'Jerusalem of Champagne'; Clement IV, 'The

Pope John Paul II at the mass held at Coventry on the third day of his visit to Britain in 1982.

dragon crushed'; Gregory X, 'The man of the serpent'; Innocent V, 'A French preacher'; Adrian V, 'A good count'; John XXI, 'A Tuscan fisherman'; Nicholas III, 'The modest rose'; Martin IV, 'From the office of Martin of the lilies'; Honorius IV, 'From the leonine rose'; Nicholas IV, 'A woodpecker among the food'; Celestine V, 'Elevated from the desert'; Boniface VII, 'From a blessing of the waves'.

For modern times Malachy predicted Pius IX, 'The cross from a cross'; Leo XIII, 'A light in the sky'; Pius X, 'The burning fire'; Benedict XV, 'Religion laid waste' (this is a particularly interesting one – Malachy saw that, indeed, with the coming of this pope in 1914, his reign was overshadowed by the holocaust of World War One which destroyed the Christian menfolk of Europe in endless slaughter); Pius XI, 'Unshaken faith'; Pius XII, 'An angelic shepherd'; John XXIII, 'Pastor and mariner'; Paul VI, 'Flower of flowers'.

In 1978 Pope John Paul I, Albino Luciani, was elected. Malachy had given for this Holy Father the clue of 'Of the half Moon'. A half-moon was over the world when he died 33 days later. Later that same year Pope John Paul II was elected, for whom Malachy had written 'From the eclipse of the Sun'. As the 263rd pastor of the Holy Church, students of Malachy believe that this is a reference to Karol Wojtyla's ability to eclipse the work of previous popes, which in his remarkable career he has managed to do.

The next pope listed by Malachy is described as 'Gloria Olivae', or "The glory of the olive'. The olive branch has always been associated with peace and Benedictines are also known as the Olivetans, which may well account for this reference. On the 24 April 2005 Cardinal Joseph Ratzinger was formally installed as Pope Benedict XVI.

Malachy lists the last pope – although he does not specify whether there will be any between 'The glory of the olive' and this one – as Petrus Romanus, 'Peter the Roman'. He concludes the prophecies saying: 'In the final persecution of the Holy Roman Church there will reign Peter the Roman, who will feed his flock among many tribulations, after which the seven-hilled city will be destroyed and the dreadful judge will judge the city.' As an omen of what may happen to Rome one day, it is a sombre one.

MOTHER SHIPTON
Prophetess of Tomorrow

While she was in a state of trance, Yorkshirewoman Mother Shipton foresaw the future, and was able to predict all of the major technological developments that were to come.

Mother Shipton was a legendary British prophetess, born in the reign of King Henry VII and credited with foretelling the deaths of Cardinal Wolsey and Lord Percy, as well as painting a remarkable portrait of the shape of things to come in the modern world. Her most famous rhyming couplets depict an H.G. Wells-type world that was remarkable for its accuracy:

'Carriages without horses shall go, And accidents fill the world with woe. Around the world thoughts shall fly, In the twinkling of an eye. The world upsidedown shall be, And gold be found at the root of a tree, Through hills man shall ride, And no horse be at his side. Under water men shall walk, Shall ride, shall sleep, shall talk. In the air men shall be seen, In white, in black, in green. Iron in the water shall float, As easily as a wooden boat. Gold shall be found and shown, In a land that's now not known. Fire and water shall wonders do, England at last shall admit a foe. The world to an end shall come, In eighteen hundred and eighty one.'

It was later learned that the final lines, about the end of the world, were an unscrupulous addition to her premonitions by a publisher hoping to cash in on her fame in a publication of her works in the 19th century, but in one short poem, Mother Shipton captured all of the major technical innovations that humanity would perfect over the coming years. She spoke of cars – and the accidents they caused – the telegraph system, motorcycles, diving suits and submarines, flying machines, gold in South Africa and the harnessing of energy for humanity's benefit. It was the Victorian bookseller Charles Hindley who, in 1862, published the latter verses in a pamphlet that was itself a reprint of a 1684 booklet entitled *The Life and Death of Mother Shipton*.

The information is sketchy on Mother Shipton – certainly, her life, simple as it was, never achieved the scrutiny of countrymen like

John Dee. The wife of a Yorkshire carpenter, born in 1488 at a place known as the Dropping Well, near Knaresborough, Yorkshire, she was baptized Ursula Southell, changing her name when she married Toby Shipton. She was, by all contemporary accounts, an ugly woman. An account written of her prophecies in 1797 describes her thus: 'Her stature was larger than common, her body crooked, her face frightful, but her understanding extraordinary.' A hunchback, by all accounts, some believe that the Punch and Judy shows beloved of British children at seaside resorts and fetes have Mr Punch modelled on Mother Shipton. However, it is for her prophecies, rather than her physical traits, for which she is best remembered.

Mother Shipton did not conform to any accepted occult or mystical practices for her prophecies. Rather, she went into trance-like states for hours and would wake up to tell friends and family who had been waiting for her predictions what had occurred. In such a manner she successfully foretold the success of King Henry's routing of the French at Agincourt, Cardinal Wolsey's arrest for treason, the Caesarian birth of Edward VI, the reign of a maiden queen – Elizabeth I – and the beheading of a widowed one, Mary, Queen of Scots. She also, like Nostradamus, successfully predicted a 'great fire consuming London'.

A Punch and Judy show, similar to the ones that travelled all over Britain in the 18th and 19th centuries.

In 1641 a pamphlet appeared entitled *The Prophesie of Mother Shipton, in the Raigne of King Henry the Eighth, Foretelling the Death of Cardinal Wolsey, the Lord Percy and Others, As Also What Should Happen in Insuing Times.* Four years later the famous astrologer William Lilly published a collection of Ancient and Modern Prophecies which included what he called 'Shipton's Prophecy' of what would happen in the world.

She died in 1561; undoubtedly, had she been more highly born, more of her remarkable life would have been chronicled. As it is, little survives as testimony to her strange powers.

JOHN DEE
Unscrupulous Rogue or Brilliant Astrologer?

Tudor scholar John Dee became personal astrologer to Queen Elizabeth I before apparently losing his powers and falling from favour.

Charlatan, rogue and impostor – or brilliant mathematician, astrologer and crystal gazer, true sage and worthy of the praise that his believers heaped on him? Researches into this intriguing man have left the argument unresolved after almost four centuries.

Dee, born in 1527 to a noble Welsh family in Mortlake, received a fine education. At the age of 15 he went to Cambridge University where his zeal for study astounded his contemporaries.

After graduating he plunged into astronomy, deciding to pursue the study of the stars in Holland and Belgium. He returned to England with newly devisd astronomical instruments, and also with books on magic and the occult. He began casting horoscopes and was much influenced by Geronimo Cardano, the Italian physician and astrologer. He amassed a vast library of works on astrology and mysticism and was soon commissioned by Queen Mary I to read horoscopes for her and her future husband, Philip of Spain. Through his cousin Blanche Parry, maid of honour to Princess Elizabeth, he came into contact with the future queen. He drew up her horoscope and compared it to that of Mary. Mary, he told her, would die childless while Elizabeth's own future was a bright one. Unfortunately for him, a spy in her camp sent word of his account to Mary and he was arrested and spent two years in jail on the charge of 'trying to take the life of the monarch through magic'. Following Elizabeth's accession he was appointed 'hyr astrologer'. His first task was to predict a suitable day for her coronation. He chose 14 January 1559. The weather was fine and sunny – reinforcing the queen's view of his powers. He travelled extensively abroad, buying massive libraries of occult and astrological works, and greatly increased his scientific and mathematical knowledge. Indeed, he is credited with foreseeing the invention of the telescope by studying the refraction of light, and suggested its military use. He returned to a house at Mortlake-on-Thames provided for him by the queen. Here he became famous for his astrology and his prophecies. He found the lost basket of clothes of a neighbour after having a prophetic vision in a dream. He also helped a butler locate his master's missing silver in the same way. He began crystal gazing – the practice of staring into the point of light

John Dee – the man upon whom Shakespeare is said to have based the character of Prospero. Dee was truly 'connected' to the high and mighty – but the debate about his talents still rages.

at the centre of a sphere of glass – from which bounce back telepathically received ideas, hallucinations or images transmitted by supernormal means. However, he had minimal success with gazing and decided to use the services of mediums.

Edward Kelly joined his household as a crystal 'scryer', or reader, at a salary of £20 per year after summoning the angel Uriel to appear in the ball for Dee. Kelly is widely regarded as the person who chiefly devalued the scholarly Dee's reputation with his hocus-pocus and his mystical incantations in which he summoned up the spirits of the dead. But there appears to have been something to him; believers in Dee feel that his interplay with the angels was genuine and that he attained telepathy and spiritualism with a nether-world never previously reached. Dee laboriously wrote down the conversations he had with numerous angels summoned forth by Kelly.

In the margin of one book, four years before she was executed, Dee drew an axe next to the name of Mary Queen of Scots – and got the date of her execution right. He also predicted 'A sea full of ships' after Uriel revealed plans about a foreign power preparing a 'vast fleet against the welfare of England'. Queen Elizabeth was grateful to Dee for warning her of the Spanish Armada.

In 1583 Dee brought Prince Adalbert Laski, representative of

The destruction of the Spanish Armada. Queen Elizabeth I is understood to have obeyed the warning of her seer, who said the fleet must be destroyed in British waters.

the King of Poland, to Mortlake to observe his angel-summoning sessions with Kelly. During one seance an attendant to the prince burst into the room uninvited, much to the displeasure of Dee and Laski. Dee said the angel told him that within five months the boy would be 'devoured by fishes'. Sure enough, five months later, the boy drowned at sea. Laski stayed on in the house searching for the mythical formula that turned base metals into gold, before he departed with Dee and Kelly on a six-year odyssey to the Continent. While abroad they earned the patronage of counts and princes, an offer to reside in Moscow from the Russian royal family, and a rebuke from the pope about their 'unchristian' activities.

Elizabeth, missing 'hyr astrologer', consulted him about how to defeat the Spanish Armada which he had foreseen. Her military advisers urged her to attack the Spanish ships while still in foreign ports, but he said a consultation on her horoscope had shown that the Spanish fleet must be defeated in English waters. The advice was heeded and he returned to England in a splendid coach provided by his monarch, but the relationship with Kelly was shattered over his command that an angel had informed him that Dee was obliged to share his wife with him!

In England, Dee's fortunes rapidly went downhill. His library had been ransacked by a mob during his absence abroad and he was facing poverty. He tried to recapture his earlier successes from the crystal ball, but nothing seemed to work. Eventually, Elizabeth tired of him and in 1595 she gave him the Wardenship of Christ's College in Manchester, a post he held for ten years before he returned to Mortlake, where he died in 1608.

Richard Deacon, who has made an authoritative study of John Dee, said: 'Some writers have depicted him as the foolish dupe of Kelly. Others have suggested that both he and Kelly used crystal gazing to obtain money fraudulently from Laski. But if it was through greed that Dee exploited the crystal then why reject the Czar's magnificent offer?' Deacon thinks that Dee was a spy for Elizabeth, passing back intelligence on his last mission – perhaps bolstered with astrological readings - to her court. He concludes: 'Dee... was a sincere seeker after knowledge, a mystic at heart but a scientist in his mind, and in many respects a pioneer in a variety of scientific fields.'

CAGLIOSTRO
Prince of Quacks?

Famed in France as the 'Divine Cagliostro', this versatile count conducted experiments in a search for the key to the secrets of the Universe.

Sometimes branded a showman – and cruelly dubbed a 'Prince of Quacks' by Thomas Carlyle – Count Alessandro Cagliostro was an enthusiast of the occult and the mysterious. He was a genuine seeker after knowledge, who strived to unravel the 'heavenly magic' which he believed held the key to the secrets of the Universe.

Little is known of his early life and education. He arrived in London in 1776 with his young wife, Sarafina, whereupon he made contact with Freemasons' groups intent on turning base metals into gold. He held seances, summoned up spirits, and on three occasions at least predicted the winning numbers of a lottery. His main interest, however, was divining the affinity between the Church, Freemasonry and other religions.

His first supernatural experiments are chronicled as having

A brutal and enduring symbol of the French Revolution. Madame Guillotine was never unemployed during the dark days of 'the Terror' which followed the overthrow of the House of Bourbon.

taken place in 1779. Using an Egyptian method of clairvoyancy he had discovered, he hypnotized a child, causing him to see visions and utter prophecies. As the subject was induced into a trance-like state, Cagliostro strove for his 'heavenly magic' by summoning angels to speak for him with God.

In one Egyptian rite ceremony Cagliostro employed the nephew of the Countess Elsa von der Recke. Cagliostro had earlier asked the husband of the Countess what sort of vision he would wish the boy to have. He suggested it be of his mother and sister who were some kilometres away in another village. Ten minutes later the boy – having no idea who he would see under Cagliostro's 'spell' – cried out that he saw his mother and sister, and that his sister was holding her 'hand to her heart as if in pain'. Cagliostro later sent an emissary to check on the family. It was discovered that the sister had recently suffered such violent heart palpitations that she thought she was dying! It is worth pointing out that Cagliostro was privately wealthy and never charged money for any of these seances.

Soon afterwards he moved across France, before arriving in Paris where he was lauded as the 'Divine Cagliostro'. Here, fresh from his successes, he assumed the role of a master magician and held many seances in which phantoms and angels were invoked in glass vases of water. This led to an introduction to King Louis XVI and he performed the same spectacular feats at Versailles.

Cagliostro also possessed seemingly remarkable powers of healing. There exist numerous accounts of the potions and elixirs that he dispensed to the sick. He was also one of the earliest believers in the powers of crystal healing. With his massive library of books, which included pharmaceutical and herbalist works, it is likely that many of his potions were used in tandem with the crystals. And again, he refused all payment for his services.

Cagliostro moved on to prophecies. At a masonic meeting held at the home of a noted occultist he expounded the theory of Gematria – that all letters of the alphabet have a numerical value and that a person's future could be foretold from the total of the digits his or her name represented. For the king he forecast a violent end to his life as he neared 39; for the queen, Marie Antoinette, he said she would become 'prematurely wrinkled through sorrow', would languish in prison and then would be beheaded on the scaffold. For her close companion, the Princesse de Lamballe, he said she would die on the corner of the street named Rue des Ballets. ALL of these predictions turned out frighteningly true.

And there was more – he predicted that a Corsican would end the Revolution and that his name would be Napoleon Bonaparte. Although a victorious general at first, Cagliostro said Napoleon would finish his days 'pacing the circle of a melancholy island' – an accurate reference to his exile to Elba.

Cagliostro's downfall came when he was falsely accused of stealing a necklace worth hundreds of thousands of francs. He spent nine months in the notorious Bastille before being found not guilty in a trial which inflamed the passions of the poor against the nobility, and upon his acquittal he was ordered to leave France by the king himself. It was 1786, three years before the French Revolution would sweep away Europe's old orders forever. He returned with his wife to England where he published a pamphlet predicting the Revolution, the storming of the hated Bastille gaol, and the downfall of the French monarchy.

Seeking fulfilment and peace elsewhere, the couple moved to Rome. Here, Freemasonry was banned but Cagliostro wanted to recapture his fame and fortune. He held one illegal seance with some Rome noblemen before he was arrested. At the seance in 1789 he used a young girl as the conduit with the spirit world. She uttered words about a mob armed with sticks, racing towards a place called Versailles: she had accurately predicted the start of the Revolution which did not take place for a further

Louis XVI, king of France from 1754 to 1793, granted permission for Cagliostro to summon up the spirits of dead ancestors – in the great Hall of Mirrors at Versailles Palace!

three weeks. The French ambassador, the Cardinal de Bemis, was among those present at the seance; he was outraged at the prediction that his lord and master was about to be destroyed. 'I am sorry, my Lord Cardinal,' said Cagliostro. 'But the prophecy will be realized.'

The vengeful ambassador told the Inquisition about him and Cagliostro was placed under close supervision before being arrested on 27 December 1789. He endured horrific tortures before being tried and found guilty of heresy, sorcery and Freemasonry. The pope commuted his sentence to life imprisonment, the same fate prescribed for his wife. She died in captivity in 1794, he a year later following a fit. Had he lived for two more years the French, under the warrior Napoleon whom he foresaw, would have liberated him.

CHEIRO
Prophet of the Politicians

From an early age Cheiro had astounding powers of prediction. Later he travelled widely and was consulted by the world's leaders.

Cheiro, born William John Warner, is probably the most successful of clairvoyants from the 19th century. Born on 1 November 1866, he found himself at an early age blessed with strange gifts. He found he could easily read the palms of his classmates and teachers. Later, after his father was ruined by a disastrous land deal – as Cheiro had foretold – he read the palm of a stranger on a train. He told the man he was another Napoleon, with a great destiny, but that he would meet his own 'Waterloo' in the shape of a beautiful woman. Years later the man, Charles Stuart Parnell, was brought down in the divorce of Katherine O'Shea.

Cheiro travelled to India, where he delved into transcendental meditation and out-of-the-body experience. He stayed for three years before inheriting a fortune from a relative, and then returned to London.

One of his successes was in helping to solve a murder in the East End. Police called upon him to 'read' a bloodstained palmprint left on a door jamb at the scene of the killing. Cheiro said that the palmprint was that of the murdered man's illegitimate son, whose existence was not known at that stage by the police. Three weeks later the son was arrested and charged with the murder. Cheiro soon became bored with London and took himself off to the temples of the Nile where he acquired the severed hand of a mummified princess. The hand travelled with him constantly after he returned to London to try to become a full-time teacher of occult studies. The name Cheiro, from the Greek word cheir for hand, came to him in a premonition and he became permanently known by it.

Arthur James Balfour, later the Tory prime minister, was one of his first clients, and he brought along with him a wealthy and fashionable clientele, but fortune telling, as defined by law, was illegal under laws dating back to Henry VIII. Police warned him to cease his practice within a week or face prosecution, but thanks to influential friends he managed to keep going. He went on to read the palms of several members of the nobility. A famous reading occurred in the home of a friend, Blanche Roosevelt, who insisted on him reading the hands of someone through a curtain. He said:

Oscar Wilde. The dandy author and playwright had his hand read by Cheiro without revealing his identity.

456

'The left hand is the hand of a king, but the right that of a king who will send himself into exile.' The owner of the hand asked when, and was told, 'A few years from now, at about your fortieth year.' Cheiro later learned he had foretold the future for Oscar Wilde.

Cheiro moved to the USA in 1894 and became an instant hit after reading the palmprints of several prominent Americans. One of them was of a man who had recently been arrested for murder. Without knowing the man, a D.T. Meyer of Chicago who was poisoning his patients with potions, Cheiro predicted that he would die peacefully in prison after many years behind bars. On the eve of his execution Cheiro again read his hand – and said that he would be reprieved. The next day the Supreme Court commuted his sentence to life imprisonment. He died in jail 15 years later.

Another stunningly accurate prediction was to a Mrs Leiter of Chicago who gave him a print of her daughter's hand. He prophesied that the girl would marry a man from another country and then 'lead the life of a queen in the East, but she will die young'. Mary Leiter became Lord Curzon's wife and later Vicereine of India. Tragically she died young.

Cheiro spoke all over the USA, saying that a baby an hour old has lines on its hands that foretell its future. Eventually, richer but bored, he returned to England, fed up with the questions from clients who mostly demanded to know how they could be richer and when it would happen.

Even King Edward VII consulted Cheiro at the Belgrave Square house of an American society friend. At the reading Cheiro told the king that the numbers six and nine would be the most significant in his life. He died in his 69th year. Cheiro also accurately foretold the month the king's coronation would take place: August 1902.

King Leopold II of the Belgians was another client who consulted Cheiro – but the news was grim. Cheiro said the king's death in 1909 would be caused by serious problems with his digestive tract. He died on 17 December that year, the cause of death given as 'the complete breakdown of the digestive organs and intestinal obstruction'. Another reading for the Czar of Russia was foreboding but true: 'He will be haunted by the horrors of war and bloodshed... his name will be bound up with some of the most far reaching and bloodiest wars in history, and in the end, about 1917, he will lose all he loves most by sword or strife in one form or another, and he himself will meet a violent death.' Cheiro had predicted the end of the Romanov dynasty and the Russian Revolution.

Georgi Rasputin, the evil monk who held so much sway over the czarina, was also a client. Cheiro told him that he would be a power for evil, holding enormous sway over others. He told him he would die by bullets and would finally be dumped in the Neva river – exactly, as it turned out, how Rasputin did meet his end.

Herbert Kitchener, the great Lord Kitchener of Sudan, consulted him on 21 July 1894 at the War Office. Cheiro said he would be in great danger in 1916, caused by a storm at sea. Kitchener died that year on board a vessel bound for Russia that struck a mine.

Cheiro went on to predict the election result for a Conservative MP in a marginal seat, the Wall Street Crash of 1929 for a businessman and saved the Shah of Persia from an assassination attempt. He did not, however, manage to predict the crash of his own fortunes, which came when he made a disastrous business deal involving the purchase of an American newspaper.

After World War One Cheiro foretold the treaty in 1926 between Soviet Russia and Germany, the General Strike in Britain in May

Lord Kitchener, Chief of the General Staff at the outbreak of World War One. He consulted Cheiro, who told him he would be in great danger in 1916. That year he died at sea en route to Russia.

1926, the breaking out of civil war in China and an earthquake in the Channel Islands. All came true. In 1927 he published a book of world predictions, stunning in their accuracy. He foretold the return of the Jews to Palestine in a state they would call Israel, World War Two and the spread of communism throughout the world. In 1930 he went to live in Hollywood with the intention of becoming a scriptwriter, but he wrote only one screenplay – about Cagliostro – and it was never made. He ran his own school of metaphysics there until his death in 1936.

WOLF MESSING
Stalin's Psychic

A Polish Jew had such powers of mental gymnastics that he acquired the patronage of no less a person than Josef Stalin.

Josef Stalin, history's bloodiest dictator, at one time placed his faith in Wolf Messing, who was undoubtedly Russia's greatest-ever seer. Messing, who discovered his gifts as an 11-year-old boy, is regarded by many as one of the great psychics of the 20th century.

Born a Polish Jew near Warsaw on 10 September 1899 Messing was a subject then of Imperial Russia and its last czar, Nicholas II. He ran away from school when he was 11 and boarded a train for Berlin with no ticket. He was caught by a brutal ticket collector who asked him repeatedly for his ticket; Messing ended up handing him a scrap of paper from his pocket – and thereby performed his first conscious act of mental gymnastics. He recalled: 'Our gazes crossed. How I desperately wanted him to accept that scrap of paper as a ticket!... I mentally suggested to him: "It is a ticket... it is a ticket... it is a ticket..." The iron jaws of the ticket punch snapped. Handing the "ticket" back to me and smiling benevolently he asked me why I had been sleeping under the seat when I had a valid ticket. It was the first time my power of suggestion manifested itself.'

After suffering grinding poverty and chronic malnutrition in Berlin, Messing gradually managed to carve himself a living as a mind-reader in city theatres. By placing himself into a light trance he found he could concentrate on the thoughts uppermost in a person's mind. He earned the grand sum of five marks a day.

Soon his mind-reading abilities brought him into the orbit of the truly great men of his day – Albert Einstein and Sigmund Freud. There is a famous story of how Freud told Einstein that he would 'think' a command for Messing to interpret. On a given day all three were seated in Freud's Vienna salon and Messing, now 17, went into a trance. Soon, he sat upright, walked across to a pair of scissors lying on a desktop, picked them up and proceeded to clip three hairs from Einstein's moustache.

Messing had interpreted the mental orders with absolute precision. Messing toured South America and the Far East during World War One and returned to his birthplace, now in an independent Poland, in 1922. After compulsory military service he took up travelling throughout Europe, again performing his mind-reading stunts to amazed audiences. One of his most appreciated performances was the ability to drive a car while totally blindfolded as he received telepathic instructions from a chauffeur about directions.

It was with the coming of Hitler and World War Two that Messing fled to Moscow – even though the racial policies of Stalin were often just as harsh as those of Hitler. In 1939 he found himself in a squalid apartment in the capital – and in a quandary about how to make a living. Stalin had banned those who practised extrasensory perception and other psychic arts, his paranoia leading him to distrust anyone with powers he could not understand. Messing did obtain work as the last act in various nightclubs but on more than one occasion found himself as a guest of the police or the KGB for a night.

Finally, one night, after he was arrested at a club in the town of Gomel, he was presented to someone of 'immense authority'. That person was Stalin himself, and at the meeting he was cordial, asking Messing questions about his life in Poland and the situation there. A few days later Messing was collected by the KGB and subjected to a special test, on Stalin's orders, of his abilities. The 'test' consisted of asking an official of the state bank to hand over 100,000 roubles, presenting him with a piece of blank paper at the same time. Messing said: 'It was essentially a rerun of the test I had on the train.'

There followed several audiences with Stalin in which Messing spoke of his foreboding that Hitler planned war on the USSR. Messing told Stalin that he had had a vision that war would come in June 1941. On 22 June that year the full weight of Hitler's mechanized armies fell against the USSR.

During the war years Messing was allowed by Stalin to perform his mind-reading feats in morale-raising public appearances. Later that year he was summoned to the Kremlin where Stalin asked for a personal display of his powers. He recalled: 'He said he did not think anybody could make a fool of him and that I would not be able to leave the Kremlin without a pass signed by him… He telephoned the guards to say I could not leave without a pass and ordered his private secretary to follow ten paces behind me.

'I entered my deepest state of trance that I can ever recall. Several minutes later, I walked right out on to the street past the guards, who remained standing at attention and looking up at the window of Stalin's study. "Maybe I should blow him a kiss," I thought mockingly.'

Stalin looked upon Messing as his personal seer, and he was forever inviting him to his private apartments in the Kremlin. But the

Josef Stalin, the Kremlin overlord who liked to test Wolf Messing's abilities. More attention to Messing might have shortened the war and saved untold thousands of lives.

'Man of Steel' did not heed his advice on the war. Stalin seems to have regarded him more as a personal pet, but it was a powerful patronage and one that Messing was keen to engender for as long as possible.

In the 1950s Messing underwent extensive testing at the hands of Soviet scientists, on Stalin's orders, to probe the workings of his extraordinary mind. Until then belief in the paranormal was attacked in Soviet society as being 'bourgeois, materialistic and pseudoscientific' but with Messing they decided that electrical impulses in the brain were acting as radar signals which he bounced off similar strong thought patterns from individuals whose minds he endeavoured to read. Messing was less scientific and said: 'All I know is that I was born with this gift and have always been able to utilise it.'

In his later years Messing toured the USSR, deriving most pleasure from performances of his powers in small villages, where he also gained a reputation as a faith healer. In the early 1970s his health began to fade and he died from a heart attack in 1972, by which time his fame was so widespread within the USSR that he was accorded a hero's burial.

KARL ERNEST KRAFFT
and the Hitler Horoscopes

At first at risk of harassment by the Nazis, Krafft attracted the attention of the leaders of the Third Reich by predicting an attempt on the life of Hitler.

Many dark forces shaped and defined the Third Reich during its 12 years. But lurking in the background was a little-known astrologer called Karl Ernest Krafft. Historians now believe that if Hitler had listened to Krafft more closely, the final outcome of the war might have been very different indeed.

Born in 1900 in Basle, Krafft was a brilliant young man with a genuine gift for figures and statistics, but his greatest love was the study of the planets and astrology. After graduating from university in mathematics, for the best part of ten years he worked on a massive book entitled *Traits of Astro-Biology*. This expounded his

Deputy Führer Rudolf Hess was an occult enthusiast. When he flew to Scotland the times became harder for Nazi seers like Karl Ernest Krafft.

own theory of 'Typocosmy' – the prediction of the future based on the study of an individual's personality, or type. By the early 1930s, when Hitler had come to power, Krafft enjoyed a unique status among occultists and prophets in Germany. But ironically, it was the Nazis – later to become his greatest patrons – who at first posed the biggest threat to him. Occultists, like Freemasons, were among those harassed and vilified by the Nazis.

However, while publicly the state may have persecuted astrologers, privately men like Hitler, his right-handman Rudolf Hess and the SS chief Himmler were all in favour of consulting them. Krafft moved directly into the orbit of the higher echelons of the Nazi elite in November 1939 when he made a remarkable prediction. He predicted that the Führer's life would be in danger between 7 and 10 November. He wrote, on 2 November, to a friend called Dr Heinrich Fesel who worked for Himmler, warning him of an attempt on Hitler's life. Fesel filed the letter away, unwilling to become enmeshed in something which he felt could become extremely dangerous.

On 8 November, a bomb exploded at a Munich beer hall. There were many injuries, but the man who was targeted, Adolf Hitler, was unscathed. When newspapers reported the near-catastrophe Fesel despatched a telegram to Hess, drawing attention to Krafft's prediction. Krafft was instantly arrested and brought to Gestapo headquarters in Berlin for questioning. Questioning soon proved that he was innocent as far as the attempt on Hitler's life went. After his release he was summoned to the offices of the Reich propaganda ministry, run by Josef Goebbels. Goebbels had recently taken to poring over the historic prophecies of Nostradamus, trying to squeeze from them the maximum amount of propaganda to portray the Third Reich in flattering tones. Krafft, he felt, had the weight and authority to begin work on deciphering the often cryptic quatrains. In January 1940 the Swiss astrologer began work on a pro-German evaluation of Nostradamus.

Krafft was convinced that the prophecies of Nostradamus boded well for the Third Reich. Tens of thousands of pamphlets based

Montgomery of Alamein, who truly did have the mettle, in the end, to take on Rommel and drive him all the way out of Africa.

upon his interpretations of the quatrains were circulated in various languages and he soon came to the attention of the Führer. In the spring of 1940 he gave a private horoscope reading for Hitler to an aide, but he never met his leader. Later he boasted to friends that he mentioned that the time for an attack on the USSR was some way off. Hitler, who was impatient to launch Operation Barbarossa (the conquest of the USSR) after he had dealt with the West, in fact delayed his operations in the east until the following June. The stunning success of the early days of Barbarossa convinced him that Krafft had great powers.

British intelligence became so concerned at the thought that their opponent's war was being conducted by a mystic that they, for a time, hired the services of the astrologer Louis De Wohl to divine the kind of prophecies that Krafft was divining for the Nazis. De Wohl was quietly dropped after several months, having failed to procure any hard evidence about Krafft's work.

Krafft warned the Reich leaders that for victory to be certain, the war MUST end for Germany in 1943; in this, it turned out, he was entirely correct. By the end of 1942 Germany was at the zenith of her victories, but after that date the full might of the Allies, with the USA behind them, could not fail to eventually swamp the Fatherland.

Krafft's star was still in the Nazi ascendancy when Rudolf Hess made his astonishing flight to Scotland in 1941. Hitler was outraged. He knew that Hess was the biggest occult supporter of them all and, in his fury, ordered a massive purge of astrologers, occultists and other sages. Even Krafft was caught up in this and he languished in prison for a year before being released. This time he was sent to work on horoscopes of Allied generals and admirals. One of his predictions when seeing the charts of both Rommel and Montgomery, adversaries in the desert war, was: 'Well, this man Montgomery's chart is certainly stronger than Rommel's.' History proved him to be correct.

Krafft's health began to fail and he developed a persecution complex. He wrote to a senior official predicting that British bombs would very soon destroy the propaganda ministry in Berlin – another true statement. The letter was passed on to the Gestapo who viewed it as treasonous. He was incarcerated in foul conditions, contracted typhus and eventually died on 8 January 1945.

JOAN QUIGLEY
The Power behind the President

For six years socialite and astrologer Joan Quigley played a major part in world events.

When the story first broke about Joan Quigley's involvement with the Reagan administration in the White House, the impact was shattering. If what was being alleged was true, then for close to six of the eight years that Ronald Reagan ruled as the world's most powerful man his destiny – and therefore humanity's – was linked to Quigley's interpretations of the Universe in her role as an astrologer. Not since medieval times has a soothsayer had so much influence in power politics.

Quigley was an educated, soft-spoken spinster who lived on San Francisco's luxurious Nob Hill and was considered a major player on the city's social scene. But what drove her was her love for, and her gift of, interpreting the stars.

Plotting future events by the alignment of the heavens was at first an escape for Joan, and then something of a permanent

Joan Quigley. The world was shocked to learn of her stargazing in the White House, which subjugated the most powerful man in the world to the will of the cosmos.

challenge. In the late 1960s and early 1970s she began reading the horoscopes of wealthy Republican friends.

She was introduced to the Reagans in 1973 and soon Nancy Reagan was calling her up on a regular basis. Quigley claimed: 'From 1973 on I drew up horoscopes for both the then governor and Mrs Reagan annually. When I first saw Ronald's horoscope I knew it was world class.'

Reagan became the single most powerful individual on earth with his triumph at the polls in 1980. His rule would lay the foundations for the most cataclysmic changes in world history since the end of the war and herald the beginning of the end for the USA's old arch-enemy, the USSR. During Reagan's first 15 months in office Joan Quigley had little influence, but after he miraculously survived an assassination attempt in March 1981, she became a force to be reckoned with within the corridors of power. For a fee of 3,000 US dollars a month she would soon be running the affairs of a superpower – or if not running them, certainly having a major say in them.

Later Joan would recall: 'Nancy was interested in everything, not just the president's safety. She was interested in her image. She wanted me to improve it.' In effect, Quigley became an ex officio cabinet member. In regular telephone conversations, Quigley would hammer out every nuance of the president's schedule. Nancy became obsessed with working out when would be the most propitious time for him to undertake any aspect of his job. By her own admission Quigley was a powerful force: 'For over seven years I was responsible for timing all press conferences, most speeches, the State of the Union addresses, the takeoffs and landings of Air Force One. I picked the times of Reagan's debates with Carter and Mondale and all of his trips. I delayed the president's cancer operation and chose the time for Nancy's mastectomy.' Using what she calls 'analysis' on the data provided by astronomers, and charts calculated by computers, here's what Quigley also takes credit for:

• Overturning Nancy's initial hostility to Gorbachev. Quigley says her examination of Gorbachev's horoscope proved to her that his Aquarian planet sign was in such harmony with Reagan's that they would share a 'beautiful vision'. Quigley credits herself with forcing Reagan to drop his 'evil empire' rhetoric against the Soviet leader.

• Defusing the crisis over the visit by the Reagans to a cemetery in the German town of Bitburg in May 1985 that contained the graves of Nazi SS officers. She completely threw the scheduling into disarray by saying that the planets were only favourable for a visit at 2.45 p.m. instead of two hours earlier as planned. 'The Bitburg visit was brief,' she said. 'And the controversy soon died down. I defused it for him.'

• Foreseeing also in 1985 the president's need for surgery. She says that on 10 July his horoscope proved conclusively that he needed an operation for cancer. The doctors that day found out and wanted to operate immediately, but she told Nancy that an operation wouldn't be successful until noon on the 13th. Nancy obeyed her and Reagan did not need further cancer surgery during his entire time in office. But Quigley said: 'Had they not listened to me they would have risked not removing the cancerous growth completely.'

• Staging the announcement in Washington of a controversial Supreme Court Justice. Right-winger Anthony Kennedy's election was not a popular one with moderates and liberals, so Quigley says she used a unique astrological device to pick the exact right

Ronald Reagan, 40th president of the United States and the first ever to have a daily schedule worked out around the signs of the horoscope.

time for Reagan to announce his choice. Nancy, she says, went along with her advice and Anthony Kennedy was later installed without fuss or rancour.

• Smoothing over the fuss about Irangate. She claims that between January and August 1987, when the scandal about the arms dealing-for-hostages was at its zenith, she re-organized Reagan's schedule to make it 'practically impossible' for hostile media representatives to get to the president with embarrassing questions.

• Securing the president's safety while airborne. She says that many times she contacted Nancy while Air Force One was transporting President Reagan around the world, dictating flying patterns and landing and take-off times. She remains convinced that his life could have been in jeopardy if her advice had not been heeded.

• Advising him on the most momentous single act of his presidency – the bombing of Libya because of Colonel Gaddafi's continued sponsorship of world terrorists.

Quigley's interpretation of the pageantry of the zodiac may have been vital to Nancy, and even to the president, but it was viewed by professionals within the White House as calamitous. Donald Regan, the chief-of-staff who blew the whistle on the entire affair in 1990, says her stargazing created a hammerlock on business. On his desk he was forced to keep a colour-coded calendar to chart the president's 'good', 'bad' and 'iffy' days and on at least one occasion she gave him a list in which large chunks of time were marked 'stay home' or 'be careful'. Regan claims Quigley chose the most auspicious time for the Aquarian Ronald to meet the Piscean Gorbachev.

'I wanted secrecy more than Nancy,' she said. 'That's why I stayed so much in the background.' However, Regan's book about the stargazing years set the media hounds on the trail and Quigley claims she was forced to go public to protect her own reputation. It caused a rift with Nancy Reagan, but she says she could not lie, not even for the former First Lady.

Quigley also takes the credit for what she calls 'PR by astrology' – smoothing the image of the 'great communicator' and his sometimes frosty wife, but perhaps her greatest claim of all is that she kept Reagan ALIVE. She points out: 'From William Henry

Washington on, every president elected in a zero year has died in office except for Reagan. I think I had something to do with that. In fact, I know I did.'

After she no longer worked for Reagan she was so upset about the rift with Nancy that she pledged never, ever to read the horoscopes of an American again.

After she quit working for the Reagans she tried to drop back out of the public limelight, although occasionally she would offer up some predictions on public figures whose horoscopes she was already acquainted with. A year before the abortive August coup in Moscow by hardliners she said this about Gorbachev: 'He's going to have more troubles from his generals and more food shortages. There is going to be a loss of power for him.'

Quigley never made any dramatic predictions for the end of the century. She did, however, offer up one Hollywood prophecy: that volatile couple Ryan O'Neal and Farrah Fawcett might not be together by the year 1999. They split in 1997.

J.Z. KNIGHT AND JACK PURSEL
Channellers of Wisdom

Thousands of her supporters follow the teachings of Seattle housewife J.Z. Knight, who claims to be the channel for a warrior from ancient Atlantis.

In a remote mountain ranch in Washington State the faithful adherents of 'channelling' gather like pilgrims every weekend for £500-per-time mind sessions with the most famous channeller of them all. Judy Z. Knight was a Seattle housewife until she was visited in 1977 by the spirit of a long-dead warrior from the long-lost continent of Atlantis. His name was Ramtha and ever since he has been sending his prophecies and his wisdom to numerous believers – among them *Dynasty* star Linda Evans and Hollywood legend Shirley MacLaine.

The concept of channellers is as old as the centuries – only the term is relatively new. It describes practitioners of prophecies who turn over control of their bodies to spirits of the dead, or to extraterrestrial beings, who in turn proffer their wisdom, coupled with portents of things to come. J.Z., as she is known to her devotees, has become wealthy and influential through her connection to Ramtha – a Cro-Magnon man, 35,000 years old. The channelling movement offers an exotic way towards spiritual fulfilment and Ramtha is credited by thousands of people as having totally changed their way of living. His 'teachings' seem to consist of bits and pieces of Buddhism, Hinduism and Christianity.

'Ramtha helped me find happiness,' said Hollywood celebrity Linda Evans. 'For me, he has been a powerful teacher. And J.Z. is one psychic who has certainly changed my life.'

Evans first heard Ramtha speak through J.Z. Knight in 1985. She took a day off from the set of soap opera *Dynasty* and drove to a Ramtha seminar near Los Angeles. She said, 'I had been exploring psychic phenomena for close to 20 years, but when I first

J.Z. Knight – rich, successful and powerful, thanks to her 'channelling' with the spirit of a long-dead warrior from the lost kingdom of Atlantis.

471

heard his voice speak I felt it was adding wonderful bridges that I had never come across.

'In the beginning I was totally suspicious. I wanted proof that the channelling wasn't just trickery. I wanted to protect myself. I didn't want to be misled after all I had been through in my personal life. But he holds you in the moment – holds a truth or emotion until you can totally feel and know it. He puts the information in front of you to see. He made me see first off that I could no longer put all the blame on my husband John Derek for leaving me. I had to take responsibility for my part.'

Why did Ramtha decide to impart his knowledge to a Seattle housewife? J.Z. – married five times and recently involved in a messy divorce – said: 'I have no idea why he chose me. I am the medium for him. He speaks and the words come out of my body, but it is not me speaking. It is his voice. When it happened I had mixed feelings. I knew that there would be days that would not belong to me any more. I am his tool. But I have learned so much wisdom from him, which others have too, that I never regret that day.'

Just what does Ramtha offer, other than self-enlightenment, contentment and advice for people to look inside themselves for the clues to the secret of the Universe? At any given session, channelling disciples will ask many wide-ranging, worldly questions – and Ramtha always gives an answer. A man at a seminar in 1990 asked what the best investment for his cash was. Ramtha told him to buy Taiwanese dollars (at the time, a sound investment bet). He predicted the San Francisco earthquake of 1989 and takes credit – through J.Z., of course, for predicting the worldwide recession of 1992. Literally thousands of people have taken the advice of his central philosophy for the 20th century – that people must abandon the cities for a more rural life. That rural life for many is in the surrounding countryside near to J.Z. Knight's home where Ramtha instructs them to 'keep to high ground' and store up to two years' food supplies in the basement for the coming unspecified catastrophe.

Shirley MacLaine is another big-name celebrity who has consulted with Ramtha on numerous occasions as part of her quest for 'new age enlightenment'. She insists that Ramtha is the summoning of a powerful, relevant force that needs to be listened to and reckoned with. MacLaine, who believes she has been, at various times in the past, a Peruvian Inca child, a Mongolian maiden and an Indian princess, says that Ramtha has provided her with many valuable lessons.

'I just knew he had been my sibling in a previous existence in Atlantis,' said MacLaine. 'He was profound.' Profound, too, is the acceptance that Knight has gained with her ancient guru from among both sceptics and students of the paranormal in the USA. Although at times the media have portrayed Knight as everything from wily cult leader to harmless psychotic to dangerous manipulator, those who have examined Ramtha's teachings find that, for the most part, his wisdom is sound and his predictions true. Arthur Hastings, who studied dozens of channellers for his book *With the Tongues of Man and Angels*, said: 'I am deeply impressed.' Even Charles Tart, author of *Open Mind, Discriminating Mind*, who questions the value of channellers, agrees: 'No high-minded entity, including Ramtha, has ever come up with a carburettor design that would help improve gas mileage, something that would concretely help civilisation. Still, much of what he says makes good common sense.'

Barry Manilow subscribes to the teachings of Lazaris, a disembodied spirit summoned up by Floridian channeller Jack Pursel.

If J.Z. Knight is the most famous, and richest, channeller, Jack Pursel from Palm Beach, Florida, runs her a close second with a celebrity client list every bit as good. He summons up Lazaris, a disembodied spirit - not a warrior-god like Ramtha – who calls himself 'the consummate friend'. Lazaris appears to channel his thoughts and predictions through former insurance adjuster Pursel, who quit his climb up the corporate ladder after being visited by the unincarnate spirit six years ago. Celebrities Sharon Gless, Michael

York, Barry Manilow and Lesley Ann Warren – all have credited Lazaris with helping them.

Gless, who won an Emmy award for her role as a New York cop in the *Cagney and Lacey* show, even thanked Lazaris in her acceptance speech when she received the award! Like Ramtha, he works on the basis of inner love and a re-evaluation of the Universe to improve life and health, rather than specific predictions. But at seminars, almost identical to those held by Knight, Lazaris is summoned to speak, where he offers wisdom on such practical matters as health care and finances. One woman suffering from pancreatic cancer credits him with saving her life after telling her to recuperate in a yellow room. Another, a man, claimed Lazaris accurately predicted a fall in certain share prices.

Like Knight, Pursel can give no reason why this force in the spirit world should have chosen to visit him. He added: 'If we can add to the sum total of knowledge, though, in the world, and its happiness, surely that can't be a bad thing, can it? He has a great deal of wisdom for us all to share.'

JEANE DIXON
The Celebrities' Clairvoyant

For 70 years devout Roman Catholic Jeane Dixon has predicted private and national events with outstanding accuracy.

Jeane Dixon is one of the most remarkable clairvoyants who has ever lived, a prophet of outstanding perception and accuracy who in her lifetime has literally changed the   s of the world's most powerful people as well as the views oι those who often refuted her powers. She correctly predicted the death of John F. Kennedy, the airplane deaths of Hollywood actress Carole Lombard and United Nations secretary-general Dag Hammarskjold, and the suicide of Marilyn Monroe. A devout Roman Catholic, she believes that her gift of second-sight comes directly from God as part of his 'divine plan' for each and every one of us.

Born Jeane Pinckert in Wisconsin in 1918, she moved to California with her parents as a toddler. As a five-year-old she said to her mother that her father would be bringing home a black and white dog that day. Her father brought a puppy home as a surprise and was baffled about how she knew about it. On another occasion she told her mother that she would shortly be receiving a 'black letter'. Two days later a black-bordered envelope announcing the death of a relative in Germany arrived through the post. It was when she was eight years old that a gypsy travelling near her home came upon her and told her mother: 'Your child is blessed with great sensitivity and wisdom.' The gypsy left the young Jeane with a crystal ball, which she went on to use as a means of concentration so that her mind became receptive to telepathic visions of future events. That gift all those years ago led to her title today of 'Seeress of Washington'. She keeps none of the money she earns from her books and lectures, preferring instead to contribute it to her non-profit-making Children to Children foundation.

Jeane Dixon is perhaps America's most successful and respected clairvoyant, with a career spanning many years and many influential clients.

As a little girl she was soon doling out advice to family and friends after gazing into her crystal ball, but it wasn't until she was married during World War Two and living in Washington that she began crystal reading with intensity. She started doing psychic readings for servicemen at parties, but once word of her abilities began to spread she moved into a higher circle of diplomats, congressmen and other dignitaries. She was invited twice to the White House for private consultations with President Roosevelt, but she has never revealed what she foretold for the great wartime leader.

She went on to predict major events with stunning accuracy. With the exception of 1960 she correctly foretold the outcome of each presidential election in America since 1948; she foretold the partition of India, the assassination of Mahatma Gandhi and the coming of Red China. But it was in 1963 with the murder of John F. Kennedy, that she achieved international fame. It was back in 1956 that Dixon predicted that a Democratic president 'with thick brown hair and blue eyes' would be assassinated by a man whose name began with an O or a Q. Dixon said the vision of this president's death had first come to her in 1952 when she prayed before a statue of the Virgin Mary in Washington's St Matthew's Cathedral. Dixon has always said that her premonitions came to her in three ways – by crystal gazing, by handling the treasured possessions of a person or in direct messages from God The last was the case in the prophecy of the murdered president.

It was four years until her vision was revealed to an American journalist. In 1959 she told a communist official visiting Washington from an Iron Curtain country – his name is not revealed but his identity authenticated by Dixon biographer Denis Brim – that the next president of the USA would be called Kennedy and that he would be assassinated in office. As 1963 approached, many people in the Kennedy circle were warned on numerous occasions about his impending doom, including one of his secretaries and a secretary to his sister. Shortly before his fateful trip to Dallas, Texas, on 22 November 1963 she tried to get him to cancel his visit as the man with the name beginning with Q or O came to her in a vision. The warnings were ignored and Lee Harvey Oswald snuffed out the life of the best and brightest politician in the world with a high-powered rifle.

After his death she became known throughout the globe; her reputation was further enhanced the following year with the publication of a biography which chronicled her remarkable gifts. By 1966 she was an established international celebrity – and about to make another world-shattering prophecy.

America's manned space flight programme was within three years of putting men on the moon when Jeane suddenly had an awful premonition about the fate of the astronauts aboard an Apollo rocket. Jeane had become friendly with a woman named Jean Stout, wife of the chief of missions operations at the Office of Manned Space Flight. In December 1966 she was lunching with Mrs Stout in Washington

The sex goddess to end them all. Her tragic death was foretold by Dixon.

when she suddenly had a premonition that something terrible was about to happen to the Apollo programme. Holding her hand Jeane Dixon said: 'There's something strange about the floor of the capsule. It seems so thin that it almost resembles tinfoil. I am afraid that a tool dropped on it or a heel pushed firmly against it would go right through it. Under the floor I see a great clump of tangled wires... I see a terrible fiery catastrophe. And it will cause the astronauts' deaths. I sense their souls leaving the blazing capsule in puffs of smoke...' On 27 January 1967 an uncontrollable blaze snuffed out the lives of three astronauts as they tested the Apollo capsule at Cape Kennedy. Electronic malfunction was cited as the cause of the disaster.

Hollywood was naturally drawn to Jeane Dixon like paperclips pulled to a magnet. She read for the Reagans – long before Ronald Reagan as president would become reliant on a seer called Joan Quigley to chart his days for him – and Bob Hope. The famous comedian once tried to test her skills by asking how many strokes he had made during a game of golf earlier that day – but he didn't mention the name of his partner on the links. Without hesitation, she replied: 'You took 92 strokes and Eisenhower took 96.' She was correct on both counts. She once told a client, actress Carole Lombard, not to travel by plane for a six-week period. Lombard chose to ignore her and died in the wreckage of her aircraft.

She has gone on to successfully predict the deaths of Martin Luther King, Marilyn Monroe and Robert Kennedy. When some of her prophecies have failed – like World War Three which she forecast would break out in 1958 - she says that the basic information from God was correct and that she was merely wrong in her interpretation of the signals she received.

It is the prophecies that Mrs Dixon wrote down for the end of the 20th century that interested most observers. She predicted a great war with Russia in the Middle East and then a mighty war with China – an apocalyptic clash between good and evil which will result, by the year 2025, in China's conquest of most of Russia, Finland, Norway, Denmark, Libya and much of central Africa. On the good side, she predicts that Western Europe will not feature in China's war plans and that salvation for the world will come after the war in the shape of the Second Coming of Christ.

'When that time comes,' she said, 'and it will come, we will all be united in the Brotherhood of Christ under the Fatherhood of God.'

MONSTERS & MYSTERIOUS PLACES

WHAT LURKS IN THE LAKE?

For over 1000 years there have been authenticated sightings of a monstrous creature living in one of the Earth's deepest lakes. Now scientists have finally begun to take the stories seriously, and are using state-of-the-art technology to get to the bottom of the icy black waters of Loch Ness and the secrets they hide ...

There can hardly be a person in the civilized world who has not heard of Loch Ness in Scotland and its famous monster. Possibly rather less commonly known is the fact that Nessie is but one of an army of such unexplained lake monsters. There are about 250 lakes, world-wide, which reputedly harbour creatures that, according to conventional science, should not be there – or anywhere - at all.

The first intimation that something strange might be living in Loch Ness came in St Adamnan's 7th-century biography of St Columba. In about AD 565 the latter apparently confronted a water monster living in the River Ness with the sign of the cross and so, according to Adamnan, caused it to depart the neighbourhood at speed. Over the centuries other sightings were made, although some have the curious feature that the creature was seen on land, not swimming in the Loch itself.

In 1771, for instance, one Patrick Rose saw what he described as a cross between a horse and a camel in the Loch. In 1907 (or 1919, according to some accounts) a group of local children at Invermoriston, which is about five miles from the southern end of the Loch on its western side, saw a 'light brown, camel-like quadruped' slip into the murky depths of this strange stretch of water.

A GAPING RED MOUTH

A curious event occurred in 1857 at Loch Arkaig, which is some 20 miles south-west of Loch Ness but linked to it by the same river system, so there may well be a connection of another kind with the creature reportedly living in Loch Ness.

Lord Malmesbury, a solid, bewhiskered gentleman rolled from the stoutest Victorian makings, went shooting deer near Loch Arkaig that autumn. His memoir of 3 October 1857 reads:

'This morning my stalker and his boy gave me an account of a mysterious creature, which they say exists in Loch Arkaig, and which they call the Lake Horse. It is the same animal of which one has occasionally read accounts in newspapers as having been seen in the Highland lochs, and on the existence of which the late Lord Ellesmere wrote an interesting article…

'My stalker, John Stewart, at Achnacarry, has seen it twice, and both times at sunrise in summer on a bright sunny day, when there was not a ripple on the water. The creature was basking on the surface; he only saw the head and the hindquarters, proving that its back was hollow, which is not the shape of any fish or of a seal. Its head resembled that of a horse.'

Local folk, then, were not unfamiliar with the presence of odd animals in the inland waters of the Highlands. Most witnesses described something with two humps, a tail, and a snake-like head. They often noted a V-shaped wash behind the creature, and commonly reported such details as a gaping red mouth and horns or antennae on the top of its head.

Children of the villages around Loch Ness were told not to go swimming in its waters lest the creatures that lived there attack them, but word of what might be in Loch Ness did not travel far. The bombshell, as far as the world outside was concerned, came in 1933. Up to a point, this has a simple, material explanation. In that year a road was dynamited into existence along the Loch's north shore, and the view across the water 'improved' by sawing away the vegetation. Tourism into the area immediately increased. So did sightings of the thing in the lake, but now they were not being made simply by local people.

While St Columba was in the Highlands, preaching to the Picts in the late 6th century, he chanced on a monster in the River Ness.

'PREHISTORIC ANIMAL'

On 14 April 1933, a Mr and Mrs Mackay catapulted the Loch Ness monster into the headlines. The *Inverness Courier* reported their account of seeing an unknown creature in the Loch that 'disported itself for fully a minute, its body resembling that of a whale'. More sightings, and photographs to prove them, followed rapidly.

At 4 p.m. on 22 July 1933, Londoners Mr and Mrs George Spicer were driving along beside Loch Ness on the new road, on their way back from a holiday in northern Scotland, when their car nearly struck a huge, black creature with a long neck. The 'prehistoric animal', as Mr Spicer described it, shambled across the road, slithered through the undergrowth, and splashed into the Loch.

On 12 November 1933, an employee of the British Aluminium Company, Hugh Gray, watched an unusually large 'object' rise out of the Loch. When it had raised itself two or three feet out of the water, Gray photographed it. He estimated the length of the thing to be about 40 ft, and described it as having greyish-coloured, smooth and shiny skin.

His photograph is, to say the least, ambiguous: it's not difficult to see in it the image of a labrador-like dog with a largish piece of wood in its mouth. But in late 1933, a little frivolity from the Highlands was good news to a world wearied by the Depression and worried by Hitler's recent rise to power. The picture was published in papers all over the globe, and the Loch Ness monster became a permanent fixture in the popular imagination. In the year after the release of the Gray photograph, there were over 50 reported sightings of 'Nessie'.

In 1934 two more photographs were taken of the creature. One was by Colonel Robert Wilson, a London doctor. Labelled the 'surgeon's picture' by the British press, Wilson's photo was clear and distinct in comparison with Gray's. It seemed to show the head and neck of a plesiosaur-like creature rising out of the water. In the summer of that year, Sir Edward Mountain organized an expedition to the Loch to investigate the stories and the sightings. A member of the group snapped a picture of something strange breaking the surface of the Loch on 13 July, but hardly any details are visible.

POMPOUS JOKE?

Since then, there have been many pictures taken of things that may or may not be mysterious animals in Loch Ness. Several have been definite hoaxes. One – taken by a notorious self-publicizing 'investigator' – was nothing more than a part-submerged fence post with a sock, or possibly a collapsed Wellington boot, stuck on top to look like the head of a monster. This kind of joke hardly forwards the cause of disinterested research.

Others, even some of those taken by reputable and impartial scientists, have been ambiguous at best, although not necessarily because of what they seem to show. The classic examples are the underwater pictures taken by Dr Robert H. Rines of the Academy of Applied Sciences at the renowned Massachusetts Institute of Technology during thorough surveys of the Loch in 1972 and 1975. One of the computer-enhanced photographs, taken in 1975, seems to show an animal that fits the standard description of Nessie – something rather like an aquatic dinosaur. The other, taken in 1972, apparently shows the creature's flipper.

The 'surgeon's picture' of Nessie, taken on 19 April 1934 by London doctor Colonel Robert Wilson, showing the classic plesiosaur-like profile of the mystery animal.

The doubt arises not just because there is, inevitably, no background or other detail by which to judge the size of the image – Loch Ness's waters are extremely murky thanks to the amount of peat suspended in them – but because of the pompous scientific name dreamed up for the purported animal by the naturalist Sir Peter Scott. Impressed by the rhomboid shape of the flipper, Scott coined the Latin name Nessiteras rhombopteryx for the animal, a 'christening' that was taken at the time to be a sign that Nessie had been accepted into the hallowed groves of establishment science.

Then someone – who must have been either a genius with dyslexia or a fanatical crossword buff – realized that the letters of the Latin name could swiftly be rearranged to read 'Monster hoax by Sir Peter S'. Was it a joke? A revelation? A bizarre coincidence? Scott never said, while sceptics have pointed out that the image in the Rines photographs could have been of nothing more mysterious than a lump of wood.

STRIKING CONSISTENCY

If the photographic evidence is largely dubious, the circumstantial evidence that some very odd animal is alive and well and living in Loch Ness is very good. Since 1933, there have been more than 3,000 sightings of the creature. There is, to begin with, a striking consistency in reports of what people see. Most describe a long-necked, humpbacked animal that can move very fast when it wants to, whether its head is up or down, and that, at other times, will simply rise quietly to the surface for a few minutes and then sink silently below.

It is also a curious fact that apart from Loch Ness itself the worldwide sightings of lake monsters that resemble Nessie (which no living animal known to science does) have all occurred around the isothermic line of 50°F in both northern and southern hemispheres. The animal, or animals, whatever they are, thus conform to a rule of zoology in having a distinct distribution within a specific environmental pattern. They don't pop up just anywhere, and if they did there would be grounds for suspecting that they were more a figment of the imagination (or folklore) than an elusive fact of nature.

Veteran cryptozoologist Bernard Heuvelmans commented crisply: 'One could hardly wish for better circumstantial evidence for their existence.' The unanswered question remains: what might these animals actually be?

INEXHAUSTIBLE APPETITE

There are numerous theories as to the animal's identity. Candidates have included the zeuglodon, a prehistoric, snake-like primitive whale, an unknown type of long-necked seal, giant eels, and more prosaically walruses, floating mats of otters, diving birds and even – someone had to say it – mirages. A favourite contender has always been the plesiosaur, a marine reptile that has officially been extinct for the last 70 million years. The 'extinct' label affixed by science is not necessarily proof that a species has in fact died out, however; it simply represents the current state of accepted knowledge. Until 1938 the coelacanth, a singularly ugly but otherwise inoffensive prehistoric fish, was reckoned extinct because there were no fossils of it less than 70 million years old and no living specimens had been seen; but then coelacanths were found thriving, and no doubt thoroughly indifferent to the opinions of scientists, in the Indian Ocean. So it is possible that a community of plesiosaurs has survived in the same way.

They would have had to survive in the sea for the major part of that time, but they could have found their way into Loch Ness with little or no difficulty in the last 10,000 years. Then, after the last great Ice Age ended, the glaciers retreated, and the Great Glen fault – which divides the Scottish Highlands, and of which Loch Ness is a part – opened up to the sea. On the other hand, they would have had to have adapted from being geared to a saline marine environment to survival in the fresh water of the Loch in a very short time (in evolutionary terms). But that again is not impossible.

Loch Ness is a fairly sterile place, partly because of its depth (up to an estimated 1,000 ft), its darkness, and the lack of nutrients flowing into it. But a plesiosaur could survive there on a healthy diet of fish without disturbing the Loch's basic ecosystem. At least, it could as long as it had an inexhaustible appetite for fresh salmon.

This is because the mature salmon that enter the Loch from the sea, by way of the River Ness, simply don't eat, and so don't affect the rest of the food chain in the Loch. Still more convenient, salmon come into the Loch all year round, so there is a reasonably consistent and plentiful supply of food for any predator that might depend on them for survival.

THE LAST DINOSAUR?

What militates against Nessie being a leftover plesiosaur is the rarity with which it seems to appear on the surface, for the creature would have to live in the top 125 ft or so of the Loch's waters, not only because that is where the food (of any kind) is, but also because below that level the temperature drops dramatically – too low for a cold-blooded reptile (even of the 'monster's' reported size) to survive. Even the warmer level of the Loch is at the extreme end of such an animal's range. On top of that, reptiles have lungs, not gills: they need to breathe fresh air. So why aren't the 'reptiles' of Loch Ness seen on the surface more often?

Most reptiles, too, would have to come – and stay – ashore for a brief period at least once every year to lay their eggs. No one has

The plesiosaur, which of all known animals most resembles 'typical' lake monsters as seen in Europe and North America.

seen that happen yet at Loch Ness. It is, of course, again possible that the creatures move from the Loch out to the ocean for some of the year, perhaps especially in the breeding season. Nevertheless, it's surprising that this hasn't been seen happening on some rocky Scottish shore by someone at some time.

Even the possibility that the creature's elusiveness – not to say virtual invisibility – is the result of there being only a very small family of monsters in the Loch, is hardly a conclusive argument. To be viable, there would need to be a community of an average of at least three monsters alive at any one time. The Loch's surface area is no more than 45 square miles, that is 15 square miles of surface water for every monster. The surface area of the Mediterranean is some 900,000 square miles, or 20,000 times bigger. The estimated population of the rare and endangered monk seal in the Mediterranean is between 300 and 600 or, at best, one every 1,500 square miles – 100 times the area for each Loch Ness monster. Seals are mammals and have to breathe air; they surface to do so. And they are seen every year, at all seasons, and recognized with delight for what they are, by all kinds of people all over that huge inland sea. There is no mystery about the monk seal, although they are far more sparsely distributed over a much vaster area than the extremely mysterious Loch Ness monster would seem to be.

A SWIMMING ELEPHANT?

None of that, however, is a conclusive argument against there being something – or some things – living in the Loch. It may not be a reptile at all. It may be a fish of a rather unusual variety. It may be something utterly unexpected. In August (not April!) 1979, two highly qualified academics, Dr Dennis Power and Dr Donald Johnson, suggested in the columns of the august journal *New Scientist* that the creature of Loch Ness might be a swimming elephant. While this may have started as a lighthearted article, a correspondent to *Fortean Times* gleefully pointed out a fine, ironic coincidence with this proposal. Ancient Pictish rock carvings showed (among many recognizable creatures) an animal that scholars had been unable to identify and had called either just 'the

Pictish beast' or – here it comes – 'the swimming elephant'.

Certainly one of the odder aspects of the Loch Ness monster is its apparent ability to travel over land. In June 1990, retired Colonel L. McP. Fordyce published an account in *Scots Magazine* of his experience in April 1932 – some 12 months before the event usually credited as the first 'modern' sighting of the denizen of the Loch. He too mentioned the resemblance to an elephant.

Colonel Fordyce and his wife were driving south in their six-cylinder Morris Isis, along the minor road on the south side of the Loch from Foyers to Fort Augustus. At one point the road leaves the shoreline and winds through woodland. Colonel Fordyce wrote:

'Travelling at about 25 mph in this wooded section, we were startled to see an enormous animal coming out of the woods on our left and making its way over the road about 150 yards ahead of us, towards the loch.

'It had the gait of an elephant, but looked like a cross between a very large horse and a camel, with a hump on its back and a small head on a long neck.'

Colonel Fordyce was not a soldier for nothing. He got out of his car and followed the animal on foot 'for a short distance. From the rear it looked grey and shaggy. Its long, thin neck gave it the appearance of an elephant with its trunk raised.'

THE MONSTER BITES BACK

So, the mystery deepens and, in its way, becomes almost as murky as the peat-ridden waters of the Loch itself. But one of the most persuasive arguments that a large, strange animal of some kind is living in (or near) Loch Ness is the variety of different traditions and sightings from other, similar lakes around the world that share certain geographic and topographical features with Loch Ness. For the mystery animals are all reported from lake and river systems that either are connected to the sea or have been in the past, and they all either harbour or once harboured migratory fish. Many of the lakes that fit this pattern are also deep and cold.

One such is Lake Storsjön in central Sweden, which is connected by river systems to the Gulf of Bothnia, a spur of the

Baltic Sea. For 350 years or more there have been reports of a monster in the lake, and since 1987 alone the local Society for Investigating the Chat Lake has collected over 400 reports of sightings. Few, unfortunately, are consistent, so there is no clear idea of what the creature might really look like. Some witnesses have seen an animal with a large neck that undulates back and forth and looks like a horse's mane. Others described a large worm-like creature with distinct 'ears' on its head. According to reports, the beast's size may vary from 10 to 42 ft in length.

By a brilliant irony, one famous sighting was made by a local fisheries conversation officer, Ragnar Bjorks. The 73-year-old official was out checking fishing permits among anglers on the lake in the 1970s when he had the fright of his life. A huge tail suddenly broke the calm surface near Bjorks's 12 ft rowing boat. The creature that owned the tail seemed to be 18 ft long, and was grey-brown on top with a yellow underbelly. Bjorks struck at it with his oar and hit it on the back. The creature reacted by slapping the water mightily with its tail: Bjorks and his boat were ignominiously hurled about 10 ft in the air. During his brief flight Bjorks became a convinced believer in lake monsters.

WAKING VENGEANCE

Inconsistent reports also come from Ireland, where in Connemara a wilderness of rocks and peatbog is broken up by a patchwork of loughs of all sizes. Here, as in the Highlands of Scotland, it's possible that the unidentified denizens of the loughs move from one to another. Such migration would help explain why so many very small stretches of water in Connemara seem to house so many animals and such large ones to boot. But there seem to be several kinds of the creatures, if the witnesses' reports are accurate.

In the evening of 22 February 1968 farmer Stephen Coyne and his son were gathering peat beside Lough Nahooin, a tiny peat tarn, only some 100 by 80 yds in extent, near Gladdaghduff. Alerted to something weird in the water by the behaviour of their dog, Coyne sent the boy to fetch the rest of his family to watch it. The seven-strong family were joined by four other local children.

They agreed that the creature was probably about 12 ft long, hairless, with 'eel-like' black skin. It had a 'pole-like' neck, in diameter about 12 in, and apparently horns on its head that may have been protuberances housing its eyes, and a pale mouth. When it put its head underwater two humps showed above the surface. The group caught only glimpses of a tail.

This is entirely different from the animal spotted in Lough Dubh, another small lake in County Galway, near Glinsk. Three men saw a monster there in 1956, and in 1960 three of them were seen in the lough. One day in March 1962, schoolteacher Alphonsus Mullaney and his son Alphonsus Jr went fishing there for pike, and took rod and line stout enough to handle these hefty fish. Mullaney caught more than a fish:

'Suddenly there was a tugging on the line. I thought it might be on a root, so I took it gently. It did not give. I hauled it slowly ashore, and the line snapped. I was examining the line when the lad screamed.

'Then I saw the animal. It was not a seal or anything I had ever seen. It had for instance short thick legs, and a hippo face. It was as big as a cow or an ass, square faced? with small ears and a white pointed horn on its snout. It was dark grey in colour, and covered with bristles or short hair, like a pig.'

The thing, hurt and furious, was trying to get out of the water and wreak vengeance on its hapless fishers. Mullaney and his son fled. A posse of local men later returned with guns to search for the creature, but they found nothing. Nothing like it has been reported since from Lough Dubh.

Different again was the monster seen in Lough Auna, three miles or so north-east of Clifden, the 'capital' of Connemara. Air Commodore Kort, who had moved to Ireland after retiring from the Royal Netherlands Air Force, was about to go indoors at the end of a barbecue party in the summer of 1980 when he and one of his guests saw what seemed to be the sawtooth, reptilian dorsal fin of an animal moving slowly across the lough. The fin was about 5 ft long and stood 12 in out of the water. 'The uncanny thing about it,' said Kort, 'was the gliding movement without any disturbance of the water on the surface.'

WATER SERPENT

In North America, monsters such as the frequently seen but so far unidentified inhabitant of New Brunswick's Lake Utopia and 'Manipogo' of Lake Manitoba in Canada, and those of Lake Erie (where there were many sightings in 1991) and Hathead Lake in Montana, were all locally renowned long before 'Nessie' grabbed the world's headlines.

One such lives in the 109-mile long Lake Champlain, which adjoins New York State, Vermont and Quebec. Lake Champlain's monster, nicknamed 'Champ', has been sighted over 240 times, nearly half of them since 1982. The first really detailed report came in July 1883. The Sheriff of Clinton County, New York, Captain Nathan H. Mooney, was on the north-west arm of the lakeshore when he saw a huge water serpent about 50 yds from him. The creature rose about 5 ft out of the water, which was rough. He reckoned the animal was 25 or 30 ft long. Its neck was about 7 in in diameter, with visibly contracting muscles, and was curved like that 'of a goose when about to take flight'. Mooney noted that there were round white spots inside the creature's mouth.

An early effort to trap the creature of Loch Ness – a huge steel cage, built in 1933.

Candidates for the identity of 'Champ' are identical to those offered for the Loch Ness monster, with the plesiosaur leading.

There are a number of photographs of the creature. Perhaps the most significant was taken on 5 July 1977 by Sandra Mansi of Connecticut, who described the thing as a 'dinosaur' with its neck and head some 6 ft out of the water. The Mansi photograph has been examined by scientists and declared to be a genuine original of something in the water. But what?

THE 'REMORSEFUL ONE'

The best-known Canadian lake monster, 'Ogopogo' of British Columbia's Lake Okanagan, also made its debut long before Nessie. Reports go back to 1850, although the local Indians were familiar with the beast long before that, and indeed named it the 'remorseful one'. Indian legend says the creature was once human – a murderer turned into a serpent as punishment for his crimes. In 1926, the editor of the *Vancouver Sun* wrote of the creature: 'Too many reputable people have seen it to ignore the seriousness of actual facts.'

A recent sighting shows how witnesses are convinced that there is indeed something odd in Lake Okanagan. In the summer of 1989, hunting guide Ernie Giroux and his wife were standing on the banks of the lake when an animal about 15 ft long surfaced from the calm waters and swam 'real gracefully and fast', as Giroux later told reporters. The creature had a round head 'like a football'. Several feet of the creature's neck and body came up out of the water. The Girouxs saw the monster at the same spot where, a few weeks before, British Columbian car salesman Ken Chaplin had taken a video of what he described as a dark green, snake-like creature about 15 ft long.

Wildlife experts who saw the video said the animal was more likely a beaver or a large river otter than a 'monster'. Ernie Giroux was unimpressed.

'I've seen a lot of animals swimming in the wild and what we saw that night was definitely not a beaver,' he said bluntly.

At the other end of the Americas is 'Nahuelito', the denizen of

Nahuel Huapi Lake at the foot of the Patagonian mountains in southern Argentina. The lake, which covers 318 square miles, is in a popular resort area. Dozens of tourists and local people have seen the creature.

Accounts of the animal vary. Some describe a giant water snake with humps and fish-like fins; others speak of a swan with a snake's head, while yet others liken it to the overturned hull of a boat or a tree stump. Estimates of the creature's length range from 15 to 150 ft. 'Nahuelito' seems to surface only in the summer, when the wind is still. A sudden swell of water and a shooting spray usually precede a sighting.

Patagonia, mountainous and desolate at best, has long been the source of tales of monstrous animals, and even human giants. Patagonian Indians told the first colonists of a huge lake-dwelling creature without head, legs or tail. The rumoured existence of a Patagonian plesiosaur was given additional fuel in the early 1920s, when a gold prospector named Sheffield followed an unusual spoor and found a bizarre water beast at the end of the trail:

'I saw in the middle of the lake,' he reported, 'an animal with a huge neck like that of a swan, and the movement in the water made me suppose the beast to have a body like that of a crocodile.' An expedition, led by Dr C. Onelli, Director of the Buenos Aires Zoo, set out to catch or photograph the animal, but sadly failed.

Operation Deepscan in 1987 was a massive attempt to 'catch' Nessie. A score or so of launches equipped with sonar dectectors made a sweep of the entire Loch. Such a method may, however, have succeeded only in frightening any animals below into hiding.

THE LATEST TECHNOLOGIES

What would solve the mystery of the world's lake monsters?

Naturalists are agreed that only the capture of a live specimen or the discovery of a carcass (scientists tend to disapprove of investigators 'acquiring' dead specimens by ballistic means) would admit the monsters into the charmed circle of conventional science. But hunting lake monsters is not the world's easiest task. No live monsters have been caught, yet.

No carcasses have been found either that might be anything other than recognizable animals. Dead specimens may be elusive because the typical monster haunt is a very deep lake. A dead monster would sink to the bottom, where the water pressure would slow down the rate of decomposition – leaving time for eels and other creatures to consume the remains.

Giant nets, submarines, underwater cameras, sonar, lake and loch-side crews of observers have all failed to come up with unambiguous and unimpeachable evidence that would prove to the world that there is an actual monster in any of their reputed haunts. If the animals as reported do exist, they are quite possibly frightened away by the sounds made by the very devices that are being used to track them – as well as by engine noise from the boats.

But until that solid evidence turns up, these strange animals will remain classic mysteries. And credible witnesses will continue to report them, take fuzzy photographs, and keep the lake monster legends alive and swimming.

NOT QUITE HUMAN

As he began his descent down the mountain through the heavy mist, the professor thought he was hearing the echo of his footsteps. Terror seized him when he realized that the footsteps belonged to something different – to something malignant…

Abominable snowmen and other horrid hairy man-beasts are strictly contained in the Himalayas, the wilderness of the USA, and the remoter parts of China. Or so you thought.

At 4,296 ft Ben MacDhui is the highest peak in Scotland's Cairngorm mountains, and the second highest in the country. Many who have scaled Ben MacDhui are convinced that a malignant entity – which locals call Am Fear Liath Mor, the Big Grey Man – lives on the mountain.

The first report from anyone outside the area that something sinister haunted Ben MacDhui came in December 1925 at the Annual General Meeting of the Cairngorm Club. Professor Norman Collie told his suitably astonished audience that in 1891 he had been climbing through heavy mist down from the summit of Ben MacDhui, when, he said, 'I began to think I heard something else than merely the noise of my own footsteps. For every few steps I took I heard a crunch, and then another crunch as if someone was walking after me but taking steps three or four times the length of my own.'

At first he thought his imagination was working overtime, but the sound persisted, although whatever was making it remained hidden in the mist. Then, as the eerie crunching continued, Collie said, 'I was seized with terror and took to my heels, staggering blindly among the boulders for four or five miles.'

Collie vowed never to return to the mountain alone, and remained convinced that there was 'something very queer about the top of Ben MacDhui'.

His chilling account was soon picked up by the newspapers, with the result that other mountaineers came forward to record that they too had had similar experiences of uncontrollable and inexplicable fear and panic while on Ben MacDhui. Some had barely managed to avoid lethal falls in their compulsion to get away as quickly as possible from the terrifying presence.

This sounds like a paranormal presence, but some witnesses have actually seen the thing, reporting a huge, man-like figure, and many accounts mention the same heavy footsteps with the unusually long stride that Collie heard.

Plenty of explanations have been put forward for these experiences. They range from the presence of yeti-like man-beasts and optical illusions to the (inevitable) 'base for extraterrestrial aliens' and (more plausibly) hallucinations brought on by lack of oxygen. This latter most probably accounts for some of the more exotic reports of the Big Grey Man, which mention strains of ghostly music and sepulchral laughter wafting across the mountain during its appearance.

But leaving the wonkier propositions aside does not mean dumping the 'man-beast' explanation entirely. There is a long tradition that hairy man-beasts inhabited the British mainland in the past. Known as 'woodwoses', or more mundanely as 'wild men of the woods', their images can be seen carved into the decorations in many old East Anglian churches. There is not much forest on Ben MacDhui, and it is a long way from East Anglia, but the possibility that a colony of these legendary creatures has survived in Scotland remains to tantalize the imagination.

FOUL ODOURS

Although conventional zoology says that one wouldn't expect to find apes of any kind, let alone 'ape men', living in South America or Australia, any more than in the British Isles, both continents can boast plenty of eyewitnesses who would swear that the contrary is true and that the scientists are wrong.

Australia's man-beast is known as the 'yowie'. Most reports have come from New South Wales and Queensland, and the creatures have been seen by settlers since the mid-19th century at least. The Aborigines have known about them since long before then. Like North America's 'bigfoot' and 'sasquatch', the yowie can remain remarkably unperturbed when surprised. When George Summerell, who was riding a horse, came upon one bending down to drink from a creek near Bemboka, New South Wales, on 12 October 1912, it simply 'rose to its full height, of about 7 feet, and looked quietly at the horseman', according to an item in the *Sydney Morning Herald*. 'Then stooping down again, it finished its drink, and then, picking up a stick that lay by it, walked steadily away... and disappeared among the rocks and timber 150 yards away.'

Footprints around the shore of the creek showed that the creature had been there at least a fortnight before, as well, and that the animal had only four toes – a feature of other man-beast prints taken around the world. But the yowie has two other features commonly reported by witnesses of the North American man-beasts: no neck, and the ability to emit revolting smells at will. In early 1978, an Australian National Parks worker was cutting timber near Springbrook in Queensland when he saw 'this big black hairy man-thing' about 12 ft away from him.

'It had huge hands,' he said, 'and… a flat, black shiny face, with two big yellow eyes and a hole for a mouth. It just stared at me and I stared back. I was so numb I couldn't even raise the axe I had in my hand. We [were] staring at each other for about 10 minutes before it suddenly gave off a foul smell that made me vomit – then it just made off sideways and disappeared.'

THE BEASTS ATTACK

The most intriguing and controversial encounter with a South American man-beast took place along the Tarra river on the Venezuela–Colombia border in 1920. A 20-strong team of geological surveyors, led by Swiss geologist Dr François de Loys, had set out in 1917 but at the end of three years had been reduced to a handful by disease, venomous animals, and the poisoned arrows of hostile Indians. One day in 1920, this ragged band saw coming through the foliage ahead of them two 5 ft tall, ape-like but tail-less creatures, walking upright on their hind legs.

When the beasts – one male and the other female – saw the geologists, they became plainly agitated, tearing angrily at the vegetation around them. They got so excited that both defecated into their hands and flung their excrement at the scientists. Then they moved forward – as if to attack, it seemed to the geologists, who responded with a hail of small-arms fire. The female died instantly. The male fled.

The geologists examined the carcass, noted its details, and photographed it. Most of the pictures were lost when the party's boat capsized later in the expedition, but one survived. On returning to Europe, De Loys showed it to the French anthropologist Professor George Montandon. He was convinced that it showed a species comparable to the Old World's apes – chimpanzees, gorillas, orang-utans and gibbons. He formally named it Ameranthropoides loysi – 'Loys's American ape'. Other scientists were less impressed.

The creature did look somewhat like an oversized and tail-less spider monkey, and most zoologists maintained that it was some form of spider monkey. Some even hinted, none too subtly, at a hoax. Montandon answered all the criticisms in painstaking detail, but his critics were unmoved: as far as establishment science was concerned, De Loys's find was not an ape, and the issue was soon simply ignored.

But there is plenty of circumstantial evidence in favour of creatures like the one De Loys shot and photographed. Indian tribes in the jungles all over South America have long believed in the existence of ape-like beasts that walk upright and lack tails. And among the ruins of various South American and Mexican ancient cities are sculptures of gorilla-like creatures quite unlike any known New World primate – but they do resemble the South American ape woman shot by De Loys's party. Further, there is no ecological reason why such an ape should not be able to survive in the South American environment – but conventional science always prefers to ignore awkward little questions and hairsplitting logic like that.

OUT OF AFRICA

In contrast to the areas we've looked at so far, it would make sense if hairy man-beasts were to be found living in Africa. Apart from its vast areas of wilderness in which such creatures could roam free, with little risk of being detected by people, the continent is now known to be the 'cradle of mankind' – the place where humans, Homo sapiens, evolved.

The oldest African fossils of hominids are the australopithecines, which first appeared over three million years ago. Some types were notably slender, others more robust – and so it is just possible that these or other ancient evolutionary forms, somewhere between apes and men, have survived out of sight in Africa to this day. And if one goes by the huge dossier of eyewitness reports, Africa is indeed home to an enormous variety of unidentified man-beasts.

Living specimens of slender australopithecine would look like several unidentified man-beasts as witnesses have described them. Among these are Zaire's 'kakundakari', the 'fating'ho' of Senegal, and Tanzania's 'agogwe'. According to witnesses, the agogwe is small, russet-furred and man-like, and sometimes mixes with other primates such as baboons. Elders of the Mandinka tribe of Senegal speak of the fating'ho as if it were just as real as any of the known animals inhabiting their lands, though it is rarely seen nowadays (perhaps simply because it has become rarer).

The enigmatic female beast shot by members of a geological survey team led by François de Loys on the Venezuela–Colombia border in 1920. Controversy still rages over the true nature of the creature.

Other man-beasts seem to resemble the robust species of australopithecines. Among these are the 'kikomba' of Zaire, and Sudan's 'wa'ab'. These may even be surviving examples of humanity's direct evolutionary ancestor, *Homo erectus.*

The French anthropologist Jacqueline Roumeguere-Eberhardt has concluded that there are no less than five different species of man-beast living in Kenya. She has cautiously dubbed them 'X One' through to 'X Five'.

X One is a typical bigfoot-like being, hairy, huge, and possibly social, since it's been seen carrying buffalo meat rather than gorging it on the spot. It also defends itself with a kind of sardonic gentleness. A young hunter who was cornered by the beast said it simply removed his arrows from their quiver, broke them up and put them back.

X Two is a cave-dwelling creature with a hairless, beige-coloured body with curly black hair on its head. A noticeably humanoid beast, it is tall and thin, and seems to live in nuclear families.

X Three is tall, and uses tools for hunting. Males have been seen to fell buffalo 'with an uprooted tree with its roots carved into spikes'. The beast then wields 'a spear-like knife' to cut out its prey's internal organs, 'which are then eaten on the spot'.

X Four is a hairy-chested, fat-bodied pygmy-like hominoid that, witnesses say, is often to be seen carrying a digging stick which it uses to uproot tubers.

X Five is exclusively vegetarian, a man-beast that carries bows and arrows and is apparently capable of making leatherwork bags.

Despite the wealth of sightings of African man-beasts, no one has yet caught or killed one, or found a skeleton that would provide conclusive proof of their existence. But Africa has given zoologists plenty of surprises in the 20th century alone. As the saying goes, 'There is always something new out of Africa.' So, perhaps, as the English cryptozoologist Dr Karl Shuker has put it, the most secretive of continents may be saving its most sensational surprise for the future.

THE INCREDIBLE HULK?

As far as the West is concerned, the granddaddy of all hairy man-beasts is, of course, the so-called 'abominable snowman' or 'yeti' of the Himalayas. The existence of what, correctly translated, the local people call 'a man-like living thing that is not a human being' first came to the West's attention in 1921, when Lt Col C.K. Howard-Bury was surveying Mt Everest for a forthcoming attempt to reach the summit. On 22 September that year he came across huge footprints on a snowfield where, earlier, he had seen dark, man-like forms moving around. News of these two events sped round the world, and have been reinforced by sightings from virtually every mountaineering expedition into the area since.

The term 'abominable snowman' is not only a mistranslation of the Nepalese term for these creatures – it's irritatingly misleading. There seems to be nothing particularly abominable about the yeti, and they appear on the high Himalayan snowfields only when making their way from one hot and humid valley, where they seem to spend most of their time, to another. And the term also implies that there is only one of these creatures. Not only are there many individuals, if reports are to be trusted, but there are at least three different kinds of yeti.

The word yeti itself is a Sherpa term that means, roughly, 'That-thing-there'. Investigator (and oil millionaire) Tom Slick was the first to conclude, from his expeditions to the Himalayas in 1957 and 1958, that there were at least two types of creature that local people had seen.

The 'original' yeti is the *meh-teh*, a man-sized creature that sports a conical head set on a stout neck, with a jutting jaw and a wide, lipless mouth. The body is covered in thick, reddish-brown fur. Prints show short, broad feet. Meh-teh eat plants and small animals, including birds, which they hunt in the upper forests of the mountains.

There is also a pygmy man-beast of the Himalayas, *teh-lma*, which means 'man-like being'. Standing about 3–4 ft tall, these creatures live deeper in the valleys than meh-teh, surviving on a diet largely of frogs and insects. Their thick fur is dark red, with a slight mane on the back.

The third species of yeti is known in the Himalayas, but only by repute. Called *dzu-teh* – 'hulking living thingy' – these beasts are huge, far taller and bulkier than a human, with a dark shaggy coat, a flat head with beetling brows, long powerful arms and hands, and large feet that leave prints with two pads under the first toe, which points out and away from the others on the foot. They live not in the Himalayas but in eastern Tibet and northern China, on a mainly vegetarian diet.

This matter of the two pads (and other features) showing in the dzu-teh's footprint is important, and so is the animal's habitat. American cryptozoologist Loren Coleman first pointed out that both plant and animal species in the areas of China where dzu-teh (called 'yeren' in China) are consistently reported bear an uncanny resemblance – they are often related to, or the same as – those found in the Pacific Northwest of North America. And this is where bigfoot and sasquatch are most often seen. And the footprints of yeren and bigfoot are strikingly similar in the configuration of their pads, ridges and disposition of the toes.

ALMOST HUMAN

So, are bigfoot (alias sasquatch) and yeren (alias dzu-teh) related - or even separate communities of the same animal? And if so, what animal?

The favourite candidate is a species of giant ape, named Gigantopithecus, which lived in southern China until it, apparently, became extinct 500,000 years ago. Its anatomy is somewhere between ape and human. Gigantopithecus, as its name implies, was huge. Males probably weighed around 806 lb and females around 500 lb. This is easily the largest primate that ever lived. Gigantopithecus also, almost certainly, stood and walked in a human manner.

Humans and all apes share a unique set of anatomical traits in the arms, shoulders, and thorax, since all evolved to swing through trees. Humans gave up this form of personal transport long ago, preferring walking horse-riding and eventually the Ford Model T. As a result they lost their tails. Gigantopithecus also belonged to this group of higher primates, but it was too large to swing through trees, and probably, therefore, also lost its tail. Its wide chest, broad shoulders, and lack of tail would make it conspicuous among apes – and remarkably like a human in appearance.

Gigantopitheces had an ape-like face and was covered with body hair. Their faces would have had the ape's retreating forehead and blunt nose, but with a more human set to the mouth and jaw. They did not make tools and had less-than-human intelligence. They probably did not live in close social groups. All these features are remarkably consistent with the reported appearance and behaviour of bigfoot/sasquatch.

Most authorities presume that Gigantopithecus is extinct because the most recent fossil teeth (from northern Vietnam) are 300,000 years old. Other finds date back a million years. But one early Gigantopithecus jaw from India is at least five million years old. Thus, the animals survived for four million years although we have no direct physical evidence that they did. So they could have survived during the 300,000 years since the owner of the most recent fossil remains died off and still leave no sign of being here.

A frame from the famous movie of a bigfoot filmed by Roger Patterson on 20 October 1967 at Bluff Creek in northern California. Expert opinion says the film was not faked.

'I RAN OUT OF FILM'

Although many American Indian tribes of the Pacific Northwest tell tales of bigfoot, and in them treat the creature just as they do less elusive animals, it was not until 1958 that the American public at large became aware of the bigfoot phenomenon. In the summer of 1958 strange, giant footprints cropped up around some road-making equipment at Bluff Creek in northern California. The tracks appeared several nights in a row, alarming the workers who found them. Once the major San Francisco papers picked up the story, it soon got national attention. Bigfoot had become the ultimate reclusive media star.

The next major sighting, which also netted a major piece of evidence, came in 1967. On 20 October that year Roger Patterson and Bob Gimlin of Yakima, Washington, went to Bluff Creek in the hope of catching sight of a bigfoot after hearing that tracks had been seen again in the area. They went on horseback, and were 40 or 50 miles from the nearest road when they rounded a bend on the trail and came to a creek. In Gimlin's words: 'Here this thing stood by the creek, just stood. We were on one side of the creek, the creature on the other and our horses went crazy. Roger's little horse just went bananas.'

Patterson managed to haul out the 16-mm movie camera, loaded with colour film, that he was carrying in his saddlebag.

'This creature turned,' said Gimlin, 'and started to walk away from us, just slow like a man would if he were just walking down the street, but as it did this, Roger ran across the creek behind it, but then he stumbled on a sandbar... He was shooting the camera while he was running. He hollered back for me when he stumbled and fell. He said, "Cover me!" and, naturally, I knew what he meant.

'So I rode across the creek on my horse and took my .30-06 rifle out of the saddle scabbard and just stood there (pointing but not aiming the rifle at the beast). When I did this, this creature was... about 90 feet [away] – and it turned and looked at me; just turned as it was walking away. It never stopped walking. And then... I heard Roger say, "Oh my God, I ran out of film.'

Gimlin remains adamant that he and Patterson saw a genuine bigfoot that day. Two things support his contention. First, Patterson is now dead, and Gimlin has more to gain financially from a confession to a hoax than stoutly maintaining the opposite – after all, he owns no rights in the film.

Second, the oft-mentioned possibility that a third party hoaxed the two bigfoot-hunters seems highly unlikely. To begin with, such a prankster would have had to have anticipated the pair's moves over many miles of rough country, seeing them but not being seen. Even if the hypothetical hoaxer had managed that feat of fieldcraft, only an idiot would risk getting in the way of a shot from Gimlin's powerful hunting rifle; the .30-06 round will bring down a bear.

And some expert scientific opinion backs the men's claim. One expert who studied the film, Dmitri Donskoy, Professor of Biomechanics at the Soviet Central Institute of Physical Culture in Moscow, noted that the creature's gait was that of an animal with enormous weight and strength, and that the movement of the whole body was fluid and confident. 'These factors... allow us to evaluate the gait of the creature as a natural movement without any sign of the artfulness that one would see in an imitation,' he concluded. 'At the same time, with all the diversity of locomotion illustrated by the creature of the footage, its gait as seen is absolutely non-typical of man.'

Another expert, Donald Grieve, Reader in Biomechanics at the Royal Free Hospital in London, was similarly impressed, but had a reservation. He felt that if the camera speed – which Patterson did not know for sure – had been set at 24 frames per second, the film could be showing a large, walking man. But if the film had been shot at 18 frames per second, no human being would be able to match the movements shown. He concluded with rare honesty: 'My subjective impressions have oscillated between total acceptance of the Bigfoot on the grounds that the film would be difficult to fake, to one of irrational rejection based on an emotional response to the possibility that the Bigfoot actually exists.'

The leading US authority on bigfoot, Professor Grover Krantz of Washington State University, made a detailed analysis of the movie in 1991, and concluded that it was indeed shot at 18 frames per second. The animal's movements, he believes, were impossible for a human to imitate, and convincingly show the creature's massiveness and strength. And he noted that its huge size, and muscles to match, were well outside the normal range of human variation. In other words, if Patterson's bigfoot had been a man in a fur suit, he would have been a giant who had pumped an awful lot of iron.

DEAD OR ALIVE

As shown by this artist's impression, bigfoot towers over an average-sized man.

More impressive evidence for the reality of bigfoot comes from a set of footprints that were discovered and cast by US Forest Service workers in 1982, in the Blue Mountains along the Washington– Oregon border. The prints were made in very fine soil that was slightly damp. All the casts show ridges on the skin under the toes and on the soles. These are just like fingerprints, and only the palms and soles of higher primates have them. Forty police fingerprinters have studied these casts over the years, and have all concluded that the footprints must have been made by one or more genuine bigfeet.

Opinion among anthropologists and primatologists who have seen the casts is mixed. Many suggested that the casts had been made from human footprints that had somehow been enlarged – a latex mould of a footprint will expand by 50 per cent when soaked in kerosene. This trick also expands the spacing between the ridges by 50 per cent. All the fingerprint experts noted that the ridges on these footprints were spaced just like those on the skin of other primates.

Despite all this circumstantial evidence, the only thing that will convince mainstream science of the reality of bigfoot will be part or all of a specimen itself, dead or alive. Professor Krantz remarks that 'a single lower jaw would be enough to establish not only its existence, but whether Gigantopithecus is still with us'.

INFESTED WATERS

Bigfoot is by no means the only mystery man-beast in North America, nor the strangest. The prize for the most bizarre has to go to a nightmarish creature nicknamed Lizard Man.

Witnesses describe it as 7 ft tall, walking upright like a man – but with green scaly skin, glowing red eyes, three toes on each foot and three fingers – each sprouting a 4 in long claw - on each hand. This grotesque animal, or apparition, first introduced itself to humanity around 2 a.m. on 29 June 1988, near Scape Ore Swamp, outside the one-horse town of Bishopville in Lee County, South Carolina.

Seventeen-year-old Christopher Davis had just finished changing a flat tyre on his car when he saw 'something large' running towards him across a nearby field. As the creature came nearer, Davis leaped into the vehicle and tried to slam the door – only to see the thing seize it and try to wrench it open. Davis had plenty of time – more than he would have liked – to note the fine details of its unlovely appearance. Davis eventually got the car going and made his getaway. When he got home, shaking with fright, he found long scratches on the car roof, and the wing mirror in serious disarray.

Others encountered Lizard Man that summer, but none helped solve the mystery of what the creature was. However, records show that scaly and apparently aquatic man-beasts have been reported before, in many parts of North America.

Such creatures sound like a fantasy, or a hoax, or merely the effect on surprised witnesses of a person in a diving suit. But there is an odd twist to the Lizard Man tale, especially if one bears in mind the possibility that bigfoot and its international relations may be a surviving form of the officially extinct Gigantopithecus. In 1982, palaeontologists Drs Dale A. Russell and R. Skguin of the Canadian National Museum of Natural Sciences published a paper in which they set out what a dinosaurian equivalent of a human being may have looked like, had the dinosaurs survived to the present. They suggest it would have been a two-legged creature with three-fingered hands, and in general would have looked startlingly like Lizard Man.

MONSTERS FROM THE DEEP

Since pre-biblical times, sailors have returned home from long voyages with tales of huge monsters and cunning sea serpents. Many stories can be attributed to the lonely nights at sea, and alcoholic solace, but should these include the testimony of senior naval officers, and the unidentifiable carcasses washed up upon remote shores?

'He had a large body and a small alligator-like head. The neck seemed to be medium size, matching the size of the head. The body was very large, shaped somewhat like a seal. There was a mane of bristly hair or fur which ran down the middle of his head.

'He would surface the upper part of his body and glide out of the water with the lower part of his body remaining submerged. The portion of his body which was visible measured about 40 feet in length. We estimate his weight to be between 35 and 40 tons over all.

'At no time did the whole body show. He stayed on the surface no longer than 40 seconds at a time. You could hear the heavy weight of his upper body when he dove below, creating a large splash and a subsequent wake. He surfaced four times in 20 minutes during which we were trying to stay clear of him. The Captain changed course to steer away from him and the queer fellow surfaced on our starboard beam...

'Another peculiar thing about him was that when he'd surface he would turn his head looking towards us and it seemed to us he was playful and curious. Another point was that on the upper part of his body there were two flippers, similar to those of a seal.'

So runs part of a report of a sea-monster sighting on 3 September 1959 by the cook, Joseph H. Bourassa, of the scalloper *Noreen*. The ship was 120 miles out from Bermuda, east of Pollock. Bourassa had been at sea for 20 years, and had never before seen anything like what he saw that day.

NAVAL REPORTS

What are sea monsters? How many kinds of them are there? Compare Bourassa's account with this, from an officer of the Imperial German Navy who was aboard the U-boat U28 when, during World War One, the submarine blew the British *Iberian* out of the water in the North Atlantic:

'A little later pieces of wreckage, and among them a gigantic sea-animal, writhing and struggling wildly, were shot out of the water to a height of 60 to 100 feet... the animal sank out of sight after 10 or 15 seconds... It was about 60 feet long, was like a crocodile in shape and had four limbs with powerful webbed feet and a long tail tapering to a point.'

If this creature bears little enough resemblance to the animal in the first account quoted, try this one:

'Then I saw this great eel-like monster rear its head like a Scotch terrier struck by curiosity. Its eyes were red and green, like the port and starboard lights of a ship. It was about ninety feet long. As we approached within 200 feet, it rose out of the water, with its seven humps like a camel and its face like a cow, and didn't make any noise, but I thought it should have mooed. Then it uttered an eerie bellow, like a bull whale in its last agony and reared up, perhaps thirty feet, perhaps fifty, and flopped over on its back. Along its flanks was a phosphorescent glow. By this time we had five searchlights on it, and it turned to the side and dived.'

The report came from First Officer A.E. Richards, who witnessed the episode from the bridge of the liner *Santa Lucia* in the long thin dawn light of 21 October 1933. The ship was off Sheringham Point near Victoria, in Cadboro Bay, Vancouver Island, British Columbia. The bay is famous for its resident sea monster 'Caddy' or, more pretentiously, Cadborosaurus.

One more example will drive home the point to which we are making so laborious a pilgrimage:

'It looked like an elephant waving its trunk, but the trunk was a long neck with a small head on the end, like a snake's head. It had humps on the back which moved in a funny way. The colour was black or very dark brown, and the skin seemed to be like a sealion's... the animal frightened me... I do not like the way it moved when it was swimming.'

'The animal' is called morgawr, the Cornish Celtic word for 'sea giant'. It made many appearances off the Cornish coast in the 1970s, and this particular witness, known only as Mary R, actually managed to photograph it, in February 1976, as it played in the sea off Rosemullion Head near Falmouth. The creature bears a striking resemblance to the popular image of the Loch Ness monster, and for all anyone knows may be of the same family, although Mary F. estimated its length to be no more than 15–18 ft – a veritable infant beside Nessie, and a positive midget compared to the monstrous 'eel-like' animal that First Officer Richards saw disporting itself off Vancouver Island.

PANDORA'S BOX

And there lies the rub. On the face of it, no one sea monster seems to bear much likeness to another. So what are we dealing with? The usual catalogue of possibilities and explanations presents itself unbidden – hallucinations, misidentifications, bored sailors livening up a ship's log to bemuse posterity, tired and emotional witnesses (considerably less of a rarity at sea than monster sightings: many long-haul freighters are navigated through a sea-fog of alcohol).

Or are we back in the world of officially extinct or simply officially overlooked animals? There is some reason to believe that some apparently extinct creatures have survived in the sea. The ostensibly freshwater Loch Ness monster, for instance, may be a marine animal, a surviving plesiosaur, that merely visits the Loch on occasion. On the evidence, there is no compelling reason to suppose for an instant that scientists have catalogued all the animals that live in the world's oceans. The waters, after all, cover roughly two-thirds of the surface of the Earth, and they keep on presenting little surprises to our friends in the laboratory coats. Just to cite three examples: in 1958, a previously unknown species of porpoise, now called the 'cochito', was found in the Gulf of California; eight years later 'megamouth' was discovered, hauled up on the anchor of a Hawaiian survey ship – a shark so different

A German U-Boat of World War One vintage. When one such craft torpedoed a British freighter, a 60 ft long sea serpent was blown out of the water at the same time.

from other sharks that zoologists had to create an entire new family to accommodate it, and it duly entered the record books, too, as the third largest known species of its kind; and in 1983 a new species of killer whale, the Prudes Bay, peculiar to the Antarctic, was added to zoology's roll of honour.

Honest scientists know that they have not plumbed the depths of the riches of life hidden in the oceans. The same honesty makes their hair, quite rightly, stand on end at the thought that untold biological riches are being destroyed in the Amazon rainforests every day. Biologists do not know what we may be losing as the fires of greed consume trees, herbs, insects, mammals and birds by the square mile every minute. They only know such a vast and fecund area must be a living treasure house. So it is with the seas of the world. There have to be creatures there waiting, willingly or not, to be discovered, but the seas of the world are harder, vaster, more expansive and more treacherous to explore than any rainforest, and that is the scientists' problem.

*A massive sea serpent was spotted from HMS **Daedalus** in 1848, and this engraving was based on an eyewitness's drawing sent to the Lords of the Admiralty by Captain M'Quhoe, the ship's commander.*

MONSTERS OF THE BIBLICAL SEAS

Our problem, for the time being – perhaps in the forlorn hope of persuading scientists to recognize that there is a potentially fruitful field of research waiting to be taken up – is to make sense of such material as we have. There is plenty of circumstantial evidence that sea monsters exist: but how good is it? Leaving aside the mistakes, hallucinations, hoaxes and misperceptions of drunken sailors, we are left with two basic possibilities as to the origin or reality of sea monsters.

First is the possibility that some, at least, of the reported sightings are of animals that have survived their official 'extinction'. Second is the possibility that these are creatures – some rare, some perhaps less so – that have simply eluded the eyes of science. They are not 'unknown' or 'unexplained' animals, but simply unidentified ones.

Whatever we are dealing with, there is nothing new about them. Large and terrifying animals have been known to exist since Old Testament times, and from the days before those ancient texts were written as well. Jonah was swallowed by a 'whale'. The other monster of the biblical seas, Leviathan, is also mentioned in greater or lesser detail in various places in the Psalms of David, and the Books of Isaiah and Job. One senses that these passages reveal what only the Lord can know of creatures that swim beneath the face of the deep.

'HUGEST OF LIVING CREATURES'

The most extensive description of Leviathan comes in Chapter 41 of that dark, bejewelled hymn to an ancient existentialism, the Book of Job. In this, the Lord continues to upbraid Job for his presumptions, and paints a picture of such power that one cannot help feeling not only that the passage seems to be celebrating the tremendous vitality of this creature, but that it is revered even by the one that created it:

'Canst thou draw out leviathan with an hook? or his tongue with a cord which thou lettest down?

Wilt thou play with him as with a bird? or wilt thou bind him for thy maidens?

Shall the companions make a banquet of him? shall they part him among the merchants?

Lay thine hand upon him, remember the battle, do no more.

Behold, the hope of him is in vain; shall not one be cast down even at the sight of him?

None is so fierce that dare stir him up ...

Who can open the doors of his face? his teeth are terrible round about.

His scales are his pride, shut up together as with a close seal.

The flakes of his flesh are joined together: they are firm in themselves; they cannot be moved.

When he raiseth himself up, the mighty are afraid: by reason of breakings they purify themselves.

He esteemeth iron as straw, and brass as rotten wood.

The arrow cannot make him flee: sling-stones are turned with him into stubble.

He maketh the deep to boil like a pot: he maketh the sea like a pot of ointment.

He maketh a path to shine after him; one would think the deep to be hoary.

Upon earth there is not his like, who is made without fear.

He beholdeth all high things: he is a king over all the children of pride.'

All the elements of a sea-monster sighting seem to be here: the terrific size, the sense of its enormous strength and invulnerability, the confident - even casual - indifference of the creature to its puny human observers, and its sheer, awe-inspiring strangeness.

A 17th-century English poet, John Milton, a mere bricklayer in comparison to the Hebrew architect of language, was also entranced by this creature, but he could only grope blindly to recapture the drift of his predecessor's magnificent vision:

'There Leviathan Hugest of living creatures, on the deep
Stretch'd like a promontory sleeps or swims,
And seems a moving land.. . '

But what was Leviathan? Can we tell, at this distance in time?

A TWISTED SERPENT

The translators of the Anglican Church's Authorised Version of the Bible appointed by King James did not actually translate the original Hebrew word, which was livyathun, probably because they could not connect its meaning to anything they knew in their own world. Literally, it means 'twisted serpent'.

The 5th- or 6th-century BC Jewish poet who recorded the trials of Job seems himself to have had only a sketchy idea of what Leviathan was. The ancient Hebrews, curiously, were not a seafaring nation, although they were always within reach of the Mediterranean Sea. Possibly all sea beasts were somewhat mysterious to them, although they would have been aware that some were of unnaturally large size.

The vision of a monstrous sea animal that possessed the poet who wrote the Book of Job was possibly, and in part, derived from sightings of whales or sharks. The most likely source was probably foreign sailors' accounts of sperm whales, the animals on which the neighbouring Phoenicians – known in the Bible as Canaanites, and living in what is now Lebanon – based their whaling industry.

The biblical story of Job is based on a Middle Eastern (not Hebrew) legend much older than the poet who re-created it, and his notion of Leviathan was almost certainly influenced by regional tales of dragons. Images of monsters mentioned in the myths of Egypt or Assyria, such as Tiamat and Apophis, would also have influenced the poet's vision. 'Leviathan', then, means any great sea or land monster.

The Belgian zoologist Dr Bernard Heuvelmans, who has made the most detailed study of sea-monster reports in modern times, suggests that Chapter 41 of Job, quoted in part above, suggests not the whale but a melodramatic account of a long-necked sea serpent.

The phrases describing a creature that 'raiseth himself' up out of the water and 'beholdeth all high things' certainly suggest an animal with a long neck. And 'the flakes of his flesh [translated elsewhere as 'the members of his body'] are joined together' may be a half-explanatory reference to the sinuous humped appearance of these creatures that (now as then) so many modern reports of sea monsters also mention.

This aspect of Leviathan rather qualifies the possibility that the true source of its reputation is the sperm whale or sharks. This is also the moment to remark on the sceptics' claim that the 'humps' of sea monsters are really a misperception of dolphins leaping in line. This is the kind of dozy (and pretty desperate) rationalization that could only come from people who have never seen dolphins in the sea. They are unmistakable for anything but dolphins.

Was Leviathan no more than a compound of mythical beasts, hearsay, and ignorance? Or was it all that, but with the hearsay relating directly to actual sea monsters? This seems at least possible. Leviathan, then, is at least partly a genuine unidentified creature.

BEEF-RED FLESH

In June 1983, amateur naturalist Owen Burnham was on holiday with his family on the coast of the Gambia, West Africa, taking a break from their home in neighbouring Senegal. During the night of 11/12 June, a large unidentified animal was washed ashore on the beach near where they were staying. They heard about this the following morning. At 8.30 a.m. Burnham, together with his brother and sister and father, went down to the shore to look for the creature. They found it easily enough, along with two Africans who were trying to sever its head so that they could sell the skull to tourists.

The animal was battered, distended with internal gas, and smelled foul, but it was essentially complete and had not begun to decompose. It had not been dead long. Burnham was familiar with all of the major land and sea creatures native to the region, but he was unable to identify this one. The group persuaded the two native entrepreneurs to stop for long enough to let them measure the animal. Burnham, lacking a camera, also made sketches of it and counted the teeth.

The animal was smooth-skinned, with four flippers. One hind flipper had been torn off, and the other damaged. Its overall length was about 15 ft, of which 5 ft were taken up by a long, pointed tail whose cross-section was like a rounded-off triangle.

The animal had a slightly domed forehead, and at the end of its 18 in long snout were what looked like a pair of nostrils. Thinking it might be some form of marine mammal (a whale or dolphin), Burnham looked for a blowhole, but found none. Nor could he see any mammary glands. If there were any male organs they were too damaged to recognize. The creature's long, thin jaws were very tightly closed; Burnham said he had 'a job' to prise them apart. He counted 80 teeth, which he noted were evenly distributed, very sharp, and similar in shape to a barracuda's but whiter and thicker.

The alleged sea monster photographed by Robert Le Serrec at Stonehaven Bay, Hook Island, Australia, on 12 December 1964.

The flippers were round and solid. There were no toes, claws or nails. When the Africans returned and completed their work of removing the head, the witnesses could see that the animal's vertebrae were very thick. It took the men 20 minutes' dedicated hacking with a machete to sever it. The animal's flesh was dark red, 'like beef'.

Burnham speaks Mandinka, the local language, fluently and asked the men the name of the animal. They told him kunthum belein, Mandinka for 'cutting jaws'; this is what the coastal fishermen call dolphins.

Burnham later described the unknown animal to many native fishermen in the area in the hope that they might be able to identify it, but none had ever seen anything like it. He concluded that the butchers on the beach had called it a 'dolphin' because it looked vaguely like one.

Burnham then wrote to various authorities on wildlife to try to get further leads, but got no real help. Most suggested animals that he had already been able to rule out thanks to his familiarity with the denizens of the region. Burnham also said that he 'looked through encyclopedias and every book I could lay hands on' in trying to identify the mystery animal. Eventually, he found a photograph of the skull of the extinct Australian *Kronosaurus queenslandicus*, which he felt was the nearest thing he had seen so far. However, he noted that that skull was 10 ft long: clearly it was not the same as the creature he had seen.

AWESOME

Burnham's detailed reports of his find, and the sketches and measurements he made, were analysed at length by zoologist Dr Karl Shuker in the mid-1980s. Shuker rapidly ruled out a number of near-contenders, and realized that the only creatures that at all resembled Burnham's find had long since died out – and, what was more, had been extinct for more than 60 million years. One was the pliosaur, a family of short-necked plesiosaurs that included the Kronosaurus whose skull Burnham had recognized but rejected. The other was a group of non-scaly sea crocodiles, called thalattosuchians, who had slender bodies and four paddle-like limbs. Their tails had a dorsal fin, but a thalattosuchian whose fin had been torn off or scuffed away would look amazingly like the beast of Burnham's sketches. And if thalattosuchians had survived into the present, it is possible that they would no longer have such a fin.

Without any physical remains for direct examination, however, the Gambian creature cannot be positively identified one way or the other. But the Gambian find suggests, at least, that not all of the reptiles of prehistory died out with the dinosaurs.

Burnham himself says: 'When I think of the coelacanth I don't like to think what could be at the bottom of the sea. I'm not looking for a prehistoric animal, only trying to identify what was the strangest thing I'll ever see. I couldn't believe this creature was lying in front of me. Even now I can remember every minute detail of it. To see such a thing was awesome.'

ESCAPING DETECTION

The magnum opus of sea-monster studies is Belgian cryptozoologist Dr Bernard Heuvelmans's *In the Wake of the Sea Serpents*. In this, Heuvelmans analysed 587 sea-monster sightings made between 1639 and 1964. After disposing of hoaxes, misidentifications and reports too vague to be useful, he was still left with 358 sightings, and was able to sort these into nine basic types.

These are the 'long necked' sea serpent – the most often-reported of all sea monsters, with four flippers, a cigar-shaped body and a capacity for swimming very fast indeed – which grows to between 15 and 65 ft long; marine saurians, seen only in tropical waters in mid-ocean, which may reach 60 ft in length; merhorses; many-humped monsters; super-otters (not reported since 1848 and possibly now extinct); many-finned monsters; super-eels; fathers-of-all-the-turtles; and yellowbellies. The last Heuvelmans believes may be an as yet unidentified fish, possibly a shark.

There is no logical reason why the seas should not be hiding any number of unidentified species of animal (especially if they are both shy and few in number) from the official catalogues of marine science. They will doubtless continue to roam the oceans, bemuse and astonish those few who are lucky enough to spot them, and be overlooked by the guardians of orthodoxy. Probably the creatures themselves would prefer it to stay that way.

PAGAN PLACES,
PAGAN POWERS

*The ancient remains of powerful pagan civilizations cast
long shadows into the present. The bright light of
scientific investigation only deepens the mysteries
surrounding the strange occurrences and unnerving
experiences, and makes the shadows darker still…*

While the Earth is full of strange, unexpected and inexplicable creatures, it is no less replete with mysterious and enigmatic works of mankind itself.

The ancient remains of lost civilizations – the great monuments of Stonehenge in England, Carnac in France, the Serpent Mound in Ohio, USA, the stone circles of West Africa – are only the most renowned of a myriad of such sites whose purpose is still obscure and whose meaning has been all but lost with the passing of those who built them.

Yet the world's mysterious places exercise a perennial fascination. They do so not simply because we still do not really understand them, or because they are awesome in themselves; but partly, at least, because we sense that they were enigmatic even to the people who created them.

Very strange things are traditionally said to happen at ancient sites. Very strange things still happen in such places today.

THE PETRIFIED MAIDENS

According to the pioneeering 'Earth mysteries' researcher Paul Devereux, a number of people have had bizarre experiences while passing along a particular 300 yd long stretch of a country lane that runs past the ancient stone circle called Rollright in Oxfordshire, England. One, a member of the Dragon Project research group, was watching a car containing two people approach the stone circle along the road – when the vehicle vanished. On another occasion, a scientist saw a huge, dog-like creature with coarse grey hair momentarily appear and then vanish. Another witness, a woman, saw an old-fashioned gypsy caravan briefly appear and then disappear in much the same way.

Odd occurrences have been associated with such megalithic sites since time immemorial, and the stones, then as now, have been held to possess mysterious powers. There is nothing new about stone circles attracting, or generating, spectres, visions of fairies and other odd creatures from folklore such as black dogs (an instance of which was, presumably, what was seen by the scientist noted above). At the Bryn-yr-Ellyllon mound near Mold in Wales, for example, a huge golden figure has been seen on many occasions – and the name of the barrow itself means 'hill of the goblins'.

It is commonly believed that the number of individual stones in certain circles cannot be counted, although many sites are associated with specific numbers, most often the key mystical figures of three, seven and nine. Possibly one reason they cannot be counted is that, so the legends say, they can move of their own accord. Many stones are reputed to resist any attempt to move them but, if they are shifted out of place by some means, will put themselves back where they came from. Others are still more independent. One such is the Enstone near Oxford – it is particularly regular in its habits: it reputedly takes a drink every midnight at a neighbouring stream.

There may be a connection between this kind of belief and the tradition that many standing stones, especially groups of them, were once people, now petrified. The Merry Maidens in Cornwall are so called because that is what they once were – a mite too merry, perhaps, as they danced themselves to exhaustion and turned to stone where they collapsed. Nearby are the musicians, presumably responsible for whipping them into their frenzy: the Two Pipers, and the Blind Fiddler, now pillars of granite. The Rollright

The Rollright Stones in Oxfordshire, which have been known to exert very peculiar influences on people in their vicinity.

Stones are reputedly a king and his knights, petrified by a witch.

Not all the powers associated with the ancient stones are so spooky: many have the reputation of being able to heal or impart healing properties. Water that has been splashed on the stones at Stonehenge will cure ailments. Sick children were traditionally passed through the hole in the famous Men-an-Tol in Cornwall. Other sites have the same capacity, especially those associated with water such as holy wells and ancient spas. There is evidence that the baths at Bath, for instance, have been regarded as curative for some 7,000 years.

All these unexpected properties have one thing in common: they suggest that there is something strangely alive about these places. They are, in other words, places where a peculiar kind of energy concentrates. This half-hidden idea is reflected in another tradition about ancient places – that many of them are associated with dragons. Stories, myths and legends occur in virtually all cultures, all over the world, of a serpent, worm or dragon whose qualities are, to say the least, peculiarly ambiguous. So it is worth taking a brief survey of dragon-lore before pondering how it fits into the puzzle of the ancient sites.

THE DRAGON GUARDS

In the oldest Indian and Babylonian myths, which are roughly 4,000 years old, the destruction of an enraged dragon brings the release of life-giving waters. These myths are not moral fables, but creation myths – poetic accounts of how the world was made. The importance of the dragon in these stories is that it releases an indispensable source of life and energy into the world – but at the price of having to confront the creature.

Everyone familiar with Genesis is aware of the double nature of the serpent in the Garden of Eden. It is an actual, physical presence, and also it represents a singular moral dilemma. To follow the path of the serpent, as Adam and Eve do, is to lose paradise and innocence but to gain knowledge and moral responsibility – free will.

This theme runs through all serpent myths, all over the world. In Anglo-Saxon Britain, the epic – and essentially pagan – poem *Beowulf* revolves in part around a fire-breathing 'worm' – in other words, a dragon – who is enraged because one of the aging Beowulf's subjects has stolen a cup from the hoard of treasure it has guarded for three centuries. (The poet makes a point of saying that dragons seek out and hoard treasure.) In killing the dragon, Beowulf is mortally wounded. Once again, the serpent is associated with something desirable and yet destructive. His power is also, finally, irresistible, and is potent in the cause of both good and ill.

Anglo-Saxon culture, like any other, had many roots. What we see in *Beowulf* is the fruit of tendrils that reach back to Norse and Celtic mythology, and beyond that to legends that have their known beginnings thousands of years ago, in the mythology of the Indo-European peoples of Central Asia. From the point of view of an investigation of prehistoric sites, what is also significant in this European dragon tradition is its connection with another piece of lore about the sites themselves: that is that many of them are reputed to be built on hoards of buried treasure.

Circular, holed stones like this one at Men-an-Tol, Cornwall, are reputed to have mysterious powers of healing.

The golden spectre seen at Bryn-yr-Ellyllon may be a reflection of this folk memory. Like the stones themselves, some hoards have minds of their own. At the neolithic mound of Willy Howe in north-eastern England, there is a tale that local people once attempted to dig out the chest of gold concealed at its centre. They tried to drag it from the earth with horses, but the chest simply burrowed deeper into the ground. As might be expected, many such prehistoric hoards are said to be guarded by dragons.

TREACHEROUS ELEMENTS

It's clear that in Western and Middle Eastern dragon-lore, the creature has both a material and a spiritual energy, but it is one that is neither simple nor entirely trustworthy.

Take the paradox that these fiery creatures have an affinity for water, for example. Water is the most treacherous element as well as the most vital. The same may be said of fire, the other 'element' that is inseparable from any concept of dragons. One hidden lesson here seems to be that both the most basic materials of survival and the great abstractions like moral freedom have a potential for both good and evil. Another hidden message is that struggle is inherent in all our dealings with the contradictory forces of life, despite the fact that we depend on them – or perhaps because we depend on them.

The most fundamental lesson that underlies these perceptions is that these are eternal verities; they are the very basic stuff of life. And so the spirit of the dragon never entirely dies. Indeed, in the Babylonian myth, the dragon was also the mother of all living things and, despite being slain, continues her immortal existence as a monstrous serpent who makes herself visible in wild storms at sea.

Dragons are everywhere associated with the most fundamental aspects of life. In the Mayan culture of Central America, which flourished between about AD 150 and AD 900, the serpent was 'lord of fire and time', and was also responsible for causing floods, earthquakes and storms. It is strange, given the distance between the Americas and Asia, that Chinese dragons are so similar in this respect.

In China, a vast and intricate dragon-lore grew up that detailed not only how long a dragon might live (5,000 years) and how many scales it had (81 or 117, depending on the school of thought) but the medicinal virtues of its teeth, liver or saliva and the significance of its behaviour as an augury of the weather.

Chinese dragons are, by Western standards, quite benevolent, but they too have an ambiguous nature. They are capable of shape-shifting, appearing in the guise of familiar animals at will, and, most importantly, they control the weather – which, as everyone knows, is neither predictable nor always benign. And to this day the Chinese believe that their dragons must be appeased and placated. The art of feng shui, which means 'wind and water', is entirely devoted to avoiding any disturbance to the 'paths of the dragon' (lung mei) when siting buildings in the landscape. Expert geomancers – 'earth diviners' – make elaborate calculations to ensure that this balance of nature is maintained. A famous modern example of their work is the alignment of the Hong Kong and Shanghai Bank in Hong Kong.

One of the most baffling and yet fascinating of all the enigmas associated with prehistoric sites and 'Earth mysteries' studies is the universal nature of dragon-lore. That the same image should reflect so many similar intuitions in so many different cultures, separated by huge gulfs of time and geography, suggests that we are confronted by something absolutely fundamental in the human psyche. And more: that this in turn suggests that the human mind has grasped something crucial about the nature of the Earth itself.

We have, in the dragon, an extraordinary concentration of ideas: a mythical beast that guards material or spiritual riches; the energies of the elements; and a connection with sites of 'Earth energy'. Researchers have also established that there is a connection between the ancient sites, the so-called ley lines that often connect them, and UFO sightings. Is it possible that dragons and UFOs are different forms of the same 'Earth energy'? And if so, are they shaped by the mind into the form most suited to a particular epoch – or do they cause the mind to perceive them in the most acceptable way?

That there are energies in the Earth, that they are most powerful around prehistoric sites, and that they have real effects on human consciousness, is attested not only by the feng shui geomancers and the long traditions of folklore – but by modern reports too.

WEIRD SENSATIONS

Paul Devereux collected one such account from local government official Peter Thornborrow. He was walking through the stone circle called Long Meg and Her Daughters in Cumbria, when he was suddenly assailed by a bizarre sensation of dizziness. He felt, he said later, as if he was 'not really there... not really in the same time'. He leaned against one of the stones to recover his normal senses. It responded by giving him what he could only describe as 'an electric shock'.

Devereux has also recorded that in 1986, as a young couple were driving on a country lane beside Cam Ingli, a peak and sacred site in the Preseli Hills in Pembrokeshire, west Wales, the girl felt a weird sensation of physical discomfort. She was sure the feeling was caused by the peak. The pair decided to test the idea. They drove on until the girl felt normal again, and then turned the car around and drove back over the same route. Once again, as they neared Carn Ingli, the strange and uncomfortable sensation returned.

Modern experience and traditional lore thus combine to confirm the strangeness of prehistoric sites. There is a long-standing belief that experiences like the two recounted above and the legacy of folklore clinging to these ancient places indicate that some form of paranormal or psychic energy is at work in them. Since the turn of the century, psychics have attempted to pick up the local 'vibrations' at standing stones, circles, barrows and mounds, and since the 1930s dowsers too have tried to unravel the secrets of these places. Unfortunately, the claimed results and 'discoveries' at any one site have been as many and various as the number of psychics or dowsers who have tried their skills there.

The aptly named Dragon Project was launched in England in 1977 to bring a comprehensive set of research methods to bear on the question of what kinds of energies might be present at prehistoric sites. The project decided to pursue two parallel lines of investigation: there would be room for dowsers and psychics to follow their own form of detective work, while a variety of scientific detection instruments would be used to search out and record the more conventional physical attributes of the sites.

This has involved recording levels of magnetism, radioactivity, infra-red radiation, among known physical forces, as well as recording and studying unexplained but theoretically conventional effects such as the strange light phenomena that have long been reported at or near many ancient sites. The psychic side of the research has been as inconclusive as any of the other attempts to use mind power to probe the secrets of the ancients, but the second, scientific line of enquiry has thrown up some intriguing results. Although this kind of monitoring deals in the standard scientific measures of physics, the actual levels discovered at the sites have been by no means conventional or consistent with normal, average ('background') levels for the areas concerned.

Science has begun to confirm folklore.

SECRET KNOWLEDGE – SECRET PURPOSES

At Long Meg, where Peter Thornborrow had the bizarre experience described earlier, Dragon Project researchers found that several of the standing stones there had small patches on them that were emitting a constant stream of gamma rays – in short, they were radioactive. The stones concerned were granite, which is naturally radioactive, but not to the degree of these particular stones. And it is distinctly unusual for granite to emit radiation of any kind from concentrated energy points such as these stones possessed.

This may or may not have been responsible for Thornborrow's experience, but researchers have noted that in places where natural radiation – from granite or other radioactive minerals, or from radon gas seeping from the ground – is higher than normal, some people have experienced apparently altered states of consciousness. Monitoring the radiation levels around the Rollright Stones revealed a fascinating fact about the 300 yd stretch of country lane where at least three people – whose accounts we gave above – had reported seeing spectral visions. Geiger counters showed far higher than normal background readings of radiation here.

Its source, the researchers concluded, was probably in energetic rocks in the hardcore used to lay the road's foundations.

This, like the stones at the ancient site, had come from local quarries – which suggests that whoever put the Rollright Stones in place was aware that the local rock had very special qualities. Those qualities were interesting to them because they serve their purposes. The key question after that is: what were their purposes? Some other odd qualities of ancient sites may help to get us nearer the answer to this crucial question.

Dragons might be defeated by the most irreverent means, but gaining the treasure of knowledge in their keeping would always bring fresh challenges.

RADIOACTIVE BURIAL CHAMBERS

People have experienced different strange effects at other sites with greater than the usual 'background' natural radiation. At Boleigh Fogou, an Iron Age underground stone chamber or 'souterrain' built from granite in Cornwall, a psychologist saw mysterious swirls and points of light moving over the inner rock surfaces. Similarly, inside the 5,000-year-old Cornish dolmen called Chun Quoit, archaeologist John Barnatt and photographer Brian Larkman both saw bands of light flashing along the underside of the capstone.

Most of Europe's ancient underground chambers of this kind are in areas whose basic rock formations are of granite, or where uranium has been found, so it can hardly be insignificant that in North America, Pueblo Indian underground ritual chambers, known as 'kivas', were likewise built in uranium-rich areas of what are now the Southwestern States. Bearing that in mind, it comes as no surprise to learn that the King's Chamber in Egypt's Great Pyramid was specially clad in granite, and that when members of the Dragon Project monitored the King's Chamber they found enhanced radiation levels there, at levels at least as high as those found inside the granite monuments of Britain.

The great stone sites of the ancient world are not unique among ancient monuments in registering unusually high – although by no means dangerous – levels of nuclear radiation. Holy wells, too, can be mildly radioactive, and there is evidence to suggest that at such 'homeopathic' levels nuclear radiation is actually beneficial, not harmful. As mentioned earlier, the famous hot springs at Bath, England have been known as healing waters for some 70 centuries, and are mildly radioactive. The waters of Chalice Well, Glastonbury – one of the holiest places in the world, if the legends are to be believed – are said to be radioactive. Dragon Project researchers have also recorded higher-than-average readings from geiger counters at a number of holy wells in the Celtic fringes of Britain in Wales, Cornwall and Scotland.

MAGNETIC MAGIC

Ancient sites, stone circles and solitary standing stones have all been known for decades to have strange effects on compasses and lodestones. Go to a standing stone or similar ancient site and the chances are it is in a place where there are peculiarities in the Earth's local magnetic field, or that it throws the standard measuring equipment – the gaussometer – out of true by a marked margin.

The Dragon Project found that scattered about Carn Ingli were areas where there were powerful anomalies in the local magnetic field. In these places, compass needles point south instead of north, and gaussometers show unexpected readings. As for individual stones creating bizarre magnetic effects – or being carefully placed where those effects are most marked – there is a host of instances. At Castlerigg, Cumbria, only the westernmost stone, alone among 38 stones at the circle, affects a compass needle. At the Gors Fawr stone circle in Wales, the outlying pillar, which indicates the direction of the midsummer sunrise, is also the only magnetic stone at the site. A serpentine outcrop on Mount Tamalpais, San Francisco (a magical place for the local American Indians), similarly causes compasses to spin. There are many other examples, and they can be found all over the world.

Even stranger is another magnetic anomaly that Dragon Project researchers have found at many ancient sites. They discovered that some standing stones show sudden fluctuations in their magnetic fields that last for only a few hours. Similar effects were found, quite independently of the Dragon Project work, at the Rollright Circle by the retired engineer Charles Brooker, who reported his discoveries in the international journal *New Scientist* in 1983.

Stonehenge, the most elaborately built of all the ancient megalithic sites.

The nature of these short-lived magnetic pulses is not understood by modern science, so what significance they may have had for the ancients so many thousands of years ago must be today entirely a matter for speculation. But then so is the means whereby the peoples of the ancient world, lacking modern instrumentation, recognized these qualities in the sites and in the stones they chose, in the first place. And why they chose them for these qualities is another question altogether.

THE STONES ARE SINGING

Some of the unexplained phenomena at ancient sites would not have needed any exotic instruments to detect. One is the often-reported appearance of peculiar and apparently intelligent lights in, around or near prehistoric remains. Another is the persistent presence of inexplicable noises at these places.

While alone inside Stonehenge one early morning in 1983, Gabriele Wilson heard a 'ringing' sound from one of the stones. At midsummer in 1987, Michael Woolf and Rachel Garcia heard 'a sudden, muffled thunderclap' that seemed to come 'from beneath the earth' at the 11 ft tall Blind Fiddler stone in Cornwall. Other researchers at the Rollright Stones have reported curious clicking noises issuing from the ground at night.

The ancients themselves witnessed such odd sounds at their sacred sites, as well. The two 60 ft tall statues known as the Colossi of Memnon, in the Valley of the Kings in Egypt, were cracked during an earthquake in 27 BC. After that, the northernmost of the two statues began to emit a strange sound at dawn each day. The noise was variously described as 'soft' and 'bell-like', 'a musical note' and even (by contrast) like 'a cord snapping'. People flocked from far and wide to the massive statue in the belief that it would act as an oracle. The sounds stopped when the cracks were eventually repaired.

Whatever the cause of these particular noises, modern researchers have long known that sounds at extremely high 'ultrasound' frequencies – well beyond the range of normal human hearing – can be detected at dawn coming from standing stones.

In January 1987 Dragon Project workers discovered that a 3 ft band around the middle of the tallest stone at the Rollright Circle was the source of a signal being picked up by their ultrasound receiver. The signal always ebbed away as the day wore on. It is possible that these signals were the by-product of transmissions from nearby military telecommunications stations, resonating in crystals in the stones. There is nothing secret or occult in the fact that crystals are sensitive to radio waves. On the other hand, the effect could be caused by some unknown process occurring in the Earth itself.

CENTRES OF POWER

The folklore interpretation of the weird sounds and lights that have been heard and seen around ancient sites has been quite logical, but it has also probably been back-to-front.

People who have intuitively recognized something strange about the ancient places have attributed other signs of their uniqueness to the spirits, ghosts or even fairies to whom they feel these places belong. But almost certainly this view is the wrong way round. It is much more likely that the sites for stone circles, burial mounds, kivas and other ceremonial centres were chosen exactly because they were (in the eyes of the builders, those who saw them first) already magical. Throwing out strange noises and weird darting lights, such sites were advertising themselves as ideal for magical purposes.

As we have seen, these signs were also signals – that even stranger effects would take place in these places on the minds of those brave enough to enter them. How those effects were taken advantage of and controlled is one of the central mysteries of the purpose of the prehistoric sites.

This mystery may not be entirely unsolved, but even to glimpse the solution, we must first look at the stars, the Sun and the Moon, the tree at the centre of the world, and at mysterious patterns on a parched desert floor.

CELESTIAL SIGNS IN SACRED PLACES

Stonehenge, with its toppled stones and sad grandeur, is but the last in a series of sacred temples which changed drastically in both appearance and purpose over several thousand years. The original Stonehenge was a place of earth and timber – and rotting corpses.

The curious physical qualities of the sites where the ancients built their sacred places must have had specific advantages for those who used them. But what did they use them for?

One tenacious myth that has taken hold in many a mind is that the prehistoric temples and stone circles were used as astronomical observatories. This idea has been going the rounds since the late 19th century, when archaeologists first recognized the way that Stonehenge, on Salisbury Plain in England, was built to coincide with a number of seasonal astronomical events. It was full of 'sightlines' between the stones to significant sunrises, sunsets, phases of the Moon, and movements of the stars.

Many of the conclusions drawn by the early pioneers of astro-archaeology have since been found to be – not to put too fine a point on it – wildly wrong. In spite of this, their ideas were revived in the 1960s. It is in fact illogical and outmoded to believe that a place like Stonehenge could have been used to watch and mark the behaviour of the Sun and Moon and stars.

The illogic of such an idea is easily exposed, for to build these sites in the first place, someone must have known beforehand all the astronomical phenomena to which their stones are so precisely aligned. The builders of the great prehistoric monuments had already made their observations of the sky and taken their measurements on the ground long before they laid a single stone. It is an especially piquant notion that such a massive construction as Stonehenge could ever have had the flexibility that is essential to a real observatory. Such places are not evidence of some kind of primitive science, as the first researchers believed, and as many who mourn for the 1960s still do today.

'No astronomer-priests surveyed the skies there,' Professor Aubrey Burl has written plainly of Stonehenge. 'Superstition, not science, dominated the minds of its builders. '

COSMIC DRAMA

Not only did the ancients see the material world in a different way from us, they seem to have found a link between space and time, and between solid reality and the realm of the spirit. Ancient astronomy was a religious quest, and Stonehenge is one of the most dramatic and visible pieces of evidence of that. Its role was not that of being a record or marker of a scientific view of the Universe and the Earth within it. It was built as a stone stage set for a cosmic drama. But by the time it reached its most complex form in stone, it was not even the greatest of such constructions in the ancient world.

Stonehenge seems to be a symbol of enormous stability, and that it is a monument to an apprehension of cosmic reality that has long since been lost only makes the splendour of the place, emptied now of its original meaning, all the more moving. But the toppled stones and magnificent relics of grandeur that we see today are in reality the last and, amazingly, the least complicated of a series of temples that were built on this single site over a period of some 16 centuries.

A TEMPLE OF DEATH

The very first Stonehenge was made not of stone, but of earth. Around 3200 BC the skin-clad peasants of the farming tribes of Salisbury Plain dug out a wide circular earthwork known as a henge. It had an inner bank broken by what seemed to be two entrances. One was 35 ft wide on the north-east arc of the henge. The second was narrower, and was set precisely south of the centre of the henge. The builders probably found this point by halving the distance between the points on the horizon where the midwinter Sun rose and set.

Stonehenge is perhaps the most impressive of all megalithic monuments – yet its architectural splendour hides the slow spiritual decay of those who built it.

In 1723 the antiquarian William Stukeley (who also discovered the other great prehistoric site in southern England, Avebury) noticed that the south-west to north-east axis of this original construction, and thus the north-eastern 'entrance', was almost in line with the midsummer sunrise. Later researchers realized that Stukeley had made an error. The builders had been interested in another heavenly body: not the Sun, but the Moon.

Outside the north-east gap in the earthwork each year, they had set up a post in line with the most northerly rising-point of the Moon. Unlike the rising-point of the midsummer Sun, this moves gradually across the horizon between two extremes, over a period of 18.61 years. The ancient builders had recorded this slow motion over six cycles and more than a century of observations, until they were certain of the most northerly point where the Moon rose. They aligned one side of the north-east 'entrance' with this point.

The first Stonehenge was a temple to the Moon. It was also a temple of death.

ROTTING CORPSES

For more than a millennium the ancestors of the first builders of Stonehenge had buried their dead in long barrows that pointed to the Moon somewhere between its midwinter rising-point in the north and its midsummer rising in the south. For these people, death and the Moon were inextricably bound up together.

The north-east 'entrance' was in fact a window, one side aligned to the midpoint of the Moon's arc, the other to its northernmost rising. Marking these lines of sight were pairs of tall stones at the edges of the causeway. On its eastern side the middle of the lunar cycle was marked by the now-fallen Slaughter Stone. The famous Heel Stone, beyond it, was never a pointer for the midsummer sunrise. It was always a lunar marker.

At the centre of the first Stonehenge was a 100 ft wide roofed building where corpses were laid until their flesh had rotted, and then the bones would be buried in the long barrows on the plain outside. This rite was long practised in Neolithic Britain and was always associated with the Moon.

The power of this strange holy mortuary was enhanced by more dead, deliberately acquired. In ditches at the ends of both entrances through the earthwork lie the bones of adults and children, sacrificed to the cold-faced, sky-sailing, shape-shifting silvery goddess of death that these people worshipped.

A TEMPLE OF THE SUN

Around 2200 BC, a new people arrived in the region and converted Stonehenge into a temple of the Sun. Whether they were a branch of what archaeologists call Beaker Folk or not, their characteristic remains are bright-red, geometrically patterned beaker pots. Teams of men bagged Welsh bluestones into the already ancient earthen enclosure and set them up in two concentric circles. Some of the slabs were shaped as lintels, imitating the earlier timber building.

The stones themselves had come from the Preseli mountains in south-west Wales. Legend said they were brought the 200 miles from those bleak, rainswept hills by none other than Merlin, the mysterious guardian mage of Camelot and King Arthur. Later, theories as elaborate as any concocted to account for the building of the pyramids in Egypt sprang fully formed from the brains of unwary academics to explain the logistics of moving the giant blocks to Salisbury Plain in an age that lacked the wheel. The favourite theory had copper prospectors hauling the things on logs and floating them down rivers.

The real history of Stonehenge is full of surprises. The intrepid-stone-age-trucker theory is even less likely to be true than the rather more pleasing image of Merlin wafting the stones across the Severn with his wand. Archaeologists have found a Welsh bluestone in a barrow that was abandoned ten centuries before Stonehenge was built, yet only seven miles from the site. The prosaic truth is that the bluestones were literally lying about the local landscape, waiting to be used by anyone who was minded to do so. They were dumped there by glacial action, perhaps as long as 8,000 years before Stonehenge was even thought of.

The people who brought the stones changed the axis of the henge. They widened the right-hand side of the north-east 'entrance', so that the middle of the break in the earthwork was now in line with the midsummer sunrise. On either side of the Heel Stone, they dug an avenue that led downhill towards the River Avon.

For these people, beakers and Sun worship went together. Tissue-thin discs of gold have been found with the pots in their distinctive round barrows and are decorated with circles and crosses, and they seem to be symbols of the Sun.

The newcomers placed four stones at the corners of a large rectangle around the unfinished stone circles. Now called the Four Stations, these created three sightlines. The short side of the rectangle they made indicated the midsummer sunrise, while the long side pointed to the northern moonset. Down the line of one diagonal one saw – can still see – the point on the horizon where the Sun sets on May Day, later to be celebrated by the Celts as another Sun festival, Beltane, which means 'the shining one'.

Death was still the essential reason for the existence of the rearranged temple. The burials round about, in the new round barrows, continued apace, dug with sweat and toil from the chalky downland. And on the new axis of the henge, not far from the centre of the stone circles, the newcomers dug the grave of a man, and laid his bone in it with the head to the north-west, looking towards the midsummer Sun. His life gave life and strength – it consecrated – the magical place on the borderline between here and there, the present and the future.

THE SUNSET OF STONEHENGE

At the height of the Early Bronze Age, around 2000 BC, Stonehenge was remade yet again – into the form whose battered and crumbling remains we can see today. By then, great cemeteries of round barrows were crowded into the landscape around the temple. In them lay the bodies of chieftains and their women, clothed in finely woven wool, with their weapons, and household items made of bronze, copper, jet, amber, faience and gold. In a few centuries Stonehenge had changed from being a simple peasant mortuary chapel to a grand cathedral, the exclusive last resting-place of the rich, the powerful, the hard and the mighty.

One might speculate easily on how the new Stonehenge was pressured into being. Possibly the warrior chieftains had grumbled about the poor place the temple was, until their demands forced a monument befitting their status from a servile priesthood and a crushed people. Possibly the priests themselves had become the real powers behind these tiny thrones, and flaunted their power in this last grand architectural gesture. In any case, Stonehenge was rebuilt, but it was no longer a place for the common people. It became weighty and overwhelming, with room only for the priests, their acolytes, and the privileged.

The Moon, not the Sun, was the most important heavenly body to the builders of the first Stonehenge.

The bluestones were torn out at the roots. From the Marlborough Downs, 20 miles away, gangs of the faithful or coerced somehow found the energy to drag massive sandstone blocks to the site, where they were shaped and erected in the circle that everyone now knows as Stonehenge. Thirty uprights supported 30 lintels. These stones, bizarrely, were finished by using carpentry techniques – as if no one knew how to dress stone, and as if the builders could not tear themselves away from the memory that this site had once sported a timber building. Inside this forbiddingly atavistic ring of stones, in a monstrous horseshoe pattern, were set five trilithons, five separate, towering archways, each of two pillars topped by a lintel.

The axis of the henge was reversed yet again. The horseshoe of trilithons was open to the north-east but rose in height towards the tallest of them, to the south-west, where the Sun would be seen setting at midwinter – but only by the few for whom there was room in this spectacular but now cramped and darkened place. Astronomically, it was, quite literally, but a gigantic shadow of its former self. The only cosmic matter of interest to its priests was the single alignment to the midwinter sunset.

Whole epic novels might be written about how the mighty slowly but surely toppled after that. The process took 1,000 years, and no doubt the last of them were the most tragic, dramatic, bloody and meaningless. The system decayed; the great stones became empty at the heart. By 1000 BC Stonehenge had been deserted. The place was left to the shrieking crows, the wind, and the teeth of the rain – and to the curiosity of those who came nearly 30 centuries later, and wondered what the place had ever been for.

ANCIENT LIGHTS

The builders of the ancient sites did not create them all solely as places from which to peer out and watch the Sun and Moon performing in predictable order. The events and effects they designed them for may have been predictable, but they could be far more spectacular than a mere moonrise or a sunset. One of the ways the ancients celebrated their festival days was to create dramatic lighting effects within the very monuments themselves.

These ancient lightshows, as veteran Earth mysteries

researcher Paul Devereux has dubbed them, needed a dark stone interior for their full effect to be seen and felt, and, without exception, they were designed to form part of some kind of religious ritual. A good example of this mixture of exploiting astronomical observation and religious significance can still be seen at Burro Flats in the Simi Hills, near Los Angeles, California. Here, a panel of Chumash Indian rock paintings marks the site of a long-dead medicine man's shrine. The paintings are of centipede-like creatures, winged human forms, clawed animals, and handprints. These are traditional and ancient signs of sanctity in American Indian lore.

For most of the year, rock overhangs shelter the paintings at Burro Flats but, on midwinter's day, the rising Sun sends a shaft of light through a natural gap in the rocks that surround the shrine, pointing a pencil of light across the paintings. Thus the inner world of the Earth and of human art, spirit, the emotions and the mind – and the outer world of the sky and its heavenly bodies were linked.

Nowhere is this link between the inner and the outer universe made more clearly or more spectacularly than at the complex of monuments in the Boyne Valley, Ireland. The best known of these is the vast Newgrange mound, which is a huge construction penetrated by secret passages and chambers whose ultimate purpose can only be guessed at. Inside the mound, a passage 60 ft long leads to a high stone chamber at the heart of the mound. Here, the rising midwinter Sun sends its light through a roof-box built above the entrance to the passage. Only on midwinter's day can the beam of sunlight reach to the back of this central chamber.

On the Loughcrew Hills of Ireland, US artist Mark Brennan and his research colleagues found that at the equinox – the two days in the year when night and day are of equal duration – the rising Sun shines into a cairn there, and that it frames a rock carving at the back of the inner chamber. The carving was a neolithic symbol for the Sun. The eight rays emanating from its centre represented the eight ancient divisions of the year.

The temple builders of Neolithic Europe used this kind of effect in many sacred mounds. The entrance passage of Maes Howe, Orkney, for instance, is aligned with the midwinter sunset. The passage forms part of an intricate web of alignments that cover the whole island.

Inside the 5,000-year-old stone chamber of Gavrinis in northern France, a block of quartz stands exactly halfway along the length of the entrance passage. It can hardly be an accident that it was placed at a point where the beams from the sunrise, pouring down the passage at midwinter, would intersect those from the Moon at a key point in the 19-year lunar cycle. Archaeologist Aubrey Burl suggests that the builders of Gavrinis used quartz in this place because it would glow dramatically white when the Sun and moonbeams played on it.

THE HEART OF THE EARTH

Similar effects were put to work at the temple of Karnak in Egypt. Much of the surviving temple complex dates from the New Kingdom (1567–1085 BC), but the place was regarded as sacred for centuries before that. Through all its long history, the major astronomical axis of the site remained the same. In the 1890s, the astronomer Sir Norman Lockyer calculated that this axis pointed towards the midsummer sunset. He pictured the dying rays of the Sun reaching in to illuminate the image of the god kept in the darkened sanctuary that lay on the axis deep within the temple.

In the southern hemisphere is the Torreon, in the Inca citadel of Machu Picchu, Peru. The north-eastern window of the inner sanctum of the temple was cut to receive the beams of the midwinter sunrise (which occurs on 21 June in the southern hemisphere). Beneath this inner window is an altar-like rock that has been carved so that a sharp cleft, at right angles to the window, divides it in half. When the Sun rises at midwinter, its light floods in through the window, falling parallel to the cleft. It is possible that originally a frame hung from the carved knobs that protrude from the otherwise featureless wall in the Torreon, supporting a plumb line that would have thrown its shadow along the cut edge on the altar stone at the same time as the slice of sunlight lit it up.

On a ledge near the top of the 430 ft high Fajada Butte in Chaco Canyon, New Mexico, three fallen slabs of rock allow sharp shafts of sunlight through onto the rock wall behind them. A thousand years ago the Anasazi Indians (who lived here and to whom the

545

place was sacred) carved two spirals into the rock face so that these 'Sun daggers' would cast their shadows on them in distinctive patterns at the equinoxes and at midsummer and midwinter.

Further west along Chaco Canyon is the ruin of the Anasazi's great kiva, Casa Rinconada. This 12 ft deep, 63 ft wide circular ceremonial structure was built so that it lay north–south, east–west, and like Stonehenge has an opening in its wall to the north-east. The rising midsummer Sun casts a beam of light through this aperture onto the opposite wall of the kiva, illuminating one of six irregularly spaced wall niches.

The stepped pyramid at Chichen Itza, Mexico, comes alive at the equinoxes as light and shadow create a representation of Kukulcan, the feathered serpent to which it is dedicated.

The ancient builders thus symbolized how the outer universe of Sun and Moon always penetrates to the heart of the Earth. But this truth, which is reminiscent of the black and white dots in the ancient Chinese yin/yang symbol, was a fact of life to these people, whose lives reflected the constant interaction of both. Earth and sky were but aspects of the same thing to them.

THE HITCHING POST OF THE SUN

As the Sun gives light, so it also casts shadows. This fact was not lost on the ancients in their ceremonies and in the way they built their sacred places.

In Mexico, the Indians used shadow in a particularly flamboyant fashion, and with perfect symbolism. The so-called Castillo at Chichen Itza on the Yucatan peninsula is a Toltec-Mayan stepped pyramid originally dedicated to Kukulcan, the feathered serpent god. A spectacular light-and-shadow picture forms on the Castillo at the spring and summer equinoxes. In the last hour before sunset, the stepped, north-west corner of the pyramid throws a serrated shadow onto the west-facing balustrade of its northern staircase. This produces a pattern of sunlight and shadow that looks strikingly like the body markings of the rattlesnake common to the region. At the bottom of the balustrade are serpents' heads, carved in stone. To these the shadow attaches itself, completing the image of the sacred snake, writhing down the holy pyramid.

In the last refuge of the Incas, the mountain-peak citadel at Machu Picchu, Peru, the small but highly significant Intihuatana is carved from a granite outcrop that sits on a naturally pyramid-shaped spur. The Intihuatana is an upright pillar, no more than a foot high, projecting from a complex, asymmetrical platform made up of a variety of odd surfaces and projections.

The name Intihuatana means 'hitching post of the Sun', which is a sure indication that this strangely fashioned (or adapted) feature must have played a vital part in the major Inca festival of Inti Raymi. This took place every winter solstice – the shortest day of the year – to 'tie the Sun'. The ritual prevented the Sun from moving any further north in its daily round and stopped it being lost for ever.

SHADOWS OF THE SUN

At Ireland's Newgrange, the American artist Martin Brennan noted something else besides the entry of the midwinter sunbeam into the great mound. He found that the entrance stone and another 'kerbstone 52' were part of the solar alignment of the site, and that some of the stones in the huge stone circle surrounding the mound also play a part in creating astonishing light-and-shadow effects on that crucial day of the year. And it was crucial: the prehistoric people of the Old World, like the Incas in Peru half a world away, also feared that the Sun might disappear for ever at midwinter.

At midwinter sunrise, as the roof-box at the entrance directs the Sun's rays deep into the mound, the shadow of one of the circle's stones points like a finger to the entrance stone and its vertical marking. At the same time, the shadow from a nearby stone strikes another carved kerbstone. With the complex interplay of shadow and light at the site, it is, as one commentator has said, 'almost as if the builders of Newgrange have left software running in their hardware'.

At nearby Knowth, another mound built like Newgrange with an inner passage and central chamber (and at about the same time, around 3700 BC), Brennan discovered that when the Sun sets at the equinoxes and sends its light down the entrance passage, a standing stone outside likewise throws its shadow onto the vertically grooved entrance stone.

At Castlerigg stone circle in Cumbria, England, photographer John Glover saw an extraordinary phenomenon during the midsummer sunset in 1976. Just as the Sun was sinking to the ridge on the horizon, Glover glanced behind him, and was amazed to see that the tallest stone of the circle was throwing a huge shadow right across the valley.

When the path of the shadow was surveyed later, the researchers found that the slope of the ground beyond the site was such that the shadow fell parallel to it and so extended far beyond the immediate ground. A conifer plantation stands in the way today, but originally it would have stretched for more than two miles across the moor.

THE LIGHT IN THE DARKNESS

Can we deduce anything from these alignments and angles, the subtle interplay of light and shade, or even from the final dark centuries of Stonehenge, with its fixation on midwinter and death, about the meaning of these astonishing constructions?

The answer is, tentatively at least, yes. As was remarked earlier, the symbolism of these ancient places indicates that for those who fashioned them with such care and attention, Earth and sky were not separate, but parts of a whole. There is more to be quarried here, however. Even the monumental morbidity of Stonehenge speaks of a fixation with wholeness – and by implication with balance, as if the ancients had anticipated and written in stone and ritual the words of Cranmer's prayerbook: 'In the midst of life we are in death...'

In the same way, the penetrating light of the Sun at sites all over the world is balanced by shadows; the dark created by light, the light known only in the darkness of a hidden chamber. Earth and cosmos were tied together by threads of light and a network of shadows in a kind of symbiosis. The one could not exist without the other, the ancients saw, and dramatized their intuition in their sacred architecture.

To them, Earth, Sun and Moon coexisted in a cosmic marriage. Part of the drama played out by the stones is conjugal: the long hard light of the Sun penetrating the secret passage of the Earth; the phallic shadow stretching itself and growing across the surface of the Earth's vast body. This was not a crass cartoon, a huge slide-show of sex and fertility, but an enactment of ultimate cosmic union.

And wherever this celebration of balance, of wholeness, of cosmic passion took place, the people could see that they were at the centre of the Universe, for here all things met as one. The ancient places were at the core of all existence.

THE MYSTIC LANDSCAPE

For the ancients the Earth was a woman – a mother to be worshipped and cherished, and a lover to be erotically embraced. The secret places of her body were the most sacred sites of the pagan religions, but their true purpose remains mysterious…

A sense of centrality inspired the builders of the world's ancient monuments: they treated their creations as if they truly were at the centre of things, and placed them where the whole surrounding landscape reinforced and reflected that feeling. If need be they would mould whole landscapes to underline the importance of a particular site.

The image of the world's centre took a number of forms in the ancient world. One was the omphalos, the navel of the world. Another was the 'world egg'. Another was the 'world tree'. Derived from the Tree of Life were any number of more portable icons and symbols: particular, living, sacred trees, or so-called totem poles, or even a simple rod stuck in the Earth. Wherever these were, there – for the purpose at hand - was the centre of the world.

Marking that central point of the world was the first great magical act in creating sacred geography. Its spiritual importance is nowhere better illustrated than in the creation myth of the Zuni American Indians of New Mexico, who are probably descended from the Anasazi who built Chaco Canyon.

According to their myth, the first Zuni wandered for a long time, looking for a place of peace and stability, where they would settle. Frustrated in their search, they finally summoned *K'yan asdebi*, the water-skate, because his long legs could point in all the directions. A centre of a kind himself, he could surely identify the centre of the world.

This he did. He rose into the sky and stretched out his legs in the six great directions: the four cardinal points of the compass, and above and below. Gradually he came back to Earth, saying, 'Where my heart and navel rest, beneath them mark the spot and there build a town of the midmost, for there shall be the midmost place of the Earth-mother, even the navel...'

A VIEW OF THE GODS

The idea of the sacred centre is really an extension of the individual's perception that he or she already exists at the centre of his or her own world. Each of us looks out upon the world with an intuitive idea of six basic directions: front, back and sides, with the Earth beneath our feet, and the heavens above us. Wherever we are, we are always at the centre of our world.

At its deepest level, the meaning of a sacred site made itself felt through the action of the landscape on the mind, and the reaction of the mind to the landscape. Ultimate reality could not be apprehended without this exchange between mind and landscape. The place represented a whole that fused together three things: time – made visible as a result of the astronomical alignments of the place, and its play of light and shadow; space, in the form of the landscape that reflected the work of the gods; and man-made imagery, the sign of human consciousness and awareness.

The sacred centre was sacred exactly because it was the place from which the movements of the Sun and Moon were observed and measured against the skyline, and because it was the place from which the actions of the gods – sometimes, even their very shapes – could be witnessed. It was the centre because all things were joined there.

THE ORACLE OF DELPHI

The best-known omphalos in the Old World is the temple complex, sanctuary and ancient home of the oracle at Delphi, Greece. According to Greek myth, Delphi was founded after the chief of the gods, Zeus, sent out two eagles from the far ends of the Earth; where their flights crossed would be the centre of the world. The eagles met over Mount Parnassos, on whose southern slopes Delphi was built.

Reflecting this legend, some classic depictions of omphalos stones (which existed at numerous sacred sites in ancient Greece) show two birds perched on them, facing in opposite directions. Two such stones survive at Delphi today. One is in the complex of temple ruins and is a cone of grey stone shot through with quartz veins. The other is now in Delphi's museum. It is egg-shaped, about 3 ft high, and covered by a delicate interlaced pattern carved in bas-relief.

THE STOREHOUSE OF THE DEAD

The Andean Indians have a very different concept of the stars in the sky from the Western notion of a series of constellations like a picture-book of mythical beings. To the Quechua Indian community of Misminay, who live near the Vilcanota river, about 30 miles north-west of Cuzco, Peru, the Milky Way is the key feature of the night sky.

They call the Milky Way Mayu, 'River'. They see it as the heavenly version of their River Vilcanota, which flows from south-east to north-west, and in Quechua myth is said to dump its waters off the edge of the Earth into the encircling void of the heavens. These waters are collected in the north-west by the Milky Way which carries them through the sky before letting them fall to Earth and rise again in the east. As the waters are carried overhead, some of the moisture drops to Earth again as rain. The terrestrial and celestial rivers fertilize land and sky.

From Misminay (as from any fixed point on the Earth), the Milky Way appears to swing across the sky, so that every 12 hours its southern and northern ends respectively appear to rise from the

Sioux Indians in an ecstatic dance, with their medicine man or shaman in buffalo hide. The centre of the cosmos for the Sioux is Mount Harney, and the shaman's staff is also a symbol of the 'world axis' around which Heaven and Earth revolve.

south-east and north-east. In a 24-hour period, this apparent movement draws two lines across the sky that intersect directly overhead. The Quechua call this zenith point Cruz Calvario, the 'cross of Calvary', borrowing the term from Christian missionaries, whose work among them was not entirely successful.

This division of space by the Milky Way is reflected on the ground in the layout of the Misminay settlement itself. Two footpaths and irrigation canals running side by side form an X-shaped cross on the ground. Their intersection is called Crucero, 'the cross'. This corresponds to the 'crossing point' of the Milky Way in the sky overhead – Calvario. Crucero is the place in Misminay from where the horizons of the 'four quarters' of the world are marked by the local people. Each direction is meaningful in Quechua mythology, and the meaning of each is reflected in house groupings in the village and in the significance the people give to certain sacred peaks beyond. The north-west–north-east quarter, for example, is associated with the ancestors, and the holy mountain on the horizon in that direction is called Apu Wanumarka, the 'Storehouse of the Dead'. Here again we have a linking of Earth and sky, life and death, past and future, the interpenetration of space and time in which each part gains its meaning and nourishes the spirit only because it is part of the whole image of the Universe that the people entertain.

THE GOLDEN NAVEL OF THE EARTH

Most ancient peoples possessed some concept of the sacred centre, and it could take many forms. It could be stone, as at Delphi or Delos in Greece, a holy city like the Incas' Cuzco (the name means 'navel' in the Quechua tongue), or a rock, as it is for the Semangs of the Malay Peninsula, where Batu-Ribn emerges at the centre of the world. It is a rock, too, at Jerusalem, that great centre sacred to Judaism, Christianity and Islam alike, and it is a rock too in Mecca.

The world centre could also be a peak, a 'world mountain'. To the Sioux Indians of the American Great Plains, the centre of the world was on Mount Harney. Israel may boast three world centres including Jerusalem – Mount Tabor, whose name may mean 'navel', according to the historian Mircea Eliade, and Mount Gerizim, which, Eliade maintains, was 'undoubtedly invested with the prestige of the centre, for it is called "navel of the earth". Buddhists too have their world centre in Mount Kailash in Tibet, the legendary 'Mount Meru', centre of the cosmos to believers. People still make pilgrimages to the remote mountain, to make a ritual tour around it. Some even make the circuit on their knees. In Japan, the volcanic cone of Mount Fujiyama is sacred; the Shinto religion centres on living earth mysteries.

The notion of the holy peak is deeply embedded in the human psyche. Croagh Padric in the west of Ireland, sacred to the great Christian saint of the island, is likewise a centre of pilgrimages and rituals, which are possibly not Christian at all in origin but an adaptation of a far older tradition.

Besides appearing in stones, rocks and mountains, the centre of the world might be represented by a pole, or even a pit dug in the ground. The 'world tree', in particular, was a universal form of the sacred centre. The world tree connected the heavens and the underworld, but was also the axis from which the middle world, the Earth, orientated itself. It was the 'still point of the turning world', but also a kind of conducting rod between the upper and lower parts of the whole cosmos.

The Yakut tribes of Siberia believe that at the 'golden navel of the Earth' stands a tree with eight branches. In Norse and Old German mythology, the world tree was named Yggdrasil, and trees that symbolize the sacred centre live on in traditions as diverse and distant from one another as those of the Australian aborigines and American Indians.

Like the sacred mountain, the roots of the world tree reach into the human mind, and the sap still rises in this ancient image. It is found in (relatively) modern opera, in Wagner's reworking of the German myths in *The Ring*, and even in English literature. In *Women In Love*, written in the 1920s, D.H. Lawrence was still conjuring with the tree of life as a symbol of growth, wholeness and spiritual stability, at whose roots gnaw the corruptions of modern 'civilization'.

A SLEEPING BEAUTY

Gazing out from their cosmic centre across the landscape, the ancients saw a very different world from the one we think we are looking at. Agriculture, where it existed, was neither a cosy calling pursued by a romanticized minority nor a business, but a battle with nature that involved most of the tribe most of the time. Nor were the deserts dead but photogenic places. The whole of the landscape was alive.

Since Earth and the heavens enacted a cosmic marriage, it is not surprising that many ancient peoples around the world saw in the hills and moors, deserts and mountains around them the shape of a vast goddess, the Earth Mother. She did not give life to the land; she was its life, and they saw her in it.

The island of Jura off the west coast of Scotland has a range of mountains called the Paps: the central peaks are symmetrical and rounded like breasts. At Ballochroy, on the Kintyre peninsula on the mainland, the central stone of three menhirs has a smoothed side that faces the most northerly of the Paps, Beinn Corra, 19 miles distant across the sound. Behind this peak the Sun sets at midsummer.

On Lewis, the most north-westerly of the major Hebrides islands, the Pairc Hills are known locally as the 'Sleeping Beauty': they resemble the profile of a woman lying on her back. From the

Mount Fujiyama, Japan's sacred mountain whose volcanic nature makes it a prime symbol of the raw power hidden within the Earth.

cluster of stone circles and settings known as the Stones of Callanish, it seems that when the Moon rises at its most southerly point during its 19-year cycle, it comes forth from the Pairc Hills. At this one time in the cycle it is as if the Sleeping Beauty gives birth to the Moon.

Two symmetrical, rounded hills near Killarney, Ireland, are known as the Paps of Anu. In the Irish myths, Anu is the mother of the last generation of gods to rule the Earth, the legendary Tuatha de Danaan. According to Celtic scholar Dr Anne Ross, these hills are still regarded with awe today. They 'personify the powers of the goddess embedded in the land', and Anu 'is still regarded as the local fairy queen'.

From the Greek island of Poros, off the north-east coast of the Peloponnisos, the mountains on the mainland are seen by local people as outlining the form of a woman lying on her back. 'The resemblance is indeed persuasive,' says the American historian Vincent Scully almost primly in *The Earth, the Temple and the Gods*, although he notes with some relish the shapes of 'the head low on the north, a long neck, high breasts, arched stomach, long legs with the knees drawn up'.

UPLIFTED BREASTS

In *Symbolic Landscapes*, Earth mysteries scholar Paul Devereux draws attention to the vast number of Bronze Age Cretan figurines that exist of a goddess with her arms raised in a characteristic and apparently curious gesture. The best-known example is the faience Snake Goddess found at Knossos, the heart of the ancient Minoan empire on Crete. Both the figure's upraised arms and its breasts, emphasized by an open bodice, create a cleft shape that is a direct echo of the sacred landscape of the island. The courtyard of the palace at Knossos opens to the distant, cleft-peaked Mount Yiouktas. The palace's propylaia or entrance is precisely aligned with the mountain.

The Minoan bull ritual, in which young men and women seized the horns of a charging bull and were propelled over its back, also echoed the horned peak of Mount Yiouktas. We know about the ritual because it is detailed in frescos found at Knossos, and it was performed under the eye of the horned mountain.

'The landscape and temples together form [an] architectural whole,' Vincent Scully wrote of the ancient Greeks' perception of their surroundings. He believed that the Greeks had 'developed an eye' for 'specific combinations of landscape features as expressive of particular holiness'.

This perception of the interchangeability of land and spirit was not confined to Knossos by any means. Other Cretan palaces were built in a deliberate relationship with horned mountains. Among them are Mama, which points toward Mount Gikte, and Phaistos, which is aligned to Mount Ida. At Gournia, the palace faces two hills that Scully described as 'so close and rounded that a more proper analogy would seem to be more directly to the female body itself and they do closely resemble the uplifted breasts' of the goddess. He remarked too that the enclosed landscape around Gournia gave the 'inescapable impression' that the palace was being embraced in the arms of the Earth Mother.

Similarly, the characteristic gesture in representations of the goddess is found throughout the Mediterranean. The small terracotta goddess figurines of Mycenae on the Greek mainland have the same raised arms. Tombs in the Castelluccio cemetery in Sicily were carved to show a powerful figure with upraised arms, breasts and head. Pieces of pottery of the same period from Sicily, the Lipari Islands and southern Italy all have horn-like handles to create an image of a goddess with raised arms.

The motif is thousands of years old. Female figurines and pottery decorations from pre-dynastic Egypt, for instance, feature this sacred gesture of upraised arms. The psychologist Erich Neumann has suggested that this universally repeated gesture of the Earth Mother indicates prayer, invocation or a magical conjuring of the deity. What he might have added is the reflection that it also reinforces the impression that the ancients saw their world as a cosmic union in which spiritual energy is constantly cycling through the whole of creation.

For it can hardly be insignificant that the goddess is always portrayed as herself in an attitude of worship. The Earth Mother was not separate from the rest of the Universe complacently receiving its supplications but herself takes part in a mutual – and mutually invigorating – reverence. Time and space, people, gods, spiritual energy, Earth, Sun, Moon and landscape were all aspects of one another. The world was whole, and holy.

HOLY LINES

Of all the conundrums posed by the anciet world's mystical landscapes, the most baffling is the fact that most are built on, or in, straight lines of one kind or another. This puzzling feature takes many different forms around the world. Every one of them brings us back to one of the most familiar, yet most fundamental, of the 'Earth mysteries': the riddle of 'ley lines'. The usual story is that leys were discovered by Alfred Watkins one sunny June afternoon in 1921. As the 66-year-old businessman was sitting in his car, gazing out over his native Herefordshire from Blackwardine, he glanced down at the map in front of him. It was then, in a sudden epiphany, that he realized that the prehistoric mounds, earthworks and standing stones of the country before him were arrayed in arrow-straight lines across the landscape.

The Old Sarum ley in Wiltshire. The photograph shows the ruin of Old Sarum with Salisbury Cathedral in the distance.

Watkins was not, in fact, the first to notice this. Numerous researchers had recorded their findings prior to Watkins's 'discovery' of 1921. As early as 1846, for instance, the antiquarian Edward Duke had proposed that Stonehenge and Avebury, some 20 miles apart, were part of an invisible straight line across the countryside that passed through another stone circle and two prehistoric earthworks. Other scholars throughout the 19th century noticed similar alignments, and in 1904, Hilaire Belloc published *The Old Road*, in which he described medieval pilgrimage routes linking old churches in England and, drawing on his observations while travelling in the USA, the straight tracks of American Indians.

The 'Cliff Palace', the largest of the Anasazi settlements perched high within the escarpment at Mesa Verde in southern Colorado.

Watkins, however, provided a comprehensive account for the ancient lines on the land. He believed they were the remaining signs of prehistoric traders' trackways, and they were straight because they had been laid out by line-of-sight. Watkins kept finding distinctive boulders on the lines he explored. He was convinced these were part of the original, prehistoric survey, and consequently called them 'markstones'. He also found old churches and crosses on the alignments which, he argued, were pagan – i.e. prehistoric – sacred places that had been commandeered by Christianity.

Watkins called his alignments 'leys' because he noted the word recurring in placenames on the lines. It comes from the Welsh word llan, which originally meant 'sacred enclosure'. The possible significance of this passed Watkins by, possessed as he was, like any good Victorian merchant, with the idea that the leys must have been trade routes. But the point was not lost on his contemporaries, the German researchers Josef Heinsch, who noted lines linking hills and old churches, and Wilhelm Teudt, who called the German alignments he discovered *heilige Linien*, 'holy lines'.

MYSTERIOUS ROADS TO NOWHERE

As Hilaire Belloc had realized, mysterious straight lines running through the landscape between ancient sites, and utterly regardless of their practicability as paths as they shot up sheer inclines and blithely disappeared over precipices, were not an exclusively European phenomenon. And as research and surveying and archaeological digs continued, it became apparent that nowhere are there such enigmatic lines in the landscape as in the Americas.

The American Indians of antiquity made what are literally old straight tracks – they too ignored practicality for the sake of a ruler-like precision – and equally straight lines of sacred sites, shrines, holy rocks and wells. The remains of this curious practice can be seen all over the Americas, and it obsessed many diverse and distant American Indian cultures. One of the most intriguing of all these prehistoric straightline systems is in the American South-west: the 'Chaco roads'.

These are centred on Chaco Canyon, in the high mesa country of north-west New Mexico. They were made by the Anasazi, whose name is actually a Navajo Indian term meaning 'the enemies of our ancestors'. The Anasazi thrived in the Four Quarters area of New Mexico from about AD 800 to about 1300; some of them, in these latter years, clashed with the Navajo as they migrated into the region from AD 1000. The Anasazi developed a distinctive style of flat-roofed buildings made of mud, rock and wood, called pueblos.

Chaco Canyon was the prime Anasazi ceremonial centre. Here, the culture reached its height. Over the years, the pueblos grew into multi-storeyed terraced complexes now known as 'Great Houses', with walls, courtyards, and 'Great Kivas' – very large ceremonial chambers. There are nine Great Houses within Chaco Canyon itself, all built between AD 900 and 1115. The largest was Pueblo Bonito, covering some three acres.

CARVED THROUGH LIVING ROCK

The Anasazis' mysterious roads radiate in straight lines for many miles around Chaco Canyon. They are fully engineered, a fairly constant 30 ft wide, with spur roads about half as wide. At their borders are earthen ridges, lines of stones or drystone walls. Their surfaces were laid with compacted earth – or cut straight into the bedrock. The true extent of the Chaco roads became apparent only in the 1970s, when aerial photography revealed how vast the network was. With ground surveys and digs, archaeologists have now mapped some 400 miles of these enigmatic highways.

Like similar sacred 'routes' elsewhere, the Anasazi roads are no respecters of difficult terrain if it stands in their way. When they reached the canyon walls, the Anasazi engineers carved staircases up to 25 ft wide from the living rock, straight down the canyon sides.

The Chaco roads throw up a host of questions. Why did a people with neither horses nor the wheel need these elaborate highways? Are they roads as such at all? Recent computer-enhanced infra-red aerial pictures taken by NASA only deepen the mystery. These have revealed the existence of rows of sections running parallel to the roads. What were they for?

There is a consensus among archaeologists and scholars that the roads were ceremonial or sacred ways that linked the Great Houses, which seem to have been ritual centres. Fragments of pottery have been found in limited areas along some of the roads, notably near Great Houses. Breaking pottery vessels has been an act of consecration in numerous societies in widely distant places all over the world. It was often associated with the dead. It is possible that the Anasazi considered the roads themselves to be holy. It remains – officially at least – a mystery as to who used them, and why they were so broad and so finely made.

INVISIBLE HIGHWAYS

Virtually every sacred site in the prehistoric world was linked with others, major or minor, by a radiating network of straight lines. Few were as elaborate or as easily detected in their heyday as the Anasazis' strange highways. Most were invisible, like the leys of Europe – which makes them, in a way, all the more mysterious. In rare cases like the Ohio effigy mounds and the vast drawing-board that covered the desert floor at Nazca, Peru, entire sites were devoted to creating miles of straight lines and, still more bewildering, very precise pictures that could be appreciated only from the air.

In cultures that enjoyed such a comprehensive world-view, and that had such a magical sense of the continuous life rolling through the whole of creation – which today we sterilize and alienate by calling it the 'environment' – the lines, visible or invisible, had to have meaning. Where do they fit in the weft and warp of this most tightly woven of all mythologies?

This has been the greatest enigma of all in the study of the ancient sacred places. It was also, as a handful of researchers have now realized, the biggest clue of all to the meaning and use of the prehistoric sites, and it was staring them in the face all the time.

A MAP FOR THE MIND

Fault lines, strange lights, magnetic and gravitational abnormalities – how do all of these fit together in the world's mysterious places?

So far, we have gathered up various enigmatic bits of information about the world's mysterious ancient places. They were most often built on fault lines, and these are places where strange lights and magnetic and gravitational anomalies abound. We've seen that these places can have bizarre psychic effects on people. Research by Professor Michael Persinger of Laurentian University in Ontario has even suggested that individuals become especially receptive to extrasensory perception in the presence of the phenomena that cling to the ancient sites.

We know too that these places were seen by the people who built them as cosmic centres on which the Sun and Moon were deliberately focused. Most probably, the cosmic light shows were arranged to reinforce the sense of universal centrality of the shrine - its place between the Otherworlds. At the sites, too, the here and now was strangely interfused with the spirit world – whether in the form of the Earth Goddess or through the link between Heaven, Earth and Underworld that was symbolized by the 'world tree' or some other equally potent image. Many sites are associated with the dead. Finally, we have seen that these perplexing places are linked, or infested, by straight lines both visible and invisible.

How, or where, do all these aspects fit together? What is the missing link? A brief tour around one of the most problematic of these baffling monuments may let slip a few more clues.

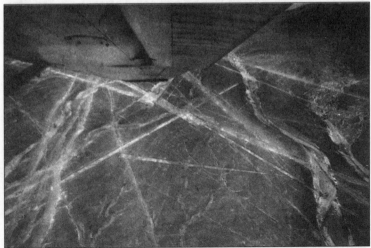

The complexity of the lines and patterns at Nazca becomes clear when they are seen from the air. But why?

DESIGNS IN THE DESERT

Probably the most famous of American Indian straight lines are the markings on the desert pampas around Nazca, Peru.

The Nazca lines were drawn by removing the desert surface to reveal the lighter soil beneath. The lines can be anything from a few dozen yards to several miles long, and pass straight over ridges. Intersperzed among the hundreds of straight lines are a variety of line drawings, made in the same way, of animals, sundry geometric forms and irregular and regular abstract shapes.

It is easier to say what the lines and drawings at Nazca are not than to summarise what they might be. That they are not and never did form a landing-strip for 'ancient astronauts' is a statement scarcely worth making: the idea was never worth ten seconds of anyone's time. Nor are the lines aligned to the heavens in any more conventional archaeo-astronomical sense. Work in the 1980s co-ordinated by Anthony F. Aveni of Colgate University, New York State, confirmed the finding by Gerald Hawkins of the Smithsonian Institution in the 1960s that none of the lines had any significant astronomical function.

Aveni and his colleagues did find that there is some pattern to the apparently random layout of the lines on the ground. Nazca's resident researcher Maria Reiche had noted what she called 'star-like centres', from which lines radiated like rays from a sun. Aveni's team identified over 60 of these centres. They are set on natural hills or mounds, and at least one line from each centre connects it with another.

At these 'star-like' centres are deposits of small stones, shells and broken pottery fragments: signs of some kind of offering to the dead, as were found along the 'roads' in Chaco Canyon. In the 1920s, an elder of the Navajo Indians made the cryptic remark to archaeologist Neil Judd that although the Chaco lines looked like roads, they 'were not roads'. The Nazca lines are not tracks, although they look like tracks. They start nowhere and end anywhere.

And the most impenetrable fact of all about Nazca is the line drawings. Why spend energy, which could barely be spared from the hard business of survival, on making pictures that no one could see?

Or could someone see them? And if so – how could they?

PATHWAYS FOR THE SPIRITS

Now let us go back to the straight lines. These are traditionally significant in other contexts. Here is another clue to the hidden meaning of the lines on the Earth – and of the ancient places themselves. There is a very ancient tradition that spirits – good and bad - move in straight lines. There is a huge global lore concerning the usefulness of knots in defending oneself against evil spirits, for instance. But straight lines can be used to encourage the intervention of the most beneficial spirits – most interestingly, in many widespread traditions, by using threads to provide a path for them.

Seen at close quarters, the lines at Nazca seem almost insignificant. Yet enormous energy and devotion went into their design and maintenance. But how did their makers get to see the full effect of their work?

Among some Australian Aboriginal tribes, a healer would treat a sick person by running a spider thread from the head of the 'patient' to a nearby bush. This, said the healer, was where the sufferer's spirit had fled from the ailing body. The filament provided a path for the spirit to return, making the patient whole again and banishing the illness.

Similarly, when dealing with sickness, the shaman (colloquially known as the tribal 'witch doctor' or 'medicine man') of the Buryat peoples of Siberia would place an arrow on the ground beside the patient's head and lay a red thread in a straight line, out through the entrance of the sick person's tent, to a birch pole that he had previously stuck in the ground outside. The pole stood for the world tree, the link between this world and the realms of spirit, while the thread gave the sick person's soul a route along which to return to the body. The principle is almost identical to that of the Australian tradition.

A yarn picture made by the Huichol Indians of central Mexico. In the upper left of the picture are shamans, directing the life force of the Sun's rays as they fall on a cornfield.

Among the Maoris of New Zealand, the stem of a plant could be taken as a spirit 'line'. The tohunga ('healer') put the stem on a sick person's head and called on the evil spirit that was causing the illness to leave by the 'road' offered by the stem of the plant.

In terms of straight lines, the spirit world and ancient places, the most provocative of all these traditions of healing belongs to the Kalahari !Kung people. When they hold a trance dance, which involves hours of rhythmic movement and continuous chanting in the hypnotic presence of a fire, it's not uncommon for people to leave their bodies – to have what we would call an out-of-the-body experience. The !Kung call this state kia. Once in it, they can climb 'threads' up to 'where God is'. When they are with God, they can become healers. The !Kung say that then they are able to gaze into people's bodies with X-ray vision to see where any disease has taken root, and can then pull it out.

Here is a very clear indication that straight lines, contact with the spirit world and a state of trance are all closely related.

THE THREE WORLDS SYSTEM

The key that unlocks the mystery connecting straight lines and the sacred sites lies in the central fact about the ancient places themselves. That is: they were, exactly and literally, central to existence. The sacred centre was not only a place from which to make and take earthly bearings. It linked the 'middle world' of the here and now with the worlds above – Heaven – and below – the Underworld. The realms above and below were kingdoms of the spirit. Anthropologists call this cosmology the 'three worlds system'. It seems to have originated, possibly hundreds of thousands of years ago, with a form of religion known as shamanism.

When and where shamanism began is anyone's guess, but it probably arrived in the Americas with the peoples who migrated across the old land bridge over the Bering Straits somewhere between 15,000 and 25,000 years ago. The shamanic tradition remained strong and healthy among the American Indian tribes until very recent times because the Americas did not suffer the same cultural changes over the centuries as Eurasia did.

What is a shaman? The term itself comes from saman, the word the Tungus peoples of Siberia had for the 'elected member' of the tribe who could journey to the spirit worlds seeking healing for tribal members, finding lost or confused souls or seeking help for those in this world by divining the future or peering into the remote past. The shaman was the intermediary between the tribe and the Otherworld of spirit, and he went to the Otherworld through an out-of-the-body experience. To his conscious self, this experience seemed to be the equivalent of flight above the Earth.

We can infer that this experience of flying was universal from many pieces of evidence. To begin with, shamans all around the world use strikingly similar metaphors to describe their journeys to the Otherworld. They say their spirits rise on smoke, ride along a rainbow, follow a flight of arrows, travel up a sunbeam – and so on. A particularly common image they use is the ladder, stretching from Earth to Heaven – just as Jacob's does in the Bible. He, significantly, also slept on a sacred stone.

ROUTES TO A TRANCE

The shaman used – and still uses – a variety of techniques to achieve the trance state. Among them were prolonged dancing, fasting and chanting. This last, incidentally, was not ordinary chanting. A large choir of Russian Orthodox monks sounds like a tin whistle with the croup in comparison to a shaman in full voice, and the greatest cantor in Brooklyn might as well be a mosquito.

There are few sounds in the world more unearthly than the vocal performance of a Siberian shaman as he prepares to leave the mundane world. Bizarre but distinct whistlings come down from his sinuses and out of his nose and mouth, while he uses an astonishing, fundamental muscular control to produce a grim, low, rhythmic roaring from the diaphragm. On top of these various abnormal noises and mesmeric drones, he manages to produce a conventional human chant, often of eerie beauty, to distract the astounded listener. It comes as something of a surprise to discover that this last, most recognizable, sound is not actually coming out of his ears. The whole effect is both hair-raising and hypnotic, as well as inhuman – as it is surely meant to be, for him as much as for his audience.

Shamans may use other ritual tools at the same time or separately to induce trance. They include exposure to extremes of heat or cold, and a range of more or less horrifying methods of inducing pain and, hence, sensory deprivation. Shamans may also use hallucinogenic plants, foods or smoking mixtures (the 'peace-pipe' had a number of applications, but the ultimate effect was usually very peaceful, not to say positively dreamy).

The hallucinogens that the shamans used are interesting because many of these drugs gave their user a strong impression of flying. One 19th-century explorer into the South American interior described how he felt himself going on 'an aerial journey' as a result of drinking ayahuasaca, a potent Indian tincture made from a hallucinogenic vine. Modern dope slang reflects something of the same experience: among other things, one gets 'high', goes on a 'trip' and gets 'spaced out'.

The mental imagery induced by drug use and trance became central to many tribes' art. Among the rock paintings in a Chumash Indian shrine at Burro Flats, near Los Angeles, California, there is a series of geometric forms – dots, lines, crosses, circles and concentric rings. Similar patterns are found in rock art all over the world, and can be seen carved into the rock at many megalithic sites in Britain.

The biblical image of Jacob's ladder as a connection between the spiritual realm and earthly life is echoed in shamanic traditions throughout the world.

The source of these patterns is the human brain. The Tukano Indians of Colombia in South America (who use trance-inducing drugs in religious ceremonies) employ similar imagery as a basis for the decorative work on their pottery and clothing, and freely admit that these are based on the colourful but geometric forms they see under the influence of the drugs. The San (Bushmen) of the Kalahari, too, make no secret of the fact that the patterns and motifs in their own rock paintings are based on what their shamans see when in trance. These patterns were probably the original inspiration for another enigmatic pattern found at endless numbers of sacred sites all over the world: the labyrinth or maze.

Most significantly, the shaman moved from normal awareness to the Otherworld to the endless beating of a magic drum, which was covered in signs and symbols to protect him on his 'journey' elsewhere. He called his drum his 'steed' or 'canoe' on or in which he would travel to the spirit realm. One of the more intriguing discoveries made about these drums is that they produce sounds at extremely low frequencies – as few as four cycles per second. These affect the so-called theta brain waves, which are somehow involved in the deeper levels of dreaming, trance and meditation.

In the Siberian tribes, the shell of the shaman's drum was, in theory, made from a branch of the world tree (usually, in fact, a birch). Because of this magical link and through his hypnotic drumming, the shaman is 'magically projected into the vicinity of the Tree', as the anthropologist Mircea Eliade put it. In the tribes of central and northern Asia, the shaman would actually climb a birch tree during his trance, to show his spectators that he was indeed ascending the axis of the world and passing into the realm of spirit.

BIRD-MEN THROUGH THE AGES

Once up the tree, he flew. In some tribes, he waved his arms like a bird's wings when he got to the top. During his trance, the Yakut shaman of north-east Siberia also made dance movements and gestures to imitate the flight of a bird.

The image of flight was the unmistakable sign of a shaman in the ancient world, and still is in those cultures that have remained prehistoric and pre-industrial in spirit. The most frequent is the form of a bird perched on a stick (standing for the world axis or tree). From this token, the almost unimaginable antiquity of the shaman tradition becomes evident, for among the Cro-Magnon cave paintings of Lascaux, France, there is one of a bird-stick next to a man in a bird mask, who is apparently in trance. The painting may be a quarter of a million years old.

The Mississippian people, who flourished between about AD 900 to 1500, left many examples of pottery decorated with human-bird figures. Siberian shamans wore bird-clawshoes, and the Hopewell Indian shaman would decorate his robes with bird-claw shapes cut out of mica. In China, Taoist monks were called 'feather scholars', which reveals their original role. In Ireland, the Celtic Druids were believed to be able to take wing through applied magic. While North American shamans most often identified with the eagle, the ancient Indian text 'Upanishads' calls the out-of-the-body spirit or soul 'the lone wild gander'; and the image flies from the tropics to the Arctic Circle, for geese figure prominently in Eskimo accounts of magical flight.

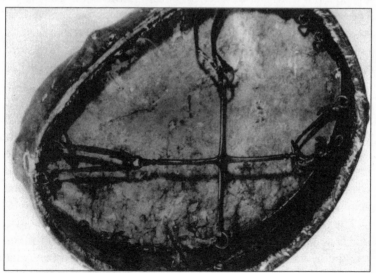

A Siberian shaman's drum. His trance partly induced by its rhythmic reverberations, the shaman believed that the drum became a steed or canoe on which he rode to the Otherworld.

COSMIC CROSSING POINTS

The spirits, as we've seen in the accounts of healing techniques, for example, move in straight lines. Thus, the lines on the landscape and the straight flight of the shaman's spirit are almost certainly versions of one and the same thing. Whether the lines on the landscape ('They look like roads, but they are not roads') were put there to guide and protect the travelling spirit – a kind of safety net for the soul – or were put there to celebrate and consecrate shamanic flight, or were a record of these journeys in spirit, we shall probably never know.

But these various threads running through magical and religious lore, and the various clues at the ancient sites themselves, all point to the conclusion that the sacred centres were shamanic centres, with the life of the Universe – the Earth Goddess, the Sun, the Moon – focused upon them and throwing into relief their significance as crossing points between this world and that of spirit. And it seems clear that the lines radiating from them or linking them were highways of the soul in its out-of-the-body flight. The lines may well have been intended also as markers and guides for the spirits of the dead. The association between death and the ancient places is too strong, and the cultures that built them were too comprehensive in their symbolism, for there to be no connection.

The other mysterious aspects of the sites now fall into place. The pictures on the ground at Nazca, and the effigy mounds in Ohio, were made to be seen during an out-of-the-body experience. Again, we shall probably never know for sure whether they were seen purely in the mind's eye of the entranced and drugged voyager, or if his soul did literally wing its way along the leys and spirit paths laid out on the ground.

The geological abnormalities of the ancient centres too begin to make sense. Not only did the 'earthlight' effects around them, created by the anomalies in the Earth, proclaim them as unusual, but the enhanced magnetism or radioactivity of the stones in turn catalysed the trance of the initiated. Paul Devereux, who pioneered this interpretation of the ancient sites, speculates in *Earth Memory*:

'We can perhaps envisage the megalithic shaman, in an altered state of consciousness, lying or sleeping in head-contact with the stone of power at a site. This might have helped to engender special visions… in the way that [the Welsh holy man] St Byrnach … used the magnetically anomalous Carn Ingli to "speak with the angels".'

A witch flies above the rooftops. The image is a buried folk-memory of the days when Scandinavian female shamans were said to be able to fly, and were pictured riding the sky on broomsticks.

MAGIC JOURNEYS AND MODERN TIMES

In Europe and much of Asia, the early tribal societies that built the ancient sites developed into more complex forms. Shamans became priests, and the priests became kings. But they did not lose all their old associations with the old shamanic world.

The connection between the straight lines of spirit and the holy office of kingship can still be seen in a word like 'ruler' in English, which means both a straight-edge and a political chief. The word derives from an ancient Indo-European word, reg, which means 'movement in a straight line'. From the same root we also get the Latin *rex* (king) and thence the English 'regal'.

Look about the land, and one will see other relics of shamanic lines in regal institutions. Royalty has always surrounded itself with architecture that bristles with ceremonial ways, boundaries, royal routes and imperial avenues. Even the ceremonial ways of kingless Washington DC are laid out in straight lines. In London, the Mall is the broad way leading to and from Buckingham Palace. A sense that a straight way symbolizes a special power associated with rulership has thus survived.

Buried in the folklore of modern Western societies are other relics of the shaman's magic journey. The cosy image of Father Christmas flying in his reindeer-drawn sleigh through the magic midwinter night is a jolly version of the flight in spirit of Arctic European and Siberian shamans. The tribes there were reindeer herders. Their minds grew wings with the aid of the hallucinogenic fly agaric fungus – whose distinctive red and white cap is the colour of Santa Claus's robes. It may be significant, too, that Santa Claus lives at the North Pole – the axis of the world.

Another relic of the shaman's magical flight is the witch flying on her broomstick. Medieval witches took 'flying ointments' or 'witches' salves', which were made from hallucinogenic herbs that also created the sensation of flight by generating an out-of-the-body experience. The broomstick is an echo of the world tree; it also recalls the habit (still practised in the Americas) of sweeping clean the spirit paths on the ground to make the space sacred. The archetypal image of the witch may come from a Scandinavian sect of women shamans who practised a form of prophecy, known as seidhr, while in trance. They wore feathered garments to indicate their ability to fly when in this altered state of consciousness. They, too, were often pictured flying on broomsticks.

As a final provocative footnote to this labyrinthine tale, there is a strong hint in the Norse mythology that it was actually women who first taught men to 'fly'.

The world is a stranger place than it seems – an even stranger place than it already seems.